an Eames anthology

an Eames anthology

articles, film scripts, interviews, letters, notes, speeches
by Charles and Ray Eames

edited by Daniel Ostroff

Yale University Press
New Haven and London

www.eamesoffice.com

yalebooks.com/art

Designed by Mark Thomson
Assisted by Rob Payne
Set in Arnhem and Fakt
Printed in China by Regent Publishing Services Limited

Library of Congress Control Number: 2014937866

ISBN: 978-0-300-20345-5

A catalogue record for this book is available from the
British Library.

This paper meets the requirements of ANSI/NISO
Z39.48-1992 (Permanence of Paper).

10 9 8 7 6 5 4 3 2 1

Contents

This book is dedicated to

Lucia Eames, 1930–2014, designer and sculptor, only child of Charles Eames and only stepdaughter of Ray Eames; and to her children: Byron Atwood, Lucia Atwood, Eames Demetrios, Llisa Demetrios, and Carla Hartman, who have operational responsibility for the Eames Office.

And to my father, Nathan Ostroff (Yale B.A. ’32, Yale LL.B. ’35), 1910–1983, international trade expert and United States Commerce Department attorney who worked with and greatly admired Charles and Ray Eames. He first encountered them in connection with his work at the American Exhibition in Moscow in 1959, where the Eames film *Glimpses of the U.S.A.* was presented. In 1964, he was Deputy United States Commissioner of the New York World’s Fair, where the Eames IBM Pavilion was such a great success. Because of my father’s position at the fair, my mother and I were given VIP passes to all of the exhibitions, and we went to most of them. The only one I remember, and I remember it vividly, is the Eames People Wall.

Daniel Ostroff
Los Angeles

Foreword

THE MISSION of the Eames Office today is to communicate, preserve, and extend the work of Charles and Ray Eames. Hearing that, I am confident most people think first of furniture, other folks perhaps of the films or the Eames House—all quite tangible projects. Meanwhile, I find myself drawn to the ideas the Eameses championed: the guest/host relationship, constraints, or Charles's beautiful comment, "After the age of information comes the age of choices."

These ideas were as much a product of the Eames Office as any of the compelling objects, images, and films that they created. And, although ideas are generally reckoned as abstract, at the Eames Office they became very real. In this book you will see that the iterative process that honed and fine-tuned their chairs was used with their ideas.

Much has been hiding in plain sight. A visitor to the Eames House notices immediately how comfortable in nature this emphatically manmade structure feels. Even if one does not know that Charles and Ray redesigned the house to preserve the meadow, the respect for the landscape is utterly present in the sensitive posture of the structure and the incorporeal but vividly present indoor-outdoor rhythms of its use. In other words, you can see the idea of the house.

You can see this gift too in the way the film *Powers of Ten* is as much about the power of constraints as it is about science—and how the Eames Aluminum Chair not only expresses but *is* way-it-should-be-ness. And perhaps all this suggests that design is less tangible than we think. The Eames LCW chair is not one specific chair—hundreds of thousands of originals have been made. It is actually the *idea* of that chair, particularly the idea that the chair Charles and Ray were designing is the authentic chair that will be made tomorrow.

I have always believed that you could literally see the ideas in their work, and as you read these pages you may find Charles giving voice to the forces that have compelled you from the start of your design awareness.

Like their chairs, these words are a product of Charles and Ray's collaboration—with all the intangibles that implies.

Charles Eames was born in 1907; thirty-four years later, in 1941, Charles and Ray arrived in Los Angeles and began their work together; thirty-seven years later, in 1978, Charles Eames died. Ray followed in 1988. Thirty-seven years later, we have this book; their working partnership has now been gone as long as it was together. This is the perfect moment to look into the heart of their designs.

A month after Charles died, their dear friend I. Bernard Cohen wrote to Ray, "[Charles] was a superb exemplar of what in the 17th century was called an 'intelligencer'—a far more apt word for him than any of those words related to the cold expression 'communicate.' To be able to command the universal respect of the scientific and engineering community as Charles did, and even educate that community in matters of taste—that really was the sign seal of his genius and the greatness of his personality!"

What you are about to enjoy is the *real* reason that design matters, not the flash, not the tendency to confuse it with style, but observations like this: "At all times, love and discipline have made for a beautiful environment and a good life." Indeed, what makes these ideas truly essential is that we can all use them in our lives as insights and inspirations, signposts and cautions.

Prepare to be intelligenced by masters.

DANIEL OSTROFF

Acknowledgments

FIRST, I must thank Eames Demetrios, director of the Eames Office, who blessed this venture at the start and facilitated my work in many ways. He gave me unfettered, unprecedented access to the Eames Office archives in Santa Monica, including those primary source materials that he collected when preparing his book, *An Eames Primer*. His scholarship sets a standard and provides a framework for all subsequent Eames research.

He asked Herman Miller and Vitra to open their archives to me; he also requested that the Library of Congress give me access not only to all of the processed Charles and Ray Eames papers but also to the five hundred boxes of unprocessed texts. I am also grateful for a grant from the Eames Office, which helped to cover my travel expenses and time.

At Herman Miller's corporate headquarters in Michigan, Mark Schurman, director of corporate communications, and Marg Mojzak, director of retail operations, and their colleagues in the archives, Linda Baron and Gloria Jacobs, helped me locate historic correspondence and some previously unpublished interviews, and sent me off with boxes of photocopies. Of equal importance was Andreas Nutz, archivist of the Vitra Design Museum, who kindly provided rare photos and some handwritten Eames notes.

At the Library of Congress, my guide was Meg McAleer, who organized the thousands of pages of Eames papers. Her on-line finding aid is invaluable; she deserves praise for this seventy-eight-page index, which includes a detailed timeline. Meg took time away from her work on the unprocessed material, directing me in minutes to speech transcripts that I would have otherwise needed months to discover. She also provided the bibliographic notes for many unpublished documents.

Three candidates for the Smithsonian Associates M.A. in the history of decorative arts volunteered to assist me during my visits to the Library of Congress: Kaitlin Handler, Grace McNicholas, and Amanda Asmus. They helped me navigate the library stacks, searched for specific texts, and made countless scans and photocopies.

Jehane Burns Kuhn worked for Charles and Ray Eames for twelve and a half years. We reviewed her Eames files together. Her advice guided some of my choices. Most helpfully, she provided a perspective as my work on this book extended from a planned six months to more than four years. She told me that when she worked at the Eames Office, there was a six-and-a-half-day workweek, and if the office hadn't closed she would never have left. I correlate this with my own feelings: never once, in all of the hours and days I worked on this book, immersed in what the Eames grandchildren call the "beautiful details," did I ever experience anything other than pleasure in the work.

The idea for this book germinated during my reading of Ralph Caplan's various Eames essays, in which he made liberal use of excerpts from Eames speeches. It was from Ralph's 1976 book *Connections: The Work of Charles and Ray Eames* that I learned that not only did Charles and Ray Eames have meaningful things to communicate and teach, but that their words were as elegant and eloquent as their designs are useful and beautiful.

One can't publish Eames texts without images, and a consideration of the "language of vision," a concept that Charles and Ray promoted. I could not have sourced many of the images for this book without the help and experience of the Eames Office archivist, David Hertsgaard. David read some of the texts and located, among the images at the Eames Santa Monica office, exactly the right ones. Eames Office general manager Genevieve Fong and chief financial officer Ric Keefer offered additional assistance and support.

Eames dealers Steve Cabella, Joel Chen, and Gerard O'Brien, and collectors John and Lynne Kishel kindly lent me copies of their precious, rare *Arts & Architecture* magazines for scans.

In terms of time and attention to detail, my friend Ruth Blair was truly heroic. She reviewed every single text, and she helped make sure that every edit made sense.

Final thanks go to everyone at Yale University Press, and designers Mark Thomson and Rob Payne, who gave me many necessary lessons on how to prepare a book for publication.

DANIEL OSTROFF

Introduction

FOR THE BEGINNING of a film about their molded plywood chair—the one designated by *Time* magazine as the "design of the century"—Charles Eames and Ray Eames wrote: "The problem of designing anything is in a sense the problem of designing a tool. And as in designing a tool it is usually wise to have a pretty clear idea of what you want the thing to do. The need it is to fill, its particular objective."[1]

By approaching their work with this attitude, as simple as it may seem, and by committing themselves to a "nuts and bolts" process, the Eameses had an extraordinary impact on our world. They created a well-documented legacy of architecture, furniture, toys, films, exhibitions, books, and graphic design.

My objective with this book is to present another important aspect of their legacy.

In addition to all of the "good goods" that they produced, the Eameses were prolific as educators, making many important contributions to the world of ideas.

Underlying all of their work is the principle that design should not be an act of creative self-expression but rather a process of problem solving. This book is a guide to the Eames process: how, in their own words, they did what they did.

Process texts are found among their handwritten notes to themselves, published articles, interviews, film scripts, letters, commissioned reports, and speeches. I selected texts from any Eames source where they provided lessons, and where the inspirations that guided them or the insights that motivated them are revealed. As design historian Ralph Caplan once said, "Charles Eames was not always teaching, but when you were with him you were always learning."[2]

Charles and Ray worked on a great variety of projects over the years and these texts are presented chronologically. In 1977 Charles told a group at the Smithsonian Institution: "Most any time I'm asked to talk about a general subject, I find I can only go through with it if I can relate it in some way with actual current work that's going on in our office."[3] The chronological presentation of their texts provides a useful guide to their work and allows for the widest possible range of subjects. Charles observed that regardless of the product, "the formula is the same for everything."[4] Here we see how this "formula" applied to a variety of creative problem-solving tasks.

The Eames Office had three kinds of clients: businesses; public organizations, which included museums, libraries, and government agencies; and teaching institutions. Examples of all of their work, jobs where they purveyed not only designs but also ideas, are found throughout this volume.

Clients in the business sector included the furniture companies Herman Miller and Vitra, plus IBM, Westinghouse, Polaroid, and Boeing. Public sector clients included the governments of the United States, India, and Puerto Rico, and the Secretariat of the United Nations.

The Eameses gave exemplary service as visiting professors at many universities, including the University of Georgia, the University of California, and Harvard University, and they delivered lectures at many more.

The communication of ideas was a fundamental aspect of their work, and it involved the same kind of iterative steps that they used to develop their designs. In this volume are texts on the development of the Eames House, as they first sketched it in 1945, as they modeled it in three dimensions in 1948, and as it was completed in 1949. In another part of this book are all seven of Charles's drafts of their design process diagram.

They often used the phrase "nuts and bolts" when talking about their work, and this is a better reflection of their efforts than any attempt to categorize them by style. When they applied themselves to product design they developed the techniques and machines by which their products are still produced today. When they created an exhibition they were responsible for every aspect, from the research and creation of the didactic material to the conception and construction of displays. Their exhibitions were presented all over the world, including at the Louvre, the British Museum, the National Museum of Poland in Warsaw, the

Metropolitan Museum of Art, the Los Angeles County Museum of Art, and the Smithsonian Institution. As testimony to the lasting quality of this work, the 1961 Eames exhibition Mathematica is on permanent display at the Boston Museum of Science and the New York Hall of Science.

The Eameses' writings are free of theory because they weren't adherents of a particular ideology of design or philosophy of aesthetics. This is evident in their furniture, as Eames Demetrios points out in *An Eames Primer*. "Their La Chaise chair and their ESU were done within two or three years of each other. One is all curves, the other all right angles."[5] In the words of their friend Bill Lacy, "There is no Eames style, only a legacy of problems beautifully and intelligently solved."[6]

Some have classified the Eameses as modernists. In fact, they insisted that they were not "-ists" of any kind.[7] Although the word "function" appears throughout these texts, it's also imprecise to think of Charles and Ray as functionalists because of their delimited view of function. As Charles told the AIA, "I'm thinking of function in terms of ultimate service to the particular individual."[8]

With regard to "ultimate service" they fully committed themselves to the consideration of "everything" in their analysis of needs, and the use of all the tools and information they could access. In response to a line in an E. E. Cummings poem, "who cares if some one-eyed son of a bitch invents a machine to measure spring with?" Charles countered, "I care."[9] They had a conviction that "you have to use the rational methods as far as possible. You must be a fool to decide in favor of less information instead of more."[10]

The Eameses believed in evolutionary rather than revolutionary design, and their emphasis on the important role of evolution in design is as closely linked to the natural order of things as one can imagine. What they applied from their study of the natural world is that it is the attributes that work that endure. Reference this exchange from a Q&A with Charles after that same speech about architectural design to the AIA:

QUESTION *You assume all parts (of a design) function?*

EAMES Oh, my God, yes. I mean, don't you think you are functioning when you smell something?

QUESTION *Beg pardon?*

EAMES Well, it's functioning in that it smells . . .

I mean, there's the passive and the active thing. A rose is functioning when it smells, and a rose knows darn well it is functioning or else it wouldn't get the bees there.[11]

Function was never about theory for Charles and Ray, it was about designs that work, that provided "service and performance" to those "particular individuals" who would use their products, see their films, and attend their exhibitions. Charles said that the "role of the architect or the designer is that of a very good, thoughtful host, all of whose energy goes into trying to anticipate the needs of his guests—those who would enter the building and use the objects later."[12] Eames chairs are distinctively strong and lightweight with people-friendly radius edges. Eames films are characteristically short and to the point, and often use humor to get ideas across. To the extent they considered the appearance of things, it was in this way: "The decisions that produce a really functional environment are no different from those that set the aesthetics of that environment, unless one has an extremely limited or brutal view of function."[13]

When asked by the mother of a young man what would prepare her son for a creative career, Charles suggested that painting and drawing the boy could do on his own time. However, he said, "if he does take any art courses, they should be in history and appreciation."[14] It was from their own studies of historic examples that Charles and Ray derived one of their most important insights. They deconstructed the process by which great things were traditionally produced and observed that these were created in a context of constraints. Their writings are filled with historical references to all of the arts, including Paul Revere's silverware, Native American Kachina dolls, Mayan temples, Chartres Cathedral, the hand ax, and the Windsor chair.

In 1958, Charles Eames was one of eight architects and designers who responded to a magazine editor's request for a statement on furnishing the home. All of the other contributors illustrated their responses with photographs of contemporary interiors furnished with their own current designs. Charles was the exception; instead of showing how he would design a room using his furniture, he submitted a photograph of a nineteenth century Indian pueblo. His point was not that this was a style to be copied; rather, he was demonstrating how limitations could result in good design.[15]

This must have raised a few eyebrows in the charged consumer world of the late 1950s, but the application of constraints is a subject to which the Eameses returned often. Contributing to a 1969 exhibition at the Louvre, titled What Is Design?, the Eameses wrote, "Design depends largely on constraints."[16]

Charles often talked about the time in the early 1960s when several noted architects participated in a study about the nature of creative work. Each was given a collection of one-inch square tiles of many different colors and asked to create a design of one square foot. Philip Johnson, describing his own efforts, said: "I used only black and white—what else?" Turning to Eero Saarinen, Johnson asked, "Eero, what did you use?" Saarinen replied, "All white."

Celebrating his colleagues' decision to self-impose limits, Charles commented, "This incident gives a clue to how far the sophisticated architect or artist will go to define the restraints of the problem he attacks. If limitations are not apparent, he will search for them or he will create them. This is no trick and no accident. It is one of the few ways that a concept of unity and structure can be maintained in the face of unrestricted choices and the foggy or non-existent limitations that are characteristic of our time."[17]

Today we continue to grapple with this defining design problem. We live in the age of choice. New technologies are introduced without pause; newly sourced materials present designers (and consumers) with an endless array of options. Many technological developments allow us to lead safer, healthier lives. Yet they can bring confusion and chaos. There's also the problem of the allocation of resources: many of the materials and technologies that characterize our time are inconsistent with good environmental stewardship. In a 1971 interview Charles noted, "The scary fact is that many of our dreams have come true. We wanted a more efficient technology and we got pesticides in the soil. We wanted cars and television sets and appliances and each of us thought he was the only one wanting that. Our dreams have come true at the expense of Lake Michigan. That doesn't mean that the dreams were all wrong. It means that there was an error somewhere in the wish and we have to fix it."[18]

The Eameses' approach to design as problem-solving, disciplined by an informed application of constraints that relate to peoples' needs, contextu-alizes their work in the continuum of world history. Rather than take credit for doing something new, the Eameses argued, by referencing history and nature, that they were focusing their attention on a process that has always led to good results.

It's reassuring that constraints are not inconsistent with great productivity. Between 1947 and 1984, Charles and Ray introduced 25 furniture product lines; of these, 19 are in the permanent collection of the Museum of Modern Art, and 17 are still in production. Fifty years after winning the AIA 25 Year Award, their house in the Pacific Palisades, California, inspires new generations of architects. Their films are referenced by Hollywood directors and video game designers.

A detailed list of the kinds of design constraints recommended by Charles and Ray Eames is found in "The India Report," in which they outline the process that led to the development of the *lota*, that country's ubiquitous brass vessel. They listed more than forty factors, both practical and emotional. It's a checklist that all designers and architects would do well to consider, including: "How pleasant does it feel, eyes closed, eyes open? How pleasant does it sound, when it strikes another vessel, is set on the ground or stone, empty or full, or being poured into? What is its cost in terms of working? What is its cost in terms of ultimate service? How does it feel to possess it, to sell it, to give it?"[19]

The kind of thoughtful constraints advocated by the Eameses do not lead to sterility or austerity. The world envisioned by Charles and Ray was not barren of color or pleasure. "Who would say that pleasure is not useful?"[20] they asked. During an AIA seminar Charles celebrated the jukebox: "If any of the more sensitive type people would design a jukebox, the thing would fade away in the corner, nobody would see it, and it would get no nickels. Its function is to get nickels and play the music. . . . It would be a bad jukebox design if it disappeared into the surroundings."[21]

This volume is the product of the application of constraints. Charles and Ray left us a huge array of writings. Charles delivered speeches regularly throughout his career, and the pair wrote, produced, and directed over 100 films. There are more than 130,000 documents archived at the Library of Congress. The Eames collection finding aid runs to 78 pages, and this details only the first 293 containers that have been processed. The work is so voluminous that 500 additional containers are yet to be catalogued: this is an ongoing effort for the library staff. With the Eames files taking up more than 120 linear feet at the Library of Congress, the collected Writings of Charles and Ray Eames could easily fill 40 volumes. To make their writings as accessible as possible, I made the decision to limit my choices to a comprehensive selection that would fit in one volume. When specific images are referenced in the texts, those images are included, and when an image appeared with a caption, wherever possible the original caption has been used.

I further constrained the contents of this book by beginning in 1941 with those texts produced after they first met and worked together at the Cranbrook Academy in Michigan. Both Charles and Ray accomplished much before Cranbrook. Ray (then Ray Kaiser) had worked with Hans Hofmann for six years. She was a founding member of the American Abstract Artists Group. Her work was exhibited in major museums alongside such other painters as Ad Reinhardt, Burgoyne Diller, and Lee Krasner. Charles was involved in an architectural practice throughout the 1930s and was responsible for designing five houses in St. Louis and two churches in Arkansas.

When Charles talked about the history of his work, he often began his narrative with 1941, the date he first worked with Ray, and the year he and Eero Saarinen garnered two awards at the Museum of Modern Art for furniture designs, for which Ray contributed the presentation drawings. Charles, who had attended the Washington University School of Architecture, noted that until he went to Cranbrook, he had "no conception of what a concept was."[22] For her part, when asked why she gave up painting, Ray said: "I never gave up painting. I changed my palette."[23] Ray began the process of changing her palette when she married Charles and they moved to Los Angeles in 1941. This anthology begins when their collaboration began.

While only a few of the texts in this book are officially attributed to Ray Eames, she was very much her husband's co-equal, which is how Charles repeatedly referred to her. He began many speeches and interviews by saying, "She (Ray) is equally responsible for everything that comes out of this office."[24] In a speech to the American Institute of Architects Charles explained that Ray preferred to work under the "brand name"—an important clarification given the fact that for many years their pieces were marketed with the words "Design by Charles Eames."[25] We don't know why

Ray felt most comfortable with this decision, but we do possess enough information today to recognize her full partnership with Charles. Their partnership extended to their written words. In this volume are three texts, formally attributed to Charles, that were actually written in longhand as first drafts by Ray.

Their oft-stated objective, "getting the best to the most number of people for the least," is another reason I chose to begin this anthology with the beginning of their collaboration.[26] It was in 1941 that they began work on the first design for which they developed the means of mass production: a molded plywood leg splint for the U.S. Navy Medical Department. Charles and Ray worked on the splint together, in their very first apartment, and the speed of that accomplishment (by 1942 the splint had been accepted by the U.S. Navy) was a harbinger of the great productivity ahead of them. Each leg splint bears a stamp, "Patent Pending Eames Process." Their "process"—the subject of most of the texts in this volume—was a synthesis of the contributions they both made to the finished products.

Mass production was central to their thinking. Ray said, "Anyone making one thing—that's very nice, to make one thing. But to be able to keep the quality in mass production is the only reason we've been working so hard. Because we could easily turn out a nice thing, and another, and another. But to figure a way that the hundredth, and the five hundredth, and the thousandth would have the original character."[27]

Mass production wasn't the end in itself; it was one of the means by which they set out to achieve their objective. For a 1953 San Francisco Museum TV show they wrote, "Mass production has the possibility of bringing more concern, more sweat, more blood and tears to the service of the individual consumer than the craft era could ever dream of."[28] As advocates of mass production it was important to them that an Eames product "would have in its appearance the essence of the method that produced it," and that it "would be produced by people working in a dignified way."[29]

Los Angeles Times reporter Dorothy Townsend documented Charles Eames's participation in a 1963 UCLA panel, "Problems of the Creative Artist": "Charles concluded that the problem the artist faces in making decisions is one of morality, because, 'we impose our creations on society.'"[30] It was characteristic of the Eameses to focus on others. In describing the boundaries within which they could work with "conviction and enthusiasm," Charles and Ray included the "concerns of society as a whole."[31]

This book features many previously unpublished texts, including ones relating to this aspect of their work process. In a personal letter to Ian McCallum of *Architectural Review*, Charles explains that at first they declined to participate in an Alcoa marketing initiative for which various designers were invited to make new products from aluminum.[32] The Eameses accepted the commission only after they came up with an approach that they felt had social value. They produced a kinetic aluminum toy powered by solar cells. This not only met their client's brief but also provided a delightful public demonstration of the virtues of a sustainable, renewable source of energy: the sun.

Charles and Ray are very well known for their chairs, and of course this book includes numerous texts about chair design; these bear as much attention as any of the variety of subjects they wrote and talked about. Ralph Caplan addressed this in his book *By Design*: "I do not believe that any chair, however elegant, contributes significantly to life or solves problems that can seriously be considered major. However, the Eames *approach* to chairs (and to anything else) is an approach we can bring to activities more important than taking the weight off one's feet."[33]

Writing as a visiting professor to his UC Berkeley School of Architecture students, Charles gave the following provocation, which provides a good context for approaching these writings: "The great thinkers and doers in architecture seem often to stand as personalities of style and form. But we believe much more reliable clues to their big direction can be found in the way they thought and among the things of which they were most fond."

"To really benefit from the work of these men, look to their loves—be interested, be enthusiastic, become involved."[34]

1. Charles Eames and Ray Eames, "The Development of the Molded Plywood Chair," film by the Office of Charles and Ray Eames, 1953, 16mm.
2. Hugh De Pree, *Business as Unusual* (Zeeland, Mich.: Herman Miller, 1986), 50.
3. Charles Eames, Frank Nelson Doubleday Lecture, Smithsonian Institution, May 1977, Part II: Speeches and Writings series, Charles and Ray Eames Papers, Manuscript Division, Library of Congress, Washington, D.C.
4. Charles Davenport, "Designer Charles Eames: Chairs, Fairs, and Films," *Los Angeles* 3, no. 1 (January 1962): 24–27.
5. Eames Demetrios, *An Eames Primer* (New York: Universe, 2007), 9.
6. Max Underwood, "Inside the Office of Charles and Ray Eames," *Ptah* 2 (Helsinki: Aalto Foundation, 2005), 49.
7. Deborah Sussman, former Eames Office staff member, in conversation with this editor, December 16, 2010.
8. Charles Eames, speech, October 10, 1952, American Institute of Architects, Kansas City, Missouri, Part II: Speeches and Writings series, Charles and Ray Eames Papers, Manuscript Division, Library of Congress, Washington, D.C.
9. Bob Specht letter, copy to Ray Eames, December 16, 1982, Eames Office Archives, Santa Monica, California.
10. Simon M. Pruys, "Eames," trans. Jordan Sowle, *Algemeen Handelsblad* (Amsterdam), June 14, 1969.
11. Charles Eames, speech, October 10, 1952, American Institute of Architects, Kansas City, Missouri, Part II: Speeches and Writings series, Charles and Ray Eames Papers, Manuscript Division, Library of Congress, Washington, D.C.
12. Digby Diehl, "Q&A Charles Eames," *West Magazine/Los Angeles Times* (October 8, 1972), 14–17.
13. Charles Eames, report to Howard W. Johnson, president, MIT, Container I:218, Folder 6, Charles and Ray Eames Papers, Manuscript Division, Library of Congress, Washington, D.C.
14. Charles Eames to Mrs. Paul Tornheim, March 7, 1961, "T" miscellaneous folder, Part II: Office File (1960–1969) series, Charles and Ray Eames Papers, Manuscript Division, Library of Congress, Washington, D.C.
15. Frances Evans, "If I Could Tell a Woman One Thing About Furnishing a Home . . ." *Family Circle* 52, no. 3 (March 1958): 33.
16. Charles Eames, design drawings and statement for What Is Design? August 29, 1969, Eames Office LLC Archives, Santa Monica, Calif.
17. Charles Eames, "Design: Its Freedoms and Its Restraints," speech, New York Art Directors' Conference, New York, April 1963, Part II: Speeches and Writings series, Charles and Ray Eames Papers, Manuscript Division, Library of Congress, Washington, D.C.

18. Anthony G. Bowman, "The Designer as Renaissance Man," trans., October 19, 1971, *Ameryka*, Eames Office LLC Archives.
19. Charles Eames and Ray Eames, "The India Report," April 1958, National Design Institute, Ahmedabad, India, Container I:45, Charles and Ray Eames Papers, Manuscript Division, Library of Congress, Washington, D.C.
20. Charles Eames, design drawings and statement for "What Is Design?" August 25, 1969, Eames Office Archives, Santa Monica, California.
21. AIA Seminar transcript, October 10, 1952, American Institute of Architects, Kansas City, Missouri, Part II: Speeches and Writings series, Charles and Ray Eames Papers, Manuscript Division, Library of Congress, Washington, D.C.
22. Olga Gueft, "3 Chairs/3 Records of the Design Process: 1. Charles Eames Leisure Group," *Interiors* 117, no. 9 (April 1958): 118–22.
23. Eames Demetrios, *Changing Her Palette: Paintings by Ray Eames* (Venice, Calif.: Eames Office, 2000), 1.
24. June Lee Smith, "Designer Charles Eames Tests Prize-Winning Furniture in His Own Home," *Christian Science Monitor* (June 22, 1949), 10.
25. AIA Seminar transcript, October 10, 1952, American Institute of Architects, Kansas City, Missouri, Part II: Speeches and Writings series, Charles and Ray Eames Papers, Manuscript Division, Library of Congress, Washington, D.C.
26. "Sympathetic Seat," *Time* 56, no. 2 (July 10, 1950): 45–46.
27. Charles Eames and Ray Eames, interview by Perry Miller Adato, "An Eames Celebration: The Several Worlds of Charles and Ray Eames," PBS, 1975.
28. Charles Eames, handwritten and typed script notes, *Discovery* television program, San Francisco Museum of Art, Part II: Projects file series, Charles and Ray Eames Papers, Manuscript Division, Library of Congress, Washington, D.C.
29. Diehl, "Q&A Charles Eames," 14–17.
30. Dorothy Townsend, "Designer, Choreographer Discuss Creativity in Arts," *Los Angeles Times* (April 8, 1963), section V, page 1.
31. Charles Eames, design drawings and statement for What Is Design?
32. Charles Eames to Ian McCallum, November 14, 1958, Part II: Office File series, Charles and Ray Eames Papers, Manuscript Division, Library of Congress, Washington, D.C.
33. Ralph B. Caplan, *By Design* (New York: St. Martin's, 1982), 205.
34. Charles Eames, "Architecture 1 and 2," *Ark Annual* (Student Chapter of the American Institute of Architects, College of Architecture, University of California, Berkeley, 1954), 29–31, Part II: Speeches and Writings series, Charles and Ray Eames Papers, Manuscript Division, Library of Congress, Washington, D.C.

an Eames anthology

Part One

1941–1949

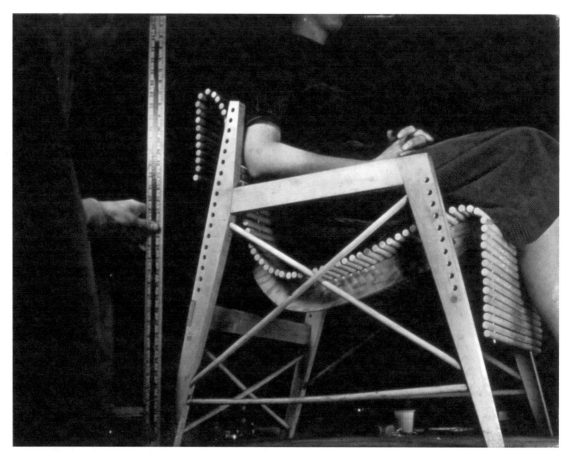

Determining the character of support
needed by the body—the first step
in designing a chair. Copyright
Cranbrook Archives. Richard G. Askew,
photographer, 5681–7.

CHARLES EAMES

"Design Today"

DESIGN TODAY presents the same problem as it always has. The need has changed but the equipment necessary to solve the problem is still the same. The designer should be capable of forming in his own mind a clearer conception of the NEED he is to fill and he should possess a vocabulary of facts regarding materials and techniques adequate enough to enable him to fill the need appropriately and with feeling. It seems obvious that he should possess these facilities and yet the classic training, which many claim deals with the fundamentals and common denominators in creating art, often forces upon the young designer a system of sterile formula, or makes him so conscious of self-expression that he ignores completely the help he can get from physical and natural law.

The first step in design, that of determining the need, is a very hazardous undertaking. It is not simple, even the most sincere can easily confuse the actual need with the traditional idea of need and be led off on a hopeless tangent. To face this problem in the complex world of today, we find young designers preparing themselves, not with involved theories, but with all the understanding, facts, and experience that they can obtain. In the manual experience of work, they develop an attitude of feeling as well as proficiency. From tools they learn vital lessons in "fitness to need," balance, and relation of form to the human scale. They discover that the work done with a tool is only as orderly as their attitude while using it. Working with the healthy discipline of economy, in materials and forms, they develop a natural feeling for the appropriate.

It is possible for them while working and designing in a limited variety of materials and media to develop a "habit of approach" that can be applied to virtually any creative work. They may so prepare themselves that they can approach any problem with the least possible loss of energy no matter how new to them its requirements or materials. They will intelligently determine the need, and then fill that need inventively and appropriately.

In the airplane one feels strongly the appropriateness of its streamed lines and they seem healthy and good. This effect is very different from that of the streamlined vacuum cleaner or inkwell where the designer has fallen into a habit of form and has the mistaken idea that it would be good to streamline everything. People instinctively recognize the goodness in a sailboat, an axe, an airplane or a huge dam and, consciously or unconsciously, get from them a feeling of esthetic satisfaction. The modern designer tries to refine his work until it contains as much of that goodness as possible. In his case it is mostly a conscious effort but the goal is still the same form of goodness that all people sense intuitively to some degree. In it there is no room for pretense or snobbery or for value results by the costliness of materials used. Certainly the future cannot be considered hopeless as long as designers continue to honor the accomplishment of producing a very inexpensive article that can serve well and bring pleasure to a million housewives.

Source: Charles Eames, "Design Today," *California Arts & Architecture* 58, no. 9 (September 1941): 18–19.

CHARLES EAMES

"Organic Design"

HAD THE Museum of Modern Art's Competition been held this year instead of last, a possible program would have required the competitors to design furniture restricting themselves to the materials and techniques not absorbed in National Defense. That would have been quite a trick but the Competition was held last year and the Museum's view was a much longer one. It was attempting to put new life into an industry which had become ingrown. Their aim and the aim of every competitor, I am sure, was to provide the largest group of people with good furniture within their means.

The opportunity was a rare one because of the unique phase of the Competition, which provided contact with manufacturers and an outlet for the winning designs. When the show opened at the Art Museum and the cost of the pieces announced, it was held by many that the main purpose had been defeated and that most of those for whom the furniture was intended could look but not afford to buy. To some, the obvious reason was the high cost of "Merchandising"—that great difference between the cost of manufacturing and the cost to the consumer. It is part of a complicated system that is to the uninitiated a complete mystery, and no matter how illogical and costly it may seem, it applies to virtually all furniture—that of the Competition suffering no more than any other.

Had the sole effect been to produce immediately acceptable and reasonable pieces, it could have been accomplished by closely studying the processes of mass production in the furniture industry and designing strictly within these techniques. These are techniques which had attained an almost incredible efficiency in the production of forms originally conceived as wood handicraft. Joints belonging to the hand technique are made by machinery, and machinery covers them with the decoration that for centuries hands have formed. It would be perfectly possible to eliminate some nonessentials and create pleasing proportions but the design could never deviate from the ingrown production pattern. The danger here is that the change is apt to be superficial and lead further up a blind alley.

There is another approach to the problem—one that should pay the greatest dividends in the long run, but it presents various immediate obstacles, economic and otherwise. That approach is to ignore all materials and techniques to determine as completely and clearly as possible our needs in furniture. *Then* to search for the materials and techniques which can most appropriately fill this need. Because of quantities involved these are apt to be found in factories where the efficiency of mass production is essential and form submits to no compromise. Factories making electrical equipment, airplanes, tools, or any of the many useful things which have never had "art tradition."

In the three-way curve laminated shell construction and the rubber weld Eero Saarinen and I felt that we had found processes that would go a long way toward filling our ideas of the chair need. Techniques not long out of the laboratory stage, they were developing rapidly along mass production lines and in a few years would surely be producing efficiently and economically.

That they were being used primarily in defense production was significant because it insured their growth and promised great possibilities when the war needs let up.

With no preconceived ideas of form we worked simultaneously with factory technicians and many experimental sitters, and as the chair forms developed we, too, were surprised and as we worked with them, we found them pleasing.

Priorities and the time limitations forced many compromises, but the Museum of Modern Art, having broadened the horizon of an industry, enabled this type of solution to be manufactured and merchandised, a process which otherwise would have taken years of propaganda and persuasion.

It will be several years before the full value of the Competition can be judged, but if its influence has made it easier for new and appropriate structural systems to be used for comfort in our home life, a great deal will have been achieved. That this comfort will be accompanied by aesthetic satisfaction we have no doubts.

Source: Charles Eames, "Organic Design," *California Arts & Architecture* 58, no. 12 (December 1941): 16–17.

Winning furniture designs by Saarinen and Eames from the Museum of Modern Art Competition. Installation view of the exhibition Organic Design in Home Furnishings. Museum of Modern Art, New York. September 24 through November 9, 1941. Photographic archive. The Museum of Modern Art Archives, New York. Gottscho-Schleisner, Inc. Digital Image © The Museum of Modern Art/Licensed by SCALA/Art Resource, NY.

Covers for *California Arts & Architecture*, 1942

California Arts & Architecture 59, no. 4 (April 1942), *California Arts & Architecture* 59, no. 5 (May 1942): cover, 15. Cover: Ray Eames in designing this month's cover has used the structural elements and drab green that we have all seen with reassurance actively defending our coast. Photograph by Charles Eames.

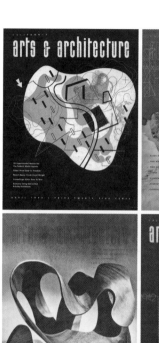

California Arts & Architecture 59, no. 8 (September 1942): cover, 10. Cover: A piece of wood sculpture by Ray Eames designed in a complex form to take advantage of a system of molding laminated wood developed by Charles Eames. In its practical application in the defense and commercial fields an important feature of the system is its principle of mass production.

California Arts & Architecture 59, no. 9 (October 1942).

California Arts & Architecture 59, no. 10 (November 1942). The Ray Eames cover for the November issue: The clearest and most concise forms often come directly out of and are a part of our most serious work. The source material of the November cover is an example of the beauty of these forms. Those shown relate to the solving of the airfoil; the basic formulas governing the motion of a fluid, curves representing lift and drag, and the airflow itself. These are the tools of the aerodynamist.

California Arts & Architecture 59, no. 11 (December 1942).

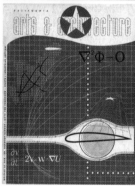

RAY EAMES

Covers for *California Arts & Architecture*, 1943

California Arts & Architecture 60, nos. 1–5 (January–June 1943), nos. 7–10 (August–December 1943).

California Arts & Architecture 60, no. 6 (July 1943): cover, 15. Cover: The blue, an American eagle, is a photograph by Ralph De Sola of the Federal Writers' Project; the black is an early American wood carving by an unknown sculptor said to have been a sign for Eagle Tavern, Pawtucket, Rhode Island. Photograph of wood carving courtesy Museum of Modern Art. Cover design by Ray Eames.

 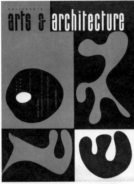  

CHARLES EAMES

"City Hall"

Editor's note: The issue of Architectural Forum *in which this article appeared was devoted to "New Buildings for 194X," an optimistic look ahead to "postwar design trends."*

IN A TYPICAL American community with 70,000 people, about 27,000 are registered voters. In 1943 only 12,000 voted in a municipal election.

WHY?

Among the several important reasons: A lack of the facilities by which the people can educate themselves to understand the techniques of government.

A city government should—must—be housed as the center of a mutually cooperative enterprise in which: THE GOVERNMENT TALKS TO THE PEOPLE. AND THE PEOPLE TALK TO THE GOVERNMENT.

The administration of government is the business of the people.

The obligations of the people in a democracy consist not only of an exercise of franchise, but participation in and active direction of the rules or laws by which government exists.

The city hall must properly be considered the heart of any community, the house of government. A building in which provision is made not only for the administration of rules and regulations, but a building which must contain facilities for the expression of the *idea* of government, which is never static and which can never be complete

without the direct participation of the people who create it.

It should be impossible to think in terms of the juvenile court without thinking in terms of the children's clinic, without thinking in terms of a Board of Education. Such a Board of Education can best function through activities within the house of government itself by presenting in active cooperation with all departments: exhibitions, motion pictures, study and lecture groups, open forums.

TO THE END THAT WHEN THE GOVERNMENT TALKS TO THE PEOPLE AND THE PEOPLE TALK TO THE GOVERNMENT—IT IS ONE AND THE SAME VOICE.

The design of the city hall is conceived as an integral part of the city plan. Located at the end of the new mall, it fits admirably into this natural position. The inter-penetration of public spaces, parks and the purely administrative functions of government symbolizes a truly democratic type of community, of which this group of buildings becomes the center.

Source: Charles Eames, "City Hall," *Architectural Forum* 78, no. 6 (May 1943): 88–90.

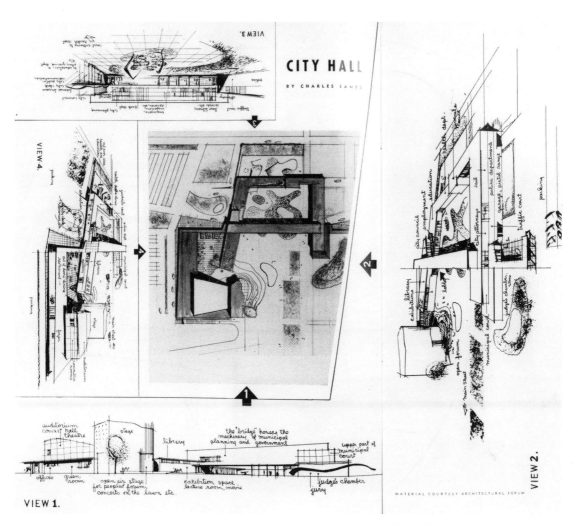

CITY HALL
BY CHARLES EAMES

City Hall by Charles Eames.

Top: Photo collage by Ray Eames.

Bottom: Paintings by Ray Eames:
"Space and the relationships of space
become so engulfing. So important that
objects in themselves lose values. Two
left-hand gloves."

RAY EAMES

"Line and Color"

LINE AND
COLOR DEFINE
VOLUME
THAT VOLUME
CAN BE TANGIBLE
OR NOT BUT THE
SPACE BETWEEN
TWO TANGIBLE
VOLUMES IS
NEVERTHELESS
    A VOLUME

it is impossible to talk about painting without bringing up the whole weary subject of aesthetics   philosophy   and metaphysics.

the fact is that without any talk we are influenced by the world in which we live and by the synthesis of the experiences of the world by all creators • the engineer   mathematician   sculptor   physicist   chemist   architect   doctor   musician   writer   dancer   teacher   baker   actor   editor   the man on the job   the woman in the home and painters

for the past many years the western world has been working back through the maze of surface decoration and meaningless gloss to the fundamentals of form • sometimes this has been an economic necessity as in the present war years, other times it comes from an aesthetic demand • where the people through the sensibilities of the creators find it necessary to rediscover the nonessentials • hindrances of the past

why is it that today we are more concerned with the materials and design of a chair than with its covering or ornament? why are we more concerned with the quality of the music than with the personal idiosyncrasies of the conductor? why are the uniforms—the word itself becomes strange—so varied and differ so radically from those of former wars? why are our houses being designed from the inside out rather than fitting the living to a predetermined style on the outside? why indeed do we not only accept but also admire and feel intensely proud of the jeep? a superb example of a healthy direction of thinking and feeling

in spite of prejudice and confusion we are becoming aware slowly of true and good and vital and therefore beautiful form

my interest in painting is the rediscovery of form through movement and balance and depth and light • using this medium to recreate, in a satisfying order, my experiences of this world with a desire to increase our pleasure   expand our perceptions   enrich our lives.

Source: Ray Eames, "Line and Color," *California Arts & Architecture* 60, no. 8 (September 1943): 16–17.

WENDELL G. SCOTT AND CHARLES EAMES

"A New Emergency Transport Splint of Plyformed Wood"

EARLY IN 1942 work was started on the development of a new type of splint for the immediate treatment and transfer of patients with injuries to the lower extremities. The need for such an "emergency transport splint" was suggested by the reports of medical officers serving in the combat zones. In the "front line" zones the medical efforts are principally emergency measures for saving a man's life, alleviating pain, and preserving an injured part until the casualty can be evacuated to a base. In such combat zones the hospital corpsmen render a large part of the initial emergency treatments, which should always be reduced to the simplest, safest, and quickest methods. It was in the hope of simplifying the initial treatment and evacuation of men with lower extremity wounds under combat conditions that the "transport" splint was produced.

"Plyformed wood" is the copyrighted name given to wood veneers that are bonded together by a resin glue and "molded" or shaped to any form by a process involving heat and pressure. By this process it is possible to shape the bonded veneers into compound curves without straining or breaking the strips of veneer. For the purpose of description plyformed wood may be considered as a type of plywood that has been molded into a desired shape. It is light but very strong for its weight. The veneers and resin glue are not critical materials. This laminated wood does not warp[,] as the adjacent strips of veneer are placed so that the grain in each runs at right angles to the other. These were the features that suggested the feasibility of using this material for a surgical splint.

Our object was to make a simple splint that could be applied quickly and efficiently by untrained personnel without causing additional damage to the injured part and yet provide adequate immobilization of the extremity with reasonable comfort to the patient. A series of molds and measurements was made of many lower extremities of various shapes and sizes. From a study of them it was possible to make a single posterior molded shell splint of plyformed wood that would support any lower extremity. It was made large enough to be used without removing the trousers or the heavy field shoe of the casualty. The splint is fastened in place by means of cross tapes made from strips of 2-inch or 3-inch gauze bandage or even strips of cloth torn from a shirt. The proximal end is flared and convex so that the weight of the body anchors the splint against the ischial tuberosities. The squared base of the flared end together with the wide bottom of the heel rest prevents the splint from rolling sidewise. A stirrup was formed into the foot of the splint so that if traction is necessary, it can be applied either by wrapping a bandage about the ankle in a double half hitch and, after applying traction, tying the free ends about the stirrup, or by threading a strip of bandage through a slit in the shoe just above the sole at the instep and bringing the free ends about the stirrup and fastening securely. Countertraction is obtained by fastening one end of a padded roll to the inside slot at the upper end of the splint and bringing the other end up against the crotch and over the groin and securing it to the opposite slot on the outside. Effective countertraction can be maintained by using a piece of 3-inch bandage tied in a hitch between the splint and patient's belt, as illustrated.

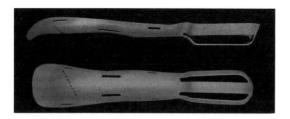

Emergency Transport Splint. Side view: The molded contour of the splint is designed to fit the shape of the posterior aspect of the buttocks, the thigh, the popliteal depression, the calf, and the heel support. The slots may be used to hold the cross tapes in place or to obtain countertraction. Viewed from back: The splint is constructed in one piece, without joints, appendages, or "gadgets." It is finished in a smooth, hard surface. Specifications: Length overall 42½ inches; width at heel 5¾ inches, at hip 8 inches; depth for heel 3¾ inches, for thigh 1¾ inches; thickness of the veneers vary from ⅛ to ¼ inch, depending on the need for strength. Weight 1½ to 1¾ pounds.

While [the accompanying] figures illustrate the use of the splint with traction, it is primarily intended to be used as a transport splint without any traction.

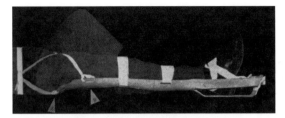

Temporary traction can be obtained by using the countertraction hitch devised by Captain J. W. Ellis (MC) U.S. Navy. The tape tied at slot B crosses over the thigh and is fastened to the belt on the left side. A second tape is fastened on the medial side of the splint in the slot opposite B and runs across the grain and is tied to the belt on the right side. Tapes from the uppermost slots at A are secured to their respective sides of the belt.

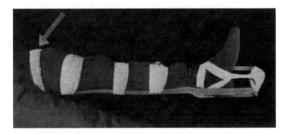

Splint applied using padded roll for countertraction. Immobilization is obtained by cross tapes of 3-inch bandage placed either through the slots or wrapped around the splint. A double half hitch is used about the ankle for securing traction. A safer method is to cut a slit in the uppers of the shoe, just above the instep, run a piece of gauze through the slits, lace the shoe on the foot, apply traction, and then tie the free ends about the stirrup.

SUMMARY

1. This is a universal splint: (a) Fits either the right or left lower extremity. (b) Fits lower extremity of any size with trousers and shoes worn.
2. It is quickly and safely applied: Can be applied quickly by untrained personnel without risk of further injury due to application.
3. It provides immobilization for any fracture of the lower extremity: Fractures at any site can be immobilized from the foot to the hip.

4. Supports the entire lower extremity and protects it from extraneous movement: No part of the leg comes in direct contact with the ground or stretcher, which eliminates certain imparted movements and jiggling to the leg during the rapid transfer and transportation of the casualty via stretcher, jeep, landing barge, airplane, etc.
5. "Padding" and "fitting" are practically eliminated, as the splint is molded to fit the contour of the leg.
6. Means for applying traction are available: While this splint is primarily for use in transporting the casualty, countertraction can be obtained by the physician when necessary. The safest method is to remove the shoe, make a slit through the uppers just above the sole at the instep, thread a piece of bandage through it, lace the shoe on the foot, and apply traction to the ends of the bandage, which are then secured to the stirrup.
7. Simplicity: Constructed in one single piece. No adjustable joints or connections. No mechanical "gadgets" or features to deteriorate, lose, break, or get out of order. No appendages, hooks, or appliances.
8. It is easily carried and stored: The splints nest one within the other, just as spoons are stacked, making it easy to carry 6 to 12, and for the same reason they can be conveniently stored in a small space.
9. It is easily cleaned for prompt re-use.
10. It is translucent to x-rays: The splint can be left on during x-ray examinations.
11. It is light in weight: Entire splint weighs about 1½ pounds.
12. It is resilient and durable: Will receive shock without splintering or cracking. It is tough, durable, and strong.
13. It is waterproof and warp-proof: Can float for any length of time without its form or strength being affected. Will not warp.
14. It is constructed of noncritical materials: The supply of plywood veneers and resin glue is accessible.

Source: Wendell G. Scott (Lieutenant Commander [MC] U.S.N.R.) and Charles O. Eames, "A New Emergency Transport Splint of Plyformed Wood," *United States Medical Bulletin* 41, no. 5, (September 1943): 1424–28.

Covers for *Arts & Architecture*, 1944

Arts & Architecture 61, no. 1
(January 1944): cover.

Arts & Architecture 61, no. 2
(February 1944): cover.

Arts & Architecture 61, no. 3
(March 1944): cover, 11. Cover by Ray
Eames, a portion of which is taken
from a drawing by Hans Hofmann.

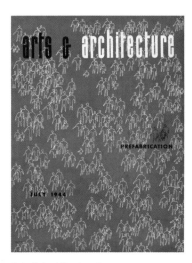

Arts & Architecture 61, no. 7
(July 1944): cover.

Arts & Architecture 61, no. 8
(August 1944): cover.

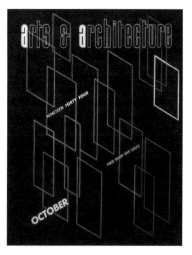

Arts & Architecture 61, no. 10
(October 1944): cover.

Arts & Architecture 61, no. 4
(April 1944): cover.

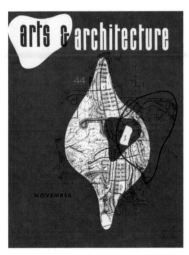

Arts & Architecture 61, no. 11
(November 1944): cover.

CHARLES EAMES

Mass-Produced Housing

Editor's note: Context for this chart is provided by the text on a preceding page of Arts & Architecture *magazine in the article "What Is a House?" by the magazine's editorial staff, which included Charles Eames and Ray Eames.*

IT HAS BEEN estimated that one million five hundred thousand houses each year for a period of ten years will be needed to relieve the urgent housing problem of this country alone. In the world at large, fifty million families will be in need of shelter as the result of war. The enormity of such a need cannot even be partially satisfied by building techniques as we have known and used them in the past. Large scale industry would seem to be the only logical means by which we can achieve an enterprise of such proportion.

Source: *Arts & Architecture* 61, no. 7 (July 1944): 34 (chart by Charles Eames), 26–27 ("What Is a House?" by magazine staff).

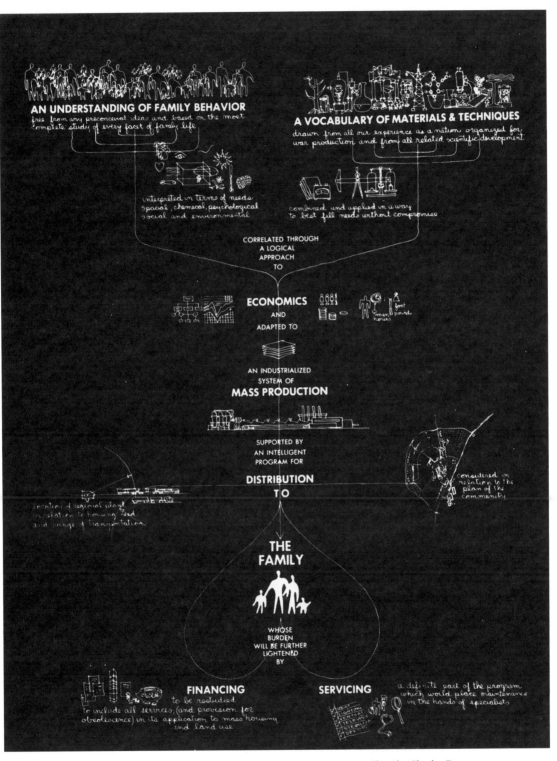

AN UNDERSTANDING OF FAMILY BEHAVIOR
free from any preconceived ideas and based on the most
complete study of every facet of family life

A VOCABULARY OF MATERIALS & TECHNIQUES
drawn from all our experience as a nation organized for
war production and from all related scientific development

interpreted in terms of needs
spacial, chemical, psychological
social and environmental

combined and applied in a way
to best fill needs without compromise

CORRELATED THROUGH
A LOGICAL
APPROACH
TO

ECONOMICS
AND
ADAPTED TO

foot
man pounds
hours

AN INDUSTRIALIZED
SYSTEM OF
MASS PRODUCTION

SUPPORTED BY
AN INTELLIGENT
PROGRAM FOR

DISTRIBUTION
TO

considered in
relation to the
plan of the
community

location of regional plant
in relation to housing and
and range of transportation

**THE
FAMILY**

WHOSE
BURDEN
WILL BE FURTHER
LIGHTENED
BY

FINANCING
to be restudied
to include all services, (and provision for
obsolescence) in its application to mass housing
and land use

SERVICING
a definite part of the program
which would place maintenance
in the hands of specialists

Chart by Charles Eames.

RAY EAMES

"No man is an illand"

Editor's note: This text is from an article on a Los Angeles County Museum of Art exhibition of the works of eight artists: Grace Clements, Ray Eames, Antonin Heythum, Frederick Kann, Gina Knee, Helen Lundeberg, Knud Merrild, and Vincent Ulery. Ray Eames uses the phrase "No man is an illand" as an echo of the magazine's introduction to these works, which concludes: "Perhaps in the broadest sense of the word, all art is intended for some use, if no more than a decorative one. But the implication is ever present that Art is for Art's Sake when it is not for tangible use and it may well prove to be that the greatest single shortcoming of our philosophy is that which has made of art a superstition and not a way of life. 'Ours is perhaps the first society to find it natural that some things be beautiful and others useful,' but ours is also a society capable of re-discovering that 'NO MAN IS AN ILLAND, ENTIRE OF IT SELFE.' And when we better realize this kind of wisdom it is possible that art may once again become great in the fusion of both spiritual and material usefulness to man."

PAINTING TODAY is not the expression of the inner working of an individual pointed to confound the public and to publicize the artist.

Man is an entity in a universe and he is striving to find order in himself in relation to that universe —the difference between the approach and a flat design is the quality of life—growth; one must live—expand—grow—or one is dead, dead.

We desire a perfect understanding—a perfect balance—a full rightness in life and an expression of impulse can be found in any medium—why should the painter with his background of technique limit his experience of nature to visual reproduction when the experience of nature includes such stirring things as the soaring of a bird—the warmth and intensity of a friend's greeting—a fire in the night—"the remembered of things past."

These experience nothing when photographically reproduced [and] in fact are impossible to reproduce, but the intensities—the relationships— the warmth of life—these are not lost—they only become fully realized by what the artist does in terms of his medium.

Source: Ray Eames, "Los Angeles Museum's Third Group Show," *Arts & Architecture* 61, no. 10 (October 1944): 19–22

Ray Eames, "For C in Limited Palette,"
1943.

"Case Study Houses 8 and 9" (1945)

Charles Eames and Eero Saarinen, Architects

THIS IS GROUND in meadow and hill, protected on all sides from intrusive developments free of the usual surrounding clutter, safe from urban clutter; not, however, removed from the necessary conveniences and the reassurances of city living.

Two houses for people of different occupations but parallel interests. Both, however, determinedly agreed on the necessity of privacy, or the right to choose privacy from one another and anyone else.

While these houses are not to be considered as solutions of typical living problems; through meeting specific and rather special needs, some contribution to the need of the typical might be developed. The whole solution proceeds from an attempt to use space in direct relation to the personal and professional needs of the individuals revolving around and within the living units inasmuch as the greater part of work or preparation for work will originate here. These houses must function as an integral part of the living pattern of the occupants and will therefore be completely "used" in a very full and real sense. "House" in these cases means center of productive activities.

Case Study House 8: For a married couple both occupied professionally with mechanical experiment and graphic presentation. Work and recreation are involved in general activities: Day and night, work and play, concentration, relaxation with friend and foe, all intermingled

personally and professionally with mutual interest. Basically apartment dwellers, there is a conscious effort made to be free of complications relating to maintenance. The house must make no insistent demands for itself, but rather aid as background for life in work. This house—in its free relation to the ground, the trees, the sea—with constant proximity to the whole vast order of nature acts as re-orientor and "shock absorber" and should provide the needed relaxations from the daily complications arising within problems.

The house is built between two trusses. The floor and ceiling help to stiffen the top and bottom cord of the truss, and together with the truss form a box beam. The end walls keep the box beam from collapsing sideways. The structure rests on two steel supports, these being set in so that the end of the box forms a cantilever. This shortens the span and develops a negative moment over the support which makes for a more economical truss. Cross bracing between the steel supports gives added strength.

Case Study House 9: In this house activities will be of a more general nature to be shared with more people and more things. It will also be used as a returning place for relaxation and recreation through reading and music and work—a place of reviving and refilling, a place to be alone for preparation of work, and with matters and concerns of personal choosing. A place for the kind of relaxed privacy necessary for the development and preparation of ideas to be continued in professional work centers. The occupant will need space used elastically where many or few people can be accommodated within the areas appropriate to such needs. Intimate conversation, groups in discussion, the use of a projection machine for amusement and education, and facilities for self-indulgent hobbies, i.e., cooking and the entertainment of very close friends.

Object to enclose as much space as possible within a fairly simple construction. The four columns in the middle are so placed to allow for cross bracing as well as continuity. Most of the joist load is transmitted to the outer rim of the rectangle, and all carrying members inside carry a fairly light and equal load. Because of this the ceiling does not need girders projecting below the joist but is a simple flat slab.

While the land is intended to be used communally, each house is so oriented that it has complete privacy within its own indoor-outdoor needs. The road follows the natural contour of the hill and will be allowed to gather leaves and regain the natural surface of the land. It serves each of the two houses, expanding for necessary turning and parking areas.

House Number 8 is independent of the ground, a point in space looking directly at the mass of the sea. It is related to the ground only through the terrace areas over which it hangs. House Number 9 incorporates the meadow of which the living scheme is an integral part. It, too, has direct and unobstructed view across the meadow through trees to the sea.

Source: Charles Eames, "Case Study Houses #8 and #9," *Arts & Architecture* 62, no. 12 (December 1945): 43–51.

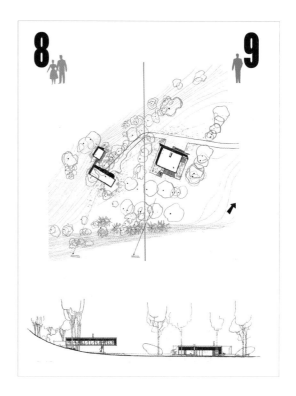

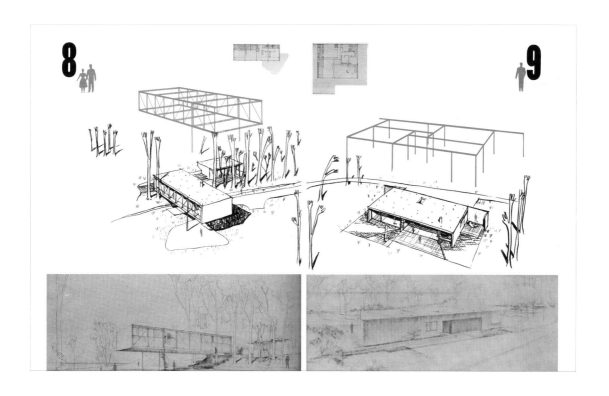

Evans Molded Plywood Products

IN ORDER to determine if there is a realistic way for Evans to profit from the furniture program these factors might be considered—

A. The development so far is to place emphasis on the "design," a great deal of the energy has been directed toward other phases

1) perfection of details easy for mass production
2) standardization and interchangeability of parts, knockdowns for shipping, etc.
3) development of equipment that would make production beginnings possible without complex setup
4) development of two practical and desirable finishes
   one natural indoor
   one completely waterproof outdoor
5) adaptation to various accessible materials

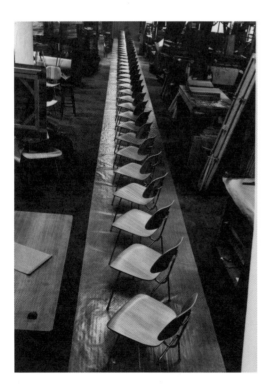

B. Graduated Production

1) Product has never been considered—division—whole hog or nothing. The first degree of production could be housed in our lab

   We to produce seats and backs, metal frames to be subcontracted (subcontractors asking to be delivered in 60 days)
   In this degree a sizeable production could take place in our lab
2) From this 1st degree production could graduate by clear and well-defined steps
3) It has never been considered impractical to cooperate on some basis with an assembly and distribution.

C. Timing and publicity

1) there are in this program many features of design, construction, detail, assembly and finish, which are at the moment unique. It would seem that the identity of the Evans Products Co. should be established.
2) Enough interest has been demonstrated in the program to ensure positive national and international comment immediately upon release if at the time of release its features are still unique.

Source: Charles Eames, handwritten notes on the back of an envelope postmarked February 14, 1946, Evans Products Company, Part II: Projects File series, Charles and Ray Eames Papers, Manuscript Division, Library of Congress, Washington, D.C.

Eames's molded plywood DCM chairs at Evans Molded Plywood Products, Venice, California.

Covers for *Arts & Architecture*, 1947

Arts & Architecture 64, no. 3
(March 1947): cover.

Arts & Architecture 64, no. 12
(December 1947): cover.

CHARLES EAMES

"Mies van der Rohe"

THE MIES VAN DER ROHE show itself is not a complete presentation of his work, and most of the few examples shown have been seen many times before, but somehow or other, this does not detract in any way from its greatness. The significant thing seems to be the way in which he has taken documents of his architecture and furniture and used them as elements in creating a space that says, "This is what it's all about."

Mies van der Rohe designed and arranged this exhibition of his own work in the second floor gallery in the Museum of Modern Art.

Certainly it is the experience of walking through that space and seeing others move in it that is the high point of the exhibition. It comes off wonderfully in so many ways.

In the sense of volume.

In the sudden change of scale from a huge photo mural of a small pencil sketch, to a quarter-inch-to-the-foot model, to man, to twice-life-size photograph, to actual pieces of furniture.

In the simultaneous effect when the natural perspective of the planes of the room are combined with the perspective and planes of the life-sized photographs.

And especially in the variety and richness of the exhibition derived from the simplest plan. By moving and turning within these simple elements one feels the impact of each new relationship.

This experience forms a frame of reference from which the history of Mies van der Rohe's work can be examined. It is good that in connection with the exhibition, Philip Johnson, head of the museum's architectural department, has compiled such a comprehensive book. History, examples and chronology can be found in this monograph, but the exhibition itself provides the smell and feel of what makes it, and Mies van der Rohe, great.

Source: Charles Eames, "Mies van der Rohe," *Arts & Architecture* 64, no. 12 (December 1947): 24–27.

Photograph by Charles Eames taken
at the exhibition.

CHARLES EAMES

"Esthetic Qualities in Architecture"

Editor's note: Charles Eames was one of three speakers on the "Panel on Esthetic Qualities in Architecture" in 1948. While he did not present a paper, he submitted the following remarks after the conference. Also on the panel were Douglas Haskell, then associate editor of Architectural Record *(in 1949 he became editor of* Architectural Forum)

and Philip Will, Jr., a renowned architect of school buildings and of such Chicago landmarks as the U.S. Gypsum Company Building, the Standard Oil Building, and, with C. F. Murphy Associates, the First National Bank of Chicago Building.

BEING PRESENT at and part of "architectural talk" after five or so years in the wilderness, I was surprised to hear expressed several times the attitude that functionalism had gone as far as it could, and that at any rate it was time that the architect again express himself as an individual. The idea was even expressed that this individuality in architecture was one of the only things that could keep it from being swamped from "forces coming up from below"—I thought we used to feel that if the job of architecture as a profession were done properly that the forces from below, and I suppose that means labor, would be a support and a foundation. Somehow I found myself clinging more strongly to the old idea that we have not really begun to express true function in architecture and have only barely begun to be conscious of what the objectives are. Each year brings discoveries of new human architectural needs we have never suspected although of course have always existed.

When the chemical engineer asked if he should consult a sculptor to further the esthetic qualities of his chemical plant, we would have to (on the basis of what had been previously said about esthetics, sculpture, and architecture) say a thousand times no—at that particular moment he seemed to be the only one on whom to pin the hopes of either sculpture or architecture.

It is unfortunate that such a conference should be so dependent on the language of words. It was most strikingly true in the case of Kepes, who if given a space within to work, I am sure could have given a three dimensional experience in form and color that would have been a basis of real controversy and conviction—it would be wonderful, worthwhile, and I think very practical.

Source: *Papers Presented at the Ann Arbor Conference Esthetic Evaluation*, University of Michigan, Ann Arbor, April 2 and 3, 1948 (College of Architecture and Design, 1948), 44.

The Eames chairs lend themselves to many arrangements in a room. They are light and unusually comfortable—not surprising, since they are molded to the human body and not influenced by any former conception of a chair. Shock mounts are used where the parts are joined together. The low center table is also of molded plywood. The Eames cases are strung along the wall and piled on one another. Chairs and tables are already in production by Evans Products Company, nationally distributed by Herman Miller. Photograph by Peter Martin.

RAY EAMES

"We Live in One of the Newest Houses in California"

THE APARTMENT we live in is the direct result of a pattern of living established by our individual requirements.

A beautifully clean and simple shell was provided by Architect Richard Neutra, who designed this group of apartments. His long-developed architectural simplicities impose no style on the tenants, but leave them free to create their own surroundings through color, texture, use of area and objects and equipment needed for everyday life and activities.

In such a shell each family creates its environment without forced direction through architectural details. Our particular needs were set by a pattern of work, which made the prime function of our apartment one of providing materials of calm and rest and pleasure at the beginning and end of each day. It is intended, quite selfishly and quite necessarily, for individual needs rather than to provide a setting for entertainment. Fluidity is maintained so that objects may be brought in for study and pleasure, remaining only as long as they are enjoyed or are a necessary part of work.

Since our immediate concern is the creation of form in painting, sculpture, and architecture in relation to man and living, and as a direct result of the Museum of Modern Art's furniture design competition of a few years ago, in which Charles Eames and Eero Saarinen were awarded jointly two first prizes, it became increasingly important to find the means by which good design could be made available to many people at lower cost.

The museum did an important thing in providing for the manufacture of the winning designs, but it was soon discovered that the then-existing techniques for molding plywood were inadequate. In order to make a real saving, methods of low-cost mass production had to be devised.

So work was undertaken in California to study means and techniques for molding wood furniture. Experiments were in progress at the outbreak of the war, and research and development were quickly channeled into producing molded plywood traction splints, which the Navy used in great quantity.

Along with the work on Navy splints, there were contracts fulfilled for vertical and horizontal stabilizers to be used in aircraft. And later (as the Molded Plywood Division of the Evans Products Company), experimental work was carried out on molded sections for troop-bearing gliders.

At the end of the war, the experience gained in mass production techniques, plus the precise and varied demands of wood aircraft parts, formed an ideal background against which to carry on further work on the furniture.

Valuable wartime developments, such as weather-resisting resins permitting indoor and outdoor use, and special bonding and welding techniques have been applied to the pieces. And now the first phase of the program is under way, with mass production enabling national distribution of reasonably priced furniture—of high quality material and of simple design.

Source: Ray Eames, "We Live in One of the Newest Houses in California," *Mademoiselle's Living* 1 no. 2 (Spring 1948): 52–55, 170.

Top: Eames's and Saarinen's models
of the Case Study Houses.

Bottom: Drawings of the Case Study
Houses.

"Case Study Houses 8 and 9" (1948)

**Charles Eames and Eero Saarinen,
Associate Architects
Edgardo Contini, Consulting Engineer**

CASE STUDY HOUSE 8: The house, looking directly into the sea, is suspended over the land, existing in a free and independent relationship to its natural environment, permitting a choice of participation at the will of the occupants. Designed for the living requirements of two people with close working interests, a first consideration was convenience and simplification of the mechanics of living. Resembling a bridge in structure, it envelops the living space in a simple rectangle. A connecting workshop is placed behind a row of great trees, becoming an integral part of the professional and living activities.

Materials: Foundation, concrete; Framing, steel (open web steel joists); Roof, steel decking covered by insulation and built up roofing; Sash, fixed and ventilating steel; Floor Covering, carpet, composition tile; Interior Walls, plaster on metal lath, corrugated glass, wood; Ceiling, wood stripping; Case Goods, storage wall; Baths, tile; Heating, radiant in ceiling.

Case Study House 9: This house is in direct participation with the land, depending upon that interrelationship for an extension of space feeling and intimate association with its environment. Looking to the sea through meadow and trees, it has been designed to accommodate the interplay of extended outward interest and to expand or contract to the requirements of many or few people. The large social area divides naturally into space serving separate or organized activities; eating, living, entertaining, conversational exchange with few or many being a basic requirement of the design. Bedrooms and interior study are minimum. A large bath-dressing room opens out to a private area defined by natural screening.

Materials: Foundations, concrete; Framing, steel (open web steel joists); Roof, steel decking covered by insulation and built up roofing; Sash, fixed and ventilating steel; Floor Covering, carpet, composition tile; Interior Walls, plaster on metal lath, corrugated glass, wood; Ceiling, wood stripping; Case Goods, storage wall; Baths, tile; Heating, radiant in ceiling.

Source: Charles Eames, "Case Study Houses 8 and 9," *Arts & Architecture* (March 1948): 40–41.

CHARLES EAMES

USC Lecture on Design

IF WE TALK about design at all we must make it clear that it includes all categories of architectural and graphic design—all the other ones are arbitrary ones brought about by a world of increasing expansion. Broadly, the function of design is to supply the degree of technical advantage to the evolutionary problems of process man. The aesthetics of design will be the degree to which the solution of these problems add to the richness of process man and man's experiences.

The process man is actually this whole system that has become man's extension of himself. Buckminster Fuller describes it as the thing a man from Mars would be first aware of. Coming from outer space, he would approach the earth, and getting close enough to a thing, he would recognize a railway system, roads, etc.—the way in which man has extended himself (i.e., nest part of process bird) beyond the limiting range inherent in his body. As process man he has taken on clothes that will protect him from the elements; he has taken upon himself mechanical devices that will extend his behavior characteristics.

I can think of no phases of the aesthetics of design that are not a continuation of your own process or attitudes. But if I really felt that you thought that to be true, there would be little point in my talking to you here. Perhaps more than anything else, design has been plagued with misconceptions of creation under conditions of inspired genius, and discussions of design weighted with pat answers and preconceived ideas.

Eric Gill in an essay called "Beauty Looks After Herself," says, "Look after goodness and truth, and beauty will look after herself." In a way this is a bad starting point, for as Buckminster Fuller says, "If design can function, it is because science has functioned in prospecting for total society by taking the universe apart and measuring these parts, and studying their behavior characteristics." For example, when science isolated the phenomenon of fire and studied its characteristics, it gave us measurable elements in oxygen and hydrogen—predictable characteristics that could be made to serve man. Science having isolated chrome, nickel,

and iron, it was a function of design to put them together in such a way as to form an alloy with characteristics superior to any one of the single elements. Science isolates; design integrates. Amount of work one individual can do is far exceeded by the amount of work produced by specialized and organized endeavor.

If it is the function of design to solve the evolving problems of man (and I repeat "evolving" because man's problems are constantly changing), then the designer's first concern must be the true need. It is very difficult to determine the need without being influenced by preconceived ideas. If we really want to arrive at the true need in any given case, it involves so many subtle phases of need that it would be impossible to gather them all together in their varying degrees at any one time. But the more completely we can gather them together, the more we are assured of a realistic solution to the problem.

Science, in the role of studying and measuring behavior characteristics of man and the influence of man's environment, makes it increasingly possible to pinpoint these needs. Let's take, for example, a chair. There are many things to be considered before the problem can be adequately stated. First, the general function; it is to be used for activities and at a table for dining. We have already made the arbitrary assumption that sitting at a flat surface, 29 inches from the ground, is the best way to dine. We must determine what optimum height is needed to give the best relationship between the average human being and the dining surface. We must determine what the best tactile surface will be so that it will not be an unpleasant thing for the skin to come in contact with, or for garments to catch on. To determine surface materials, we must know what the physical conditions must be so that the material will stand up. We must study the actions of the body as one leans forward as part of the eating process, and as one relaxes momentarily and leans backwards. We must face the fact that the chair may be slid backward and forward during the process of a meal without causing undue commotion. We must consider etc., etc., etc. We must consider the relationship of the object to the other parts of the room, to the psychological effects of the color. We must determine beforehand how important an object it should be in the room, and what its result will be on the conception of space in the room.

What this all adds up to is as clear as possible a conception of a device for sitting and eating at the dining table. We cannot allow ourselves to dwell on any preconceived idea of what a dining chair should be. In such a category of needs, there is no place for a preconceived idea, nor is there a place for a desire to create something new and different. We can only be concerned with the best possible object to fill these needs.

Obviously, one of the significant requirements is apt to be that the average man be able to obtain it for himself in return for a specific number of manhours of work that would be a small fraction of the number that would be required if he himself were to produce this object single-handed. But that the resulting chair need be a whole object by virtue of its close following of function is obviously not true, when we have considered in the needs man's psychological reactions to form, color, texture, the chair's relation to the next larger thing, and its effect on man as part of his environment.

This same problem goes on in the process of graphic design and in architectural design. In architectural design, it takes on, as you can imagine, very complicated forms. At this very moment architecture is functioning for us in a way. But the degree to which these architectural forms were fashioned to serve the true needs of a mid-twentieth century university is a little obscure. They have on the surface details that are reminiscent of some of the external characteristics of what was once a great architecture, in its original form—an architecture in which the designers did their very best to fill a true need of their fellow men. That was in the twelfth century. At that time nine of the ninety-two elements were known and used, and the cipher had just been brought over from the Arabs to facilitate the study of mathematics.

At that time it had long been a habit of creative man to combine materials in a way that would best serve the needs of other men of his own time. I recall seeing an eleventh-century Romanesque building at Maria Laach Abbey between Cologne and Koblenz to which had been added a dormitory of the most fresh and realistic construction. This was before Hitler demanded conformity to the folk style we connect with that regime. The buildings had been done centuries apart, but they were done with the same attitude towards man's needs. There was no disunity, and the relationship between the two was an exciting one.

It does not mean that the Romanesque revival in this country was a completely bad thing, because in the hands of a man like Richardson, who was at his peak in the 1870s, it was not a revival of surface detail but a revival of an attitude in the solution of architectural problems. And what he did within this framework was really architectural . . . and this was in turn passed on to Louis Sullivan. It grew and flowered into great architecture, great creative thinking and great attitudes. These men were at no point concerned with the superficial details that might recall Romanesque architecture.

I understand that the Board of Regents at the university have passed rulings that the architecture of the university shall be in the Mid-Mediterranean Romanesque style. What such a group of men have in mind making such decisions I certainly cannot tell. I am sure their motives were not vicious, and probably their decisions were made because it was the line of least resistance.

Certainly it could not be because they thought it the best possible architecture in which to house twentieth-century students of science and philosophy, because a great deal has changed since the twelfth century. They can't have arrived at this ruling of uniformity with the object of building up the traditions of Harvard's Yard, because Harvard's Yard is not built that way. At this moment, Dr. Walter Gropius, one of the great creative thinkers of the world, is designing for Harvard a series of the most fresh buildings, and as completely appropriate to the mid-twentieth century as he is capable of . . . the same applies to the work of Alvar Aalto designing for MIT. . . . And the expansion program that Eliel Saarinen is developing for Yale.

The last few decades have even made us more suspicious of rulings of uniformity. In many cases they were decreed in supreme ignorance. We cannot forget that the Nazi anthropologists were allowed to work freely within their science, as long as they came up with the supremacy of the Nordic race. And recently the Russian rulings which have influenced the decision of geneticists regarding the effect of environmental conditions upon genes. We recall that at the time [William] Harvey established the theory of the circulation of the blood, it was not accepted by the English Parliament. They did rule, however, that if it would help a patient a doctor could act as if it were true, though the doctor must profess publicly his disbelief in the theory.

Source: Charles Eames, untitled speech, University of Southern California, Los Angeles, January 1949, Part II: Speeches and Writings series, Charles and Ray Eames Papers, Manuscript Division, Library of Congress, Washington, D.C.

CHARLES EAMES

Advice for Students

Make a list of books
Develop a curiosity
Look at things as though for the first time
Think of things in relation to each other
Always think of the next larger thing
Avoid the "pat" answer—the formula
Avoid the preconceived idea
Study well objects made past recent and ancient
but never without the technological
and social conditions responsible
Prepare yourself to search out the true need—
physical, psychological
Prepare yourself to intelligently fill that need

The art is not something you apply to your work
The art is the way you do your work, a result
of your attitude toward it

Design is a full time job
It is the way you look at politics, funny papers,
listen to music, raise children
Art is not a thing in a vacuum—
    No personal signature
    Economy of material
    Avoid the contrived
Apprentice system and why it is impractical
for them
No office wants to add another prima donna
to its staff
No office is looking for a great creative genius
No office—or at least very few—can train
employees from scratch

There is always a need for anyone that can do
a simple job thoroughly

There are things you can do to prepare yourself—
to be desirable
    orderly work habits
    ability to bring any job to a conclusion
    drawing feasibility
    lettering
    a presentation that "reads" well
    willingness to do outside work and study on
    a problem . . .
Primitive spear is not the work of an individual
nor is a good tool or utensil.
To be a good designer you must be a good engineer
in every sense: curious, inquisitive.
I am interested in course because I have great
faith in the engineer, BUT to those who are serious
(avoid putting on art hat) Boulder Dam all's great
not due engineer
By the nature of his problems the engineer has
high percentage of known factors relatively little
left to intuition
(the chemical engineer asking if he should call
in Sulphur)

Source: Charles Eames, handwritten notes on talks
at University of California, Los Angeles, January 1949,
Part II: Speeches and Writings series, Charles and
Ray Eames Papers, Manuscript Division, Library of
Congress, Washington, D.C.

The Neutra apartment building.

Richard Neutra Apartments

CORRESPONDENCE

March 18, 1949

Dear Mr. Neutra,

This is a thank you note I have been intending to write for the past seven years. During these seven years Mrs. Ray Eames and I have been living in the Strathmore Apartments designed by you. It is an experience that has greatly added to the richness of our lives, and it is obvious that it has had the same effect on others living in the group of apartments. Strangely enough, this feeling has no relation to the tastes and background of the tenants in that they were modern or conventional. The apartments you have developed here have given each the opportunity to develop his surroundings in the most expansive way, each feeling that he is living within his own garden, and has complete privacy.

I wish there were more like these so that people could enjoy them. Thank you again for what you have done.

Sincerely,
Charles Eames

P.S. You perhaps know that at no time has there been a vacancy in this group of apartments.

Source: Charles Eames to Richard Neutra, March 1949, Container I:81; Ray Eames, handwritten draft, March 18, 1949, Part II: Office File series, Charles and Ray Eames Papers, Manuscript Division, Library of Congress, Washington, D.C.

Ray Eames's handwritten first draft of this letter.

JUNE LEE SMITH

"Designer Charles Eames Tests Prize-Winning Furniture in His Own Home"

EAMES TESTS his furniture by living with it in his own home, and his wife, Ray, works hand in hand with her husband.

Eames says of his wife, Ray: "She is equally responsible with me for everything that goes on here. She works on the furniture program, on architectural problems, and right now she is doing a series of printed fabric designs."

Ray Eames studied in New York with painter Hans Hofmann. She has done a series of covers for Arts & Architecture magazine, and her abstractions in molded plywood have been shown in the Museum of Modern Art in New York. Daily one finds her, clad in work-a-day pinafore and practical low heels, bending over her drafting board on some new design project.

Source: June Lee Smith, "Designer Charles Eames Tests Prize-Winning Furniture in His Own Home," *Christian Science Monitor* (June 22, 1949): 10.

Charles and Ray Eames in front of their studio, 901 Washington Boulevard, Venice, California, circa 1949.

"Case Study House for 1949"

Charles Eames, Architect

ADAPTATION TO SITE—In order to make the most sense economically, this house should be on a level lot. That possibility existed here, but to place it so would have meant the destruction of a natural meadow, beautifully related to the sea. To keep that part intact and to take full advantage of the protective qualities of a truly grand row of eucalyptus trees, a new site was excavated behind these trees into the hill, saving the meadow at the cost of a 200-foot concrete retaining wall 8 feet high. The excavated earth was, in a sense, lifted out and dropped on the property line between this and the adjoining site (which is part of this program), to form a man-made mound and effective barrier.

AS A CASE STUDY HOUSE—Most materials and techniques which have been used here are standard to residential architecture. In the structural system that evolved from these materials and techniques, it was not difficult to house a pleasant space for living and working. The structural approach became an expansive one in that it encouraged use of space, as such, beyond the optimum requirements of living. However, the actual plan within the system is personal, and whether or not it solves the particular requirements of many families is not important as a case study. Case study wise, it is interesting to consider how the rigidity of the system was responsible for the free use of space and to see how the most matter-of-fact structure resulted in pattern and texture. Another interesting study, in any case, is the weighing of those ideas that did not come off against those that did. In most instances those that did not failed either because they were not carried to their logical conclusion or because the offending part was not considered in relation to its surroundings. Prominent among these are the old problems of service connections, hose bibbs, electrical outlets, flashing, valves, grills, etc. Neglected, these can easily take over the architecture through no fault of their own, but because they have not been carefully enough selected and placed.

Most of the qualities that proved satisfying were inherent in the materials themselves—the texture of the ceiling, the metal joists, the repetition of the standard sash, the change of glazing from transparent to translucent—the surprise of seeing the plane in space by the wire glass in the studio.

Relationship between the second floor bedroom and the 17 ft. high living area seems good, as does the skylight over the stair well. And again, the satisfaction, architecturally, of the relation of house to nature.

COLOR—Color was planned and used as a structural element, and while much concern was given to its use in the various structural planes, the most gratifying of all the painted surfaces is the dark, warm gray that covers the structural steel and metal sash. The varying thickness and constant strength of this line does more than anything else to express what goes on in the structural web that surrounds the building. It is also this gray web that holds in a unit the stucco panels white, blue, red, black, and earth.

All steel sections, metal sash and flashing are painted a dark neutral gray, which enclose the buildings in a sharply defined structural web.

The two bathrooms—each one bay wide and one bay deep—are crisp cubes in form and color. The floors are Voit Rubber Tile, one in black and white checkers, the other in Sea Sand. The interior walls are plain colored Micarta, the ceilings are of U.S. Plywood's bird's eye maple, applied in the baths to the under side of the Ferroboard in order to cut down condensation.

The meadow sloping away from the house toward the ocean is planted in rye with scattered wild flowers. The flowers will do their bit in the spring, and the green rye will be allowed to grow yellow during the dry season. Mr. J.A. Gooch, Landscape Architect, is acting as planting consultant, and has sensitively provided a combination of shrubs and trees that are natural to the environment.

Source: Charles Eames, "Case Study House for 1949," *Arts & Architecture* 66, no. 12 (December 1949): 26–39.

This section of the east elevation is characteristic of the buildings. Of the three stucco panels shown here, one is pure white, one is brilliant blue, and one is black behind white crossed tension rods. The small rectangular panels and the sash are the natural warm gray of the Cemesto board; the two panels above the door are covered with gold leaf. The drapes are a natural colored rayon and linen fabric.

Top: View from the northwest above the retaining wall looking toward the ocean.

Bottom: East elevation of house and studio from across the meadow.

The 11½-ton steel frame shown was
erected in a day and a half with a total
of 90 manhours.

These cross-sections through the structure and retaining wall show the joists condition at both the two-story and the 18' high bay. Extending 18'o" above the finished floor lines are two rows of 4" H columns 20'o" apart—these are spaced to form 7'4" bays. The west row is half embedded in the eight-foot concrete retaining wall. At the 18' height of each column and spanning the 20'o" width are 12" Republic steel open web joists. Approximately half the 7'4" bays are divided into two floors by open web joists at the 8'o" height. Republic's Ferroboard steel decking spans the 7'4" between joists to form the roof.

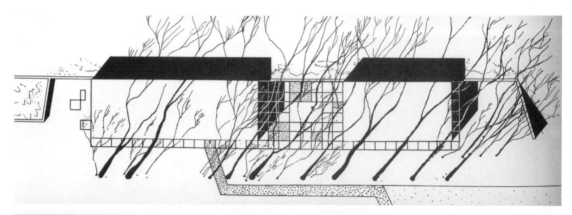

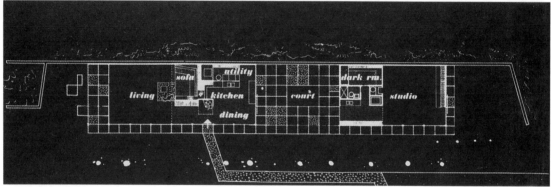

living   sola   utility   kitchen   court   dark rm.   studio   dining

Line drawings.

44

Throughout the house and the studio, with the exception of the bathrooms, the Truscon open webbed joists and Ferroboard decking form the exposed ceiling.

Top: Northeast corner of house from
north court.

Bottom: Interior of studio work room
looking north.

View from dining space area past spiral stair. At right a 14" Modernfold Door divides kitchen and dining area. The floor is Voit rubber tile in Sea Sandstone, one of the colors recently developed for architectural use.

Dividing sitting area from entrance and
next to spiral stair are storage closets
for many uses including guest wraps.
The sliding doors are prefabricated all
metal units which are now in the stages
of production development by Republic
Steel.

The development of the southeast corner of the 17' high living room. Seen in the upper right corner, the Truscon Maximair Window provides circulation in the upper part of the room. Like all other plain white interior surfaces in the building, the one shown here is covered with Walltex, stiffened canvas, unpainted.

The white rectangles shown here on the east wall of the studio are Cemesto panels set into the lower section of Truscon architecture projected sash, providing both exterior and interior surfaces. In this case they have been painted white, but in most cases they have been left the natural warm gray of the Cemesto panels, which is a sandwich of asbestos board faces and Celatex core.

Opposite: In a steel structure so close to the sea, protection of the surface becomes most important and calls for a surface covering designed primarily for industrial plants subject to the attack of corrosive fumes. Such a paint was a rubber based #5 coating of the A. C. Horn Company, from which was mixed a dark, neutral, and very satisfying gray.

The northeast corner of studio building
shows the Mississippi polished wire
glass used in this work room essentially
because of the factor of safety, but in
actuality, the plane in space described
by the wire mesh became an important
contributing esthetic element.

Exterior walls change into a gloomy cave. But glass and reflections restore transparency and add double images that become characteristic of the building.

A portion of the retaining wall.

The house by Eames and Eero Saarinen which is now reaching completion on the same site, will be shown in the final stages of construction. Contractor on both houses: Lamport-Cofer-Salzman, Inc.

At night.

Case Study Houses

TRUSCON STEEL PRODUCTS

Source: Charles Eames, "In the Words of Charles Eames Regarding the Use of Trucson Steel Products in Case Study Houses 8 and 9," *Arts & Architecture* 66, no. 7 (June 1949): 4.

Part Two

1950–1959

CHARLES EAMES

"Case Study House 9" (1950)

Architects: Charles Eames, Eero Saarinen

THIS HOUSE, planned as a project for the Case Study House program, was first published in the December 1945 issue of the magazine. In its final realization it has not substantially changed in general plan or idea. Oriented on over an acre of meadow that looks to the sea, it incorporated the land as a part of the living scheme, depending upon this interrelationship for an extension of its space feeling and establishing an intimate association with its natural environment. There is a direct and unobstructed view across the meadow through old trees to the Pacific.

In general, the purpose was to enclose as much space as possible within a reasonably simple construction. Four steel columns in the center are so placed as to allow cross bracing as well as continuity, with most of the joist load transmitted to the outer rim of the rectangle, all carrying members inside bearing a fairly light and equal load.

The large social area has been designed to serve separate or organized activities and divides naturally into the basic requirements for eating, living, entertaining, and conversational exchange with few or many.

In preparation the house progressed from idea to drafting board to model to reality with remarkable clarity of purpose and with a sure sense of concept, which when completed lacked utterly that sense of stunned surprise that very often confronts those who see their handiwork complete and real for the first time. All this comes very probably from a consistency of idea and purpose which created and carried the whole to completion. There is, of course, a sense of delight and discovery—however, for those of us who have worked with it, it is not surprising that it is beautiful and satisfying, and, in the best sense, integrated and complete within the limits defined by the need and the purpose and the objective.

This house, like the other (which is a part of the same overall project), is, among other things, · the statement of an attitude, and, as such, we are very proud of it, and feel that within its reasons for being it is immensely successful.

As is usual in such projects, it has, of course, in the actual construction been subjected to innumerable vicissitudes and a host of the customary occurring and recurring problems. However, it is one of the wonders of all such undertakings that they get done at all, and in this case we are deeply gratified that, having done it, it is not only successful structurally but that it is also a beautifully created human environment.

The house is equipped with a Talk-O intercommunication system installed by Jewell-Summer Company. Sliding panels in the record cabinets are Plyon by Swedlow Plastics Company.

The ceiling, which is continuous throughout the house, is of habillo from Penberthy Lumber Company, and lighting enclosures contain equipment from Century Lighting Company. The patterned draperies are of "The Squared Circle" by Laverne Originals. The plain draperies are of beige wool by Deering-Milliken. All draperies were made by Frank Bros. Ceiling heating vents are air diffusers by Air Factors used in conjunction with the Payne Forced Air Heating System.

General Contractor: Paul Lamport Landscaping: Evans & Reeves Nurseries; Heating: Affiliated Gas Equipment, Payne Furnace Division; Furniture: Frank Brothers, Van Keppel-Green, Herman Miller; Hardwoods: Penberthy Lumber Company; Paints: A. C. Horne & Co.; Garage floor paint: Plastik Company of America.

Sources: Charles Eames, "Case Study House 9," *Arts & Architecture* 67, no. 7 (July 1950): 26–39. Photographs by Julius Shulman, Copyright J. Paul Getty Trust. Used with permission. Julius Shulman Photography Archive, Research Library at the Getty Research Institute.

Charles Eames and Eero Saarinen,
Case Study House No. 9 (1950).

Structure over service entrance of steel
and Ferroboard roofing material.

Interior view.

Interior views. The fireplace area
showing Truscon architecturally projected windows with movable sash.
The face of the fireplace is painted
a lively orange-red.

Looking into the bedroom, above the
sofa, with the sliding door opened.

Top: View of the house from a man-made mound showing the service entrance and a far view of the large living terrace backed by a concrete block wall. The siding of the house is Truscon Ferroboard painted gray.

Bottom: Meadow side of the house showing wall of glass by Libbey-Owens-Ford with Truscon steel window framing.

Top: Section of the living room wall in Ferroboard siding painted in alternate stripes of white and grey.

Bottom: Case Study House 8 as seen from the front of Case Study House 9.

Case Study Houses

CORRESPONDENCE

Peter Blake, associate editor, *Architectural Forum*,
to Charles Eames, New York
August 9, 1950

Dear Charlie:

Here are some specific questions about your house. I imagine there will be others before I am through.

1. Do you have any trouble with condensation?
2. Have you made any studies that would indicate whether or not there are any money savings as a result of less labor time in assembling standard industrial materials or whether the higher cost of these materials actually raises the over-all cost of a building such as yours?
3. What was the actual time of assembling the building? Did any of the operations go unusually quickly as a result of your having used prefabricated units?
4. I notice there are no interior shots of the studio building. Has this been left unfinished so far?
5. Do you believe that the frame of your building is sufficiently cross-braced?
6. I like the way you use sheet materials other than glass in standard projecting sash. Did you run into any trouble there? What materials did you use?
7. What made you decide to employ bolted rather than welded connections in so many places? Was it greater ease of assembly?
8. Would it be correct for me to say that one of the principal esthetic differences between your house and John's house is that you have in a sense allowed space to flow both vertically and horizontally whereas John's house is more Miesian in concept and plays with space only in a horizontal direction?
9. What is the barber pole stripe on the side of John's house?

Many of these questions may be answered as soon as I get your blueprints. In which case, why don't you just say please see drawings. Otherwise I would appreciate one or two comments.

I am having lunch with Edgar [Kaufmann, Jr.] this week. He will, I hope, give me some of his first-hand observations.

All best to you and Ray.
Sincerely,
Peter Blake

Charles Eames to Peter Blake
August 15, 1950

Dear Peter:

1. We have been through one complete winter and one half through a summer, and condensation has been no problem at all. The steel decking is exposed in everything but the bathroom, where condensation would be the greatest. Here a panel of birdseye maple waterproof plywood is separated from the steel decking by a layer of Celotex. There is 2 inches of Celotex above the decking, and evidently the heat rises during the day to the underside of the ceiling. The temperature of the steel is kept high so that there is no tendency for moisture to condense, and even under the most extreme conditions there has been no evidence of it.

2. The structure as it exists in our house would cost just about what it would to build a conventional house of good quality. That 8 foot retaining wall 200 feet long is responsible for more than its share of the cost, and we discovered that very definite reductions in cost could be made by not spanning the steel the short way, as we did in our house, but rather the long way, reducing connections, etc.

3. All the steel was erected in 48 hours. The steel decking and sash followed in short order, but the fussing with finishing details was as bad as it ever is.

4. The light and feeling in the studio is actually quite wonderful. Perhaps the reason is the one unfinished thing—that is, a ship's ladder to the second floor which is planned but not installed. Access at the moment is still gained by a painter's ladder. This balcony will be used for storage, guest room, etc. In the shot of the living room

Photograph taken by Charles Eames
from inside Case Study House 8
during construction.

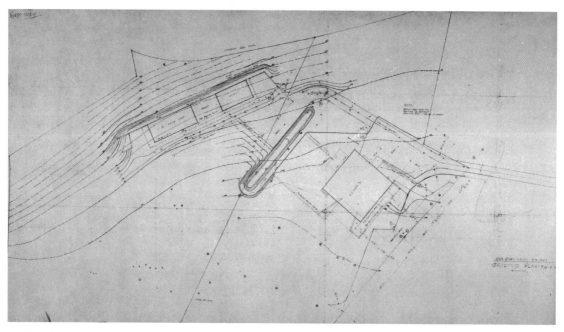

Grading plan for Case Study Houses 8
and 9.

you will probably notice a ladder which we built
in our own shop, and which is designed so that
it can hook on to the open webbed joists at any
point, giving a vertical circulation to the room.

6. We did plan the sash-filled walls like a web
which would receive surfaces of different materials—transparent, translucent, and opaque.
Color wise, as you probably saw in the sketch,
we had counted on a much greater variety
than we later found was necessary. There was
no catch in this theory. The materials we did
use were Mississippi Polished Chicken Wire
Glass—this in the very large areas of the studio,
and esthetically it was very successful in establishing the plane and still allowing freedom to
look through and beyond,—and Mississippi
Factorlite, which as a translucent glass is nice
both for its color quality and the thing that happens to night lights as they are projected on it.

The opaque material in all cases was
Cemesto board sometimes left natural, sometimes painted with a rubber base paint, and in
one case, over the front door, Ray and I covered
it with gold leaf. We had considered thin sheets
of stainless steel bonded to some core material,
and also impregnated waterproof plywood
panels. The only negative part of the Cemesto

board was that it was just about one quarter inch
too thick to use in the sash without rabbitting.

7. I believe the reason for the bolted connection is
ease of assembly.

8. Your description in 8 can very well be true,
although I believe I have thought of our house
as a great web which at the same time supports
and encloses, and within that web a play
between translucent, transparent and opaque
materials. John's house, a great square horizontal plane, is supported by thin columns. The
volume is enclosed by applying opaque and
transparent areas. Actually there is more similarity in the structural details of the two buildings
than is apparent.

9. The vertical stripes on the side of the house
are not ruled stripes, but alternate 6 inch strips
of Ferroboard steel decking painted warm grey
and white. This place was chosen to be the one
where the individual strips of Ferroboard really
stand for a unit, because in the life of the building, it is apt to be the one least seen. It is on the
side of the bathroom terrace, and when planting
is finished, it will be obscured from the road,
and from the meadow beyond. It will remain as
a surprise when one wanders around that corner
of the house.

Enclosed are some shots taken along that little special world upon the hillside of the retaining wall. I do remember on the spur of the moment, while talking with Doug Haskell, giving it some picturesque name, but for the life of me, I cannot remember it. It is not completely planted, but it should be a pleasant space.

Many of the most pleasant things about the house are things on which we had not planned, but which came one by one as surprises. The difference between the shapes of things in sunlight, twilight, and at night, and the little things that happen in relation to the trees and shadows.

In the ground we are putting plants natural to the area, and will forgo the pleasure of green lawn, etc.

The use of straight earth as a man-made mound between John's house and ours I feel was very successful, and can hardly wait to do bigger and better mounds. What it amounts to is vignetting the ground plane upward, and giving both houses at the same time a feeling of greatest space and enclosure. The mound is planted with eucalyptus bushes which will someday be large.

Sincerely,
Charles Eames

Sources: Peter Blake to Charles Eames, August 9, 1950, and Charles Eames to Peter Blake, August 15, 1950, Part II: Speeches and Writings series, Charles and Ray Eames Papers, Manuscript Division, Library of Congress, Washington, D.C. Note: There is no paragraph 5 in the original letter.

Architectural Forum 93, no. 3 (September 1950). Cover photograph by Julius Shulman. Copyright J. Paul Getty Trust. Used with permission. Julius Shulman Photography Archive, Research Library at the Getty Research Institute.

May 5, 1950

Mr. Eero Saarinen
Vaughan House
Bloomfield Hills,
Michigan

Dear Eero:

We have been all involved in a production charette,
getting the chair together and production lined up on
all the parts. I thought that by now we could have
gotten at least one to you, but everytime one did
appear, off it had to go for some special purpose.
However, as soon as possible - it should be the end
of next week - you will have one with which to see
whether or not plastics are here to stay.

I might have said this before, but I will be in Madison,
Wisconsin, the week of July 17 to 21. It may be possible
that we arrange Aspen on the way home, should that
possibly coincide with your Aspen plans. The job there
sounds like a nice change of pace.

It looks as though we are finally going to get Susan
and Sandro out here. Wish we could all be together.

Sincerely,

Charles Eames

[handwritten:] the wire bases.
we have been working
on for the chair
have been terrific
in price and weight —
and seem to be a form
that does not conflict with
the shell itself — the next step we are taking
in this direction is *very* interesting

[handwritten:] Special ♡ ♡ to Lilly —
a family of Sparrow Hawks
has moved in on us — and I
will send Lilly some Telephoto
shots we have taken of their activities

♡ — mvers

[stamp:] RECEIVED
R.
MAY 8 1950
SAARINEN SAARINEN
AND ASSOCIATES

CHARLES EAMES 901 WASHINGTON BOULEVARD VENICE CALIFORNIA

Charles Eames to Eero Saarinen,
May 5, 1950. Private collection,
Los Angeles.

72

Molded Plastic Chairs

**MoMA Low Cost Furniture Competition
Entry Panel by the Eames Office**

The form of these chairs is not new nor is the philosophy of seating in them new—but they have been designed to be produced by existing mass-production methods at prices that make mass production feasible and in a manner that makes a consistent high quality possible.

"Sympathetic Seat"
from *Time*

Last week designer Eames tooled up a brand-new $175,000 factory, turning out the first 3,000 models of his 1950 line.

Composed of a single plastic and Fiberglas™ shell mounted on legs, the new chair is more roomy, stable, and luxurious, but just as simple as, its predecessor. . . . At one time or another, Eames has tackled everything from movie sets to a molded plywood splint used by the Navy during the war. "A forerunner of our furniture," says Eames, "because it supported the body and was sympathetic to it."

Eames is pleased, but still not entirely satisfied with his new chair. It will sell for $28 and he wishes he could design just as good a chair for less. "The objective," he says solemnly, "is the simple thing of getting the best to the greatest number of people for the least."

Chairs by Charles Eames
from *Arts & Architecture*

The new Eames chair is substantially a molded plastic shell susceptible to production in many colors and attachable to a variety of bases for domestic and commercial use. The material, Zenaloy—a plastic resin reinforced with Fiberglas—is virtually indestructible and extremely light in weight. As in the first chair, the object was to use and to develop new technical means by which the best of mass production could be made available in terms of a product of wide use that could be produced with simple directness and at a reasonable price.

Sources: Charles Eames to Eero Saarinen, May 5, 1950. Private collection, Los Angeles; MoMA entry panel, 1948. Eames Office Archives, Santa Monica, California. "Sympathetic Seat," *Time* 56, no. 2 (July 10, 1950): 45–46; "Chairs by Charles Eames," *Arts & Architecture* 67, no. 10 (October 1950): 31.

Eames Office photograph
of the molded plastic chairs.

The shells are available in parchment,
elephant hide gray, light black, with
future possibility of red, yellow, green.
Bases are interchangeable, shell to be
attached by rubber shock mounts, for
numerous general and special uses.

Eames Storage Units

THE NEW Eames storage units make use of an ingenious and inventive system of construction as simple and as openly engineered as a bridge. The elements come together with a fine unforced logic and the methods and mechanics and reasons are completely apparent in the whole.

The units have been designed in such a way as to permit exceptional economies in fabrication, and it was with a practiced foreknowledge of possible complications that the designer was able to avoid the unnecessary and to use the simplest approach to the industrial techniques available. The combination of standard elements can be made to serve an infinite number of uses—in the living room, the dining room, the bedroom, or as a room divider.

Color is used with great flexibility—calm and clean—in feeling with accents of brilliant blue, red, yellow, against a background of neutral colors and natural birch and walnut.

The two standard units are forty-eight inches by twenty-four inches wide; both are sixteen inches deep and thirty-two inches high.

Source: Charles Eames, "A New Series of Storage Units Designed by Charles Eames," *Arts & Architecture* 67, no. 50 (April 1950): 34–35.

Eames storage units.

FROM *PORTFOLIO*

Designs for Kites

THE EAMESES' desire to move freely in a world of enormous and unlimited possibilities (a desire whose practical realization is often labeled idiosyncrasy) is combined with an accurate sense of discrimination and taste, an ability to select among the unlimited possibilities, and return considerable richness to the world. Ray and Charles are, in every sense of the much abused word, a team, and their best known product, the Eames chair, itself is a result of their somewhat torturous experiments together in molding plywood, when they brought

wood up to their apartment after dark to avoid a more conventional landlord, used a bicycle pump as a compressor, and worked out the process of molding plywood in compound shapes. Later, since factory machinery was inadequate to carry out the molding process, they had to work on revising and improving the machinery itself for better and more satisfying results.

Source: "Charles Eames," *Portfolio* 1, no. 2 (Summer 1950): cover, 40–50.

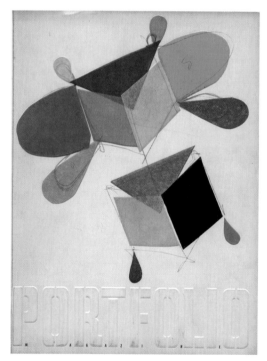

Cover: Design for a kite by Charles Eames, reproduced from his original paste-up made with swatches of colored tissue paper.

Charles Eames's design for a kite, pasted up from brilliant swatches of tissue paper, reflects the same creative organization of form and color that goes into his architecture and furniture.

Top: Ray Eames drawing for the Eames room at Alexander Girard's 1949 *Exhibition for Modern Living*, Detroit.

Bottom: Photograph of that same exhibition.

CHARLES EAMES

"Design Today"

ARBORETUM SPEECH

Editor's note: Charles Eames was one of three speakers who participated in a three-day exhibition and conference sponsored by the Arboretum Foundation of Seattle and the Institute of Modern Living in conjunction with the University of Washington. This text is an edited version of Eames's speech.

SOME TIME AGO a friend of mine and a friend of Mr. [Richard] Neutra's who was an editor of a magazine got a post card from South Carolina. It was a very simple post card and the message was very simple. . . . The message came in the form of a request, which was, "Can you please send me any free information on art?" This card and this request became sort of a hot potato which people passed back and forth and in a way rightly so, because who are we to give . . . anyone any free information on art? . . .

[The writer] had probably heard of art, and she had heard of it on radio programs, and read of it in the newspapers, and, therefore, it must have had some sort of a tangible value. And if it had a tangible value, why then it must be possible for her to get it, if, for example, she collected the correct number of box tops and sent them in to the right place, surely the value of this art would come into her hands. And what she would expect for the box tops if she sent them in would be some sort of a pat answer, a clearly stated formula which she could take and place up on the shelf and then if in the course of her daily work, there came a need for art, she could go to the shelf and open it up and take it down, and then put it back there.

And in a way, in this time of specialization, any subject which we are not familiar with, we are apt to feel that way about. That we can ask for, ask the experts for, and receive a pat answer, which we can wrap up and put on the shelf and then feel at ease, as though feeling at ease were the object and understanding had nothing to do with it. But if . . . we went to any of the great original thinkers of our time and posed the question, we would never get a pat answer; we would never get the package or the formula. What we would get would be something in the form of an attitude. And the catch

there would be that in order to use this attitude, we would have to go beyond and become involved. I mean in order to make use of the attitude which would be given to us, it would mean actual self-involvement. A sacrifice which, in this day and age, few people are ready to accept. And if we take the attitude which is given to us, why, we can't stop any place. The chain reaction. It means never thinking of one thing by itself, but invariably these attitudes involve relation of things to each other. Think of this, but not unless you think of it in relation to other things, and evaluate it by its relation and not unless you take these two things and go on and think of the next larger thing to put it in its proper place.

Actually, with such an attitude over a long period of time some of the great things have been designed. Designed by artists and scientists whose names are completely lost, by people who . . . , in the sort of the real beginning of things, are long forgotten. The designer of the ax helped the designer of the scythe, the crucible, the wheel with the spokes. Surely they are anonymous things, and the names of the designers are not known, could not be known because they were designed over a period of many centuries, and designed by many people. And yet, sort of in each one of these things, each of these people are present as individuals, because they were the ones, each as he took it, [who] sort of selected what was good and added to that, carefully isolated what was bad and took that away; in that process, sort of the shape of the ax, the shape of the scythe, the cup, the spoon, the fork, each one of those things were designed. A great system for design, and only possible if the objective is completely real and the need is actually felt.

In such an attitude toward design, why, it's pretty difficult to conceive a thing that is very popular today and that is the effort toward originality for originality's sake. To be original for the sake of being original is sort of fatal, and can only lead to something derivative. To be original, or have the desire to be original in a field which is set, and have no other desire than to create something of a group which will be new and different, is completely fatal. It is destined to be a re-hash of these elements. But, if the objective is specific and the feeling for the need is real, then this desire to be original, this need to be original and different immediately falls off because there is no room for it. If a person is intent on solving a real and specific problem, whether it's . . . [the] problem of doing the canning or getting the children ready for the costume party, or a large scale problem, to follow the direction toward a logical conclusion of any problem and to try to do that without any preconceived idea of what that solution should be, is

a path that certainly will end in something unique, or can end in something unique. The desire to do the new and different and original immediately falls away.

So, broadly, the function of design would be to apply the technical advantages developed by man to the evolutionary problems of man. And the aesthetics of design will be to the degree which the solution of these problems adds to the richness of man's life, whether it's applied on a very large scale or a very small scale. . . . What I would like to do now is to get into a series of slides which I have, which I don't believe is anything you haven't seen before. They are all things which you have experienced and they are all things which I feel have probably added to the richness of your life, and all of our lives. Certainly [the post card writer] has seen them and we have seen them, so let's start that now.

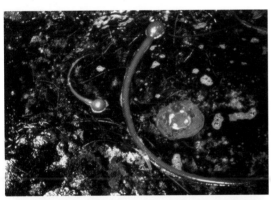

There are some things in nature . . . here are some seaweed floating on a pool and interesting in itself, but also the way it defines the various planes in the pool, you get the surface, the jellyfish and the kelp on the pool and you get the depth of the pool itself, the little line where the rock stands. Is it bright enough in the back of the room for you to see? Well, even if it wasn't, it wouldn't make a lot of difference. Actually, it probably is upside down. But the wetness of the seaweed carries through. You have the same elements here, so a relationship to each other, which is just as real as the other, yet in an entirely different way. The whole colorings and the forms are entirely different.

Here is what at first seems to be one group of people. But actually as you look at it and examine it, there are two groups of people. There is one group coming to and from the Staten Island Ferry and, passing through each other and as they do, this single group forms two groups and you

can almost feel the lines of tension between the
people, very much as you feel the lines of tension
between birds that fly in space and suddenly turn
one way or the other. . . .

Nature again working in the texture of
Eucalyptus bark, which could almost be an aerial
view of some kind of terrain or it could be a micro-
scopic view of something else. . . .

And it also happens on elephants, elephants'
heads. It's a wonderful thing the way you look
through the hair on the top of the elephant's head.
. . .

Driftwood we all know, but it is good to see it
again. And it again is sort of the result of elements
working with a consistent attitude on a given material, so that you have something that with the unity
of the working of the elements and the unity of
the materials, you have made new and wonderful
things.

In taking this, in looking at it now it almost looks like a posed shot, but it was taken up near, or on the way toward, Monument Valley, one of the earliest trading posts where they had traded with the Navajos. Just because everything was placed here with a certain amount of love, the things themselves have a relationship in the past, a unity which is given it in almost an overall texture, in a way texture, just as this is texture, the repeated form of the plant, each one like the other, yet each one different and individual, yet hanging together with straight unity.

So, the firecrackers. The little firecrackers, the lady firecrackers, baby firecrackers, greatly magnified they become something else and something rich in themselves. . .

And Rockefeller Center, we now call rich in a way; even a variation of light in the building; the difference between incandescent and fluorescent light and the accidentals of the lights turned on make a pretty pattern. The structure itself is pretty wonderful. . . . We would see the structure here and the way the skin and flesh and muscle hang on here, and sort of reflect the same orderly form that the bones themselves do, as does the skeleton

of the scenic railway on the old Venice Pier. . . .
You get a certain rhythmic pattern, that all these
members of a thing are working, just to a minimum, and here as it is being torn down, there is
another thing, where you see these nerve ends
shattered and in space. Every stage of this roller
coaster destruction was a dramatic one.

The things that go on above the sets in a movie
studio. The drawings of Piranesi, if you know
them, terribly dramatic, and in itself much more
beautiful than what is going on down below, but
a real by-product of a concentrated effort, as often
by-products of any orderly effort are bound to in
themselves show a counterpart of order.

The fire escape. It's a fire escape in Pittsburgh,
which viewed in one way, could be thought of as
sort of a homely thing, if it is seen sort of distort-
ing a preconceived idea of what a structure should
be, but viewed in another way, can actually be a
very beautiful thing and a rich experience.

The oil wells, too. This was in motion as it was being photographed. And even then, the vertical in the center, the thin line that actually connects with the pump, is a very important element, and even comes out I believe in the still, strangely enough, the latter giving the scale, and the vertical line in the center which is the reason for all this activity. . . .

A church under process of construction, and certainly this building will never look as beautiful as it does now. I haven't had the heart to go by and see what it looked like after it was put up, but never was the structural purpose of the elements more clear, I am sure, in the building than it was at this stage. . . .

A friend of ours has the habit of throwing waste paper in the fireplace. It seems that even if consistently you throw enough paper in a fireplace, why the consistency of that attitude will show up and it doesn't become a bad thing.

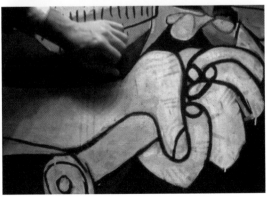

That is *Guernica*. Sorry that you can't see the whole thing and at its proper size because it's a pretty wonderful thing as you know, but even this slide gives a little of the quality beyond the black and white which it has; the elements show pretty well in their strength. And as you look at the face or hand, it is obvious that Picasso, in reconstructing the terror and the hand, sort of took it apart and put it together in a way that went beyond and transcended the inequality, which could be shown in the hand itself. And Picasso and many painters have done it and used it, and used it in this case very successfully. . . .

Bones Blondie . . . is one of the high wire men in Ringling Brothers and Barnum and Bailey Circus. The very use of his costume did the same thing. The ingeniously designed costume took the natural figure of Blondie, destroyed it, reconstructed it, and gave it this fantastic thing.

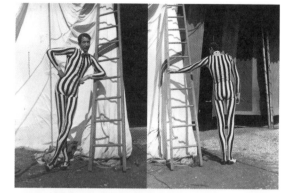

We all know Lou Jacobs, one of the most celebrated clowns. Well, in his own way, hasn't he done the very same thing with his face? I mean, that face that now belongs to Jacobs, which was created, originated by someone even prior to Jacobs, who inherited it, and he himself, as all of the designers of whom we spoke, has sort of added to it, or discarded which things were not appropriate for his new audience, and has come up with this superb make-up which stands for The Clown. . . .

A set of paper dolls, with real imaginative and creative forms, a set of paper dolls by a four-year-old girl who is at the time fascinated with cats, but the forms are so really strong and rich that you feel then the form itself, and you feel the negative of the form in the black . . .

. . . as here on a piece of driftwood you see a form of the snow, which is actually defined by the driftwood, yet is invisible when the snow is not there, yet one which is present when the snow is not there in the fact that the space itself is defined by the piece of driftwood, in a kind of negative form.

This is just a section of a painting photographed in perspective and the perspective gives another imagery to what was a flat painting. . . .

This is the figure of Andrew Jackson in the square in front of the [Saint Louis] Cathedral in New Orleans. It is a pretty good, or a very good piece of monumental sculpture; for that sort of thing the equestrian statue should be seen against the daylight or against the bright sky as this is here, the quite wonderful relationships of the form and the negative forms, as you see through the very, very crisp outline.

And another entirely different spirit of sculpture, a family group, by Henry Moore. As the Jackson thing sort of gave the sharp silhouette and the positive and negative feeling of the areas, this more actually creates the space in which it stands. And it is with the figure, the solid figure itself, which makes all the space around it count and makes the space around it work in a very agreeable way.

Here in this painting of [Paul] Klee's where by pure color, not by form, but just areas of pure color, Klee has made a volume by the advancing and receding squares. He has actually, on this one plane, created a volume in the best sense of the word, just the same as the Moore thing.

And here is the kind of double imagery thing we see while looking through a piece of glass, a kind of phenomenon you experience every day. But to stop and to look at it and then to relate it to the next thing is part of the process. . . .

[Slide not found] This is one of the objects that we talk about when we say the identity of the designer is lost, but yet, for the many designers who took part [in] it are actually present as individuals, you can see the design for the crucible, being gradually refined for hundreds and hundreds of years, and the end use, the need, the objective remaining the same, each person adding what was good and taking what was bad. It's a rich idea in the design. . . .

And so it was with this mica hand that was done by the Indians of Ohio and found there in the mounds. We are sure, well, we know that this hand is no momentary flight of inspiration by one Indian of that time. It is something that was added to and refined by people over a long period of time, and the anonymity of the designer is no less credit to it.

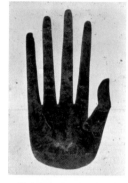

This we know I am sure. The letter and the history of the design of the character and what causes it to form, and the function of the letter is a very exciting thing. The fact that the function and the use of the thing is so clearly prescribed itself, and that within that function of communicating, using it as a communicative symbol, to have the forms be so rich, gives one pause to think of many of the things, the whole history of the use of the quill and the carved letters. The same letter which performs the function varies in character to its different uses in that you can find the best example of an adaptation of a material to a function.

And here, sort of, on the typewriter keyboard, it becomes a rich thing because the letters make no literary sense but almost for the first time you can see them as beautiful arrangements of letters to each other. And for that reason the keyboard is a beautiful and abstract relation of letters to each other. There was a time when by giving emphasis to the spoken word of a letter, I believe, after the First World War in Germany, whole sort of poems were recited through the repetition of one letter. And in our own country, some of the only examples of a true folklore are found in the devising of letters in the vegetable and market stands, numbers which are distinctive and yet which carry terrifically well. This is a more fantastic than functional example, but most of them actually are. . . .

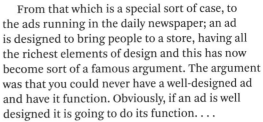

From that which is a special sort of case, to the ads running in the daily newspaper; an ad is designed to bring people to a store, having all the richest elements of design and this has now become sort of a famous argument. The argument was that you could never have a well-designed ad and have it function. Obviously, if an ad is well designed it is going to do its function. . . .

This we know—the circus thing, which has terrific impact, and is an exciting thing to see, the number of the circus itself.

The very sweet thing, the little flower, sort of the sweetest things, the most sentimental, the flower in death, the bed dried-up, withered flower, it's not better or worse, it has its own kind of beauty.

That which the beach washed up, and which the element of time, shown by this web line, occurred, adds to the quality. . . .

And the lines of tension of the telephone wires in Venice, California, which might be viewed by the city planner as somewhat of an objectionable object, and in relation to his objective, they probably are, but it doesn't mean that looking at them can't be a beautiful experience, because the whole feeling of tension, the accents, where the connection of one line occurs to another, etc., can be a . . .

very rich thing; a very pure thing is a drop of
dew on a plant, and then blown up it is a doubly
exciting thing.

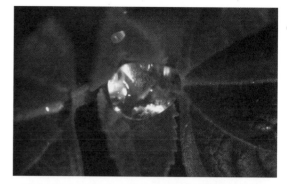

And a daisy in our laboratory put under a
hydraulic press sort of disintegrates itself and sort
of recreates itself and it's another type of thing.

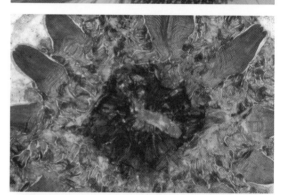

The triple image of a reflected image in a pond,
the sun, the surface, the depth of the pool and
this little edge formed by the plants on the surface
becomes a world in itself, or just a spot in the sun.
. . .

We have a few moments perhaps, and I would like to try . . . answering some direct questions from the floor, which, if they are irritating enough, will let me forget myself for the moment and probably give you something which you would like to hear. Before that I don't want you to leave with the idea all I have in mind is that you venture forth and see the dead flower in the gutter, pick it up and say "Isn't that beautiful!"—but that's all there is to it.

I'm giving you the experiences which I have experienced, and I am sure to a degree the experiences which Mr. Neutra has experienced. And in a way it forms sort of the common denominator between us all. And in the forms and the appropriateness of the forms that were arrived at in nature through construction and through the working of an attitude is also the clue to the forms that the relationships of forms may be appropriate in the work that we are doing.

One thing is that it must apply not to art as an isolated study or design as an isolated study, because if what I have shown you has meant anything, why, it will be clear that the whole business is a sort of a chain reaction mechanism that can start anywhere and go everywhere, and is commonly related to every problem, because we must see every problem as one in design, I believe.

Surely the headlines that we see in the newspapers, many of them are the result of poor design, and had every job there been carried sort of to its logical conclusion—that, is as far as we are now equipped—the state of affairs wouldn't be as they are today. And after all, isn't design sort of carrying whatever job you're setting out to do . . . to its logical conclusion? It's a very difficult thing to do, because the first thing you have is the preconceived idea. Yes, you want to solve it, and you want to understand what the true need is, but the preconceived idea is already there.

If one could, as some of the great can, see and look at everything as though we were children looking for the first time, it would be a wonderful thing, and a wonderful help, and perhaps we would be in a position to recognize the real idiom of design, the real idiom of form of our times when it comes, because where they are crystallizing now, we don't know, and none of us can predict what they are going to be, but we can certainly participate in forming them, and perhaps the smallest thing we do will be the element which will most influence the form of the idiom of anything that we do.

But one thing, let us feel secure in change and just in that, if in an institution, in a school, we can do one thing and that is to give the students, give the people going out, a feeling of security in change when they know sort of what makes this change work. . . .

Now, I believe, there is a minute or two for any questions. . . .

How do you like your house?

Oh, it's a wonderful house to live in. It's very nice. . . . In the morning there is a low or a high fog, but when the sun is out in the morning, it's quite wonderful. And this I will say about it: that the things we didn't anticipate are some of the richest and most enjoyable things of all.

[Question not audible.]

Well, the problems of man are evolutionary. To meet evolution and evolutionary problems, or a constantly evolving problem, with all the means that are at our disposal at this time, which is also an evolving thing, you see, there is no room for a cliché. I, well, there just is no room for it. The word doesn't have anything to do, because you don't arrive at a conclusion to a problem through the use of clichés. Now, you may reuse something else, but if you do it sort of knowingly, as the best solution of that problem as you see it at that time, it's not a cliché. And anyone who would avoid using something just because it has been used before would be knowingly not creating the best solution, if in his mind he knew it was the best thing to do and he was not doing it because he knew it had been done before. He would be guilty, if the man wouldn't perform the operation in such a way because that certain technique had been used before.

How do you keep from going about a design from a preconceived notion?

Very difficult, very difficult. Well, it's impossible. Though what you do is try to train yourself and certainly to train students to solve problems with which they have never been confronted before, and for which (as far as they know) there has never been a solution.

I mean, that's a training thing. If you can invent a problem. I now have a ball bearing; I will place it here, and I want it to travel the vertical distance from here to the floor but I want it to [make] as many fantastic contortions when traveling as possible. Design a piece of equipment that will do that. Such a problem will start thinking that way.

Then also I see us thinking how we want to design the glass or the cup, and the first thing, of course, is not to think of the glass or the tumbler, or of all these things which immediately come to your mind; and in the first place use the word "glass" that means one of specific material, which is entirely wrong, because you have something that holds the liquid and you need something that will get the liquid to your mouth and do all the other things.

Water in a glass is sort of a delightful thing. If it fails in making the act of lifting the liquid to your mouth a delightful thing, it fails in that respect; therefore, it is not as good as this, and therefore, you have to come up with something else.

Maybe it turns out that it isn't a receptacle's fault but rather a fancy coagulating substance.

If you free yourself from the idea "I am going to design a new and novel glass," then you have a chance. If you say in your mind, "I want this vessel to bring this liquid in the best possible way." Does that illustrate the point?

[Question not audible.]

Well, the only thing against it is that it isn't here. That's not against it. That's being cute. My opinion for it is that the best, well, if you're familiar with the house of which she speaks, Buckminster Fuller sometime ago developed a Dymaxion house which hung essentially from a post. The post was the only compression member, and he did everything possible, he put all the rest of the members into tension.

The house, a frame house, weighed about ten or fifteen pounds a cubic foot, or twenty, twenty-five. The Dymaxion house weighed about one pound per cubic foot, and the new geodesic structure, of which the young lady speaks, I believe will get up to a point to where he encloses about twenty-five cubic feet of space for every pound of material. Now, this is very important.

In a way, I wish Mr. Neutra could answer this question, because he knows he could do so much better than I can. I believe one of the most important things is that under the present method of constructing a building, a structure, it's sort of like the marching Chinese: you never catch up. Is that correct, Mr. Neutra? The point is, the shelter problem has always been there, and it grows more acute. You read less about it, that's all. I mean there are times when it's popular to write about the problem of shelter, and then you read all about this house. But it's always there, and an appalling number of people have died in the world because of a lack of proper shelter. Obviously, that's the best thing about this kind of an idea. That such thinking, that this kind of thinking, will eventually lead to the solution and the use of materials which will make real basic shelter for everyone. Whether the house is round or square or an oblong spheroid or entered through a tube doesn't make the beginning any different. The point is that you use this material, and I think I can stop answering it there.

Mr. Eames, can you tell me, have you experienced any shying away from metal furniture, because of its coldness, its hardness and stiffness?

Yes, as someone told me—I forget who it was, but he had a wonderful theory that it was the proximity of metal furniture that induced rheumatism.

The reason I asked that question, we know that mechanics, or people—the reason I experienced this was in the hardware field, the design of tools, lawnmowers, yard tools, people don't like the metal handles as well as they like the wood handles. And the same way in the design of steel chairs, and things of that sort.

Actually, the fact is that we have two types of plywood chairs. One has a metal base and the other has a wood base. Actually I have enjoyed the ones with the metal base most, because I felt in a way that it divided the function of these two elements.

And what I would like to feel is that you walk in the room and not feel conscious of a piece of furniture at all, but if you were to feel conscious of it, I would like to feel conscious of the seat and the back, just as the two would determine the need, and that the metal thing would just sort of disappear in the room. Of course, it doesn't do that, but I think that the dividing of the two elements is a fairly, in the particular case of this chair, a good thing rather than a poor one. But the use of that metal chair has been predicted to be a thing which would live on the market, predicted by really competent people in merchandising, it would live for about six months. Well, this was five years ago. And the sales curve has sort of gone like this. Well, it doesn't mean that it had very small beginnings, that it is now at any sort of a stall, like some of these steel pieces do, but the fact is that the toughness of the metal chair has gone way down here in the book, and it has gone way up beyond that of the wood chair, whether it means anything to you or not.

Now, I'm not actually speaking of the wood, the wood you actually come in contact with, but I'm speaking of the metal which you actually come in contact with.

You were talking about a metal chair and I of course thought you were talking about this chair that we had designed.

I would like to ask you a question about your own house. I wonder about the color panels and so on. Is that a conscious effort on your part of design, in the choice and the selection of colors, and the placement of them, or more or less an accidental thing that somehow happened. And also the cross bracing, is that really, honestly essential to the design?

I cross my heart, it has to be there. The longitudinal bracing for the whole house. I could say the color was accidental, but too many of you people have seen a stack of sketches this high that went into studying the color arrangements on the panels. And if it was accidental, it was studied for a long time, and Ray, my wife, and I both made many, many sketches. But certain things that they do in the light of course are accidental. The object, however, was not accidental: to use the color in a structural way, to have colors, and areas of colors that relate to each other.

There are certain lines of tension, and the advancing and receding of these planes, just like there are in the structural areas. And to use the brilliant colors of these large surfaces, we took eight colors which went through the structured steel, the whole section and the open areas, the opaque areas, tried to place them in relation to each other in such a way that the whole thing held together and didn't, you know, didn't lie apart in a way of the color structure any more than it did physically.

Source: Charles Eames, "Design Today," speech, University of Washington Arboretum, Seattle, October 1950, Part II: Speeches and Writings series, Charles and Ray Eames Papers, Manuscript Division, Library of Congress, Washington, D.C.

Japanese Tea House

Charles Eames to Soko Sen, Kyoto City, Japan
October 26, 1951

Dear Mr. Sen:

Ray and I regret very much that we didn't have a chance to see you again before you left. We and our friends have enjoyed the tea ceremony book, and we think often of you and your beautiful home in Kyoto.

It was so thoughtful of you to send by Susi Matsumoto, the lovely fan and yukata. These beautiful things will also remind us of your visit.

It is too bad that we didn't have time to discuss more the tea house and its architecture. I am sending under separate cover some photographs we took at our house when Yoshiko Yamaguchi performed the tea ceremony there.

Any feeling that I may have about the relationship of this beautiful and ancient ceremony to the architecture which houses it, can only be based on an intuitive feeling for I have no extensive knowledge of either one. If our house was as sympathetic to the ceremony as it seemed, I believe it was because it had to some degree, the elements that seem necessary in any architecture that is to form a background for such an idea. The most important thing that it (the house) has in common with the Japanese tea house, is the fact that it uses extremely humble materials in a natural and uncontrived way. The bare and unadorned I-beams and open webbed steel joists serve very much as the stripped wood structural members of the tea house. No matter what these materials are, whether they have the humble quality of the New Mexico adobe structure, or a New England wood, the attitude could certainly be there.

I must confess, though, that the intrusion on this scene of tables and chairs in a westernized version seems quite shocking to me.

I consider the architecture as creating a space through which the body moves in relation to a very few and carefully selected objects, and the introduction of furniture associated with other conflicting activities must make meditation through focus on the selected objects most difficult.

The environment of the idea must be humble, sensitive, and unobstrusive.

. . . With kindest regards and pleasant memories of your visit,

Sincerely,

Charles Eames

Source: Charles Eames to Soko Sen, October 26, 1951, "Japan" folder, Part II: Office File series, Charles and Ray Eames Papers, Manuscript Division, Library of Congress, Washington, D.C.

Footnote: Yoshiko Yamaguchi (b. 1920) is a Japanese actress and singer who made a career in China, Japan, Hong Kong, and the United States. She was elected as a member of the Japanese Diet in the 1970s and served for eighteen years.

Yoshiko Yamaguchi, interior of the
Eames House living room during the
Tea Ceremony.

CHARLES EAMES

"The Relation of Artist to Industry"

Editor's note: This speech was delivered November 1, 1951, at the University of Colorado, Boulder.

IN GENERAL when I use the term, "artist," I will use it to mean anyone who creates in his work a value beyond that which can be calculated or measured. When I use the word, "scientist," . . . I will mean all those who isolate and measure and those who use the resulting data to predict future performance and to check past performance.

Buckminster Fuller uses fire as an example of the activity of scientist and engineer. A phenomenon isolated by science, taken apart and presented to engineering as two elements, oxygen and hydrogen, measurable and performance predictable to be used to serve mankind. In the same way, science isolated iron, nickel and chromium, measurable and predictable. It was the function of the designer that combined these three elements in such a way as to form a new material, the strength and usefulness of which went beyond the sum of the three. That is a design problem.

So we have science isolating, measuring . . . engineering, analyzing and predicting . . . design combining and relating in a way to go beyond.

When we think of the pure scientist and pure mathematician, we think of them as operating on a rarified plane—the Einsteins, Minkowskis—great creative minds anticipating relationships even yet to be conceived. Parallel to these and in the same atmosphere, the great painters, poets—the Picassos, the Joyces, Mondrians—working in pure distilled aesthetics. There was a time when these happenings of the rarified plane seemed completely remote from man's everyday life. But then Alamogordo fixed that.

What is the "relation between the artist and industry"? In the time when industry was craft, the relation was, I believe, obvious. We can say that industry is, as were the crafts, the link between pure science and pure engineering, on one hand, and humanity, on the other. It is through industry that science serves the everyday needs of man, and in every case, the physical characteristics of the service are prescribed by the designer. The quality varies greatly, but in the degree to which any product of industry serves man richly and fully, the artist has functioned—be he artist-designer, artist-executive, artist-tooling engineer, or artist-merchandise manager, somewhere there was an artist and this can be demonstrated.

It can be demonstrated here in Mr. Walter Paepcke, who will speak to us today. His title may read Chairman of the Board, Container Corporation of America, but his function, the results of which we see, is that of an artist.

In any problem of design, there are, in addition to measureable factors, an infinite number of factors not yet measured and not yet isolated. *The degree to which the ultimate performance standards go beyond the solving of the measurable factors may show the degree to which the artist has functioned.*

Take any example—take a cup. There are many factors that can be measured and solved, but their combinations and relations to the human factor make the problem infinitely complex. Some are: The optimum volume of liquid to be carried to the mouth of the average person in the average situation. The balance of the cup when lifted or tilted, security when at rest. The shape from the standpoint of fluid dynamics. The shape from the standpoint of the human scale. The shape from the standpoint of production techniques. The resistance of the material to moisture, corrosive action, and impact. The degree and effect of heat transfer.

The combination of these factors is already so complex as to demand intuitive solutions, but this is only the beginning. There is: pleasantness from the tactile standpoint, texture and the acoustics. Color associations. The relation between the specific liquids to be used, the specific occasion and the form. The degree to which it holds together as a unit, its simplicity as a statement, its economy of means. The way in which it is presented and transferred to the customer.

Finally, the question of the validity of the cup at all. Liquids should perhaps be transferred from a volume container to man's stomach by an entirely different means—what can it be? So we start all over again.

This is a design concept of unlimited service—of unlimited performance standards. Broadly, the function of such design is to apply to man's evolutionary ever changing needs, the greatest degree of man's technical advantage. The presence of the artist will be evidenced in the degree to which the solutions add to the richness of man's experience. When industry as a whole starts working within such a complete service concept of design, there will be no need for thinking of obsolescence in the artificial sense.

Certainly, one of the concerns of such a conference as this must be a preparation of students for such work. I honestly cannot see the artist-designer being trained in the art departments of our colleges and secondary schools. It would be a rare thing to have a student's beginnings be so humble and sound as to prepare him for the average well-thought-out "foundation course." These beginning exercises are often very advanced and subtle experiences. Sometimes the instructor, who just recently has become aware of the fullness of tactile experience, plunges enthusiastically into presenting the tactile exercise as a basic fundamental to the beginner. Danger—words, clichés, the art type patter. . . .

While doing an exhibition in the Merchandise Mart some years ago, we had some students bring their work to use in relation to the show. I happened to be in the freight elevator with some maintenance men and a student carrying a great Lucite mobile construction. Obviously fascinated, a carpenter asked, "What the hell is that?" The student answered in measured tones, "*That*—is a space—mod-u-la-tor."

If there is to be a beginning, it must be the building of a constant awareness of quality—a constant awareness of things in their changing relation to each other—the ability to determine the immediate objective in each problem—and the ability to proceed towards it with the fewest possible preconceived ideas.

I don't believe these beginnings can happen in the art department. *But*, the art department could do a terrific job in making them come about. Call it expediting or irritating, or what you will. If the awareness of value and relationship could infiltrate every department of school and work, we would begin to have a chance—not just in our design world but in our world. Fortunately, it doesn't make much difference where you start—it is like a chain reaction.

There seems to exist, even at an early age, a general feeling that when confronted with more than one thing, one must immediately compare and judge, good, bad or best.

What do you like best? Red or blue—Bach or Be-bop? Recently I received a questionnaire in which was the question, "Which is more important—beauty or function?" *I* should make a choice between keeping my head or my heart?

Now, in any of the classes—civics, literature, economics—it can be shown that things are not better or worse but different, and what they *are* changes according to the things to which they are related. To this is added a simple lesson. There can exist two specific things—one with value "A," another with value "B." But put them in the proper relation to each other, and you have the value $(AB)_2$ or $(AB)nth$.

It can happen between a voice and a cello; light and dark. It can be shown in literature; in chemistry; in coffee and cake; or even two areas of color in relation to each other.

It may not be easy, but I believe that even the engineering department of a college would find this attitude of art not merely compatible, but an accelerating force towards their objectives—an extension of the engineering concept beyond that which can be computed.

Physics, chemistry, biology—what a world of training for the artist and the human being—relationships, discipline, economy of means, unity in the large complex, the vast world in the infinitely small.

The physics experiment and the report for the experiment make a good example, because here the objective is very clear. There are very few things the student can present where the objectives are so specific that he can proceed directly toward them. The experiment itself is clear because it is abstract. It may be calculating degrees of friction or results of a change in atmosphere, but whatever it is, the objective is clear. So every step taken by the student is one toward that end. There is no need for originality or no reason to attempt it for the sake of being original. The experiment report itself is an instrument for transmitting the procedure and results from the student to the instructor.

The more graphically sound the presentation, the better the report will be—the richer the experience in reading the report—the richer in making it.

I have used the physics class as an example, but it has its parallel in every course.

It is simultaneous and in relation to these experiences that the study of the fine arts becomes the great plus value. It is this combination of interests and involvements that helps us when the problem's complex goes far beyond what we can now measure. Here the work of the great artists, the great original thinkers, helps us recognize the moment when it comes.

From the opposite end comes no less a help— always, it seems, the toy, the fantastic, the game, has worked as a counterpart of the concentrated aesthetics of the fine arts—a constant flow from painting to toys, from toys to sculpture, from music to games, from games to poetry—and together they have fed the process man.

It is possible that we will face a future with a higher standard of living and more leisure than ever before. It is also *very* possible that we face, what will be to us, unprecedented discipline and restriction for a long time. In either case, the preparation for the artist-designer is the same, and in *neither* case is there any room for pat answers or preconceived ideas.

If nothing else, a student must get from his training a feeling of security in change. He is living in a changing world and his only *real* security will lie in the knowledge that he can deal with the new and unexpected.

Source: Charles Eames, "The Relation of the Artist to Industry," speech, November 1, 1951, University of Colorado, Boulder, Part II: Speeches and Writings series, Charles and Ray Eames Papers, Manuscript Division, Library of Congress, Washington, D.C.

CHARLES EAMES

"Design, Designer, Industry"

*[This talk was] delivered late in June this year [1951]
at Aspen in the Colorado Alps, where officials of the
Container Corporation of America invited some two
hundred business executives, product designers,
graphic designers and educators to consider the role
of design in business today. In the course of four days'
conferences, one issue stood out; businessmen considered design a good gambit in the contest for profits,
while responsible designers argued that competitive
advantages was a poor goal compared to the full
development and wide distribution of human satisfactions, both spiritual and physical.*
    —Edgar J. Kaufmann, Jr.

IN THE COURSE OF one of the earlier sessions of
this conference, Don Wallance, touching lightly
on the many facets of the relationship of design to
industry, made one observation that caused spon-
taneous murmurs to run to the audience. This was
a remark made from the consumer's standpoint
that may serve as a warning against design with
more integration than integrity. A consumer product may be so loaded with shelf-appeal that its
victory over competition is immediate, up to and
including the point of sale. But its true value will
not be known until the consumer takes it home
and lives with it. Then, one of two things will usually happen. If after he has gotten it home the
object becomes a rich and contributing part of his
life, it will take on a beauty and receive a love far,
far greater than that which caused it to be picked
from the shelf. If, however, in the proving laboratory of the consumer's home the object proves a
fraud or fails in a great degree to perform, it will
inevitably take on a sick kind of ugliness—all the
more so for its pretence to be beautiful. Nothing
could be worse, or more deserved, for the conscious manufacturer than a switch.

Two examples of the design program within
the Martin-Senour [Paint] Company were shown
to this conference by the company's president,
Mr. [William] Stuart. The first was an excellent
sample color card, the result of a sincere attempt
to raise the performance standards of a useful tool.
But the second example, the wet-paint sign, I am

afraid was not such a happy one. Perhaps in the
enthusiasm of bringing modern painting into the
program, shelf-appeal here got the better of function. Conceivably, someone would want to use that
sign as a decoration for his rumpus room. But,
functioning as a wet-paint sign, would it, in a crisis, ever stop you in time?

This is a part of the great trap, and we should
be grateful for this reminder that some things
can be so integrated and so "attractive" that they

Martin-Senour "Wet Paint" sign.
Private collection, Los Angeles.

completely fail in the specific function they should perform. This happens when clichés take over, whether they are the clichés of modern painting or of anything else. For the sake of our children's lives, let us hope that the traffic "Stop" signs never become so integrated!

The same thing often happens in the designs of building materials. In an all-out effort to make their product "attractive," the manufacturers so art it up that it becomes impossible to make it hold its place as an element in building. Such super-appeal puts the architect, who must work with the elements, in the frustrating position of a painter who, reaching for a tube of pure color, finds plaids and polka dots coming out when he squeezes it.

Here I would like to quote from the brochure describing this conference. By taking this passage out of its context, I may be doing injustice to the thought; if so, I apologize.

"American business faces a new era and a new phase of competition. Because of the levelling or equalizing processes now generally practiced throughout industry (automatic machinery, uniform wage and marketing practices), the opportunities for effective competition based on traditional factors of price and quality of product have been greatly diminished.

"Competition of the present and future must be based on new factors, on the appearance, attractiveness and appeal of the product, and on the reputation of the companies who make and sell it. This involves the use of imagination and visual appeal not only in the design of the product itself, but in everything which associates the company with its product in the mind of the public: advertising, printed matter, company offices, factories and displays."

The attitude and works of the man who made this statement are positive without question. That is demonstrated through the works of his company—the Container Corporation of America—and by our presence at this conference. But the statement itself I find scary—as, I guess, I do all conscious effort towards shelf-appeal.

"We have gone as far as we can in quality and price; therefore we will add art to make this product attractive"? This thought is diametrically opposed to everything we try to stand for and work towards.

Have we, in fact, gone as far as we can in quality and price—service per dollar—standard of performance per man-hours' work? Gone as far as we can?

We've hardly started, and everyone here knows it.

The facets of performance of any product are innumerable—some measurable, many immeasurable; some perhaps of which we'll never be aware and which will only be solved intuitively. But everyday some new need of performance is isolated and made calculable—and the way to increasing service for the dollar is made easier.

If there really is a desire to make the product good—that is, turn each consumer dollar into the highest standard of performance—then there must be goodness all the way down the line. This is the "integrated design program." To want the materials to be good, the package to be good, the delivery to be good, the printed matter, the office, the plant. And really to want the hours of each employee on the job to be good—and good for him or her; because if this is true, and the intention is really to make the life of the employee on the job a happy one, the steps are clear, and the relation of morale to goodness of product will take care of itself. But plant morale programs that start from the "let's increase the output" end often fall into the same trap we have seen in respect to "shelf-appeal." They can get to look more than to be.

Let's scrutinize our objectives, look at them big, look at them small. . . .

When we think of great imagination and far-reaching perspective combined with infinite patience and attention to detail, we think of Leonardo Da Vinci. We are often apt to think there are no Leonardos today, and as usual we are wrong, because there are. It's just that it is never a snap to apply such attitudes, even though in the long run they offer by far the greatest odds. Among such great original thinkers we must all certainly be grateful for is Buckminster Fuller. His is real perspective. I believe it was George Nelson who once said, "You know, Bucky somehow has the quality of looking at everything he sees as a child looking at it for the first time." What a great faculty that is! If any of us becomes momentarily complacent about the quality-cost ratio of our products, then it's high time to take another good look at Buckminster Fuller's attitude towards production standards— the total service he would provide per man-hours' work.

He has pointed out that originality for the sake of being original is simply no good and can only lead to something that is, in the worst sense, derivative. To this we would all agree—whether we ourselves can avoid it completely or not. But

Fuller goes further and suggests that if our objectives—our immediate objectives—are clear, and if we proceed, free from preconceived ideas, to work towards them, then the need for the originality is gone—and the work stands a chance of being as big as the objective.

Sometimes it takes a new kind of courage to stop trying to be original and instead to examine the objective closely, to see what it really may be. As another example of Fuller's perspective, he says that the great advantage that education can provide to a student is "security in change." What a great gain that is over safety in the status quo!

Herbert Bayer's ads—such as the House of Cards—certainly do not come as the result of trying to be original. His works have an immediate objective, a real conception, a big idea. They are also real advertisements, not modern paintings. His objective was certainly clear, and he moved so directly

towards its fulfillment that it enriched the thought, the product, the page and the life of the page-consumer. That's the way it should be with our own work—and I mean, you know, in every detail of our work. Not just the label on the package, but goodness in the package, the product, the plant, the people that make it, the way it is presented and thought of. No one will deny that these details, done better and to everyone's benefit, are often rewarding in unlooked for and surprising ways.

This is "Design, an Element of our Business"; this is "Integrated Design, a Concept of Order and Vision"; this is "What the Artist-Designer Offers Industry."

Let's make an honest-to-God effort to find out what good is. And if it is good, do it.

Source: Charles Eames, "Design, Designer and Industry," *Magazine of Art* 44, no. 8 (December 1951): 320–21.

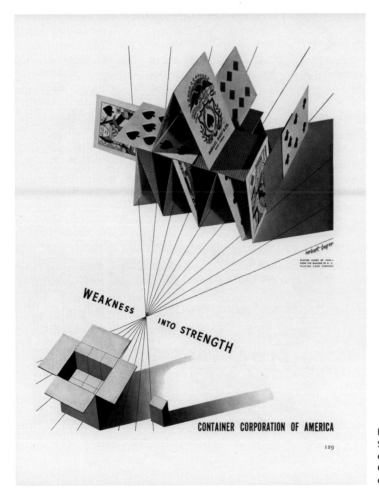

WEAKNESS INTO STRENGTH

CONTAINER CORPORATION OF AMERICA

129

Herbert Bayer "Weakness into Strength" Container Corporation of America Advertisement, 1941, Courtesy Herbert Bayer Collection and Archive, Denver Art Museum.

Packaging for Soap

CORRESPONDENCE

Editor's note: In 1952 Hubert Lewis Will (1914–1995) represented the Eames Office as an attorney at Nelson, Boodell and Will. In 1961 he was appointed a United States federal judge and served in that capacity until his death.

**Charles Eames to Hubert L. Will, Chicago
February 29, 1952**

Dear Hugh:

The Iowa Soap thing looks really very interesting. We have done some thinking and fussing on it, but I am a little at a loss as to know what should be the next step. Perhaps it should be playing with some rough ideas on packaging and outlining to you possible directions that the program might take. Yet, at this stage, presenting a few done-up packages does not seem quite right, because the idea and the conviction behind it is more than just a few super-arted-up boxes. I really feel that the service aspect of the problem could carry a quality product such as Iowa Soap a long way, and that the very consistency of the attitude would be the thing that would yield parallel dividends in editorial space in the consumer magazines, because it could involve a kind of richness in service that both the public and the publications have been starved for.

In addition to the graphics and the color, the problem of better pouring, storing, etc., would, of course, be studied. There are also aspects in the whole presentation of the performance claims that we would like to discuss. When people try to outshout each other on boxes, they all fall into a pattern of similarity and become completely camouflaged and indistinguishable, one from the other.

We are going ahead on some mock-ups of these packages just for our own interest, curiosity, and conviction in the problem. Have you any ideas as to a next step as far as Iowa Soap Company is concerned, if you still think it is a good idea?

Sincerely,
Charles Eames

Source: Charles Eames to Hubert ("Hugh") L. Will, February 29, 1952, Part II: Office File (Pre-1960) series, Charles and Ray Eames Papers, Manuscript Division, Library of Congress, Washington, D.C.

Upholstered Wire Chairs

CORRESPONDENCE

Charles Eames to L. C. Sattmus, *Domus*, Milan
March 26, 1952

Dear L. C. Sattmus:

Many thanks for the very nice cable. . . . In doing the wire upholstered chair, we tried to do a piece that would be of good material and yet immediately economical. In it, we exploited the wire systems, not only for the base, but for the structural shell itself. While it has many parts and many welds, it is so a part of the production system, the results are most economical. To provide further economies, we have made the bases on these shells interchangeable with the bases on the plastic chair, working on the same theory that we have in our other pieces and that is, that the chair has essentially two parts—one, a surface to receive the body, and two, a structure to hold that surface in proper relation to the ground.

The upholstered pad which goes on the wire shell is made by a production technique developed in our office, and is easily removed, making a pad interchangeable. As an additional economy, we have, at present, kept the coverings of these chairs down to two basic fabrics and leather. This permits the stockpiling of the pieces in production and eliminates the handling necessary for special fabrics.

We have sent you illustrations of six different versions: a pivot model of desk height—a dining or desk height model on a wood and wire structure; a dining or desk height model on a wire structure—a rocker model on a wood and wire structure—a lounge model on a cross rod base—and a very low model on a wire structure.

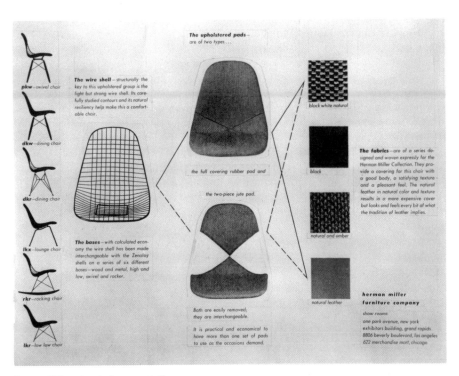

Eames Office wire chair presentation.

There was some concern that the public reaction to a wire shell would be negative, but so far, this has been no problem. The chair has been received well and the prejudices towards humble materials seem to be giving way. Most criticisms that have come in have been perfectly legitimate ones and are not based on fear of the unfamiliar.

If there is any specific information or any material you would like, please say so. We will try to get it to you without delay.

My thanks to you and the whole staff for *Domus*, which we enjoy.

Sincerely,
Charles Eames

Charles Eames to L. C. Sattmus, March 26, 1952, *Domus* folder; Part II: Office File (Pre-1960) series, Charles and Ray Eames Papers, Manuscript Division, Library of Congress, Washington, D.C.

Charles Eames to George Howe, chairman, Yale University School of Architecture, New Haven, Connecticut
March 25, 1952

Dear George:

My secretary is billing you for the two leather chairs, but before, or parallel to doing so, please let us know if there is anything wrong with these pieces, as they were from the very first to go out and often these are far from perfect. I am particularly concerned about the black finish on the wire base. In some of the bases the finish was not solved, but the later ones have been done with a zinc plating—which is very effective protection against corrosion, and a black stain over that. If there is any failure on this, let us know and we will replace it immediately.

Sorry our visit was so brief—it was a very stimulating experience for us. Ray sends best greetings.

Sincerely,
Charles Eames

George Howe to Charles Eames, Philadelphia
April 7, 1952

Dear Charles:

When those wonderful chairs arrived in Philadelphia I thought I would write you a note to tell you my high opinion of them when the bill arrived and I sent you my check. Time passes so quickly I have no idea how many weeks ago that was but it has just occurred to me I still haven't received a bill, so I must apologize for my delay in expressing my admiration before expressing it.

The chairs are totally satisfying to me. Their lightness is so agreeable to arm and eye, their shape so physically and aesthetically right, their surface so caressing to hand and buttocks. You are a benefactor *hominis sapientis et sedentis* (hope I got that Latin right).

Please let me know how much I owe you. When shall we see you again? Love to you both.

Yours,
George Howe, Chairman

Verla Schulman to George Howe
April 9, 1952

Dear Mr. Howe:

The bill for the 2 DKR leather chairs amounts to: $52.80

Very truly yours,
Verla Schulman, Secretary to Charles Eames

Charles Eames to George Howe
April 14, 1952

Dear George:

It was very thoughtful of you to send us such a nice note. I have just discovered that a bill actually has gone out to you, which was a little of a shock because before sending one, I, too, wanted to write a note—and this is what I would have said.

The chairs that were sent to you were a pair of the very earliest, and as such, may have been unsatisfactory in some detail. Since then, the handling of the leather has been improved; the joints on the perimeter pieces are skived, and the general appearance is more tailored, so that if anything is not perfectly right with the chair or the finish proves unsatisfactory, please, please, let us know immediately so that we can have a replacement sent.

It was so nice to see you for a short time. It would be very nice to see you on a visit out there. Aren't you due for one soon? Ray sends warm greetings.

Sincerely,
Charles Eames

George Howe to Charles Eames, New Haven, Connecticut
April 21, 1952

Dear Charles:

Thanks for your offer to replace my chairs by improved examples but it is to be my boast that mine are "early artist's proofs."

Yours,
George Howe, Chairman

Sources: Charles Eames to L. C. Sattmus, March 26, 1952, *Domus* folder; Part II: Office File (Pre-1960) series, Charles and Ray Eames Papers, Manuscript Division, Library of Congress, Washington, D.C. Charles Eames to George Howe, April 14, 1952, "H" miscellaneous folder, Part II: Office File (Pre-1960) series, Charles and Ray Eames Papers, Manuscript Division, Library of Congress, Washington, D.C.

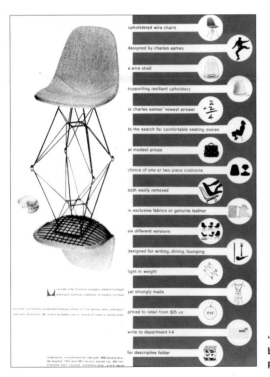

"Upholstered wire chairs designed by Charles Eames," advertisement published in *Interiors*, April 1952.

AIA 1952 Speech

Editor's note: Remarks delivered at American Institute of Architects meeting, Kansas City, Missouri, October 10, 1952.

YESTERDAY AFTERNOON there was quite a bit said about, you know, "function is all right, but . . ." It seems to me, not so long ago, that function was admitted to be respectable; and in a way, I suspect that it's a little too soon to start "butting" it out of its existence.

If the ultimate performance of a building or product is a measure of the way it has functioned, how could we damn a work because it has served mankind too well? If the telephone on our desk is a pleasure to look at and if it feels good and if it smells good and if it tastes good, and when you put it down on the receiver it sounds good, if it adds to the sort of enrichment of our life, isn't that the way in which it is functioning for us? Isn't it serving us better; isn't it functioning a little better? Then is there any possible way it could serve us better if it would function less?

I feel there are still many aspects of architecture that are calculable, but very much neglected. In the Mies [van der Rohe] house that we saw yesterday . . . there may be something wrong about that house, but if there's something wrong about it, I'm sure Mies would agree, that it's not that it functions too much. I think that any negative thing within it would be that it didn't function quite enough; and Mies would agree to that. Mies is a sensitive man.

We talked about sensitive people . . . and the architecture has been referred to as super-functional, or whatnot, and the fact that architects should become more sensitive; but if anyone has seen or heard of Mies van der Rohe arranging an exhibition, or determining some relationships of a facade, moving a column or a panel half an inch and stepping back and then a half an inch the other way and a dozen people and carpenters holding their breaths while he arranges elements of his own work, [why] the man couldn't be more sensitive. I feel that Mies's idea is to be the architect who would lay one big perfect brick, and lay it perfectly. . . .

As design problems, I feel that architecture, city planning, furniture, fabrics, pottery, etc., are essentially the same, and you might agree. They must be broken down into as many calculable factors as possible, and these factors must be solved in relation to one concept, one sort of big idea . . . take a house, or take something simple, take a cup, for example. We have to think of a cup in as many ways . . . we have to consider its fluid dynamics, and how a liquid of the viscosity of coffee or tea would slosh around, how, within the balance of the cup, how the balance of the cup relates to the hand, the ability to take it from the table up to the lips without the liquid getting out of hand, and know pretty well whether it's going to be coffee, tea, or whether it's going to be hot chocolate or something of a higher viscosity.

We also have to know something about heat transfer and thermodynamics so that you have a material that isn't impossible as far as holding a hot liquid, and that the way it's transmitted to the hand doesn't burn, etc., etc., and it has to be tactilely pleasant, or it has to be a material that is not impossible to feel good about holding. When you set down a cup it has to have a pleasant sound and, yet, it can't break. Now, that doesn't mean that it has to have the sound with which we are familiar, that it rings, which is not an unpleasant sound, except when four hundred people do it together, maybe. But that is one of the elements. The surface of the material has to be one of extremely low moisture absorption quality, and yet it also has to be one that will not stain, you have to wash it, etc., etc., etc.

Well, at any rate, point only to demonstrate that there are an infinite number of factors that have to be considered—whether it's a house, or a cup, or whatever it is, . . . all these have to be considered and broken down.

That brings us to yesterday, again, during which was said, I believe, more than once, that it was a good idea that if architecture would again take the lead over engineering, and guide the situation. Now I agree with this; I think it would be a hell of a good idea, but do you know what you are saying when you say that? You just take a look around and consider the progress being made by engineering and the physical sciences, and you will agree that architecture better start pumping. But, it is not completely bad, because architects and designers have, I believe, a great advantage. Architects are very human beings . . . very. That's why not just anybody can be an architect or a designer. And being very human beings, they have real interests and real enthusiasms, sometimes all extracurricular, but nothing is really extracurricular to an architect. He can and will look under what lies under, and find something that is essential and peculiar to the particular situation. And his enthusiasms which exist, not for some gain he might later have for them, or not, for some use that he might make of them; but for themselves alone, real enthusiasms come to his aid time and time again, and I suspect that if he is serious about taking the lead over engineering, this is going to be his greatest hope.

Enthusiasms are like chain reactions. It doesn't make any difference where they start, just so they start, it can be anything—it can be baseball. It began with an architect's mind when it's getting under the skin, looking at baseball, thinking of it as a game, relation of man to man, relation of man to the physical space, a trajectory of a ball as it is hit out, the way the direction of the ball may be varied by the prevailing wind velocity, the stands in relation to the ball field and how it would be possible to arrange it so that everybody was behind whatever plate it is necessary to be behind, and all that monkey business.

Or, it could be something, it could be magic; and all architects, like some others, like to show off in front of their grandchildren. And . . . magic is one way, it can start with a trick, and he's a sort of a great guy, but he's also getting into something else, pretty soon he discovers laws of perception, and he's well on the way to the kind of stuff he then can become interested in, which, like they're doing at Eames, real sort of beautiful and intricate ways of fooling oneself and, you know, what is it, or what you think it is, or is it what it is, which is what you don't think it is.

And this in a way has a lot to do with architecture. It's the whole business of movement in space,

it's the beautiful props, it's the balls that appear, you see them and then you don't, and the rings that clang and the very equipment with which a magician works, which is fantastically appropriate to the thing, including the gal that holds the props and all that business.

It could be anthropology, the science of man, and through anthropology, one thing leading to the other, does this man necessarily want to live in that kind of space. How does he react to something, and what does it recall from something that he doesn't remember years ago, and what has been the result of cultures as a result of either confining him in quarters or giving him open space to live in, etc., etc. . . .

Or it could be sociology, the clues to man's relation to man, and the action of man either as an individual or as a mass; it can be calligraphy, sort of wonderfully stylized stuff, things that designed what, not by an individual, never, but by thousands of individuals, working one after the other, each adding a thing that is positive, each coming upon a negative thing, and taking it from it, and there you have represented real individualism that over a long period of time. . . . Terrific anonymous products, but serving, my God, functioning. What could function more than, and in a better and richer way, than calligraphy?

Oceanography, the sea around us. Rachel Carson—boy, what a genius, what a plan, what a conception, just within that field. The whole article appeared in installments in the *New Yorker* and is now in a book, but a beginning to end, a sort of entropy of things.

Mathematics, the precision of numbers, the relation of number to number and then, within mathematics—you find that it's not infallible. The concept is really not quite right, but instead of shaking the foundation, because of the basis upon which you find that the concept is not right, why, you feel relieved because it was now one misconception less that you have to labor on, and a real feeling of security can come in a realization of such change.

The theater, sort of a heightening of basic situations, a sort of shorthand of life. You get a lot of things compressed, and yet the essential facts go across. Working within a volume in space and business. The dance, man's body is, perhaps, his closest measurement, and to have a completely non-static use of the body in relation to movement, aside from the obvious locus of points of the hands creating volumes and things like that, from that many things can be drawn.

Physics, it's obvious, as we heard yesterday, sort of the description of the electron, why, gee, for a moment, the room was quiet, you know, . . . because people were conceiving of this thing. A pea and a balloon, that was good enough, but when you had X-hundred feet out this balloon rotating, this was terrific stuff, and it made an impression, and everybody is thinking better, and his relation to his problem will be better, I'm sure, because of it.

Merchandising, fantastic stuff, if you really get under its skin, because you find out that all the monkey business, which you rebelled against in merchandising, or most of it, wasn't essentially true. That really, if one thing followed each other, not half way, but toward its conclusion, why, merchandising was a scene in which the goodnesses would out, and even a few merchants might find it out, it gets to rub off.

Astronomy, the reverse corollary to the nuclear stuff, and then all of a sudden you breathe clear again, until astronomy scares the pants off you, when you realize what it takes in—and, you know, the fantasy.

Packaging, you can't package the solar system, but you start with packaging as you may have wrapped up a package and tied it with a string. But packaging isn't packaging any more, just as salt isn't salt. Salt isn't salt until it is in the hands of the consumer going on top of a poached egg—and the thing that gets it from the mind to the poached egg is all, in a way, packaging—and the merchant that thinks it's salt is crazy as hell. Because if, for example, in distributing soap, you develop a fourth-dimensional gadget [on] which you would turn a thing and soap would just come—delivered, by the fourth dimension, to the washpan—you could sell more soap that way, merely by giving superior service.

This circus as a mobile organization, an autonomous unit from which we can all learn a great deal, and military machines, I think, has this. But here is this autonomous mobile unit that is dealing with the all-time high of personal relations, within it. The clown, the clown itself, the stylized face, the inherited thing, the thing like the calligraphy, where a face may be inherited and improved and changed, added to and taken away and sort of the complete conservation of energy in pantomime, which in itself is a wonderful thing

for an architect to experience. And then the business of destroying his own face so as to rebuild it, so as to now have a face which goes beyond, in what he wanted to convey, goes beyond what his face was before.

Picasso, the same way: to destroy an element to put it back together. And there you see it related in a way, stronger and farther in the direction than the element was before he broke it to pieces.

Home economics, we were talking about home economics at the table, and I said, "Listen to the word, it sounds like a wonderful thing, 'home economics.'" If taken literally and is followed toward its conclusion, the economy of the home, just think all it involves, and if there was really a course or a school, or whatever it is, studying the economy of the home, it could be a good thing.

Farming, gee . . . to have time to be a farmer, that would be wonderful stuff.

Geography, statistics, painting, painting, pure distilled aesthetics, and from these guys, these very, very few who can deal with pure distilled aesthetics, we, sort of, could get the clue to many things, because there you have great, great original thinking, sort of anticipating ideas which haven't really been formed yet . . . and the clue can come from there.

Sculpture, a thing that activates space itself.

Ornithology, electronics . . . pretty good stuff. Love of things, just the thing that you always sort of feel missing in young students while they're coming up, maybe because you just can't recognize it, but the kind of love, a real affection of things. And there's something that love does to a thing, just like working it over with carnuba wax or something, that helps it.

Toys, gee, the world of toys. The one field in which one man works unselfconsciously and unembarrassed. He doesn't care, so he produces a terrific thing, and the whole world of . . . what . . . where would electricity be if some architect-type maniac hadn't played with electricity for a long time just as a toy?

Where would all the things based on pneumatics be, all the things based on thermodynamics? Games, whether it's hopscotch, baseball, whatever it is, there's sort of a relationship to man and thing and object that inevitably ends up in a surrounding which is out of this world, whether it's the drawing of hopscotch on the [side]walk, that makes a much better walk out of it, in most cases, or the ball court in Palenque.

Music, pure architecture of sound, and wonderful stuff.

This can go on forever, you know, and I'm not going on forever, but I wanted to go on long enough to not only give you an idea of what the factors are in relation to the cup, but give you an idea of what the ammunition is.

You can make the list long and I think there's something from almost every item in the list that can be applied to all problems of design, furniture, architecture, etc., etc.

If such a list of applicable stuff makes us feel lost, why, it may be a good idea to sort of reorient ourselves. We look around, we might find that, again, just in the lost feeling, and considering all this stuff at hand, all the problems, how we will apply it.

I suspect it will be that we haven't looked far enough. Because we'll find that the necessity of handling complex factors is not unique to architecture and design.

We find that man is producing equipment capable of handling incredible complex data and is developing principles upon which problems and data can be organized in order to feed the equipment . . . and we find that the men, the principles, the equipment and the process of thinking have many broad aspects and specific details in common, and we find that these common denominators are so rich, and so applicable, as to not only include architecture of design and the rest of the arts, but to give them once again a clear and positive direction.

There have been some points in history [that] we refer to, the Stone Age, or the Iron Age, or the Age of Mechanization, or whatever, and what we are now entering may well be the Age of Communication and Control.

This is not fantasy, because, remember, we were talking yesterday about leading the engineers. This is what you are really up against, not in the fantastic way. It may be fantastic, but it's not fantasy . . . and the very thing we are talking about, the means for handling factors, became . . . one of the top secret things during the war, it ranked next to the A-bomb, and that was the theory of games.

You know the theory of games? The theory of games, a very important factor in the war, and it could be, I feel, a very important factor in architecture. It has to do, basically, with the relation of all factors so that you can put indeterminables in and you can get an answer.

Essentially, it's based on the duel, when applied to war, because one man has a gun and the other fellow has a gun, they walk X-paces, turn around and you have a choice, you know, you can fire and get the first shot, or you can wait and draw fire, and then have, really, time to fire, but if the guy hits you on the first shot, then it's better not to have waited; on the other hand, you don't know what his relation to the situation is.

So, it's a business of outguessing the other guy. He thinks that I think, therefore, I think that . . . etc. The duel, it's a basic thing, or, as it gets much more complex, it's the poker hand.

And the difference between the duel or matching pennies, or whatever it is, and the poker hand is terrific. Because, just from the standpoint of complexity. An example of how they do it, how it would apply to things . . . say there is a channel, submarine going through a channel, and there is a narrow part to the channel and there is a wide part to the channel. . . . It is the job, now, of aircraft to locate submarine and sink same . . . but, there is only one airplane, and they know that the submarine, before it gets through the channel, has to surface for oxygen and stuff. What, when, where will he surface?

Well, the submarine knows that if he surfaces in the narrow part of the channel he will be a better target for the airplane, therefore, he will surface in the wide part of the channel, but the submarine figures that the airplane figures that if he does this he will be a better target, therefore, that he will fool the airplane and surface in the narrow part of the channel.

Well, there are many factors involved in this statement . . . how the hell do you do it?

You gather a thing all together, and now, for the first time, due to the terrific steps in the mechanical age, this was known, this whole theory was known, but it could never be applied. It's the computer, this terrific thing, and the computer . . . it not only can handle the problem but gets to have a terrific amount in common with the man that feeds it the problem, just as we have all these factors in relation to the cup and the list of monkey business we went through. In order to solve it, we're up against bringing it down to a yes, no, stop, go, fire, no fire signal. This is what a computer has to do. It can only handle one thing, one kind of a decision; it has to be yes, no, one, zero, stop, go, you know, just the two things. But, the computer isn't so bad off, because that's all you can do either. It's all I can do.

Our whole nervous system is broken down into neurons, which can only handle one thing. There are impulses that go through there, and it's stop, go, yes, no, but the complexity of it is so great and so refined that you get these sort of terrific shades of thinking and meaning.

We have a photograph here in the magazine and it is a picture of Ed Stone, you can recognize him. Ed Stone isn't just black or white but there are gradations in shadow. Yet the printing press that printed this thing is incapable of printing anything but black.

Yes, no, it's either black or white, and if you examined this, it would be black and white spots, and so, sort of, subtle and varied shadings.

You know there has been a lot of talk lately that the Aristotle-type thinking is the bunk, that's where something is either right or something is wrong and it only leads to trouble, and sure, in the "G. O. Political" scene, it's been disastrous.

We've seen disaster, we've seen horrible examples, we know that's really the way that it's applied, because in order for us to handle this thing, if we have a yes-no thinking machine or a computer, we can't feed in a half [question] . . . we can't feed a maybe question, that's what leads to nervous breakdowns.

There is a thing that these computers operate on, which is called feedback, and that is where at all points in the operation, this thing is going ker-chunk, ker-chunk, ker-chunk, and it has to check itself as fast as it goes or else the efficiency of the machine would be only as efficient as me checking the system.

And, so that it goes and is constantly checking itself, and this sort of rotary motion is called feed-back . . . and, which is very much the same here. I reach out to pick up this cigar, heaven forbid, and as I reach out, I have no control over the individual muscles, because I don't know what they are, I wouldn't know how to get in touch with them if I had to; but they are operating on a go, no-go basis, too.

The thing either contracts or it doesn't. But there are so many of them that I can do all kinds of things. You see, I make very subtle movements, and the direction to pick up the glass is so controlled by feedbacks, or whether either by seeing or not I am constantly, as I reach out to pick up the glass, measuring and evaluating the degree to which the glass is not picked up yet. You see, this takes place until I pick up the glass. The master

feedback type designer that we have, I think, is Eero Saarinen. It is going ker-chunk, ker-chunk, ker-chunk all the time, and he's at all times measuring the degree to which the problem is not solved. And anybody that comes within range of him is sort of fair bait to try out his feedback thing.

If the feedback is decelerated, or if it's not fast enough, why, you can have a kind of a situation like ataxia, where you know, you really can't do it. On the other hand, if the feedback is too accelerated, just like in a human being, why you overshoot and you can have a nervous tremor.

And this is also true of computing machines, they operate that way . . .

There's a theory of noise, and communication engineers are working with this every day, and it's a very real thing. Noise was always a thing that, sort of, you heard in spite of, but it's something else now. Because they found in calculations, not only in communication, but in aerodynamics, you get that turbulence at the end of an air coil. You have a certain amount of predictable turbulence, but you have some unpredictable turbulence, so you would try to calculate it on the basis of the predictable turbulence and not ignore the unpredictable or all would be lost. This, in communication engineering, bothered everybody until they decided to not only calculate the unpredictable, but to calculate it as an element.

Now, as we go along here, just quick, feed this back into architectural problems, because it's not so ridiculous. Calculate the uncalcuable—I mean, consider the uncalcuable as a quantity, and so count it in the calculations—and then things begin to clear up.

The whole theory of what they call noise developed. Noise is the kind of uncalcuable thing, if anything, those factors which have no orderly pattern of any kind and, of course, in communication, the amount of information received in the presence of noise is actually, and can be proven, greater than the amount of information received in the presence of less noise, which I suspect would have something to do with this subject.

We could explore it, because this speculation is another thing.

I was talking to a group of students at K.U., and I feel that speculation has somehow or other fallen into disrepute. You know, you just don't speculate out loud, you're kind of careful what you say, so I'm going to indulge in a little of it here.

There is in thermodynamics a factor called

entropy, and there, I think, we've sort of really got a hold of something. I don't know quite what it is, but it makes things for the design world, and all the stuff that has been happening so hit and miss. . . . Entropy is a quality that makes everything in the universe sort of return to a state of shuffledness, and if there is anybody that, you know, really can clarify this better, I would really love to [hear about it] because it's quite important.

One of the physicists has referred to it as sort of "time's arrow." It's kind of the thing that by looking at it, by studying it, and relating relative entropy, you can, sort of, tell whether the movie of the world is going backward or forward. And, gee, we need something like that around. . . .

[MODERATOR] *I might raise a question. Do you think, if we take the leadership of the engineers, that we have to know all the things that they know?*

CHARLES EAMES You don't take the leadership, you earn the leadership.

[M] *Well, if we earn it.*

CE Well, that's a big if. I would figure that out when you earn it.

[M] *No, do we have to know all that they know in order to lead them?*

CE Oh, that isn't necessarily true.

[M] *What is the position, then, of an architect who directs, or whatever he can do to, an engineer?*

CE Well, in a way, that's what I've tried to point out. I think that this talk about too much functionalism. This is, if you would accept my views, my description of function, then how can you have too much of it? You just don't carry it far enough, I feel. And just tell me [whether] in a way a thing would serve you better and you would love it more if it functioned less? It may be a block, but I can't quite conceive of it, like in the Mies building. Gee, it's never that it functions too well, and there are certain aspects, just on a mechanical level, that Miesonian or the Miesophiles would sort of get embarrassed about.

There's no need to get embarrassed because Mies's house, this Farnsworth House, is a terrific statement—for which I am, and you should be, very grateful. Because he has taken one phase of a problem and really carried it toward the conclusion, and there are very few things like that, and very few guys that could do it. Mies's concept in this case was to say remove—I'm not going to say what it was—but the apparent thing is that, if [we]

removed everything from the soil, a house is a house, ground is ground and there's . . . no reason why they should be alike. Out of respect to the ground we will make the house a prismatical thing, not out of disrespect, but out of respect to the ground, and the difficult thing is following through the concept as he went down the elements, to fit every solution of every factor within that concept. This becomes, sort of, the great thing. This does not make it less of a concept or valid thing, [such] that a guy like "Uncle Frank" [Frank Lloyd Wright] would say, "Well, let's respect the ground by making it part of the ground."

One is not more or less; one is different, and they are both damn good. We should be grateful for them. Oh, that the good old days were here, when the architect did all—but, brother . . .

Naturally everybody throws up Leonardo to the architect, but, I mean, those guys had a lot on the ball, and they were human beings, and they were conscious and aware of all the nuclear physics of their time, and they were leading things.

So then, I say, all right, architect. What is he that other people aren't? He is a human being—if not, why, his public relations have certainly led the world astray, because he is a human guy, he can consider other factors, he is trained in gathering factors, his enthusiasms are natural to him. Now, enthusiasms should be natural to him, and any energy that he puts into enthusiasms will come back many times. . . .

[M] *Is function the only worthwhile consideration?*

CE Now, I did two things, I talked about a cup, lots of things. I then went down a list of conceivable enthusiasms, and in both things there were applicable factors. Now, if I left out something that deeply concerns man as a human being, it was not by a conscious effort. So, I mean, what's left out when you say, "Is function the only thing?" I'm thinking of function in terms of ultimate service to the particular individual. What do you have in mind when you say "function"? Well, I said, I said, you pick up the telephone, you want to feel it, smell it, and if by any chance you taste it, it should taste good, and would be a better telephone.

[M] *You assume all parts function.*

CE Oh, my God, yes. . . . I mean, don't you think you are functioning when you smell something?

[M] *[Question inaudible.]*

CE Well, it's functioning in that it smells. . . . There's the passive and the active thing. I mean, a rose is functioning when it smells, and a rose knows darn well it is functioning or else it wouldn't get the bees there.

Seminar Excerpt: Jukebox

Nor, is it embarrassing to say, to say that a thing has to attract a kind of attention. There's nothing phony about it if the thing functions by virtue of the attention that is attracted. If you could get the client to really set down his objectives as they really are, so as to get them to include attracting people and sort of lay his cards really out on the table.

You see we've always talked about "Ha, Ha . . . the jukebox, it's a lousy piece of design." I don't know that a jukebox is a lousy piece of design, because if any of the more sensitive type people would design a jukebox, the thing would fade away in the corner, nobody would see it, and it would get no nickels. Its function is to get nickels and play the music. . . . Now, whether you agree with the function it performs or not is beside the point, but it would be a bad jukebox design if it disappeared into the surroundings. . . .

Seminar Excerpt: Ray Eames

My wife is a painter, and a very good one, and we've been working together for, oh, twelve years now. At first I used to help and criticize things she was doing, and then she would help and criticize things I was doing, and we would pitch in and do all the jiggering for each other and get it as people do. Then, gradually, things begin to sort of entropy. Things began to get shuffled, and pretty soon you didn't know where one started and the other ended, and anything that we've looked at or talked about here, I say that I'm doing it, but actually, she's doing it just as much as I am, only she sort of goes under the same corporate type name.

Her friends in the American Association of Abstract Artists take a very dim view of the fact that Ray hasn't exhibited any paintings or, actually, hasn't done a lot of any painting lately, in the sense that you can paint something and put it into a frame.

Now, actually, I think that she has been consistently functioning as a painter, and has functioned as a painter on and above the call of duty, because her hand and everything that makes it so is a part of everything we do, just as much of architecture as anything else . . . and if you're thinking of what some color looks like on a building, or what some spot of color [looks like] in relation to something else, this is not it. This is really functioning as a painter, extra and beyond perception, stuff that is anticipatory of very real things that happen later on, and it can come into the field of engineering as anything else. The contribution of an artist can often be—by his close association and feeling and contact with nature or situations, thinking again beyond the surface—to be able to have an intuitive feeling for what the appropriate form may be. This has happened so many times . . . there are so many examples. Painting in relation to architecture.

When a painter—say, my wife, for example— suspects that within the solution of the architecture you are sort of drifting from the concept, a little bit, this isn't just a highfalutin "Art for Art's Sake" thing, because as any painter knows, or as any architect knows, if for a minute you are tempted to drift from the big concept and you try to look around, you say, "Well, it won't hurt this. It won't hurt this and it won't hurt this, therefore, I will do this," you're just kidding yourself, because a time is going to come when it will all come out, and it might not come until the building is together, and you have an element over here, you have an element over there, which in the drawings you've never seen together, and you are walking through it and you see a reflection, you see a reflection of this element here into a mirror that brings the two together, and it shows you where you fouled up your scheme. You didn't think anybody was going to know about it. Now, painters can smell this kind of a mistake, you know, they can sort of anticipate it when they're really working, and if there was a big help, I think that is the kind. . . . Whether you're interested in cash on the barrel head, or a good building, or getting the client to come back, or not having it fall down, this is all applicable, it really is, and so I just want to shout down any talk that this kind of talk is all right, but let's get down to brass tacks, 'cause this is brass tacks.

Sources: Charles Eames, speech and seminar transcript, October 10, 1952, American Institute of Architects, Kansas City, Missouri, Part II: Speeches and Writings series, Charles and Ray Eames Papers, Manuscript Division, Library of Congress, Washington, D.C.

CHARLES EAMES

"Japanese Architecture and the West"

Editor's note: For this article, Architectural Forum *solicited comments from sixteen Western architects; this is Charles Eames's contribution.*

WHETHER IT IS a paper toy or a tea house, or a garden or a palace, traditional Japanese things seem to represent a super understanding of humble materials and elements in relation to human scale and human needs. The question in applying it seems to be in recognizing just what are the humble materials in our environment— what is our scale and what are our needs. . . . We have a long way to go before we know the humble materials of our environment well enough to select from them.

Source: "Japanese Architecture and the West,"
Architectural Forum 98, no. 1 (January 1953): 143–48.

Royalties for Furniture Designers

CORRESPONDENCE

Editor's note: Henry Dreyfuss (1904–1972) was an American industrial designer who made important contributions to the products that defined such companies as Honeywell, Westinghouse, Bell Telephone, Hoover, and Polaroid. His iconic designs include the 20th Century Limited locomotive, the Princess phone, and the circular Honeywell thermostat.

Sam Maloof (1916–2009) was a California furniture designer and woodworker. His work is in the collections of several major American museums, including the Metropolitan Museum of Art, the Los Angeles County Museum of Art, the Philadelphia Museum of Art, and the Smithsonian American Art Museum.

Henry Dreyfuss to Charles Eames, South Pasadena, California
February 18, 1953

Dear Charley:

I have a young friend, Sam Maloof, who is doing some excellent furniture designing and distinguishing himself by actually building the pieces in a fine craftsman like manner. He works alone in his own shop at Ontario, California.

Sam is anxious to design and build samples which can be turned over to manufacturers for mass production. Several manufacturers have already approached him, and I would like to see him get off to a good start.

Today he came to see me to ask advice about charging for such an effort. I frankly am not familiar with this furniture design charging methods.

I know you will appreciate that Mr. Maloof wishes to abide by whatever ethical concept has been established in this field. Would you be helpful to him and give him some indication as to how he might charge?

Does he charge for drawings?

Does he charge for three-dimensional samples?

Does he get a retainer (how much)?

Does he get a royalty (how much)?

Your suggestions will be appreciated by both Mr. Maloof and me. (He can be addressed in care of this office.) Thank you.

Very kindest personal regards,

Henry Dreyfuss

Charles Eames to Sam Maloof
February 24, 1953

Dear Mr. Maloof:

Henry Dreyfuss has asked me to write you giving some information as to the standard practice in charging for work on furniture design.

I must confess I know very little about what has been standard procedure in the furniture field in general. However, recently more and more of this work has been done by individual designers and the kind of architect-designer that has been for the past 20 years more and more working back and forth across the thin line that divides architecture and product design.

I believe most of the past design work in the furniture field has been on a price for the job basis. This has many drawbacks; one, the design no longer has any relation to the designer and is usually altered ostensibly to set a production or merchandising scheme and ends up serving neither the client nor the designer. The royalty system, under which we work, as do people like Eero Saarinen and George Nelson, has proved most satisfactory and gives the designer a continued responsibility. There are several ways of working within the royalty system:

1. To work with a percentage around 1½ percent to 2 percent at the wholesale level, in which the designer is responsible only for the design and the details relative to its production, shipping, etc. In this case, it is usual to get an advance on royalties and or reimbursement for out-of-pocket expenses, travel expenses, etc., during the development period.

2. A royalty from 2½ percent to 4 percent according to the amount of work done, which would be based on the designer's continued responsibility to the product, servicing it as far as the design of literature, exhibitions, displays, public relations, etc. etc.

3. There are some cases in which the royalty is payable for the life of the design, others in which it is limited to a period of ten years, others where it is limited to a maximum amount.

4. The varying percentage of royalty is usually and should be dependent on the amount of service and responsibility the designer is willing to give the client and the amount the client is willing to accept. If the designer has an understanding of the problem and the ability to view the situation in a round way, including the points of view of the customer and the client, then the more responsibility he is willing to accept, the more valuable he will be to the client.

I hope this rambling is of some help, even though it is general. If there are any specific questions, please feel free to call. Best wishes for success in your work.

Sincerely,

Charles Eames

Sam Maloof to Charles Eames, Ontario, California
March 19, 1953

Dear Mr. Eames:

Thank you very much for your letter of February 24, which has been forwarded to me by Mr. Dreyfuss.

I certainly appreciate your giving this matter your attention and thank you very much for all the valuable information given in your reply.

Sincerely yours,

Sam Maloof

Source: Charles Eames to Sam Maloof, February 24, 1953, Henry Dreyfuss folder, Part II: Office File (Pre-1960) series, Charles and Ray Eames Papers, Manuscript Division, Library of Congress, Washington, D.C.

Rough

FILM: CHAIR TO COME AT END OF "DISCOVERY" TITLE.

LIVE: M.C. INTRODUCES PROGRAM

Rouse FILM: ("A" SECTION)

	M.C. TALK:
TREES & OCEAN	CHARLES & RAY EAMES LIVE ON A
REFLECTION OF OCEAN IN HOUSE	LEDGE ABOVE THE PACIFIC AT SANTA MONICA CANYON AMONG THE
PILINGS PAN TO	EUCALYPTUS TREES IN A HOUSE OF THEIR OWN DESIGN WHICH
INSIDE AND HOFMANNS	REFLECTS THE SURROUNDINGS, THE OCEAN, THE TREES, AS WELL
THRU DESERT PLANT FROM OUTSIDE	AS IT REFLECTS THEIR ATTITUDE TOWARD THEIR WORK, THEIR
TO INSIDE TO INDIAN BLANKET	ATTITUDE TOWARD DESIGN, AND THE WAY THEY HAVE
ZOOM TO BLK. SQUARE	COLLABORATED WITH EACH OTHER.
AND OUTSIDE	
EUCALYPTUS TRUNK	
TO THREE QUARTER FACADE	
TO SHADOWS AND WHITE PANEL	
ZOOM OF FACADE	
BELL RINGING	
LEAVES TO	
CROSS TIE ROD	

LIVE:

	M.C. TALK:
(DISSOLVE TO GUESTS AND MOLDED PLYWOOD CHAIR)	M.C.: WE WANT TO TALK TO YOU ABOUT DESIGN AND SPECIFICALLY ABOUT THIS MOLDED PLYWOOD CHAIR BUT BEFORE WE DO, I WOULD LIKE ANOTHER GLIMPSE OF THAT HOUSE OF YOURS AND HAVE YOU TELL US SOME MORE ABOUT IT.

---

live: follows B

"B" SECTION

Rouse FILM:

	MC:
SHADOWS	DESIGN IN YOUR LIFE CERTAINLY SEEMS TO
BEDROOMS	COVER MANY THINGS. JUST HOW WOULD
SCREENS	YOU DESCRIBE XXXXX OR DEFINE YOUR IDEA OF DESIGN.
RAY'S WOOD SCULPTURE & HOFMANNS	
TO CEILING AND LADDER	GUEST:
TO LAMP & MONSTERA	I THINK THAT ANYTIME ONE OR MORE THINGS ARE CONSCIOUSLY PUT TOGETHER
TO DETAILS MONSTERA	IN A WAY THAT THEY CAN ACCOMPLISH SOMETHING BETTER THAN THEY COULD HAVE
TO SHADOW TO STONES TO BUTTERFLY	ACCOMPLISHED INDIVIDUALLY, THIS IS AN ACT OF DESIGN.
TO POT AND BIRD	IT IS GOOD TO THE DEGREE TO WHICH IT IS ULTIMATELY SUCCESSFUL. THESE XXXXX
TO BUTTERFLY PAPER	TOOLS ARE EXAMPLES OF DESIGN, THESE LIGHTS AND GOBOS, AND I WOULD SAY,
ZOOM TO B'FAST TABLE	HIGHLY SUCCESSFUL.
DETAILS OF TABLE	COMBINING RYE BREAD AND SWISS CHEESE WAS A GREAT ACT OF DESIGN. THE VALUE
TO FERN	OF THE RESULT, THE SANDWICH, IS NOT THE VALUE OF RYE BREAD PLUS CHEESE,
TO STUDIO	BUT IT IS RYE BREAD PLUS CHEESE RAISED TO THE Nth POWER.
ZOOM THRU DOOR	
TO LANTERNS	X X X X IS DESIGN XXXXX IS DESIGN THE RELATION OF GOVERNMENTS TO EACH
TO STUDIO WINDOW	OTHER IS DESIGN.
TO EQUIPMENT	THE FRONT PAGES OF OUR NEWSPAPERS TODAY REFLECT THE RESULTS OF DESIGN,
CHILD'S PAINTING TO	GOOD OR BAD.
KITE WALL	
ZOOM TO CHINESE BUTTERFLY	
FROM SHAVINGS TO JOISTS	

LIVE:

LIVE (con't)

MC:
THAT IS BROAD, BUT IN THE CASE OF THE MOLDED PLYWOOD CHAIR, YOU HAD SOMETHING THAT BROKE SHARPLY WITH TRADITION - SOMETHING ABSOLUTELY NEW ......

GUEST:
PARDON ME -- I DON'T THINK IT BROKE WITH TRADITION, OR WAS ABSOLUTELY NEW. NOT IF YOU TAKE A GOOD LOOK AT THE DEVELOPMENT OF CHAIRS. THINGS SELDOM DEVELOP IN A VACUUM. FOR EXAMPLE, THE EARLY AUTOMOBILE.

FILM: ANIMATION, CARRIAGE TO AUTO

LIVE: GUEST:

ARCHITECTURE AND FURNITURE ARE NO DIFFERENT, -- IT IS A REAL EVOLUTIONARY PROCESS.

M.C.:
I WOULD LIKE TO SEE THE SAME KIND OF A TRANSITION IN THE DEVELOPMENT OF FURNITURE.

GUEST:
SORRY, I CAN'T SHOW YOU ONE. I WOULD LIKE TO SEE IT MYSELF, BUT HERE ARE A FEW EXAMPLES

M.C.:
IT SEEMS THAT PART OF THAT STORY WOULD BE THE CHAIRS WITH WHICH YOU WON THE ORGANIC FURNITURE COMPETITION 12 YEARS AGO.

GUEST:
IT WAS EERO SAARINEN AND I THAT DID THAT COMPETITION IN COLLABORATION, AND RAY WORKED ON THE PRESENTATION DRAWINGS.

M.C.:
WHAT WAS YOUR OBJECTIVE?

GUEST:
THE SAME AS ALWAYS -- AN ATTEMPT TO GET WHAT IS ULTIMATELY THE MOST OF THE BEST TO THE GREATEST NUMBER OF PEOPLE FOR THE XXX LEAST. IN THIS AND OTHER CASES ULTIMATELY IT DOES NOT NECESSARILY MEAN IMMEDIATELY AND IT IS APT TO INVOLVE MASS PRODUCTION.

M.C.:
IN INVOLVING MASS PRODUCTION, DON'T YOU FIND THAT YOU HAVE TO SACRIFICE SOME OF THE PERSONAL ATTENTIONS AND

LIVE (con't)

M.C.:
IN INVOLVING MASS PRODUCTION DON'T YOU FIND THAT YOU HAVE TO SACRIFICE SOME OF THE PERSONAL ATTENTIONS AND VALUES THAT EXIST WITHIN THE CRAFTS, WHERE THE PERSONAL NEEDS OF EACH INDIVIDUAL CLIENT WERE CAREFULLY CONSIDERED?

LIVE

GUEST:
I DON'T THINK THAT IS NECESSARILY TRUE AT ALL. IN FACT, I FEEL IT IS DEFINITELY NOT TRUE. POTENTIALLY MASS PRODUCTION HAS THE POSSIBILITY OF BRINGING MORE CONCERN, MORE SWEAT, BLOOD AND TEARS TO THE SERVICE OF THE INDIVIDUAL CONSUMER THAN THE CRAFT ERA COULD EVER DREAM OF, AND IN MANY AREAS TODAY, IT IS ALREADY BEING DONE.

WHEN WE ORIGINALLY TALKED ABOUT THIS PROGRAM YOU ASKED THAT WE DEVELOP OUR APPROACH TO THE DESIGN OF THE MOLDED PLYWOOD CHAIR. RAY AND I HAVE PUT THE ANSWER TO THAT ON A FILM. I WOULD LIKE TO SHOW THAT NOW. IT MAY ALSO ANSWER THE QUESTION ABOUT CONSIDERATION OF ALL INDIVIDUALS NEEDS IN MASS PRODUCTION.

LIVE

MC:
LET'S SEE IT.

FILM:

CHAIR: SECTION "A"
Development of Concept and Form

CHAIR: SECTION "B"
Perfecting of manufacturing techniques

CHAIR: SECTION "C"
Additional services, graphic and architectural

Break

Break

Chair Design Process

Editor's note: Charles and Ray Eames were featured guests on Discovery, *the San Francisco Museum of Modern Art's public television art survey show. Charles wrote three drafts of notes in preparation. The notes reproduced here, the last draft, are almost the only existing record of this show.*

The curators also asked the Eameses to talk about the development of the molded plywood chair. In answer to this request, Charles and Ray Eames made a 16mm film. A transcript of the narration follows.

Narration for "The Development of the Molded Plywood Chair"

The problem of designing anything is in a sense the problem of designing a tool. And as in designing a tool, it is usually wise to have a pretty clear idea of what you want the thing to do. The need it is to fill. Its particular objective.

We could have taken it as our objective the problem of how people should sit. How they should be supported to get the most pleasure and benefit from their surroundings. This would have been a perfectly good problem but an extremely complicated one.

In the particular case of the molded plywood chair, we arbitrarily decided to accept the way people do sit. Our specific objective was to provide a good piece of equipment for conventional sitting. To do it without preconceived ideas, and to have it contain some of the best qualities inherent in the mass-production system.

The people we wanted to serve were varied. To begin with, we studied the shapes and postures of many types. Averages and extremes. We retraced the steps we had taken earlier in the "Organic" competition—measuring and inquiring and relating. People may seem to differ greatly from each other. But when compared to nonpeople—mice, elephants, trees, and things, people begin to look very similar to each other and it seems more nearly possible to provide a good general solution.

In a more or less standard situation like sitting for eating or writing, we found that certain relationships of support give optimum comfort to a surprisingly large number of people. We found that comfort depended less on the perfect molding to the body shape than it did on the way the bone structure was supported. And that if the structure was supported properly, a hard and rigid material like molded plywood could provide a remarkably high degree of comfort. We limited the solution to a hard surface and concentrated on plywood. We tried ribbon shape and bucket shape, saddle seat, and a split-back one-piece shell. We tried movement and found that if the back was allowed to move in relation to the seat, the latitude of comfort was greatly increased. First, the movement was mechanical. Then it developed into the idea of a rubber shock mount, a movable connection.

In the design of any structure, it is often the connection that provides the key to the solution. The factor of movement also helped to crystallize the idea of a chair in two pieces—the seat and a back. The two surfaces developed into petal-like forms. Modeled, remodeled, tested and retested a hundred times. Contoured, repaired and lost it. And always checked with the back and seat of many people. It seemed practical to have a frame that would hold the two surfaces in relation to each other and in relation to the floor. Gradually it developed into a central spine and attached legs. First it was plywood because the unity of material seemed to be desirable. But the frame served a different function than did the seat and the back. It had no need for surface. Its job was one of point connections. If the seat was to be the target, the frame might well be deemphasized.

Solid steel rod seems the best way to get the most strength with the thinnest line. A much thinner line than even the tube that has been used in previous metal furniture. We thought that a tripod base would be a good idea because three legs would always tend to be steady when the floor was uneven. And a four-legged chair would rock. But we found that even a skilled sitter could be unseated while picking up a pencil. Putting a single leg in the rear was no help,

Sixteen prototypes of molded plywood
chairs.

you can't lean back. Four legs again seemed best; the frames began to take their final forms. The contours of the seat and back were refined in terms of the complicated functions of the edges and the relation to each other. We became more conscious of surface texture, of heat transfer, finishes, the balance, the ease of handling, the colors, the woods, and the heads of the bolts. A chair should look equally good, approached from above or from below. If it's going to be a chair, it should be a whole chair.

The molding of plywood had gone a long way since the Organic competition. But the flowing curves of this seat and back had to be formed without resorting to true compound curve. Even the mold process we had developed earlier for the molded plywood splint was too complicated for furniture production. The splint depended on gores and darts. The surfaces of the chair were designed to be formed from flat sheets of veneer without splitting or buckling. We had to face the characteristics of the bonding ring. The behaviors of the impregnating resins required trial after trial, test after test, and many disappointments.

Things that went right the first time failed for forty times after, with no clue as to the reason for the first success. The shock mounts seemed simple enough, but we could find no outside source to tackle it except at great cost. We tried it, made many mistakes, and learned from most of them. Then some encouraging results; one thing always depends on another. A rubber button could not become a shock mount until it could be attached to the plywood without bolts or screws. This meant more risk, much experiment with radio frequency, all costly, some appropriate. But eventually there was a connection that would take half a million flexes. Then the frame, more connections. This time, metal to metal. Braces, welds, working. We had only seen the heavy spot weld used on wheel wrenches. But after many trials we found the heavy spot weld an excellent and impressive joining device. Again, the connection is the same.

When a product is designed in a way that its production varies from the norm and its given field, it becomes the responsibility of the designer to help make the necessary transition. It is not so much the creating of tools and techniques as it is

the searching out of appropriate existing ones that will provide a product of greatest ultimate service to the consumer.

Sources: Charles Eames, handwritten and typed script notes, *Discovery* television program, San Francisco Museum of Art, San Francisco, Part II: Projects file series, Charles and Ray Eames Papers, Manuscript Division, Library of Congress, Washington, D.C. Charles Eames and Ray Eames, "The Development of the Molded Plywood Chair," film by the Office of Charles and Ray Eames, 1953, 16mm.

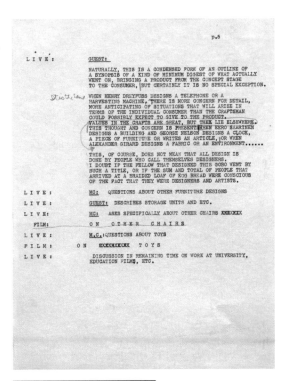

A production example of the molded plywood chair

MGM's *Executive Suite*

CORRESPONDENCE

Editor's note: John Houseman had a distinguished career as a film producer and actor. His MGM production Executive Suite *garnered four Academy Award nominations, for supporting actress, black-and-white cinematography, black-and-white art direction, and costume design.*

Eames designs are seen throughout the scenes in the story, in which the president of a furniture company dies and several individuals—the vice presidents of sales, finance, and design—vie for the top job.

Charles Eames to John Houseman, Metro Goldwyn Mayer Studios
August 10, 1953

Dear John:

I have it on good authority that the type [of] merchandise you are looking for in terms of watered-down clichéd modern can be seen at Richard's (8811 Beverly Blvd., near Robertson)— or Grosfeld House at 145 North Robertson, near Beverly.

Enclosed is a possible treatment of that scene we talked about—is this about the length you had in mind? It could, of course, get more involved.

Enclosed is a piece of Nelson case goods and a slat bench, which could stand for good, high quality modern furniture.

Sincerely,
Charles Eames

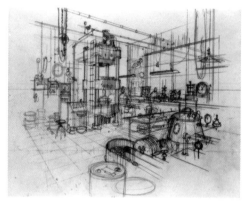

Charles Eames, sketch for *Executive Suite*, August 6, 1953.

Memo from Charles Eames "for Mr. Houseman,"
August 6, 1953

Don't try to have Don draw chair. Temptation to show chair is great, but probability of its not being stilted and boobish is zero. Anyway, it's not necessary. Show design doodles instead—unreadable except to Don—no necessity to be read by others. Characters are so black and white there is no suspense. Every candidate but Don is either sweaty-palmed, shifty-eyed, weak, bull-headed, or senile. A world of salesman and comptrollers would have a right to resent these characters.

It is not demonstrated that Don is in any way qualified to be president—(Mary would seem more likely). It is unnatural for him to *want* to be president. He should be only interested in ultimate service of product to public and company. His desire to be president under circumstances shows a weakness.

His last speech would be really positive if it backed up other clues—if he had shown ability to put the charts to work—relate the facts to the whole picture.

If a guy like Don *was* a really top designer growing in potential administrative material, his outside interests (even relative to the child) would be something other than baseball.

Growing from varied interests in things and people, he would have a super appreciation for charts, sales production, etc.

Page of Script by Charles Eames

DON: This test is going to work . . .
[starts to go away]
Then we can move this first unit in for that short
run of molded backs—

SHAW: But before you can . . .

DON: *[turns to Shaw]*
You know those material rejection charts you
posted yesterday? Compare them with last
quarter . . . and even in direct labor . . .
a process like this is the only way to *really* beat
that trend . . . and think of the quality of the
product!

SHAW: *[slowly]*
You really think it will make that production line
obsolete?

DON: *[half to himself]*
Maybe . . .

Source: Charles Eames to John Houseman, August 10,
1953, Part II: Office File (Pre-1960) series, Charles and Ray
Eames Papers, Manuscript Division, Library of Congress,
Washington, D.C.

Photograph of actor William Phipps,
left, and actor William Holden, right,
who starred as McDonald Walling, vice
president for design and development.

CHARLES EAMES

Architecture 1 and 2, University of California, Berkeley

Lecture No. 1
23 September 1953
(Given by Mr. Eames)

I.

The architect is not merely a draftsman but a combination of scientist, engineer, designer, and fine artist of a very special sort:

A. As a scientist the architect investigates and observes. No one observes enough and it is hard, especially for the young, to see the way in which everything that happens results from what has happened previously.

B. As an engineer the architect applies his facts and observations to the problems of construction.

C. As a designer the architect attempts to combine his materials so that his whole will be more than just the sum of its parts.

D. As a fine artist the architect is concerned not so much with "fine art" defined as art for art's sake without relation to utility, but rather with being an artist "fine" in the dictionary sense of "finished, brought to perfection, refined." He is like an athlete trained to a point close to the limit of efficiency—physically, mentally, and emotionally reacting as one unit.

E. Architecture is a combination of the efficient and the non-utilitarian. The course of education for the architect is the same both for the man who wants to become the very best architect and for the man who is solely interested in rapid building and making a great deal of money. The broad view the architect must learn to take of his problems would even be valuable for a housewife in solving hers.

II. The Indispensability of Involvement:

The moment one is presented with a problem he should immediately become "involved" in it, interested in the subject from every angle and in all its aspects. The student of architecture should allow himself to become "involved" and really interested in architecture. If one admires a certain architect, looking into the areas of his interest will provide a good clue to the content of his architecture.

A recording was played of a statement by Le Corbusier having much the same attitude on the necessity for involvement. He stressed the investigation of nature and observation of the harmony between nature and animals.

III. Visual and Intellectual Awareness:

An important aspect of the involvement process is learning to see things with new eyes, realizing the possibility of gaining new emotional experiences through intensive looking.

A. Capturing a scene with a camera is of value for it helps the individual learn to see. Looking at familiar objects from a different perspective, as from an airplane or through a microscope, also helps to stimulate greater awareness.

B. As an example of "intensive looking" the lecturer presented the first of his "Awareness Shows," a Trainscape, consisting of color slides made by the lecturer and his staff in a railroad yard and while en route on a train, which were shown together with a recording of sounds heard in a railroad station. In combining sight with sound the lecturer was trying to catch and develop emotional relationships.

This is an example of a creative shuffling and working of elements which must be done by the architect in his office. The architect must read the mind of his client, ask him questions, draw sketches for him; the two working together to produce a harmonious result such as the slide show.

IV. Lettering, Drawing, and Communication

A. Great emphasis will be placed in this course upon drawing as a means of communication. The architect must learn to put something on paper which the client may read and learn from, as a child learns from pictures. Drawing is also important as a means of communication to oneself as well as to others.

B. Lettering is wonderful as a means of communication; it is an individual thing, helping one person to understand another. Lettering developed over a long period of time and can be identified like an individual spoon or axe; it reflects the interests of its period and country.

C. The drawings of children are also fine means of communication. Not having lived long enough, children are naturally uninhibited and see everything as new and interesting; they are observing and associating all the time, and there are great truths in things done unconsciously by children.

A sound film of toys in action, "The Parade," was shown—a film made by the lecturer in an attempt to capture this enthusiasm and unselfconscious action of children.

D. Another fine method of creating relationships and solving problems is that of theme and variations, as seen in music. By arranging and rearranging the elements of a problem, by trying changes and reversals, the creative artist (musician, filmmaker, or architect) is able to solve his problem. All creative activities have similar problems, and the engineer, architect, painter or poet, as they develop and grow, may merge and become one.

The lecturer's film "Blacktop" was shown as an example of the theme and variations technique. The score of Bach's "Goldberg Variations" was played against closeup shots of water washing a schoolyard.

V. The Storehouse of Experience:

By continual observation and awareness of situations in life, a vocabulary of experience can be built up [along with] files in the "post office" of the mind, to draw on when needed in solving problems.

A. Photography is an excellent exercise in observation and coordination. In taking a picture one must make decisions about subject matter, composition angles, and when finally to snap the shutter.

B. There should also be developed a sense of "quality" in everything done, which requires criticism and a "feeling" for things and their relations. In the problems which will be given in the course the student should begin with drawings and develop attitudes toward his work and his objectives.

Lecture No. 2
12 October 1953
(Given by Mr. Eames)

I. An Infinite Number of Ideas Can Be Communicated Through Drawing:

A. Drawing can be used to exactly communicate anything to anyone. The type and quality of drawing contained in the UPA cartoon productions is an example of this.

B. Drawing can be used to depict sounds, and there have been competitions of drawings representing sounds. The film "Fiddle-De-Dee" by Norman McLaren was shown as an example. This is abstract in form with color drawings done directly on the film and synchronized with a soundtrack of the song "Listen to the Mocking Bird."

C. It has been said that Eero Saarinen is able to win competitions because of the quality of his presentation. However, pure slickness of drawing is not at the heart of an architecture problem. The method Saarinen used to win the competition for the Jefferson Memorial in St. Louis was to break up the problem into its component elements. He isolated each of these hundred or so parts—the organization of a washroom, that of the circulation system for the entire area, etcetera—and attempted first to solve the problems inherent in each separate element. He reached perhaps 50 possible solutions for each of the 100 elements, combining the best of these into a prize-winning scheme. This is the way solving a problem in architecture can be accomplished. Slick drawing or presentation cannot be substituted for the problem solving, which is at the heart of architecture.

II. Lettering as Communication

A. Development of calligraphy: the time span from the earliest cave drawing to the Roman non-phonetic letter as we know it is very long compared to the brief 2,000 years from Roman times to ours. Around 250,000 years of human history passed before the first cave drawings (a span which could be represented by half the width of the auditorium stage) and from then 15,000 more years till the Egyptian hieroglyphics (represented by four more feet of stage). On this scale the 5,000-year period until the first letter would be only one foot of stage width.

After this there was rapid development; in 35 years these consonant letters had spread all over Europe. They represented half pictorial ideas and half phonetics. The Phoenician took up the system and developed it into the first real concrete system of writing. The Greeks, also traders, adopted the system from the Phoenicians; the Romans received it from the Greeks and the Etruscans. (The Rosetta stone was an important find of one of Napoleon's men, for it contained the same inscription in Egyptian hieroglyphics, early Phoenician lettering, and Greek.)

The Romans wrote on everything, improving their letters. The Greeks wrote on wax tablets in single, sharp lines; the Romans used square letter formation and the Phoenicians rounded. Thick and thin lines were probably caused by use of the quill pen. The stone carver copied this in his lettering, and it was later taken up in painting.

Architects of the Renaissance modified and refined Roman and Greek lettering. Lowercase letters were developed at the end of the 5th century, and cursive writing later.

B. A film on calligraphy, "La Lettre," was shown.

III. The Problem and Its Approach

A. The tendency to be original for originality's sake is one of the big hurdles a designer must get over. There is need for a clear determination of the specific objective and for using only a limited vocabulary of technique. There is a horrible freedom in a completely plastic medium, and one with definite limitations, such as granite, will be of help in achieving better results.

B. A small structure problem was assigned: using several small dowels and a quantity of thread to support four pounds of books at a certain height. The structure is to be a unit in itself, not attached to a board, and have a certain amount of stability.

C. The student should begin by making many drawings of possible solutions. This problem is of value because its results are measurable. Also it can be done—it has been shown that dowels and thread will support twenty pounds of books.

Lecture No. 3
13 October 1953
(Given by Mr. Eames)

I. Entropy and Morality

A. One of the basic quantities of physics is entropy, the measure of the tendency toward "shuffledness," "mixed-upness," or disorder.
  1. The second law of thermodynamics which concerns entropy states in substance that in any isolated system, the probability that entropy will decrease is zero.
  2. Entropy is spreading into other fields and continues to mean in general that, barring outside interference, the probability that order will increase is zero.

B. Applied to communication, the principle of entropy indicates that the probability that a message will increase in accuracy by transmission is zero: information can only be dissipated.
  1. This does not concern the element of truth, which might increase in transmission, but only that of fidelity to the original, which will not.
  2. The principle was again demonstrated in some publicity material on the present course for which the lecturer supplied the original facts. The newspaper reported that the lecturer was interested only in design for mass production, an untrue statement caused by errors in transmission in accordance with the law of entropy.

C. The lecturer was also asked whether he advocated more international-style architecture or more indigenous architecture, to which he felt the only possible reply would be that there should be more of both. This is related to all such unanswerable questions of whether beauty or form or the heart or the head is the more important.

The subtleties of information are so easily dissipated that there is a human tendency to select the extremes and consider only an abstract "all good" as opposed to an "all bad."
  1. This is related to the child's separation of the "good people" from the "bad people" in an absolute distinction.
  2. The "good" and the "bad" are relative; there cannot be imagined a "bad" color, for instance, but only one bad in a particular relation or for a certain purpose.

3. There can be no "epitome of what is bad." Decaying flesh would not seem bad to a vulture, and objects are thought of as "good" and "bad" because of positive or negative mental associations. . . .

II. The Importance of Associations

A. The great contemporary mathematician, Von Neumann, was asked to assist in the design of an electronic calculator, and quickly solved the problem for which the machine was being built. He was unable to explain how he arrived at the answer, but he had solved the problem by recognizing and applying relationships he already knew from his work in the field.

B. In their field, architects must also build up a fund of associations for solving problems, both from drawings and observation of the scene around them.

III. Slide Demonstrations

A. The first demonstration consisted of unrelated color slides showing "scenes around town"—telephone lines, store facades, construction skeletons, brick walls, sidewalks, crowds, and market and nursery displays—designed to show various pattern relations of line, mass, and color.

Played concurrently but not synchronized with the slides was a tape recording of city and traffic noises interspersed with nickelodeon, oriental, march, and jazz music, and a reading by Gertrude Stein of selections from her own abstract poetry.

By observing the associations between the pictures and the sound a "sight-sound poem" can be created, and nondramatic elements (such as the nickelodeon) can assume either a comic or tragic character depending on the pictures associated with them. Gertrude Stein's poetry, played again in illustration, is a good example in sound of how seemingly meaningless words can suggest meaning by association.

Lecture No. 4
9 November 1953
(Given by Mr. Eames)

I. The Importance of Decisions

A. The best of the "latter" communications asked for by the lecturer—whether chemical codes, rebuses, limericks, or what not—all showed a conscious decision not only of content but as to how the message should be placed on the paper.

B. The lecturer's purpose, as stated at the beginning of the course, is to "involve" the student in architecture. This involves becoming "unbored" with the subject and conscious of every decision made as involving quality.

1. Every time anything is put down on a piece of paper a decision involving quality must be made.
2. This process of being always conscious of the quality of decisions must be applied at all times or it will not work.
3. Seeing a situation and the necessity it presents for making a decision is more important than the decision made.
4. The food one eats, the clothes one wears, and the way one's room is furnished are all the result of decisions, the quality of which reflect back upon the individual and offer a way of knowing him.

C. If the lecturer were given the task of making the student eminently successful financially in the field of architecture, or eminently helpful and handy around an office, his advice would be the same. In all professions there must be an understanding and consciousness of the standards of quality, there must be an involvement in the field. A good janitor will know how to sweep a floor properly and a good architect will know when a vertical line must be a vertical line.

D. In all activities it is necessary to have a fund of "built in" experiences upon which to draw in making these decisions and evaluations of quality. The lecturer in his "awareness shows" attempts to demonstrate some of the audible and visual association experiences the student of architecture should be aware of.

II. The Three "Awareness Shows":

The first in this series on locomotives, the second a townscape, and this one a seascape: showing awareness of what can be seen along the edge of the ocean.

The show consisted of a series of color slides, first of people at a bathing beach, and then of elements of a beach itself: sand, surf, breakers, pilings, waterbirds, seaweed and marine plantlife, encrusted rocks, coral, etc.

With the slides was played a tape recording having the continuous breaking of the surf along a beach intermixed with popular Italian, American, and French songs concerning the sea and other sounds such as an airplane, dog barking, seagulls.

At the end students were asked what they "remembered most," what affected them most negatively or positively. (Student reactions given in quotes, with additional comment by lecturer.)

— So much of it was repulsive: "slimy objects and stagnant pools." There were only a very few pictures actually stagnant, and even these were right along the coast, all shorts being made within 75 feet of the pounding surf of the sound recording. The association of stagnation with the unbeautiful is surprising. This is a personal, relative view—there are many stagnant forms of life which are necessary and beautiful, and arbitrary good and bad characters cannot be imposed on outside objects.
— "The pictures showed nature arranged very pleasingly without human design." The stones are nice examples of this. Some of the shots were close and the patterns could not be seen except through the camera, so the term "accidental" must be used advisedly. Also, natural arrangements are not really "accidental" because they result from the many laws of force, dynamics, gravity, etc., which are working on them.
— "They show the life giving and taking powers of the water, its force and strength." The pictures were taken at random but what was included and the order of showing are of course the results of decisions about building up or destroying moods. . . .
— "The stagnant pools seemed more in suspended animation, waiting for the waves." This is more what the lecturer felt about it, and was shocked when the student saw them as stagnant and repulsive.
— "The whole scene was too busy, and the noise filled up the brain." This was at least a vivid experience and can be referred to in joining other things and making future associations.
— "It would be nice to show the slides for oneself

at varying rates, leaving some on longer."
— "The stagnant scenes should be correlated with the recording by moving the sound further away." This is a little pedestrian. It is necessary to take the responsibility of observing, relating, and making decisions for oneself. This is one result of education on the secondary level where too many things are outlined and set up in a framework and too many predecisions are made for the student. Discipline is thought of as not throwing erasers, rather than something which should be built up in the individual as a working basis for associations and decisions.

III. Variations on a Theme:
This is a fine form of exercise in making associations, requiring the keeping within strict limitations of form. Each variation is not only based on the original theme but has a relation to the one before it. The process is one of the great rich and rewarding disciplines—often the means of solving seemingly impossible problems—which has been enjoyed and indulged in by great men of all times. Architects know this from experimenting with a form inside out, in its opposite, etc. It is a great tool for exploring and studying problems. The device of theme and variations is again only good if one becomes completely "involved" in it—fascinated, interested, and delighted in the work.

A valid set of limitations, such as those imposed by a theme and variations exercise, are very helpful in solving all problems. It is harder to do bad work in granite than in plastic media, for the harder material narrows down the range of decisions which may be made in working with it. Granite offers orderly resistance according to the nature of its material. The artist must have the few proper tools and must be organized himself before he attacks it—and the result is therefore more apt to be orderly. The Aztecs punished drunkenness up to the age of 50 by death, reasoning that not till this age would the man have his spirit well enough controlled, and this policy should be applied to artists working with the plastics.

A. Theme and variations by the Swiss architect and sculptor Max Bill: the theme is a geometric design of an open triangle becoming an open square, this is a pentagon, etc. Variations showed this design in colors, surrounded by circles at points of intersections, with inscribed and circumscribed circles, as colored circles, as solid geometric forms, etc., ending with the original theme again.

B. A film, "Blacktop," made by the lecturer and his wife exhibits the theme and variations idea in the flow and eddy of water washing a school-yard, using the Bach Goldberg Variations as score.

C. Interscene cartoons by UPA for the film *The Four Poster* carry the mood and story of the film and make use of the theme and variations idea in picturing the spirit of the times.

Lecture No. 5
10 November 1953
(Given by Mr. Eames)

II. The Importance of Speculation

A. One reason for the importance of science fiction literature is that it is one of the few areas today in which the art of speculation is practiced. There should be a course in speculation introduced in the public schools. Most persons are quite untrained in this field, and while they have many wishes they wish harder than wisely.

1. This is dramatically illustrated in the King Midas and Genie stories of folklore. When someone is granted a number of wishes he is usually so unprepared that he creates disaster with the first wish and uses up the remaining ones just returning to normal.

2. It is often true that if we wish for something hard enough we are apt to get it, so there is a great need for background and study in speculation.

3. We wished very hard for a weapon that would destroy whole cities, and now many persons would like to unwish it again. Had we collectively been trained in the art of speculation we might not have wished so hard on this particular subject.

B. Rationally organized speculation

1. In our wish to fly to the moon we ought to speculate on our reasons, on the amount of money and man-hours it would take to accomplish this, and on the possibility of our getting back, and decide whether getting to the moon is really worth all this.

2. There is a course at MIT in creative engineering in which the students take an existing planet, calculate its gravity, rotation, atmo-

sphere, etc., to get an idea of its environment, speculate on the type of inhabitants, and attempt to design products for export to this planet. The points of reference are changed from those on earth, so that, for example, a clock cannot be thought of in a preconceived way as Big Ben or an alarm clock but in its basic function as "a device for measuring intervals of time" because the period of planet rotation and numbering system might be entirely different.

C. In speculation one should reinforce oneself by memory and by a knowledge of all that has already been learned in the field. It is not necessary to rediscover all the laws of electricity in solving an electric problem but more important to go on from what is already known.

A good aid to speculation and a way of solving problems is to look carefully back into history, involving oneself in the situation and conditions under which people solved problems in their own society. This will be the basis of the next problem, an historical one involving drawing and organization.

III. The Historical Problem:

As an example of one of the eras the student might be working with, the remainder of the lecture is devoted to material of the sights and sounds of the Renaissance era. This serves as a clue of what exists beneath the surface of an era when one looks into and identifies oneself with it.

A. A letter was read from a student of Cardano, the Renaissance scholar and mathematician, to another scholar. The university situation was very free and a student could at any time challenge the thesis of his instructor and even take over his position. Scholars challenged each other to debates and placed side bets to supplement their incomes. The audience for one of these great debates might overflow a large cathedral, and runners would be sent outside to inform the crowd of an important point. Also the "bookies" who accepted the bets needed to keep up with all the latest theories; this was dissemination of knowledge on a very real level. Scholars wrote heated letters to each other, often indulging in personalities and insults.

B. From the film *The Titan: Story of Michelangelo*,

Form and sequence studies.

sections on the peasant rebellion against the Medicis and Michelangelo working on the Sistine ceiling were shown. . . . Michelangelo's work is a good example of limitations on art discussed previously; he was always restricted as to subject matter, cost, location, etc.

C. A recording of brass choir music by the 16th-century organist of St. Mark's, Giovanni Bagrieli, was played along with a showing of color slides recently taken by Saarinen of Renaissance buildings and town in Italy. A combination of the music, the architecture, the food, the blood vengeance codes, the husband-wife-lover triangle love code, the extremely pious highway murderers, etc., are all necessary to the Renaissance setting.

D. A film on Leonardo da Vinci was shown. Leonardo had so many enthusiasms and interests that he was always beginning new projects, leaving others unfinished. Also he was able to profit by moments of real failure and mistake— as when his covering of page boys for a pageant entirely with gold leaf so that one died caused him to set about demonstrating the use of glands of the body.

E. The UPA drawings were shown again as an example of the capturing of the essence and spirit of their own times.

Lecture No. 6
3 June 1954
(Given by Mr. Eames)

This being the last lecture of the semester, discussion of the content of the course was considered of importance to Mr. Eames, with questions and answers to give the lecturer a clue as to what is going on in the minds of the students. . . .

Student begrudged time spent in making models; that is dissipated energy and interest. Mr. Eames was surprised at this as he would like to have had the time to do such a model, the problem for which was so clearly defined, and really worked with tension and compression. He went on to say that he discussed the tent problem with Mr. Saarinen, who was much pleased with it. *Mrs. Eames* added here that things happen in making a model that never happen any other way and never happen in the drawings or sketches; that in the making of a model you experienced the third dimension, which you do not get in drawings

Cardboard towers, Arch 1N.

or sketches—you just have to make the model to experience this third dimension. That the student experiences constant critical judgment all along the line in making a model. Also that he is concerned with the matter of communication to others, a very important facility to learn.

Architecture 1 and 2

The screams of train whistles, roars of lions, beating of waves, sounds of cable cars and Gertrude Stein that came from the Architecture I and II lectures—plus the images that went with them—were not just the result of passion for taking photos and *taping* sounds. These were a part of the many things we felt desirable and necessary to the business of involving beginning students in architecture. To become involved is not easy because it means being responsible—and in architecture it means pulling all past, present, and future experiences into the act.

The object of the slides and sounds and film was to help pull such experiences into the act of architecture and to heighten the awareness of future looking, seeing, hearing, smelling, feeling, tasting, and relating. Coupled with curiosity and enthusiasm, this awareness builds a warehouse of associations; and associations are the stock in trade of any creative individual. We would have had much more and better material from many other fields of learning—not in order to give capsule courses, but to open doors and to demonstrate relationships. Approximately 75 percent of the class time was spent on the problems and exercises which required and produced an extraordinary amount of work. A real problem is the designing of a series of problems that lead to experiences and discoveries upon which one can build. The problems we presented this year were not uniformly successful as problems, but the three general principles upon which they were based we believe are sound—

1. That the object be limited
   A concise idea of the immediate objective is the greatest stimulus to real creative thinking. The danger in most problems is that the limits are so broad and the number of factors involved so compounded, that it is impossible for the student to isolate an objective and work toward it. This is often responsible for that well known rat race "originality for its own sake." This habit of limiting can help an architect recognize those aspects which are sociological, structural, sculptural, etc.

2. That the process of solution be within the scope of the student
   This to develop a habit of responsibility to all the factors involved in any problem. When structural or sociological aspects occur that are so complex that they must be ignored, it can create in the beginning student an irresponsible pattern of thinking—a habit of fakery. If a problem can be grasped completely, it will leave the student free to call upon the *whole* of his experience.

3. That there be some practical basis for evaluating the results
   Too often evaluations can disintegrate on the "I like it—you don't like it—so what" level. It would seem good in the beginning to give the disciplines so necessary to an architectural attitude, a more than even chance to come through.

To the beginning student, the great thinkers and doers in architecture seem often to stand as personalities of style and form. But we believe much more reliable clues to their big direction can be found in the *way* they thought and among the things of which they were most fond.

To really benefit from the work of these men—look to their loves—
be interested
be enthusiastic
become involved

Sources: Charles Eames, typed transcript of lecture, December 15, 1953, University of California, Berkeley, Part II: Projects series; Charles and Ray Eames Papers, Manuscript Division, Library of Congress, Washington, D.C. Charles Eames, "Architecture 1 and 2," *Ark Annual* (Student Chapter of the American Institute of Architects, College of Architecture, University of California, Berkeley, 1954), 29–31, Part II: Speeches and Writings series, Charles and Ray Eames Papers, Manuscript Division, Library of Congress, Washington, D.C.

Six-inch thread and stick structure to
support five pounds, Arch 1N.

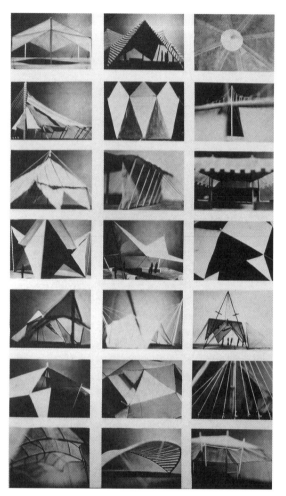

Tent structures, Arch 2N.

Washington University School of Architecture

CORRESPONDENCE

Charles Eames to Professor Lawrence Hill, Washington University School of Architecture
April 22, 1954

Dear Professor Hill:

Ray and I enjoyed so much our visit with you. After later talking with the students, we felt that the best thing that could happen to them would be to hear and receive things like you said, words and thoughts such as you gave us during the short visit. It was distressing to then hear of your coming retirement from the school. I hope that if you do go on and do work elsewhere, there will develop a kind of communication between yourself, the rich things you hold, and this youngest of all generations.

If I had a chance to choose between studying the "styles" as we were introduced to them 1925 fashion, and the frozen style that I see being taught today, I think I would unhesitatingly choose the kind you taught to us. I feel it is just as necessary today. Thank you again.

Sincerely,
Charles Eames

Charles Eames to Ethan A. H. Shepley, Washington University School of Architecture
April 23, 1954

Dear Chancellor Shepley:

We enjoyed having the opportunity of visiting with you and have not forgotten the House of Cards, which is being sent separately.

It was a warming surprise to find that you had taken time from what must be busy days to attend a lecture in the School of Architecture.

It became apparent, even in the short visit, that Washington University is not free from the danger that exists in many schools of architecture today—that of becoming, in many ways, a trade school. Trade schools are not necessarily bad, but a trade must usually be taught in terms of a more or less static art. A field like architecture is evolving and must be in its way anticipatory. Taught as a *trade* it would be obsolete before they had a chance to practice (or learn) it.

I am sure that, given the opportunity, [Buford L.] Pickens will emphasize a more liberal preparation for coping with changing problems—a security in change, instead of a security in a now existent status quo—and an opportunity and urge to develop and expand their innate abilities.

Ray joins me in greetings—and best of luck in your big new job.

Sincerely,
Charles Eames

Source: Charles Eames to Lawrence Hill, April 22, 1954, and Charles Eames to Ethan A. H. Shepley, April 23, 1954, Washington University folder, Part II: Office File (Pre-1960) series, Charles and Ray Eames Papers, Manuscript Division, Library of Congress, Washington, D.C.

How the Chairs Are Made

CORRESPONDENCE

Editor's note: Frank Newby (March 26, 1926–May 10, 2001) was a structural engineer, working with such architects as Philip Powell and Hidalgo Moya, Eero Saarinen, James Stirling, and the practice of Skidmore, Owings & Merrill.

Charles Eames to Frank Newby, in care of Felix J. Samuely
March 2, 1954

Dear Frank:

It was very good to hear from you—I would like to be looking over your shoulder and see what you are doing. . . .

As soon as we get a print of "A Communications Primer" circulating in England we will certainly direct it to you, and of course, we think of you every time we see that distinguished handwriting on the screen. . . .

1. The molded plywood chairs are molded from sheets of veneer between heated platens bonded with a thermosetting resin. (Seat and back from five sheets—legs and spine from nine.) Finish of most of these parts is in the form of an impregnating resin sprayed on the surface of the veneer and cured against the platen. Molded parts adhere to the frame by means of the rubber shock mount. The rubber shock mount is a rubber part with a metal insert molded into it. The metal insert is threaded to receive the machine screw. The shock mount is secured to the wood seat and back with a thermosetting adhesive.

   The molded fiberglass chair is made from a fiberglass preform. The fiberglass is short pieces of glass fiber roving which have been blown into a cyclone and pulled up against the preform screen by air, which exhausted through the screen. The preform is then set between male and female dies, a predetermined amount of polyester resin poured into the preform and the matched dies, then closed on this combination, and the resin is forced between the fibers and cured at a temperature of 250 degrees F. for a time duration of five minutes.

2. The finish can be seen as an integral part of the chair and is not later applied, but rather forced around the glass fibers as molded.

3. Glass fiber is made by Owens-Corning—they call it "Fiberglas," which is their trademark. Glass fiber is also made by Pittsburgh Plate Glass Co. and Libbey-Owens-Ford and some others. Zenith Plastics who mold the chairs do not use just one brand only.

4. The first molded plastic chair appeared in 1948 [Eames's "La Chaise," for the Museum of Modern Art's Low Cost Furniture competition].

5. There have been approximately 100,000 armchairs molded. Nominal basic cost of such dies is likely to be in the vicinity of $20,000.

Warmest greetings to you from all of us,
Charles Eames

Source: Charles Eames to Frank Newby, March 2, 1954, Part II: Office File (Pre-1960) series, Charles and Ray Eames Papers, Manuscript Division, Library of Congress, Washington, D.C.

herman **M**iller zeeland michigan

PKW-2
Pivot base makes this version of upholstered wire chair ideal for desk work. Wood legs.

DCM
America's most famous modern chair; molded plywood; dining, desk height.

DAR-U
Upholstered armchair dining, desk height. Bright wire base has smooth "glide" tips.

✳ DSR
A plastic side chair, available in three colors on a black or a bright metal base.

LCM
A low-cost Eames design! Molded plywood chair for relaxation, sturdy metal legs.

MSX
Practical, lightweight side chair at lounging height. Plastic shell and strong metal legs.

RAR-U
Popular rocker has shell upholstered in leather, fabric, vinyl; birch and wire base.

MAX
Armchair for reading, and for relaxation. Glass fiber reinforced plastic; metal legs.

RKR-2
Upholstered wire chair with metal base. Two-piece leather, fabric, or vinyl pad.

LAR
Lounge chair of exceptional comfort. Plastic shell; black or light wire base.

DKR-1
For dining, for desk work: upholstered wire chair, 1-piece pad; black legs and frame.

DKX-1
Versatile upholstered wire chair in dining, desk height; harlequin pad; black legs, frame.

LCW
Molded plywood "low" chair—choice of five finishes: birch, ash, walnut, black or red.

built by pioneers of the best in modern furniture, these chairs designed by charles eames are sound solutions of basic needs - chairs that are comfortable, attractive and long wearing . in many many versions, and very modestly priced from ✳ **$23.95 up** . write department LN for free folder and name of nearest dealer

send 25c in coin to department LN for illustrated booklet; ABC OF MODERN FURNITURE

"Built by Pioneers," Herman Miller, Inc., advertisement published in *Living for Young Homemakers*, November 1953.

Upholstery for Furniture

CORRESPONDENCE

Editor's note: Eames Demetrios, director of the Eames Office, has observed that Charles and Ray Eames did not believe in "delegating understanding." This correspondence is a representation of this practice. The Eameses brought in an educator to teach them and their staff how to sew upholstery, and they manufactured the first examples in their own shop. They sent the patterns and tools they developed to Herman Miller for serial production.

Charles Eames to Mr. Wood, Apparel Arts Department, Los Angeles Trade and Technical College
June 30, 1954

Dear Mr. Wood:

For several years Mrs. Maxine Turner has worked with us on research and development projects having to do with production problems in the manufacture of upholstered furniture.

Her initial work with us started with the teaching of techniques and basic principles to members of the design staff. She followed this through the development of the product for production, and those employed in the actual manufacture of pads had been students in her class.

She was cooperative in every detail and personally a pleasure to work with. Teaching with her became a real craft, and she possesses an amazing ability to analyze and criticize in relation to problems that arise.

We are grateful to Mrs. Turner for the help she has given us in the development of products for the Herman Miller Furniture Company.

Sincerely,

Charles Eames

Source: Charles Eames to Mr. Wood, June 20, 1954, filed with letter from Maxine Turner, June 3, 1954, "T" miscellaneous folder, Part II: Office File (Pre-1960) series, Charles and Ray Eames Papers, Manuscript Division, Library of Congress, Washington, D.C.

Buying a New Ford

CORRESPONDENCE

Ford convertible in front of the Eames
House, circa 1950.

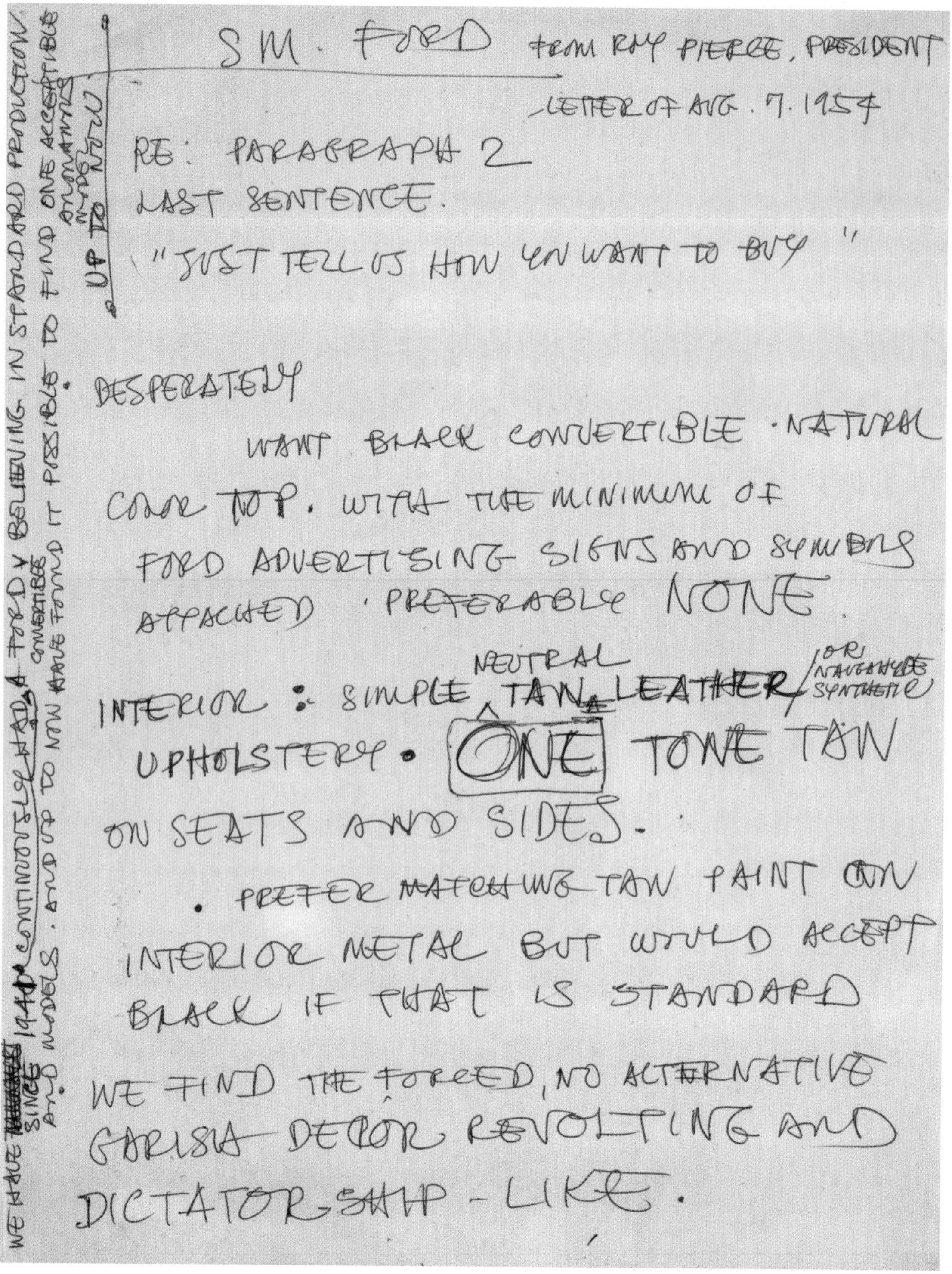

S.M. FORD from RAY PIERCE, PRESIDENT

LETTER OF AUG. 7. 1954

RE: PARAGRAPH 2
LAST SENTENCE.

"JUST TELL US HOW YOU WANT TO BUY"

DESPERATELY

WANT BLACK CONVERTIBLE · NATURAL
COLOR TOP · WITH THE MINIMUM OF
FORD ADVERTISING SIGNS AND SYMBOLS
ATTACHED · PREFERABLE NONE.

INTERIOR :· SIMPLE NEUTRAL TAN LEATHER /OR /WASHABLE SYNTHETIC
UPHOLSTERY · ONE TONE TAN
ON SEATS AND SIDES.

· PREFER MATCHING TAN PAINT ON
INTERIOR METAL BUT WOULD ACCEPT
BLACK IF THAT IS STANDARD

WE FIND THE FORCED, NO ALTERNATIVE
GARISH DECOR REVOLTING AND
DICTATOR-SHIP - LIKE.

UP TO NOW · WE HAVE THELLES SINCE 1940 · CONTINUOUSLY HAD A FORD · BELIEVING IN STANDARD PRODUCTION CONVERTIBLES AND MODELS · AND UP TO NOW HAVE FOUND IT POSSIBLE TO FIND ONE ACCEPTABLE CONVERTIBLE

Handwritten notes by Ray Eames,
August 7, 1954, Eames Office Archives,
Santa Monica, California.

August 26, 1954

~~Copy~~

Mr. Henry Ford II, President
The Ford Motor Company
Administration Building
3000 Schaefer Road
Dearborn, Michigan

Dear Mr. Ford:

I have been driving Fords continuously since 1929, and
we have had Ford convertibles since 1941.

We believe in the use of standard production models.

Up until now we have been able to find one acceptable
anonymous model.

The following is what we could consider an anonymous
model - one we would like to buy now:

>   Black convertible, natural top, minimum of
>   advertising signs and symbols attached -
>   preferably none.
>   The interior: simple neutral tan leather or
>   good neutral color synthetic material -
>   no two-tones - preferably matching tan
>   paint on interior metal, but would accept
>   black if that is standard.

We have needed a new car for some time, but have been
unable to obtain any assurance from our local agent that
our requirements are in any way possible to fulfill. On
a recent visit to the Alexander Girards in Santa Fe, we
were advised by them that our only recourse was to write
to you directly and that by so doing we would undoubtedly
obtain the information we cannot obtain here. We are
taking the liberty of following the Girards' advice, and
trust that this letter will be channeled by your office
to the appropriate department.

Thank you for the many positive things that bear the name
of Ford.

Sincerely,

Charles Eames

CE:vs

CHARLES EAMES 901 WASHINGTON BOULEVARD VENICE CALIFORNIA

Charles Eames to Henry Ford II, August
26, 1954, Eames Office Archives, Santa
Monica, California.

"A Communications Primer"

CORRESPONDENCE

Charles Eames to Ian McCallum, *Architectural Review*, **London**
September 3, 1954

Dear Ian McCallum:

We have recently finished a 16 millimeter film which we call "A Communications Primer." (It runs 22 minutes, is in color-sound.) A print has been at Edinburgh, and before shipping it back we have taken the liberty of sending it to you to view, if you are interested. (Mr. Nikolaus Pevsner saw some of the rough material when he was at Aspen.)

"A Communications Primer" doesn't pretend to "teach" anything about communications theory but is at best a door opener to some of the many aspects of this broad subject. We are now working on a sequel (not "Son of Communications" or "Communications Rides Again"—but "Theory of Feedback").

One of the reasons for our interest in the subject is our strong suspicion that the development and application of these related theories will be the greatest tool ever to have fallen into the hands of the architects or planners. One of the reasons for writing this to you is that I also suspect that the use of such a tool will reinforce those qualities which you have so richly presented in Townscapes.

If ever an art was based on the handling and relating of an impossible number of factors, this art is architecture. One of the things that makes an architect is the ability to include in a concept the effect of and effect on many simultaneous factors—and a precious tool has been his ability to fall back on his own experiences, which have somehow turned into intuitive associations. It is one reason why an architect seldom is, nor can afford to be, bored with anything.

The ability to make keen intuitive associations does not, of course, relieve the architect of the responsibility of calculating and predicting all factors of a problem that can be calculated and predicted. It is perhaps safe to say that in any architectural problem very few of the factors involved have been calculable—the relationships of factors are almost impossible to calculate—and most of the factors remain unknown.

If, however, a tool should be developed which could make possible the inclusion of *more* factors—and could make calculable the possible results of relationships between combinations of factors—then it would become the *responsibility* of the architect and planner to use such a tool. The talent for associations would be far from negated—it would be put to a much keener use. The level of creativity would be immediately raised and so would the responsibility. We may have the possibility of such a tool in the "Theory of Games."

You are no doubt familiar with the main aspects of the "Theory of Games of Strategy" or "Game Theory." (Now some 35 years old, it was of great importance during the war, and in complex organizational and industrial problems today[;] linear programming is a development of games theory.) While the big concept is great and simple, the working vocabulary gets so supermathematical as to be unintelligible, and the working mechanics would have been impossible had it not been for the simultaneous development of the present day electronic calculator.

Like *linear programming*, game theory is a pure mathematical system that can be used in relation to very human problems. By it a number of variables can be considered simultaneously and a solution calculated that has the highest probability of filling the desired requirements under the given circumstances.

How human and confidence-giving it is to learn that such answers are *not* given in terms of "a sure thing" but in terms of "high probability."

About 10 years ago John von Neumann, mathematician (and author of the theory of games), and Oskar Morgenstern, economist, co-authored a book *Theory of Games and Economic Behavior.* Many of its pages are so filled with mathematical symbolism that they look like (and are for many of us) pages of a foreign language. But very real was the method and the concept of treating human actions and needs in such a way that they can be discussed mathematically. In most any economic situation, some of these actions and needs are emotional or psychological. To discuss these aspects of a problem mathematically seems difficult but not unreasonable, when we hear that mathematics did not exist in physics before the 16th century or in chemistry and biology until the 18th century.

Here is a supersimple and interesting example of thinking taken from a footnote in the von Neumann–Morgenstern book:

> Assume that an individual prefers the consumption of a glass of tea to that of a cup of coffee, and the cup of coffee to a glass of milk. If we now want to know whether the last preference—i.e., difference in utilities—exceeds the former, it suffices to place him in a situation where he must decide this: Does he prefer a cup of coffee to a glass the contents of which will be determined by a 50%–50% chance device as tea or milk.

As the authors go step by step through the process of evaluating economic situations in mathematical terms—the very nature of the situations makes it apparent that one can substitute "planning" or "design" for "economics" and since the direction is toward high probabilities and not sure things, the factors are all open to re-evaluation on a highly creative or personal level—including nothing out.

It is unfortunate that in this time much of the really creative thinking is organizing and programming, and evaluation should be so shrouded with the panic of secrecy. Here is a useful working tool that comes to us at a time when numbers and complications seem about to obliterate the human scale. What makes this tool so handy is that it would seem to actually use large numbers and unlimited relationships to help us return to the human scale and the richness of the townscape in the terms of our times.

Of course, there will be the hidden fears of loss of individuality and creativity which tend to swamp any concept which gives greater responsibility to the individual and the creator—but of one thing we can be quite sure: the buildings and communities of the near future *will* be planned with the aid of some development of these theories. Whether or not they are planned by architects may pretty well depend on the way architects today prepare to use such tools.

Anyway, this is the background thinking of the film "A Communications Primer."

Sincerely,

Charles Eames

Source: Charles Eames to Ian McCallum, September 3, 1954, Part II: Speeches and Writings series, Charles and Ray Eames Papers, Manuscript Division, Library of Congress, Washington, D.C.

A production still from "A Communications Primer."

Visit to Germany

EXCHANGE PROGRAM OF THE GERMAN GOVERNMENT, 1954/55

German government announcement

The Exchange Program of the German Government will be continued this year. The program was established in 1952 in recognition of the hundreds of invitations extended to German citizens by the United States Government.

The program consists in a four-week information tour, including a visit to West-Berlin. The objective of the program is to give leading Americans, active in all fields of public life, an opportunity to become acquainted with present-day life in institutions in Germany, particularly in their areas of special interest.

Travel expenses from New York to Frankfurt/ Main and return by air (tourist class) are paid for by the German Government. Transportation by rail within the Federal Republic will be free. A daily allowance of DM 40.—app. $10.—will be paid, which will be sufficient for accommodation and board in first-ration hotels. The American guests will be insured against accident to the amount of DM 10.000.

The American guests will be met at Frankfurt airport by representatives of the German Foreign Office and immediately be accompanied to Bonn. The first 3 days in Bonn will be devoted to an official program, comprising the official welcome by the Federal Government and a round-table conference with representatives of the relevant federal ministries for the purpose of informing the guests about the present situation in Germany. After 3 days in Bonn the group will start on its information trip through the Federal Republic and West Berlin.

Charles Eames to His Excellency, Walter Hallstein, Secretary of State for Foreign Affairs of the Federal Republic of Germany
September 20, 1954

Excellency:

I beg you to excuse the fact that I must write this letter in English. It was an exceptional honor to receive your invitation to visit Germany as a guest of the Federal German Government. I am extremely happy to be able to accept this generous offer of hospitality.

I am, of course, interested in German painting and sculpture, both old and new, in architecture and planning, and in the theater and in motion picture films. But I am also interested in folk arts, toys, games, festivals, and music. We are planning a large exhibit of toys. Germany occupies a unique position in the history of such art. It is my hope that in travelling through Germany I might have the opportunity of seeing such examples and, if they are available, purchasing some for the exhibition and for an educational series of films we are doing.

I have recently spoken with some educators who have taken part in the exchange program, and they have been most enthusiastic about the way it was conducted by your government. I am looking forward to this experience. Again, I would like to thank you for the honor and the opportunity.

Sincerely,

Charles Eames

"Civilized Touch Forgotten"
By Harriet Morrison

This information was obtained during an interview with Charles Eames, the smiling designer with a crew cut. . . . He was interviewed here on his arrival from Germany, where he was looking around at the invitation of the West German Foreign Ministry as part of a cultural exchange program.

Mr. Eames had a wonderful time in Germany "partaking" of life and exploring his two main interests: mathematics and toys. His activities involved enjoying "small but important civilized touches" such as the loving ritual in Germany of a cup of coffee on a tray, the feel of a feather bed swathed in fine linen, the wonders of rich German pastry, and the fairyland of Bavarian Baroque architecture. "It's nice to be reminded of the dignity of civilized attitudes," he said of his trip. "Not that we've lost the civilized touch in America, but we seem to have forgotten it for a while."

The pastry was pure delight, he reports. He and his wife spent two evenings photographing the beautiful shapes after tasting their rich goodness. He was asked by the pastry shop proprietors if he were going to open a bakery in Los Angeles. He doesn't plan to but would like to feed the pastry by spoon to today's students of architecture and design. The pastry, Mr. Eames explained, is a contemporary example of the Baroque style of architecture of the early eighteenth century in southern Germany, which the designer calls "light, humorous, wonderfully thought out, and highly mathematical."

He is convinced that Baroque offers the most fruitful inspiration for modern designers. "The trouble with modern design," he observed, "is not that it's too functional, but that it is not functional enough in human terms." He said, "The future has never seemed so bright because ours will be the first culture to be able to pick and choose the best of the past and not copy it but evaluate and measure the heretofore felt but unmeasurable human and emotional factors that made it good." How will we measure? Through the field of communications, which he terms a unique characteristic of our age, "Developments in the theory of communications are the greatest tool for architects of the future," he said.

Sources: German government announcement, [1954], German Cultural Exchange Program, itineraries, Part II: Office File (Pre-1960) series, Charles and Ray Eames Papers, Manuscript Division, Library of Congress, Washington, D.C. Charles Eames to Walter Hallstein, September 20, 1954, German Cultural Exchange Program, correspondence, Part II: Office File (Pre-1960) series, Charles and Ray Eames Papers, Manuscript Division, Library of Congress, Washington, D.C. Harriet Morrison, "Civilized Touch Forgotten," *New York Herald Tribune* (December 16, 1954).

Photographs of Baroque churches by Charles Eames.

CHARLES EAMES AND RAY EAMES

Compact Sofa

Editor's note: The following text is narration for a sales film.

More and more the problems of shipping come to be considered as a part of the manufacturer's responsibility. He knows that no matter what the product is it cannot start its real life of service until it is in the hands of the consumer.

Shipping then automatically becomes the designer's problem. Any space pilot will tell us that it is not the standing or cruising that is tough on merchandise, it is the quick start and stop.

Most furniture is difficult to ship, but the size of the sofa exaggerates the difficulty. Crated as it stands, it would not only be vulnerable to damage, but it would occupy 34 cubic feet for its 110 pounds. Traffic managers like weight but they don't like volume. Volume is expensive so it makes the rates go up. The sofa compact has one-third the volume and of course the same weight. It is convenient to store, it is easy to handle, and has no vulnerable projecting parts.

After delivery to the average couple the process of decompacting offers no problem. A couple less experienced in such matters may take a little longer, but the steps are simple, clear, and few.

They have here a product that has been made with great concern for the service it will ultimately give them. It is the result of much thought and research on the part of the designer and much work, thought, and involvement on the part of many others. Mockups and models and all the problems and decisions that go with planning and preparing a product for production.

The objective was to make a full length, high back, long life, high ultimate value, compactable sofa. The three-section profile was perhaps influenced by studies made for earlier molded plywood pieces. Some of the first models we tried were in wire. The material is economical, and the end product can be made quite light. These gave way to studies of central tube schemes which had much fewer but complicated connections.

The frame that finally went into production has components that are easily stored, and the assembly requires fewer connections than did the previous models.

The covers for the foam rubber cushions were selected from materials designed by Alexander Girard for the Herman Miller Collection. These include not only fabrics, but . . . special colors in Naugahyde. It seemed good to have also available a cover that can recover from this [image of a jelly sandwich smeared on a sofa]. There's no predicting what may happen in the life of a sofa.

Source: Charles and Ray Eames, *S-73*, by the Office of Charles and Ray Eames for Herman Miller, Inc., 1954. 16mm film, 10 min. The title of this film refers to the original Herman Miller model number for the sofa. Eventually this design came to known as the Compact Sofa.

Production still from this film.

Production still from this film.

Lounge Chair and Ottoman

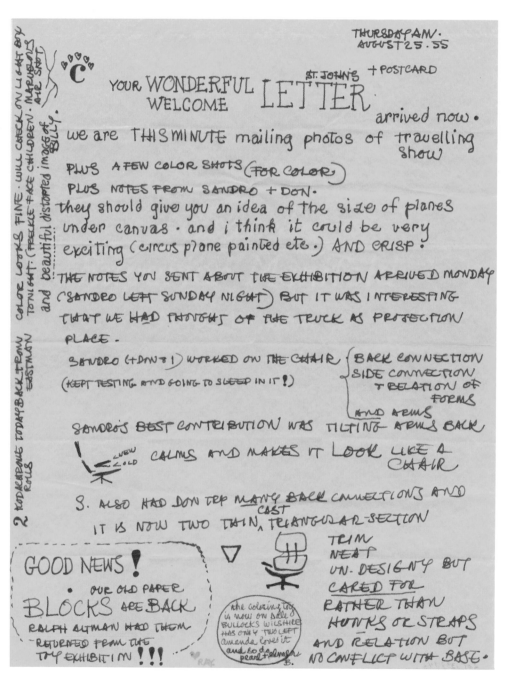

Ray Eames, letter to Charles Eames.

Home Show, NBC, hosted by Arlene Francis
Guests: Charles and Ray Eames, 1956

ARLENE FRANCIS *I wonder if you'll tell us some of the highlights of your careers in designing these chairs. How did you happen to get started with chairs?*

CHARLES EAMES Well, Ray was a painter. Ray worked here in New York with Hans Hofmann for a long time. That's a pretty good start. I'm an architect. . . . I don't know if you know, architects think that everything comes after the heading of architecture, whether it's chairs or space platforms. Everything.

AF *Yes. Even dresses and . . .*

CE By all means. They have structure. . . . The molded plywood chairs are a result of a working with a mass-production technique and in a way letting the mass-production technique show through in the result. In the case of the plastic chairs, the object was to take a material which was a high-performance material developed during the war and try to make it available to householders at non-military prices.

AF *Aha . . . And very practical, is it?*

CE Well, they make shock helmets out of it . . . that should be pretty good. The wire and the upholstered wire pieces, these are of course old materials but they are combined in a way to give a high strength light weight and the . . .

AF *Very new look . . .*

CE . . . high-performance result. The things are different but this doesn't mean the attitude is different. It's just that there was different objective in each case.

AF *I've noticed that you have some of them that revolve here.*

CE These are pivot things. . . .

AF *Is there a basic theory of design of your chairs?*

CE Well, there's one. I don't know whether I can talk about it. There's, that is, the attitude in all them is really the same. We've never designed for a fashion or with the idea of fitting in a fashion. The Herman Miller Company has never ever requested that we do pieces for a market for an annual thing.

AF *You really create your market, don't you?*

CE Yes. The timing is more or less our own. Sometimes it's too slow, but we are allowed then to follow it through the graphics presentation.

AF *Yes, you say it's too slow and yet you've done so much and so many and so much sooner than* most people have. Designing interesting furniture is of course only part of the work that Charles and Ray Eames do. As I remember, your house shows very well the way you feel about living and the problems of design. I think if we could see some pictures. Mr. Eames will tell us a little about the house. . . .

CE Ray and I worked on it. We designed it together, of course. Recently, we made a film on the house ["House: After Five Years of Living"], and it has been released at the Museum of Modern Art. It's a series of films. The music for it was composed by Elmer Bernstein, and it's a marvelous thing. Elmer just did *The Man with the Golden Arm* and the music for "House."

AF *This is beautiful and airy looking, isn't it?*

CE Well, we think so. It's sort of gotten to be like an old cave for us but . . . it's composed of standard factory units.

AF *Standard factory units that don't look very standard or very factory in those pictures. That's what your beautification has done for you and Ray. You've also done some of the most fascinating toys, not only for children but for grown-ups as well. And we have something here. I wish you'd just tell us about it.*

CE Well, it's a house of cards done from things mainly picked up around our own house. . . .

AF *Aha . . . You mean the designs on the cards?*

CE Yeah.

AF *And this is sold to provide children to build their own private house as well.*

CE Children, yes, but there's no limit on the age, of course.

AF *Adults are children in many respects, aren't they. And of course, you've been working on the picture* The Spirit of St. Louis. *I'm curious about what you did precisely with that picture, Charles.*

CE Well, I worked with Billy Wilder, the director. He's a great man . . .

AF *Indeed.*

CE . . . and it's going to be a real good picture. I didn't make the furniture for Jimmy Stewart or anything like that. I was working with Billy and directed for him some second-unit work, mainly the construction of the airplane.

AF *Is it going to be the exact replica of the one that's in the Smithsonian?*

CE Well, Charles Lindbergh couldn't tell the difference.

AF *Well, if he can't, it must be pretty accurate. Charles, we know about the materials that you have used for your chairs. They are basically molded wood and plastics as you have shown us—fiberglass, wire, and so forth, and some upholstered parts—but I think* *now it would be very nice if we could preview your newest chair. Why don't we just go up here and have a little preview of this.* [Chair is revealed, from behind a curtain] *Well, that is quite a departure, Charles, and it looks wonderfully comfortable.*

Eames Lounge Chair and Ottoman Hangtag

This envelope contains information on the new lounge chair designed by Charles Eames for the Herman Miller Furniture Company

"The upholstered lounge chair & ottoman are a combination intended to give comfort for long periods of time such as reading or conversation after dinner or just relaxing and thinking. Size and relationships of the parts are most important, I suppose, but the fact that all of the parts are allowed a bit of movement in relation to each other and that both main units are mounted on swivels gives the freedom that contributes to relaxation.

Another thing we came to realize in our search for this kind of comfort is that feathers and down are pretty good materials. Like few others, they give one the feeling of settling in, and when you get up, feathers and down do not instantly pop back into place as though you had never been there.

The leather cushions do have built-in wrinkles to start with, but that is a clue that spells comfort to come, like the warm receptive look of a well-used first baseman's mitt."

Charles Eames

Sources: Ray Eames to Charles Eames, August 25, 1955, Part II: Office File (Pre-1960) series, Charles and Ray Eames Papers, Manuscript Division, Library of Congress, Washington, D.C. "Eames Lounge Chair Debut in 1956 on NBC Complete," YouTube video, 11:22, from an episode of *The Home Show* with Arlene Francis, televised by NBC in 1956 (http://youtu.be/z_X6RsN-HFw). Charles Eames, "Eames Lounge Chair and Ottoman," product hangtag, Herman Miller Inc., Zeeland, Michigan, 1956.

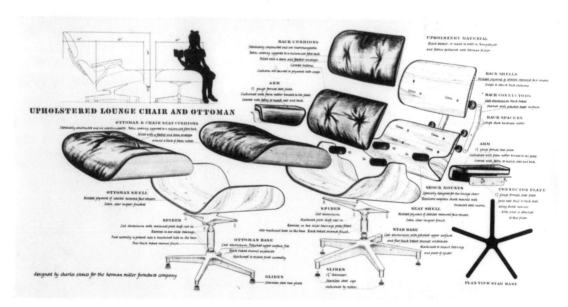

Eames lounge chair and ottoman graphic by the Eames Office, with calligraphy by Sister Corita Kent.

Charles and Ray Eames in their living room, seated on the lounge chair and ottoman, 1959. © Vitra AG Photo: Monique Jacot.

Omnibus

Editor's note: Among the Eames papers is a file of notes prepared by Charles and Ray Eames in anticipation of their appearance on Alistair Cooke's Omnibus *television show. There is no record of their appearance on the show. There are three sets of notes in the Eames archives. The first is on index cards. Here, in Charles's handwriting, is the second and first full draft of the notes, written on hotel stationery.*

Source: Charles Eames, handwritten notes for a proposed CBS *Omnibus* television program, April 1956, Part II: Speeches and Writings series, Charles and Ray Eames Papers, Manuscript Division, Library of Congress, Washington, D.C.

OMNIBUS
May 1956

Cook

Intro.

montage of chair

① give a small capsule of background

~~explain~~ that Ray comes to design thru painting
and I thru architecture —

that this should not be at all surprising since
I feel that most everything is *a form of* Architecture — certainly
all of the ~~the~~ environment that man creates for himself —
and Ray feels that painting is related to everything —
and of course I feel that painting ~~is a part of Architecture~~
comes under the heading of Arch —

This is our home in California
we did it about seven years ago —
and whether it is design — painting — or architecture
— we love it —
and we approached the problem of its design
exactly as we approach this chair, of which Mr. Cook *has spoken*
or a painting or tool or anything we tackle —

before talking about the design of a chair
for that reason it might be good to ~~first~~ show
you a little more of the house —
certainly it is the best way *that we can* to introduce ourselves to you

Omnibus first draft script pages
by Charles Eames.

②

what you have just seen is really a clip from a 10min film Ray and I did on the House

The music is by Elmer Bernstein (you have probably heard the theme from the music he did for the 'Man with the golden arm')

The music for the House film was of course composed for the film - and with the film - what is interesting is that the music itself stands as architecture - it contributes so much to the structure of the film that if you take the music away it is difficult to look at the picture - one can learn about construction while working with a composer and music

Whether it's House or film or chair - it must have a structural concept -

Our architecture as well as furniture has been likened to kites - while I wouldn't take that too literally - It doesn't seem completely unnatural since we are both interested in kites and have used them as problems for students to develop a live feeling an attitude toward architecture

③

The marvelous fact about a kite problem is that there is one area in which one can definitely judge its success or failure - that it - it will fly or it will not fly - I wish more problems could be so beautifully defined -

'Now Ray has been in the corner quietly putting what I hope are the finishing touches on a monster kite -

'lets generate some breeze and see if it will fly or if it will not fly -

fine device ...

that last was an athopter
it really flies like a bird -
How Leonardo da Vinci would
have loved one of these -
you have seen these great drawings of his
I am sure -
He must have been a very amused gentleman

⑤

Toys have an influence on design, on any culture and certainly on this chair but it is a very special kind of influence -

Toys (and with toys I include most of the festival arts - masks, floats, cake decorating and this whole wild world) have always been approached in a way that is almost completely free from embarrassment and self consciousness

It is this lack of self consciousness on the part of the real toymaker, his complete involvement with the spirit of the toy, that enables him to take the meanest material and make it sing — in its own way —
Paper like paper tin like tin —
no pretension

⑥

Here is a locomotive - it is an old american toy completely in the wood tradition its modern german and especially lovable for its sound - listen -
this locomotive - is old american
what is tin is beautifully tin - what is cast is beautifully cast and what is bell rings beautifully —

There have been, for the most part, true toys not scale reproductions of the real thing -
In the mind of the maker the objective of the toy was so real, so clear that he did not get derailed in trying to be original

ortthopter, kite, or model jet —
designing and building anything that
has such critical performance is priceless
experience for developing structural concepts
related to performance

    Examples in
    Furniture
        Frames
        Shells
        Bases etc —

BUT The influence of kites and the like
on Design should not be confused
with the influence of TOY — TOYS are something special —
Playing with kites is in the same category
as all the playing that has be done with
static electricity, and fluid dynamics (damming
up streams and gutters and such —   .

    To know so well what you want to
accomplish — that there is no pressure to be
original — this is a desirable state
whether one is designing a toy, or writing a play
or building a chair —

    Good tools are perhaps the most foolproof
against the trap of originality for its own sake —
~~~~~~~~ The familiarity with tools
and the experience of designing tools for
specific purposes — play a great part
in our attitude toward any problem
we approach — this was certainly
apparent in the chair

Toy Orthopter

CORRESPONDENCE

Charles Eames to Mr. Andrew Knox, London
June 19, 1956

Dear Andrew:

Ray and I enjoyed so much receiving your note. More than any photograph could do, it showed us how grown up you are and makes us want to see you again very much.

I am sending you a toy which is one of the best I have seen in a long, long time. Because I have enjoyed it, I believe you will, too. It makes me wish I could be able to send one also to a great man who lived four hundred years ago and also enjoyed playing with such things. Leonardo Da Vinci did many things but found time to build some of the best kites ever and made marvelous drawings of a bird-like flying mechanism almost exactly like the toy I am sending.

When you start to fly it, if it seems to "stall," bend the tail slightly down. If it seems to go into a "dive," bend the tail slightly up. It is a pretty rugged bird and can stand quite a few turns—perhaps thirty or forty—in winding.

Give our love to your father and mother. Tell them that we have sent Larry Bachmann a film based on our house and they might want to see it. Ray also sends warmest greetings.

Sincerely,
Charles Eames

Source: Charles Eames to Andrew Knox, June 19, 1956, Part II: Office File (Pre-1960) series, Charles and Ray Eames Papers, Manuscript Division, Library of Congress, Washington, D.C.

Toy from the Collection of Charles and Ray Eames. Photograph by Ric Keefer.

"Toccata for Toy Trains"

CORRESPONDENCE AND NARRATION

Editor's note: Eliot Noyes, an American architect and designer, was the curator at the Museum of Modern Art who devised the 1941 Organic Furniture Design competition and, in 1946, gave Charles and Ray Eames their first exhibition at MoMA. Noyes also was consultant design director at IBM and the designer of the Selectric typewriter. He continued his association with the Eameses over the years, commissioning many exhibitions from them, including IBM's New York World's Fair Pavilion design in 1964.

Charles Eames to Mr. Eliot Noyes
November 21, 1956

Dear Eliot:

It was very thoughtful of you to send the little glass locomotive, and I have an idea it is going to prove more useful than you thought. We are in the middle of shooting now and way, way over our ears in toy trains old and new. I do wish that you and Molly could see them because, of all the people we know, you would be high, high on the list of enjoyability.

The Museum of the City of New York was very helpful, and they sent us most all of their good things (train wise, that is). This helped in two ways: the stuff itself, and then, the priming of other sources. Now that we have got the material, it is pretty terrifying to try to handle it well enough.

Much love to all Noyes,

Charles Eames

Production still of "the little glass locomotive" from first frames of "Toccata for Toy Trains."

"Toccata for Toy Trains": Narration

This is a film about toy trains. These are real toys—not scale models. That doesn't mean that toys are good and scale models are bad—but they *are* different.

Most of the trains we have used are old, and some are quite old. The reason for this is perhaps that in the more recent years, we seem to have lost the knack of *making* real toys.

Most old ones have a direct and unembarrassed manner that give us a special kind of pleasure, different from the admiration we may feel for the perfect little copy of the real thing. In a good old toy there is apt to be nothing self-conscious about the use of materials—what is wood is wood; what is tin is tin; what is cast is beautifully cast. It is possible that somewhere in all this is a clue to what sets the creative climate of any time—including our own.

Anyway, let's take a close look at some real toy trains.

Sources: Charles Eames to Eliot Noyes, November 21, 1956; Part II: Office File (Pre-1960) series, Charles and Ray Eames Papers, Manuscript Division, Library of Congress, Washington, D.C. Ray Eames and Charles Eames, "Toccata for Toy Trains," narration, Eames Office, Venice, California 1957, 16mm, 14 minutes.

Color photographs of Charles and Ray Eames in the studio during the making of the film, and one additional still from the film.

Fine Art and Function

CORRESPONDENCE

Editor's note: Wayne Chezem was an accomplished craftsman in wood and an educator. He developed a crafts program at the Soledad State Prison and for many years taught in the California public school system.

Wayne A. Chezem to Charles Eames, Seaside, California
November 13, 1956

Dear Mr. Eames:

Your talk at Asilomar left me with the distinct impression that you are an idealistic industrial designer. Knowing that you are an industrial designer, I should not have been startled at your apparent attitude toward "fine" arts, since function is one prime concern of the industrial artist. However, I do feel that it is my duty, as a believer in the validity of more-or-less purely visual art objects, to attempt to prove this validity.

I would not be so concerned if your statements did not carry unusual weight because of your enviable prestige and fame. Because of this weight, I believe your statements should be as close to the truth as possible. Therefore, I offer the following for your consideration. The only possible basis for the evaluation of an art object is through judging the extent of unity achieved through the use of the elements of artistic composition. (You must certainly know this fact if you have ever served on a painting or sculpture competition jury.) This applies to the sound, visual, and motion art forms.

Of course, associational values in the form of past experiences, prejudices, etc., are included in every art form (as you mentioned). These associational values produce no end of trouble and confusion, as you well know. The religious insist that a work of art must have religious implications to be truly art—and so it is with politicians, social leaders, romanticists, realists, and I think industrial designers to some extent.

These associational values hamper the perception of the elements of composition in combination. One cannot fully appreciate the beauty of a symphonic passage if it reminds one of a waterfall. Likewise, one cannot fully appreciate the beauty of

an Eames chair if one becomes involved in fanciful flights about how comfortable it might be. So, it is my contention that the *function* of an object containing elements of artistic composition is an associational value. This, of course, is not to say that one should not make beautiful chairs. But it is to say that one should not require that beautiful things be made into chairs or letter openers, or colonnades or illustrations. The chair should first be made, then made beautiful. A chair is beautiful because it approaches sculpture, not because it is a piece of sculpture that functions as a chair.

A piece of sculpture that functions only as a thing to look at is valid because it contains the things that make the chair beautiful in greater quantities and kinds and with as little as possible associational values. A chair's value lies in its ability to receive the human form with ease and comfort and in its beauty. A sculpture's value lies in its unity and its ability to facilitate perception of this unity. Visual unity is secondary to function in industrial art; it is primary in the fine arts.

Function is one of the elements of composition of industrial objects; it is not in "fine" arts.

To require that all objects of art be, in a sense, industrial art objects is comparable to politicians requiring that all art be political. Art is art, politics is politics, engineering is engineering, cooking is cooking. Art can be applied to politics, engineering, or cooking; but to insist that politics, engineering, or cooking is part of art is invalid.

Art has to exist in a pure as possible form or it cannot be applied successfully, just as pure chemistry must exist before it can be applied to the manufacture of paint with success. The results of pure art are painting, sculpture, music, etc. The results of pure chemistry are new compounds. The results of applied art are more attractive political cartoons and posters, more attractive products of engineering, and tastier food, etc. The results of applied chemistry are better fabrics, cleaner oils, self-polishing wax, etc. Both pure art and pure chemistry are appreciated for themselves alone as examples of the search and occasional attainment of ideals. Their results are appreciated as products of applied ideals.

Perhaps we are in agreement and I have misunderstood the implications of your talk. In any case you have made me think once again, and I am grateful for it.

You have a standing invitation to visit our Crafts Shop at Fort Ord—not necessarily to continue this subject. I am sure our program would be of interest to you.

Yours very truly,
Wayne A. Chezem

Charles Eames to Wayne Chezem
November 29, 1956

Dear Mr. Chezem:

It was nice to receive your letter and be reminded again of the conference. There were many rich and positive things, but because of the nature of such conferences, many misinterpretations go along with them. I suspect from your letter that I would agree with more of your feelings than I would disagree with them. I, myself, have never felt any real pressure to validate beautiful things on a functional basis. Yet, if put to it, I imagine I would have a pretty hard time selecting a work of fine art from the historical past that did not have in it its functional or service aspect. Certainly nonfunction would rule out all the works involved in religion and ceremony.

An area in which we might not agree is your sentence, "The chair should first be made, then made beautiful." It is impossible for me to imagine this order of things applying to the guys that made those wonderful Windsor chairs. I am certain it would be an impossible approach for Le Corbusier, a great painter as well as chair designer. I cannot

conceive of Picasso thinking of a good chair being first made and then made beautiful. An African stool has its beauty so involved in its structural concept that making and beautifying could no more be separated in a good African stool than you could separate structure and beautifying in a painting.

No, I am afraid this is not the way to make a good chair or a good newspaper layout or a good plan or a good piece of sculpture. And one certainly doesn't write a story and then make it beautiful. I imagine the concept in the structure and the beauty are all part of the same motion. Though it might be possible that they are present in various degrees, like Vitruvius's "firmness, commodity and delight."

Charles Eames

Source: Wayne Chezem to Charles Eames, November 13, 1956; Charles Eames to Wayne Chezem, November 29, 1956, "C" miscellaneous folder, Part II: Office File (Pre-1960) series, Charles and Ray Eames Papers, Manuscript Division, Library of Congress, Washington, D.C.

Staffing the Eames Office

CORRESPONDENCE

Editor's note: Harold L. Cohen founded the department of design at Southern Illinois University. Cohen has contributed to the fields of design, psychology, psychiatry, art education, and environmental design. Since 1994 he has produced prints, paintings, and sculptures.

Charles Eames to Harold Cohen
April 22, 1957

Dear Harold:

_____ arrived either the day, or the day after, I talked to you, and Ray and I had a very pleasant visit with him. He is, as you know, charming and personable. We were, of course, impressed by the refinements in his work and what seemed to be a development of a personal taste.

In putting this to use, what forms a stumbling block is lack of a background in physics and applied mechanics along with any demonstration of the ability to select from and employ the world of catalogs.

We have a specific job in mind, which, if we could have used him, would have been the best possible experience for a young designer. And like most best possible jobs for those fresh out of school, it would have been most profitably handled with a certain judicious waste of time. That is, time and opportunity to make valid mistakes. But a system of breaking in based on valid waste and error can

only work under something like apprentice system rates, which most of the young people entering the field seem unable to afford these days. It is unfortunate because it robs them of a rich experience and robs the profession of one of their only sources of growth. That is, areas of affordable error within the structure of the profession.

The above is a general observation and comment and was not the basis of not using _____. Our problem was a combination of transferring solar energy to mechanical energy with least possible function loss and the greatest possible visual delight.

Sincerely,
Charles Eames

Source: Charles Eames to Harold Cohen, April 22, 1957, Southern Illinois University folder, Office File (Pre-1960) series, Charles and Ray Eames Papers, Manuscript Division, Library of Congress, Washington, D.C.

Art Education in Public Schools

Editor's note: This document, from the files of Annette Del Zoppo, who worked at the Eames Office for ten years, is titled "Representing: National Art Education Association Convention (Excerpts from interview with Charles Eames, international designer)." Handwritten on the document is "Received from Pauli Tolman/L.A. City Board of Education/ May 2, 1957."

QUESTION *Of what relative value do you believe art education is to the academic subjects taught in our schools?*

CHARLES EAMES It would never occur to me to consider art as a subject apart from any other in the curriculum. Art education increases in value to the degree that it is related to the whole academic picture. I see art education as a kind of thing that threads its way through every facet of academic work.

[Q] *Do you see evidence of general growth in the creativity of our youth?*

CE I am so aware of increasing potentials that I am a little blinded to whether or not youth is living up to these potentials.

[Q] *What do you advocate for better art education?*

CE First, better teachers. This involves better teacher training, better teacher preparation, higher salaries, better professional standing resulting in greater community respect. Secondly, a genuine rapport between all areas of learning.

[Q] *Do you feel more compulsory art education in the secondary schools would help eliminate juvenile delinquency?*

CE Of course it would have some effect, about the same as would compulsory religious education. Perhaps the best thing art education could do for the problem of juvenile delinquency would be to concern itself, also, with some of the disciplines that belong in its own structure. I regret that in a great measure art education seems to have abandoned these disciplines.

[Q] *What should the role of the parent and teacher be in developing appreciation of art in the child?*

CE To display in their own words and in their own actions a consistent sense of selectivity and a consciousness of quality.

[Q] *To what extent do you believe the child should be permitted to explore the medium unguided—undirected?*

CE It's up to the child—permitted or not—to find a way to explore the medium unguided and undirected.

[Q] *Do you believe in private lessons in art for the "gifted" child?*

CE I believe in private and personal *enthusiasm*. If it rises to the degree that involves additional people or training—well, fine. The help most such children need is in relating their particular talents to other areas in their life, and to areas in their life with which they are not familiar.

Source: Charles Eames interview, May 2, 1957, Private collection, Los Angeles.

CHARLES EAMES

"The Making of a Craftsman"

Editor's note: From the paperwork received by Charles Eames: "The First Annual Conference of American Craftsmen will be held under the auspices of the American Craftsmen's Council on June 12–13–14th, 1957 at Asilomar, Monterey Peninsula, California. All interested in crafts will be welcome. . . . Theme/The Socio-Economic Outlook."

Conference participants included Anni Albers, F. Carlton Ball, Margaret De Patta, Wharton Esherick, Tage Frid, Edith Heath, Vivika Heino, Michael Higgins, Jack Lenor Larsen, Harvey Littleton, Sam Maloof, Edwin Scheier, Millard Sheets, Toshiko Takaezu, Peter Voulkos, Marguerite Wildenhain, and Jackson and Ellamarie Wooley.

I DO NOT THINK there is any single group who use the words "craft" and "craftsman" with deeper respect than architects do, and if there is a name which I would like to copyright, it is the name—"craftsman." It is a name which places a tremendous responsibility on those who claim it. When I say that the papers we have just heard were prepared in a craftsmanlike way I am stating what I feel—that a tremendous amount of thought and work went into their preparation, and that they merit careful reading and thought by all of us who are concerned in any way with crafts and craftsmen.

Yesterday afternoon I dropped into the Wood Panel in time to hear some of the discussion. Something happened there that I believe must go on in all the discussions that come up at this conference. [James] Prestini was saying, "All right for so and so, and for this and that, but really, what do you feel is the place of a craftsman in our society today?"

There were a number of statements made in reply to this, and some perfectly good ones, most of them ending with man's relationship to the thing he was producing, the amount of satisfaction he got from it, and the sincerity with which he did it, as well as the value of the opportunity for individual expression. And so on. But the real question that Prestini had put remained unanswered.

In the course of the discussion Prestini was questioned about his bowls—what they mean to him, what they give him, and so on. Yet when I think of Prestini as a craftsman (and I do), his bowls are not what I think of first. Nor even second. I have to sort of work my way around to them because, fundamentally, and first and second, I think of Prestini as a craftsmanlike guy with a terrifically humble attitude to the materials that he

works with and to the problems that surround him.

I use Prestini as an example because the question he brought up is closely related to the way I think of the building of the values that go to make a craftsman. And believe me, in our world and in our time, we are deeply in need of the values which come under the head of "craftsmanship." I would venture to say that society today is more in need of these values than of any other thing.

The richness that a craftsman working for himself in a simple and direct way gradually brings to our society cannot be overestimated. Society needs this. The only contention that I would have with the individual craftsman, or with a group of them working for themselves and for the satisfactions they get from their work, is in those areas in which the individual craftsman is uncraftsmanlike. And this is the most damning thing that you can say about the majority of craftsmen.

The same thing is true of architects. Architects are just as bound as craftsmen. So are educators. So when I point the finger of uncraftsmanship to some of the craftsmen, I am pointing it all around the circle, to all other areas. This is the problem of our time. It is the problem that confronts us as a nation and it is the problem of the human race. If we are going to survive we have to become craftsmanlike people; and in that word's deepest, fullest sense.

It is urgent therefore that we start thinking and talking about craftsmen and craftsmanship in a much broader and unlimited way.

The field of design is undergoing changes. It would be interesting to see how a designer of great value to a company functions today. A great number of them, functioning as designers in the best sense of the term, for various companies producing material are not even drawing a line. It's not necessary. Nor do they consider a form. Nor do they dictate necessarily any special relationship. Very often they work within areas, and there are so many that no individual would possibly presume or want to be responsible for their form and structure himself. Such a presumption would be ridiculous.

Because of this, the responsibility for a decision—aesthetic, practical, and connected with craft—has to be set back in the industry itself. So we have the designer in industry feeding back basic responsibility to management, to the purchasing agent, to the engineer, to the analyst. There is an area in design that has to do with not taking on individual responsibility but making a sense of responsibility run through industry and management, making those who have previously thought of themselves as responsible only in those areas—management and industry—more and more responsible in the peripheral areas.

This is the sort of thing that must happen to the whole of society. There is an area in large industry which has this and that in abundance, but which lacks craft. And there is a similar lack among craftsmen in regard to what industry has. Craftsmen need to examine the mechanics of production and the results and relationships in industry. Mutual understanding will do much for both. It will help build up a feeling of craft in industry, to industry's and the craftsman's and society's benefit.

I began by speaking of architects, and now, at the close, I want to go back to architecture again just to mention Mies van der Rohe. I want to mention Mies because here is a man who is essentially a superb craftsman. It has been said of Mies that the ambition of his life would be to take the most perfect brick in the world and lay it in the most perfect bed of mortar and in the most perfect relationship to the next brick.

Mies himself has something to say which bears on this, and which bears much thinking about. He said, "I don't want to be interesting. I just want to be good."

This I think, a craftsman should have tattooed across his chest.

Forum on Design

The Forum . . . was opened by the moderator, Daniel Defenbacher, who reported that he had often, and in many parts of the country, heard the complaint that the greatest lack in crafts is in originality of design. "We, in America," he said, "have apparently developed a fantastic technical ability. When the peak work is found it always has good design as well. But, by and large, craft work in America fails because its design quality fails."

Charles Eames replied to this criticism: "My point of view is just the opposite. To my mind crafts seem to suffer more from overdoses of originality in design rather than from lack of this. Looking at something, you are frequently very conscious that somebody was very conscious of being 'original' and therefore did not know really what he was about. Too much originality, I would say. Not enough continuity. I can think of no great craftsman whom you would accuse of being 'original.' You certainly wouldn't accuse Mies van der Rohe of being 'original,' yet he is certainly one of the greatest architects today. You wouldn't accuse Sheraton of being 'original' in his generation. I wouldn't accuse Paul Revere of being 'original.' Revere was an excellent craftsman, and he put into his work many plus values. But he was not original, in a sense of 'originality.' The panic to be original is one of the evidences of a lack of knowledge. We have too much design, to my way of thinking. If you are conscious of the design in anything you look at, then there is too much. . . .

"I don't think that it can be proven impossible for a person to become an artist in any field in which he is occupied. In some of our discussions I find a feeling of apology and compromise in the craftsman's going into industry, or into business, or into mass production. This I find shocking and surprising. The added tremendous responsibilities in terms of the artistry of the craftsman as he is drawn into problems involving greater complexities can do nothing but raise his self-respect. In a way it's a sanctifying process. As it adds responsibilities and dimensions, it's a compliment. It enriches his service. To refer to it as compromise, you know, I find terribly shocking. It is as though suddenly you are doing some little thing which is for a degree of self delight, and then you are drawn into an act by which your extra-dimensional consciousness and your disciplines are brought in to affect a larger segment of society. Can anyone feel that he has lost stature by being brought into a richer field? The role of craftsmen in the future is going to be great. I can promise you that. If the people today who call themselves craftsmen are going to take a part in the society which we have and in that which we may have, it's up to them. The job is going to be done, and it is going to be done by people that I would call craftsmen; and I hope that you are going to be concerned in and about it."

Sources: Charles Eames, "The Making of a Craftsman" and "Discussion: Forum on Design," both in American Craftsmen's Council, *Asilomar: First Annual Conference of American Craftsmen*, June 1957, 64–66, 69–71.

First Annual Conference of American Craftsmen sponsored by the American Craftsmen's Council June, 1957

Cover of the publication in which these texts were published.

Stephens Trusonic Speakers

FIRMS LIKE Ampex, Packard-Bell, Stromberg-Carlson, and Stephens Trusonic are all forces to be reckoned with in the production of consumer products; and industrial design figures in the reckoning. Just how much it can figure is strikingly illustrated in the case of the Stephens Manufacturing Co. of Culver City, California.

The company was founded (in a garage, naturally) by Robert L. Stephens, whose background was sound engineering for the early "talking pictures." A pioneer in high fidelity equipment, Stephens in 1938 built a company that got and kept a reputation for quality products. But, primarily an engineer, Stephens tended to concentrate on product excellence to the neglect of sales effectiveness, advertising, public relations, and up-to-date management techniques.

When Bert Berlant and Bernard D. Cirlin took over control of the corporation about a year and a half ago, this was the general status of Stephens Trusonic, Inc.: a company with a good reputation for fine engineering, that had not developed or advanced as a sales organization.

The first problem Berlant and Cirlin faced was clear: the company was under new management, and they had to announce that. But such announcements are routine, and they felt that the change was more than routine. What they wanted was a way to dramatize the area that they were *really* under new management. The new management decided on the following divisions of labor and responsibility: Berlant, an engineer, was to be in charge of all engineering and production; Cirlin would be "general manager." One of the first engineering objectives was to replan the entire production system in order to facilitate production, and to permit standardization of parts whenever possible. This was necessary if Stephens, with sixty-one employees, was to compete in a consumer market dominated by mass-produced items. This is a common situation in electronics on the Pacific Coast, where relatively small companies sell quality products that are "semi mass-produced" in competition with gigantic corporations. Stephens already had a superior product. The problem was to carry into large-scale selling an expression of the same high quality that was by now taken for granted in their normal operation. The questions, then, were 1) How do you say "*really* under new management"? and 2) How do you articulate the inherent excellence of a product?

In both cases, Cirlin thought he knew how: design. Moreover, he knew a designer: Eames. So he called on him.

What was a new situation for Stephens Trusonic was also a new situation for Charles Eames, a designer whose whole professional history suggests the lone wolf, working on self-proposed projects that he has developed fully and engineered into a state ready for manufacture. Although he is active in policy-making for the Herman Miller Company, collaborating of this sort on a specific company project with a group of engineers was for him a new relationship.

"Of course we approached the problem with our own vocabulary," Eames says. But, as far as the specific subject was concerned, it was a very limited vocabulary. He had never designed speaker enclosures—or, for that matter, any sound equipment—before, and he had no more than a moderately interested amateur's understanding of high fidelity. So he didn't begin by designing but by sitting down with the company engineers and asking questions—partly for his own edification, partly to establish the problem.

"We challenged all the fixed ideas about speakers," Eames says. He asked very basic, even naive questions like "What is the grill cloth for anyway?" (Answer: To keep people from poking their fingers through the delicate speaker cone.) And "Why do you have to put a speaker in a box like this?" (Answer: Maybe you don't.)

As the approach described above indicates, Eames very quickly established that the problem was not simply that of providing new speaker enclosures but rather one of completely rethinking the theory of speaker structure and placement. For true bass response they wanted "backloaded coupling," piping the sound through a long path to reinforce the front wave with the pressure behind the speaker cone. In the Quadreflex design the speaker is surrounded by "tunnel space," permitting bass reflex response in a smaller enclosure than previously required.

The greatest reward in the rethinking process, according to Eames, is that it became company-wide. "The most gratifying part of the whole project is the way the engineers took to the new ideas and developed them. We would say, 'Why not do it *this* way?' And they would say, 'Well, you *could*. But if you did then you'd have to move the . . . say, maybe that's not a bad idea. Look!' . . . And then they'd go to work on it. Their contribution was by far the greatest—what we did was second best. And the creative approach didn't stop with the engineers. The whole company began thinking very actively and creatively about design, and the result will be some major changes in the techniques of sound distribution." The Quadraflex speaker, with its new backloaded coupling, points toward such changes.

If the engineers were the main contributors, what was the designer's role? Eames calls him a "random element." This suggests a new concept of the designer as a sort of industrial gadfly, prodding management and engineering departments to help think through their own design. Yet, for all his insistence on crediting engineers, Eames did design a radically different line of speaker enclosures for Trusonic. The line was too radical for many people, including some dealers, and the initial trade response to the enclosures was not overwhelmingly enthusiastic. Some dealers "made fun" of them. (One very large New York music company won't stock them because they're "too modern.") Others liked them but wouldn't stock them because they didn't see why any customer would pay an extra $100 for design when he could get the same speakers in a conventional box. Others stocked them but couldn't sell them. But still others liked them, understood them, stocked then, and sold them; and at the 1956 and 1957 Hi-Fi shows, the Eames enclosures did more than anything else to establish the new personality of Stephens Trusonic. Although they were highly praised in the more sophisticated design and electronics circles, Eames does not think of the new designs as 100 percent successful. For one thing, he did not lick the problem of the grille cloth, usually an unattractive dustcatcher, that he would have liked to get rid of. (He came closest in the Quadraflex, which has a colored woven saran

The Quadraflex Stephens Trusonic Speaker by Eames.

cloth stretched over an aluminum hoop that can be snapped off for cleaning.) But there was another element alien to Eames's customary working methods: haste. "It was a matter of doing the best we could do between now and Tuesday," he states, adding philosophically, "Still, it is important to remember that 'the best you can do between now and Tuesday' is still a kind of 'best you can do.'"

The best Eames could do turned out to be much better than Berlant and Cirlin had expected. Consider their aim: "Initially the Eames enclosures were not to set the world on fire or sell by the carload, but simply to impress the industry with the imagination of the new management." They feel that the new designs have done just that, and that there is a resultant industry-wide attitude of "look-to-Stephens-for-the-new-and-unusual," which is exactly what they wanted. Furthermore, the Eames speakers, originally figured to represent 3 percent of annual sales, already represent 7 percent. . . .

But however successful the new enclosures have been, Eames's last word on the subject is that the best is yet to come, and that it will come from the engineers at Stephens.

Source: "Under New Management," *Industrial Design* 4, no. 10 (October 1957): 106–8.

"St. Louis Train Station 1957"

Editor's note: The following is a transcript of a filmed interview with Charles Eames conducted by an unnamed, unseen person.

INTERVIEWER *Mr. Eames, we understand that one of the reasons you're in town is to take pictures of the Union Station here. I think that it would be fair to say that you are a functional or modern architect, and the building which you are going to take pictures of, if this is true, is over fifty or sixty years old. Of what interest is it to you to take pictures of a building like this?*

CHARLES EAMES First, you're saying that I'm going to take pictures of the building—I'm not. If I am a functional person, this is flattering, in a way, the railroad itself is functioning. We've been interested in doing a series of things where we've been taking photographs of—in one case, it's a railroad-scape, in one case it's a townscape—all of the little things that are incidental to the functioning of a thing like a railroad; putting them together with sounds and presenting them as kind of an awareness series. Well, this is the explanation. The fact of the matter is I'll do anything to give an excuse to take some photographs. I just like to shoot photographs, actually.

INTERVIEWER *Are you going to take any pictures of the building itself, other than the machines that are in it?*

CE Well, no. The most impressive thing, in a way, is the track system and the way of backing trains into a station. This switchback Y, or whatever they call it, is almost unique to this station. It's an old station, but one of the few stations in the country where all the railroads coming into a major city come to the same station.

So when you get there, you have an interplay of color and movement, and a complexity of a track and switching system, which is unique. It's a rich thing, this railroad. Sometime come to St. Louis and stand on the back platform of a train as it backs into that Y. It's pretty nice stuff.

INTERVIEWER *In other words, you don't find too much of interest in the building itself.*

CE No, now, this is another subject. I'm not comparing the building with the tracks. The building was built in 1903 for the World's Fair, and at that time was one of the most outstanding buildings in the country. Aside from the fact it has a very heavy, medieval-looking character the concept of handling traffic in this building at that time was a very, very modern one. I'm sorry that I forget the name of the architect [Theodore C. Link], because he did an awful lot of things in this state, and in this city, of quite a bit of importance at the time.

INTERVIEWER *You mentioned this word "scapes." Some of us have seen these in relationship to trains (which you've already done) and to a circus, which we found very effective. Are there any other areas that you've treated?*

CE Well, by the way, the use of the townscape is a descriptive term used by Ian McCallum in *Architectural Review*, and in a sense it takes in all the little relationships in a city. We have applied it to the ocean. We've applied it to a studio—a major motion picture studio.

In other words, we've taken photographs of all the objects and things behind the camera, the things that are never seen on the screen. But what I'm looking at now is much more beautiful than what the camera is looking at. And if you had a way of presenting this, why you'd have a lot of rich associations that come together to do a wonderful job; and so it is in a motion picture studio.

And parallel with these photographs of ladders and clamps and gobos and cucoloris and everything that they use, they run a soundtrack of sounds taken during the lighting and the rehearsals for a shot. Now, actually, the counterpoint that takes place between these two things (the sound and the image) adds up to some very exciting stuff. I mean, if you could play back the voices and the sounds that existed in this studio five minutes before you started rolling, it could be perhaps a little more interesting.

INTERVIEWER *You used the word "exciting stuff" to rationalize doing this type of thing. Would it be fair to ask you to expand what you mean by "exciting stuff"?*

CE On the face of it, it doesn't sound quite fair. Give me another clue.

INTERVIEWER *Well, you get an experience (many of us did) when we watched these scapes. Is this all they're intended to do, just to give us an experience? An emotional experience?*

CE Well, of course, you've already qualified it, as far as an emotional experience. If it gives you an experience, that's not all it does, I'm sure. If the circus-scape gave you an experience, why, it will change and relate other things in a way that they have never been related before. In other words, the thing that you experienced in the circus, whether it was emotional or intellectual or whatever it was never again will stand for something by itself. It will stand for things, for an experience in combination with other experiences, and it will so affect experiences to come. It's no longer a thing by itself.

INTERVIEWER *Do you intend to get that same philosophy (or are you bringing forth this same philosophy) in some of the other things you've designed, such as the cards which you hold in your hand?*

CE I could try to explain why we did the cards. Actually, we did them, first of all, because we have enjoyed the idea. The first set were a series of paper patterns, and it was because we have enjoyed using and seeing papers of all kinds: Japanese, Chinese, Swiss, English, old book papers, and whatnot. We put them on cards for a child to be able to build with.

This was a nice and successful thing, and when we started another series; why, we began to take photographs of objects which we, ourselves, cared for very much. And soon the objects began to build up a pattern. And as Ray put it, before we get through, we'll have a set of cards that will be great fun for anyone from 8 to 115 years old. And they include things like spools of thread, a metronome, and a bunch of old buttons and things.

Now this seems innocuous enough, in itself, but the fact is again you have relationships. I mean, whether it's a child or an adult looking at a series of these images in relationship to each other; why, the meanings change. Naturally the reason for doing it wasn't as complicated as that. I guess I'm just trying to answer your question in a profound way.

INTERVIEWER *Can we look specifically at those cards?*

CE Shall I start it this way? This is a kachina doll. This is a cookie. Here's a series of buttons. Flowers. Chinese firecrackers. A quilt. String. Scissors. An African comb. And you can see, as we put out a group of things, a pattern of nostalgia already takes place.

INTERVIEWER *Have you thought about making cards for adults?*

CE Well, please! I mean, if these are cards for children, why, I'm very happy. But after all, if your definition of adult includes Ray, and includes me and our friends, why then, that's why they were done.

INTERVIEWER *I see. You've been interested in doing things for children. I think that's fair. And I understand that you're working on something out in California—a playground. Can you just describe something of that? That's your most contemporary work, isn't it?*

CE Oh, so you have an inside line on our work. Yes, we're interested in children. We're in favor of children. And we're interested in play. We're interested in toys. In one way, the playground, the festival, the toys are one of the few areas where even adults can approach it with unembarrassment and unselfconsciousness. And this is getting to be a kind of a rare thing.

And if it's possible to approach a problem (play or work) in an unembarrassed and unselfconscious way, why, a lot of positive things are apt to happen. Now, of course, it's even possible to approach a toy in a self-conscious way, and we have examples of it.

When somebody says we want to design a toy or a game which will look as though somebody will have a good time with it, and then a lot of people will buy it . . . now, this is sort of doomed to failure at the beginning. Because as soon as you try to do something that will look as if it will do something, why, the phoniness immediately becomes apparent. It's such a simple thing to, in the case of a toy or in the case of a festival, to try to approach it really with the idea of having a good time; or approach a toy really with the idea of having it being fun.

In the playground (or if we call it a "kiddyland," those that exist) many of them are very satisfactory, but most are a little bit conscious of doing what the adult's idea of what a child should have a good time doing (the Mother-Gooseries and whatnot, which are all right, except they become sweet and stereotyped), and everybody is happy to think that now a child will have a chance to go to Mother Gooseland.

Now we began to approach it from a little bit the other standpoints; that is, what would a child really do, and really like to do in the sense this is what you would like to do, or what I would like to do. We would face it. And this includes some curiosity things, some aggressive things, sort of letting off steam. And so we've been building up a pattern of things to take care of the curiosity, the inquisitiveness.

One of the things is providing an area where there will be gongs the size of the ones that J. Arthur Rank opens his pictures with. You come in and just beat the gong for all you're worth. There will be devices where you can put a nickel in them, and they will just have a wonderful time doing nothing in the most complicated way imaginable. You fill in your own suppressed desires, but tell me what they are later.

INTERVIEWER *I'd like to change the subject a bit. I think that the general public associates the name Charles Eames with a chair. Let's talk about furniture, if we can, because you've been very closely associated with that industry (the modern industry of furniture making) and have had a tremendous influence on that industry. Let me ask you this question: Do you feel a person who is oriented, or is satisfied, with contemporary, so-called "well-designed furniture" is actually—can be a happier person with that furniture than one, let's say, who has in his home colonial American furniture?*

CE Well, of course, you've immediately sort of put the Yankee curse on the first category by saying if a person has sort of modern, so-called "well designed," etc. (which in itself builds up a kind of a horrific picture) and then you've compared that with some colonial furniture (which because, when you say it, you say just the word colonial; you don't modify it) it presents a pretty nice picture. So, I'm already prejudiced in favor of the Windsor chair. It's a colonial piece.

Charles Eames with an Eames House of Cards.

I don't think it ends there, of course. I think that if the piece of colonial furniture is a piece that the owner, the user, knows and loves, and it serves his purpose well, of course he'll be happy with it. If the piece of modern furniture (so-called well designed) is a piece that he has acquired in order to be "in the swim" and keep up with the Joneses; of course, he will have less of a chance to be happy with it.

We would hope that the piece of the second category—and let's think of it in terms of a piece of furniture which is not better or worse because it's old or new, but because it will satisfy his needs at the time better than the old piece of furniture satisfied him—naturally, if it did satisfy his needs better (and by this I mean his spiritual needs as well as his physical) then he'll be happier with it. I think it's as simple as that.

INTERVIEWER *You've gone into the very profound subject of communication recently. Did this desire to study communication and to make some very effective films on the subject come out of a feeling from you that people did not understand, possibly, the shapes, the forms, and are sensitive to the compositions around them?*

CE No, I don't think so. I think that shapes and forms have never consciously entered into the picture anymore than did an abstract desire to study communications. I think that one finds himself into the subject, and surrounded by the subject of communications, and it's a question of sort of studying your way out more than trying to approach it.

And as far as the film is concerned, I think anything that you come upon, or find yourself with, and you find it really rich beyond your expectations, then you want to share; and there are many ways [of] sharing it. And Ray and I [do] it with a camera around. This is one way of doing it. Had we been able to do it some other way, we would have done it. Am I getting off the subject?

INTERVIEWER *No, not at all. We were just trying to get a relationship between what you talked about before in terms of form, and images, and relationships between colors and those things, and your interest in communication—the relationship between those two fields of interest. Or are they isolated?*

CE In a way you're asking for this relationship, so I'm sort of reaching for it. But if I was going to choose a relationship, I'd say that communication and the communications field and what it offers is more akin to the unselfconsciousness of the toy-maker that I was speaking of than it is directly to form and color. I mean, it's a relationship on that level rather than on a mechanical level.

INTERVIEWER *Well, my final question would be: Do you have any comments about the way the majority of American architects are being trained in this country? And if I can place another question (which is not too directly related, but will carry through for me on this last question): What part do you think taste plays in architecture?*

CE First, again, this is bound to be a very general answer, and it's hard to sort of isolate a thing, which you want to take that place. But I would say that the danger is that the architectural schools are becoming trade schools. And this doesn't mean that a trade school is a bad thing, but it means that a trade school is a limiting thing. But my feeling is that an architectural school should be more than that, because an architect has a responsibility that is so broad that if his background isn't one that he can sort of grow with, . . . it could be disastrous.

The second part of the question?

INTERVIEWER *What part does taste play in architecture?*

CE I think that whatever part it does play is apt to be a negative part. I think that—and again, I'm using this as an example without too much thought—pieces of architecture (and by architecture I mean planning and objects and extensions of man as well as buildings) . . . often have things in common and relationships. And the good old pieces—Chartres, for example—I would say that Chartres Cathedral has more in common with a present-day cracking plant or grain elevator than it has with the Riverside Cathedral, the rose window of which is a copy. I would say that those things that we recognize as taste are often the most negative aspects of an architect's work. It's the area where he isn't sure of himself and falls back on this highly personal thing to fill the gap. I don't mean to confuse taste with an intuitive sense of what is good—I think that's another subject. Taste as we know it in general is more apt to be a negative thing than I believe it is a positive thing.

Source: "St. Louis Train Station 1957," Eames Office LLC archives, Santa Monica, California, 16mm film, ten minutes.

CHARLES EAMES

Furnishing a Home

Introductory note from Evan Frances, home furnishings editor, Family Circle: "A letter from a reader set us on the path that led to the article on this and the next six pages. In it she wrote, 'When women get together, how to decorate a home is getting to be as touchy a subject as bringing up baby. Everyone starts being opinionated, but after a while we have to admit that we're puzzled and awed by the whole business. . . . Can't you give us some practical principles that we can follow with confidence?' . . . We here bring together eight authorities (Russell Lynes, Raymond Loewy, Everett Brown, Freda Diamond, Jo Mielziner, Paul McCobb, Eero Saarinen, and Charles Eames) who speak their minds. What they have to say should help solve the puzzling job of furnishing a home."

IT IS HARD TO FIND any one thing to say to a woman about the environment of the home that will not at some stage disintegrate into ivy in the teakettle or lamps made of spinning wheels. I come to the conclusion that the best one can do is wish for her either great love or profound discipline or an equivalent combination of both. In terms of environment, neither love nor discipline is easy to come by these days. "Things," as a rule, are too plentiful and quality too casual to encourage love; they are too varied and unrestrained to promote discipline. Poverty has been an effective encouragement to discipline and to the cherishing of things, but it is not the only way. Personal involvement, and concern over inherent quality, are other ways. But whatever the way, at all times love and discipline have led to a beautiful environment and a good life.

—Charles Eames, California designer of products, films, and architecture, whose credo is "to help people enjoy the richness of simple stuff"

Source: Evan Frances, "If I Could Tell a Woman One Thing About Furnishing a Home . . ." *Family Circle* 52, no. 3 (March 1958): 27–33.

Says Eames of the Indian-pueblo interior shown, "It is of course, not intended as a model to copy. It serves only to demonstrate a quality that can come from a natural discipline combined with respect and affection for things."

CHARLES EAMES

Aluminum Group

Introductory note from Olga Gueft of Interiors: "This is the first of a series of three articles, each devoted to the design of a new chair or group of chairs. The series is not devoted to presenting the chairs, but to analyzing how each one was designed, though two of the articles, including this one, will incidentally be the first publication of the design in question. . . .

The series begins with an account by Charles Eames and his assistants of the new cast aluminium group he has done for the Herman Miller Furniture Company. . . .

Charles Eames's leisure or indoor-outdoor group, as it has variously been called, is a collection of four chairs and an ottoman, with two companion tables, which the Herman Miller Furniture Company is launching on the market. When Charles Eames was asked to relate in his own words the process of designing the group, he was about to fly to India on a mission for the U.S. Department of Commerce. As a result, the text is the direct transcript of a tape recording Eames made shortly before flight time."

I HAVE BEEN WORKING ON furniture as a part of architecture ever since I started to practice architecture in 1930. But it really wasn't until I started to work for Eliel Saarinen, and with Eero, that I had any conception of what a concept was. I believe that what we did for the Museum of Modern Art's Organic Furniture Competition in 1940 was really a statement of concept. We weren't particularly concerned with the economics of the solution, even though at the time we thought we were.

When Ray [Eames's wife] and I did the molded plywood chair, this was quite different. We set out deliberately to develop an economical and feasible method for molding plywood. This was the first step in developing a chair which we hoped would have good qualities but whose qualities we insisted would be inherent in the mass production system and have their basis in the mass production method. I don't know to what degree we succeeded in this, but I feel that we made a fairly clear statement of the handling of the connection between two different materials.

We've always been aware of not even attempting to solve the problem of how people *should* sit, but of rather arbitrarily accepting the way people *do* sit and of operating within that framework. But if we ignored that problem, we really knocked ourselves out on the technical aspects—the bonding agents, the impregnation of veneers, integral finishes, high-frequency curing, shock mounts, compounding of rubber, induction welding. We actually designed and built within our office all the presses and tools and jigs and fixtures that were used in the original production—this is still the molded plywood chair I'm referring to.

The molded plastic chair was much different. The reinforced polyester was a special technique developed for areas that demanded a high-performance material. Essentially this meant the aircraft industry, which could afford big investments for the development of material and tooling. Our object was to make this high-performance material accessible to the consumer in a chair that would ultimately give it a high performance per dollar. The problem wasn't so much one of form. The real problem was to make this essentially industrial material available at the consumer level. At first we had very clear ideas of the kind of surface we wanted to maintain, but eventually we realized that anything would do just as long as it was uniform. Uniformity, uniformity . . . eventually we realized that this was what we were striving for and that actually it was the toughest thing to get. It was in the most desperate hours, when there seemed to be no hope of getting the perfect molding for the reinforced polyester chair, that the upholstered wire chair was conceived—and in the meantime it began to look as though the thin molded shell really belong to the jet age. As far as furniture was concerned, we were still at the Wright Brothers level.

So we thought we would go to the opposite extreme and do a molded, body-conforming shell depending on many, many connections—but connections that we as an industrial society were prepared to cope with on the production level. If you looked around you found these fantastic things being made of wire—trays, baskets, rat traps—using a wire fabricating technique perfected over a period of many years. We looked into it and

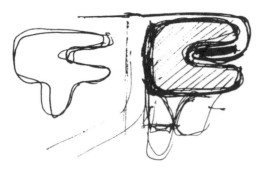

These are cross-sections of chair's side, showing groove where fabric has been inserted. When fabric is turned around edge it remains in place under great tension, without stitching or glue. This connection is basis of stretched-fabric chair.

Drawings by Charles Eames. Photos by Marvin Rand.

found that it was a good production technique and also a good use of material. Before the molded plastic chair had been solved, the molded wire chair was well under way.

Meantime, the upholstered wire chair brought with it some real attempts in another direction—towards mass production in upholstery—by fellows in our office. Don Albinson, who had been a student of mine at Cranbrook and who had worked even on the early model for the photographs we entered in the Organic Furniture Competition, took hold of this problem and developed some really ingenious techniques.

Again we were at the point where the design and production of even the machinery for making the furniture was being done in our office. Jigs and fixtures for building up the upholstered pads were made and operated in the initial production stage by fellows in our office.

This is some of the background in which we have to consider the development of the cast aluminum chair. It sounds ridiculously simple, and in that way it doesn't seem to make sense. The blood and the pain don't show. They say in the motion picture industry, "It looks easy on the screen." Well, it sounds too easy on the tape.

But the beginnings of the cast aluminum chair were entirely different. This one started when Alexander Girard, Sandro, came to visit, and we were talking about furnishing a house which he and Eero [Saarinen] had just completed, a house marvelous in concept and superb in quality, and Sandro was bemoaning the fact that there was no real quality outdoor furniture that he could get for

such a place—that is, the quality *he* wanted.

You start on a close human scale. Here is a friend who has done something. He needs something for it, and you become involved. As we were trying to analyze the reasons why there was nothing available on the market to suit him, why we were of course starting to write a program for designing the object to fill this void. That's how it started.

Well, having the program in mind, you gradually begin to stew about it—while traveling in planes and so on. The actual idea, the idea for the chair—that is, the gimmick, the device that made it possible—is something I recall drawing on the back of an envelope.

This was not like the beginnings—or even the motives—of the other chairs. The story of those was mostly of sticking to a concept through all the pitfalls of technique. This one was more like an approach to an architectural problem, where you have the program fairly well embedded and call on past experience. And like the beginning of an architectural solution, this one began with a cross section. It was in this full-sized doodle of a cross section less than two inches square that the whole framework of speculation could be built: Is it structural? Is it natural to the tools and the materials? What about the economics of tooling? Is it a monster, or is there some hope of elegance? But perhaps the real question that you must ultimately face is: Is it a function of the necessary connections? In architecture or furniture or jackstraws, it is the connection that can do you in. Where two materials come together, brother, watch out!

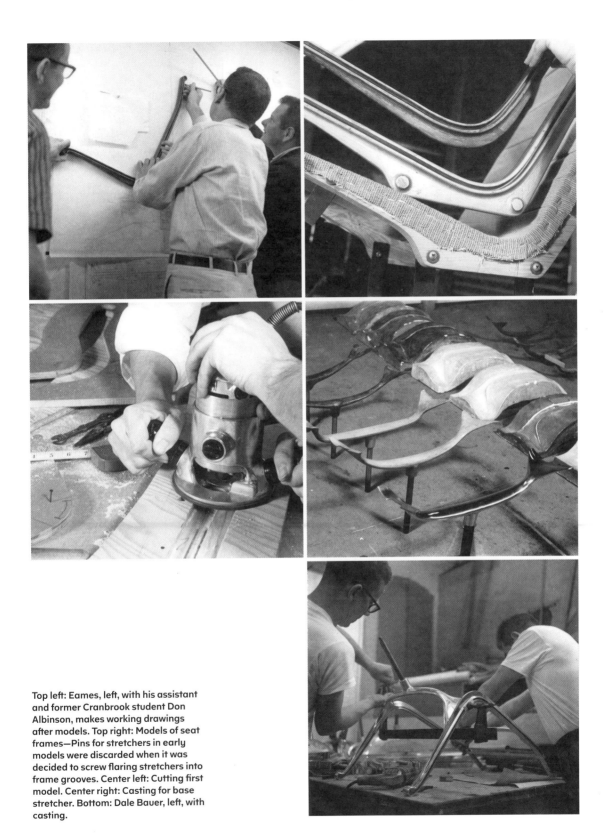

Top left: Eames, left, with his assistant and former Cranbrook student Don Albinson, makes working drawings after models. Top right: Models of seat frames—Pins for stretchers in early models were discarded when it was decided to screw flaring stretchers into frame grooves. Center left: Cutting first model. Center right: Casting for base stretcher. Bottom: Dale Bauer, left, with casting.

The cross section was really a system of connections based on tensions which served to support the body. The chair was when we applied this system to a theory of support we had developed earlier.

In the other cases we had fought our way up through technical problems. In this one we had a fair idea of what cast aluminum and fabrics would do. Don Albinson, who really fought this one out, went directly to casting in the mock-up stage. By now he and Dale Bauer in our office know about everything you can do with a sewing machine or heat-sealing device.

But there are other things. When you develop a cross section you have to develop a way of terminating it. When you develop a system of stitching it has to come to an end. There is always the problem, once having developed the system, of when do you call it off? The finial, the topper, the resolving of the problem. And there were many of these.

Also, when you've committed yourself to casting, you've committed yourself to a plastic material and the kind of freedom that can really give you the willies. If you're dealing with extrusions or rolled sections, you're really given a limitation which is pretty nice to fall back on. But in casting there are times where the definition of the problem is pretty vague. At that moment you find yourself face to face with sculpture, and it can scare the pants off you. There's the suspicion that maybe you're doing sculpture for which there is a valid, practical need—a need you've neglected in the past somewhere along the line. I know that when we were trying to cope with that phase of the job there have been times when Ray and Don and I have sort of worked and worked and reworked form, and where vagaries intruded until we found we had worked ourselves into a deep, deep hole. Whatever was it that Oppenheimer said in his interview with Murrow? Something about we work in the day and we question and correct at night. The working was in the day, the questioning and correcting at night.

Oh yes, this started to be an outdoor chair for a special client of Sandro's and Eero's. Well, I suppose it's still an outdoor chair. We've been using one for a test outside our house for the past six months. But it's also an indoor chair. Probably a high-budget outdoor chair, a low-budget indoor chair. But whatever it is, it's something that has been done really not just for Sandro's client anymore but for the people that work in the factory with us day by day who would flop down in one at the end of a hard day and from whom we would really get our feedback, our clues.

Source: Olga Gueft, "3 Chairs/3 Records of the Design Process. 1: Charles Eames Leisure Group," *Interiors* CXVII, no. 9 (April 1958): 118–22.

Trials of highly polished cast aluminium
stretchers surround Eames in
workshop.

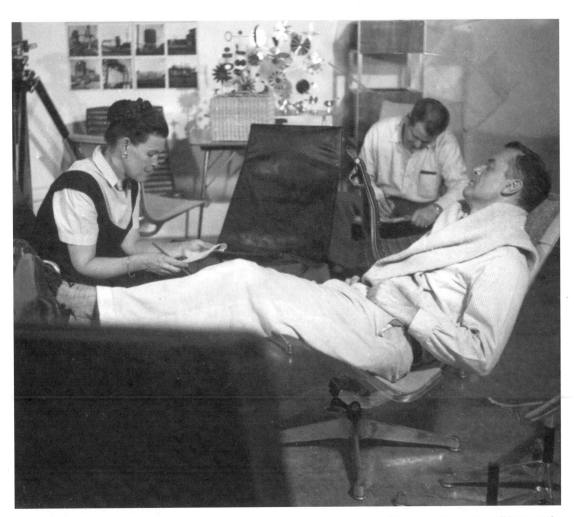

Opposite: Eames and his wife, Ray, attach three stiffening panels, later to be hidden by folds in fabric, which give the body firm support exceptional in thin fabric sling chair. Secret of non-sag fabric—Fabric held in tension is one important secret of the chair. The other is stiff strips hidden in fabric folds at three strategic points, supporting body and preventing potato-sack sag of ordinary sling chairs.

Above: Ray Eames, Don Albinson, and Charles Eames used themselves and the Herman Miller factory staffs as informal testers over a long period.

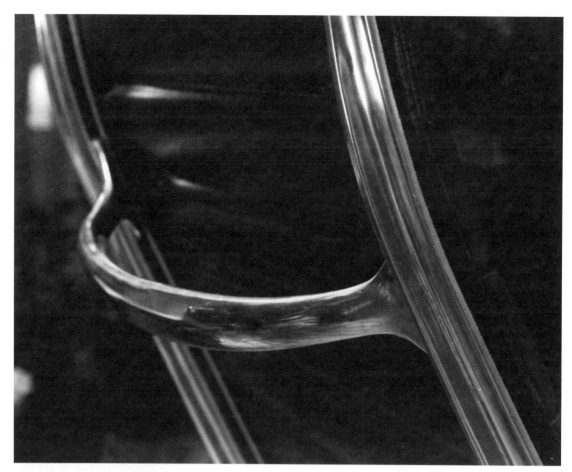

Handle stretcher gripped in frame.
The seat is supported free of its base
on stretchers which also keep the sides
apart, holding the fabric in tension.
The graceful base and back stretchers
are identical. Back stretcher also
serves as a carrying handle. Fabric with
stitched edge inserted in narrow slot
and then brought around is held with
great force when in tension. The force
increases with resistance. Protruding
back fin receives screwed-in-stretchers,
which flare at the ends. All models
are available in two fabrics, the first,
black Koroseal with horizontal trapunto
stripes executed with electronic
welding, the second a choice of neutral
Saran weaves developed by Alexander
Girard.

Complete chair model.

CHARLES EAMES AND RAY EAMES

"The India Report"

Introductory note: The Government of India asked for recommendations on a program of training in design that would serve as an aid to the small industries; and that would resist the present rapid deterioration in design and quality of consumer goods.

Charles Eames, American industrial designer, and his wife and colleague Ray Eames visited India for three months at the invitation of the Government, with the sponsorship of the Ford Foundation, to explore the problems of design and to make recommendations for a training program. The Eameses toured throughout India, making a careful study of the many centers of design, handicrafts, and general manufacture. They talked with many persons, official and non-official, in the field of small and large industry, in design and architecture, and in education. As a result of their study and discussions, the following report emerged.

FOREWORD

You have the right to work but for the work's sake only; you have no right to the fruits of work. Desire for the fruits of work must never be your motive in working. Never give way to laziness, either.

Perform every action with your heart fixed on the Supreme Lord. Renounce attachment to the fruits. Be even-tempered in success and failures, for it is this evenness of temper, which is meant by Yoga.

Work done with anxiety about results is far inferior to work done without such anxiety, in the calm of self-surrender.

Seek refuge in the knowledge of Brahman.

They who work selfishly for results are miserable.

—*Bhagavad Gita*

PART 1

We have been asked by the Government of India to recommend a program of training in the area of design, which would serve as an aid to the small industries. We have been asked to state what India can do to resist the rapid deterioration of consumer goods within the country today.

In the light of the dramatic acceleration with which change is taking place in India and the seriousness of the basic problems involved, we recommend that without delay there be a sober investigation into those values and those qualities that Indians hold important to a good life, that there be a close scrutiny of those elements that go to make up a "Standard of Living." We recommend that those who make this investigation be prepared to follow it with a restudy of the problems of environment and shelter, to look upon the detailed problems of services and objects as though they were being attacked for the first time; to restate solutions to these problems in theory and in actual prototype; to explore the evolving symbols of India.

One suspects that much benefit would be gained from starting this search at the small village level.

In order to insure the validity of such investigation and such restatement, it will be necessary to bring together and bring to bear on the question all the disciplines that have developed in our time—sociology, engineering, philosophy, architecture, economics, communications, physics, psychology, history, painting, anthropology . . . anything to restate the questions of familiar problems in a fresh clear way. The task of translating the values inherent in these disciplines to appropriate concrete details will be difficult, painful, and pricelessly rewarding. It cannot start too soon. The growing speed of production and training cries out for some sober unit of informed concern sufficiently insulated to act as a steering device in terms of direction, quality, and ultimate values.

We recommend an institute of design, research, and service, which would also be an advanced training medium. It would be connected with the Ministry of Commerce and Industry but it should retain enough autonomy to protect its prime objective from bureaucratic disintegration.

We recommend a Board of Governors drawn from the broad field of disciplines mentioned above—these must be receptive, involvable people concerned with the future of India and the image she presents to herself and to the world.

We will describe in some detail the functions and organization of this proposed institute—the faculty, the trainees, the proposed projects, service aspects, and the physical plant. First we will give a general background of this concept—some form of which must be developed—as an immediate and practical necessity. The reason for this urgency is quite apparent. The change India is undergoing is a change in kind, not a change of degree. The medium that is producing this change is communication; not some influence of the West on the East. The phenomenon of communication is something that affects a world, not a country.

The advanced complexities of communication were perhaps felt first in Europe, then west to America, which was a fertile traditionless field. They then moved East and West, gathering momentum and striking India with terrific impact—an impact that was made more violent because of India's own complex of isolation, barriers of language, deep-rooted tradition.

The decisions that are made in a tradition-oriented society are apt to be unconscious decisions—in that each situation or action automatically calls for a specified reaction. Behavior patterns are pre-programmed, pre-set.

It is in this climate that handicrafts flourish—changes take place by degrees—there are moments of violence but the security is in the status quo.

The nature of a communication-oriented society is different by kind—not by degree. All decisions must be conscious decisions evaluating changing factors. In order to even approach the quality and values of a traditional society, a conscious effort must be made to relate every factor that might possibly have an effect. Security here lies in change and conscious selection and correction in relation to evolving needs. India stands to face the change with three great advantages:

First
    She has a tradition and a philosophy familiar with the meaning
    of creative destruction.
Second
    She need not make all the mistakes others have made in the
    transition.
Third
    Her immediate problems are well defined: FOOD, SHELTER,
    DISTRIBUTION, POPULATION.

This last stated advantage is a great one. Such ever-present statements
of need should block or counteract any self-conscious urge to be original. They should put consciousness of quality—selection of first things
first—(investigation into what are the first things) on the basis of survival, not caprice.

**Photographs of lotas taken in India by
Charles and Ray Eames.**

Of all the objects we have seen and admired during our visit to India, the lota, that simple vessel of everyday use, stands out as perhaps the greatest, the most beautiful. The village women have a process, which, with the use of tamarind and ash, each day turns this brass into gold.

But how would one go about designing a lota? First one would have to shut out all preconceived ideas on the subject and then begin to consider factor after factor:

—The optimum amount of liquid to be fetched, carried, poured, and
    stored in a prescribed set of circumstances.
— The size and strength and gender of the hands (if hands) that would
    manipulate it.
—The way it is to be transported—head, hip, hand, basket, or cart.
—The balance, the center of gravity, when empty, when full, its balance
    when rotated for pouring.
—The fluid dynamics of the problem not only when pouring but when
    filling and cleaning, and under the complicated motions of head
    carrying—slow and fast.
—Its sculpture as it fits the palm of the hand, the curve of the hip.
—Its sculpture as complement to the rhythmic motion of walking or
    a static post at the well.
—The relation of opening to volume in terms of storage uses—and
    objects other than liquid.
—The size of the opening and inner contour in terms of cleaning.
—The texture inside and out in terms of cleaning and feeling.
—Heat transfer—can it be grasped if the liquid is hot?
—How pleasant does it feel, eyes closed, eyes open?
—How pleasant does it sound, when it strikes another vessel, is set
    down on ground or stone, empty or full—or being poured into?
—What is the possible material?
—What is its cost in terms of working?
—What is its cost in terms of ultimate service?
—What kind of an investment does the material provide as product,
    as salvage?
—How will the material affect the contents, etc., etc.?
—How will it look as the sun reflects off its surface?
—How does it feel to possess it, to sell it, to give it?

Of course, no one man could have possibly designed the lota. The number of combinations of factors to be considered gets to be astronomical—no one man designed the lota but many men over many generations. Many individuals represented in their own way through something they may have added or may have removed or through some quality of which they were particularly aware.

The hope for and the reason for such an institute as we describe is that it will hasten the production of the "lotas" of our time. By this we mean a hope that an attitude be generated that will appraise and solve the problems of our coming times with the same tremendous service, dignity, and love that the lota served its time.

The simplest problem of environment has a list of aspects that makes the list we have given for the lota small by comparison. The roster of disciplines we have suggested can bring about measurable answers to some measurable aspects of the problem, but in addition they must provide the trainee with a questioning approach and a smell for appropriateness; a concern for quality, which will help him through the immeasurable relationships.

In the face of the inevitable destruction of many cultural values—in the face of the immediate need for the nation to feed and shelter itself—a drive for quality takes on a real meaning. It is not a self-conscious effort to develop an aesthetic—it is a relentless search for quality that must be maintained if this new Republic is to survive.

PART 2

The Institute

The objective has been stated in Part 1. It may be restated as a desire to create an alert and impatient national conscience—a conscience concerned with the quality and ultimate values of the environment.

The functions will be research and training and service—these functions will continually overlap each other, support and correct each other.

The size should be small starting with perhaps a dozen students—but with a faculty that would more than complement them in number. Even as it grew to optimum size, this one-to-one ratio of faculty to students might well be maintained.

The effectiveness of the institute will depend on the way in which results are communicated. Effectiveness will vary as the square of the caliber of staff it attracts—and as the cube of the degree to which the staff and students become personally involved.

Having stated the objectives (in Part 1) we will treat specific aspects of the institute in the following order:

First—The Students or Trainees
  Because if we know the objectives we may do well to look around for the available raw material.
Second—The Faculty or Staff
  Because if we know the objectives and have the raw material we can select the appropriate tools.
Third—The Projects or Methods
  With objectives, raw material, and tools we can begin to plan the operation. Refinement of operation will of course call for refining the selection of tools.
Fourth—Aspects of Service
  Method of channeling results of the operation so as to affect the original objectives.
Fifth—The Physical Plant
  Housing and equipping the entire process.

1. The Trainees or Students

The purpose of training these students is to prepare them to meet problems in design, problems which have occurred many times, and problems which have never occurred before—and to meet them all openly and inquiringly. Strictly speaking, preparations for problems that have never been solved before call for education, not training.

So we must look for prospective trainees who are highly educable

180

and who have some background in the complex areas of environment and communications.

There appears to be, at the present time, only one main group of students who have been exposed to the variety of training and discipline that might prepare them for such Work—these are graduate architects. (Immediate note of warning): Graduate architects are recommended not because of their design training but in spite of it. With some few but encouraging exceptions—the architectural student's designs are an assemblage of inappropriate clichés. The students themselves seem much brighter than their designs— the disciplines of Physics and Chemistry are not unknown to them. They have in their training applied these disciplines to some sociological and human scale problems. They are aware of the use of materials and some of the functions of economics and they are apt to suspect that these have something to do with the history and development of a culture.

As a group, young architects are apt to be involvable in general social problems and in theatre, dance, music, and other aspects of communications. They tend to have a higher than average potential for enthusiasm. This is important because if they are enthusiastic enough they might discover some of the values that exist in the commonplace things that surround them. There are some good clues in the everyday solutions to unspectacular problems, in vernacular expressions that are so often ignored.

This description if carefully applied would be enough to screen the prospects.

Naturally they need not all be architects—an equally responsible young engineer, economist, doctor, mathematician, philosopher, or housewife might also be a candidate.

These students become part of a graduate school with a training period of perhaps two years. According to the development of the particular student, several things may then happen:

He may continue working in the service branch of the institute;
He may be grabbed off by private industry;
He may be invited to join some other branch of government service;
He may open a consulting office of his own;
He may return to architecture as a much needed, enriched version
    of an architect.

2. The Staff
or Faculty

We would hope that those leaving the institute would leave with a start towards a real education. They should be trained not only to solve problems—but what is more important, they should be trained to help others solve their own problems. One of the most valuable functions of a good industrial designer today is to ask the right questions of those concerned so that they become freshly involved and seek a solution themselves.

The permanent faculty would be about equal to the students in number. There would also be a liberal number of visiting critics or consultants from within the country, who would spend days, weeks, or months and be drawn from Government, Private Practice, Industry, and other institutions.

In addition to this, a few most carefully selected critics and consultants from abroad.

As we have indicated earlier, the scope of disciplines represented on the staff should be extremely broad. Those disciplines represented on the permanent faculty would depend on available men, and those not represented there would certainly be among the visiting consultants. Perhaps the real challenge of this program is that it is committed to include a wide variety of disciplines. Here is a list, which is no doubt incomplete:

Engineering	Economics
Structural	Art History
Mechanical	Political History
Production	Agriculture
Physics	Dance and Drama
Philosophy	Logistics
Mathematics	Painting
Physiology	Communications
Anthropology	Theory and Techniques
Psychology	Statistics
Architecture	Graphics
Music	Literature
Sculpture	Demography

It may be correctly pointed out that one of the most difficult things is to attract good men to a new institution. The variety of talents listed above makes it more difficult—but simple.

1. Demonstrate that mature, responsible members of the large community are personally concerned.
2. Present a prime objective and methods that are designed to give long-range benefits to the community.
3. Insure a degree of autonomy that will protect the objective from dilution and the method from deterioration.

Warning: In selecting candidates for these posts one must be extremely careful about applicants discontented with their present work or anyone who would look upon the work in the institute as his "chance to be creative." Also in this connection beware of the professional or specialist who when confronted with a problem having to do with design seems suddenly to abandon the disciplines of his own profession and put on his art hat—this can happen to those who are otherwise most rational: doctors, engineers, politicians, philosophers.

This method of bringing various disciplines together to attack a problem in a fresh way will be used in India more and more. This institute is an excellent place to start. The method is not easy—the trick is to get the specialist to bring to bear on the problem a logical extension of his framework of thinking—the nature of the design problem helps because it affords constant illustrations and progress checks.

The faculty will need a strong nucleus of exceptionally aware architects and designers to act as catalysts and preceptors, and to keep the system from oscillating too violently.

The effectiveness of the program will depend on the communication links established. Some staff members must be prepared to work and train in communication techniques—exhibitions, graphics, printing, photography, film, demonstration, writing, drama. Through these devices the institute will communicate to itself and to the nation.

The importance of the exhaustive use of communication techniques cannot be overemphasized. It brings concepts and statements out into the open, to be used, expanded, corrected. One measure of the strength of this institute will be the degree to which it is willing to stick its neck out.

The director of the institute should perhaps not be a professional designer. He should be a mature man capable of approaching administration as a nonspecialist—a man who by nature could become part of the Board of Governors and a part of the institute.

3. The Projects of Methods

To be at all meaningful, the projects must be viewed in the light of the objectives (Part 1), the description of students, and the description of faculty. The projects are meant as a possible guide to the nature of activities, not the extent.

It is very likely that the staff and students of this institute will have—and want—more work than they can handle. This is good because it produces a sense of immediacy characteristic of living groups and individuals—but not always characteristic of our institutions of higher learning. Training will be through participation in and contact with Research projects and Service projects—plus special exposure to specific disciplines.

Project "A"

There is much discussion, in India, about Standards of Living, and there are, at times, some strangely irrelevant (goods and services?) touted as contributing to this standard. In a country that faces the food, shelter, and distribution problems that India does, it might be well to take a close look at those things that constitute a "Standard of Living" in India. How do they vary according to time, place, and situation? What are the real values? To what degree are snobbery and pretension linked with standard of living? How much pretension can a young republic afford? What does India ultimately desire? What do Indians desire for themselves and for India?

Buckminster Fuller, a man of great perspective, gave this problem to a group of students: Design a package of services and effects which will be the most essential to salvage from a city about to be destroyed—the program was of course limited, but it was not an exercise in civil defense. It was a careful study of relative values—what do you take with you when the house burns down?

It will be seen that this type of research problem can only be attempted within collective disciplines such as we have listed under "faculty." It is a problem with continuity that will be going throughout the life of the institute because it will always be subject to scrutiny and reevaluation.

It will provide an evolving yardstick (meter stick) against which questions and answers can be checked. It will be a decompression chamber for the new student. It will be a perspective widener for those agencies or parties seeking service. It will be a helmsman for those working in the institute. Any institution needs such a continuous restatement of its objectives.

Project "B"   In the same way that Project "A" helped to build a foundation of values, Project "B" and ones like it will provide the framework on which the training and service programs are built.

This is the careful examination of old problems in new light and the search for the beginning of new problems and the attempt to make a valid statement of solution as of this time. It is a project that can fully exploit the broad experience of faculty and consultants.
Example:

To study the shelter and environment, all the artifacts and services required for a family in a specific agricultural community to make statements of solution in drawing and prototype.

It starts out much like the problem of the lota.

—Consider the history of the country and all its social mores.
—Consider the weather.
—Consider the local resources, the productivity of the land—its probable future.
—Consider the state of education, its future plans.
—Study available materials, available skills, the good things in the vernacular, the bad.
—Study the ventilation, devices for ventilation, food storage, sanitation, safety, security, and the kinds of pleasures these people respond to.
—Make drawings, mockups, full-sized working models of the shelter, the fittings, the devices, and every artifact involved.
—Study the economics—immediate and long range.

Detailed example: Study the problem of lighting in terms of increasing literacy and existing resources—consider the possibilities of electrical power becoming available and devise ways of making genuinely effective use of this power in terms of light—consider light uses—to banish fear, to work, to read, relax—make working models—prototypes—consider a system of wiring that will be efficient, effective and of such quality and concept that it will contribute to the whole, not detract.

The advantage of this attack on such a problem is that it clarifies the basic issues. We are searching for a device to turn power into an appropriate quality of light. We are not setting out to design a "lighting fixture" (the word "lighting fixture" is loaded with preconceived ideas). Furthermore, we are doing it for a situation of most rigid economical circumstances—where basic values must remain clear. This line of attack could end up in a highly desirable piece of equipment—BUT the chances are that it would not end up highly desirable if there was much premature anxiety (see *Gita* quote) about how desirable and saleable it would turn out.

Project "B" would then arrive at a point where there was a collection of models, prototypes, history, cost data, looks into the future, etc.— but the responsibility of the institute does not end here. In order to be a real contribution in these fast-moving times this information must be organized and communicated in a far-reaching, digestible way. This means exhibitions, films, literature, made and organized as part of the service program of the institute.

Working in these media is great discipline for making statements in a communicable way. It is also a way to quickly discover mistakes— mistakes quickly discovered and acted upon can be of great value. Such an institute must have enough autonomy to be free to make its own mistakes—free to stick its neck out.

Project "C"

The general procedure of exhaustive analysis and specific statement is much the same in this project as it was in the one above. However, the situation is of a special nature with special problem characteristics— a railroad station or a post office or an information center where the solution may in many ways be standardized but yet must be adaptable to a variety of localities.

We will take a post office as an example. This is a good problem for a number of reasons:

—In terms of values—this begins to reach out and suggest something of the symbol or image of the nation—one looks for confidence in that image and pleasure in that image and help from it.
—The pieces of equipment involved must be able to serve equally well in most parts of the country.
—Much of this equipment will parallel the requirements in other office problems.
—Because it houses a responsible government service, the building should be adaptable to the climate, unpretentious, and inviting.
—Because it is an image of the nation it should be pleasant to come upon, easy to keep clean. It should be related to a public place— the public spaces, the fittings, the hardware, the counters—the light should be as though this image really wanted to serve. The signs should give information with dignity and conviction. Ways of pro- viding other needed information should be explored—as should the uniforms, the stamps, the posters, the trucks, the printed forms, the post office pens, the poles that hold flags.
—To work on such a problem is to unearth many clues important to the prime objectives—a statement of quality values across the nation could form a contagious network. This too would make an exhibition and a film and word would be getting around in India and abroad that somewhere here in India there was growing con- cern about the quality of things—and that new and healthy values were beginning to appear.

Project "D"

Has to do with a design for an occasion.

The occasion could be:

The welcoming of some foreign dignitary, a national festival of music or dance, the investiture of some public officials, the Olympic Games, a national holiday parade, the mayor's birthday.

This kind of problem has in it many unique characteristics of value to the other projects, to the general direction of the institute—but they are not easy to state. Like most problems in design and architecture it is a problem in true *speculation*—*before* the act relive, the act before and evaluate many possible courses of action.

The great opportunity in the occasion is that it involves mood, symbolizing a kind of faith and a limited time span—the limited time is important. Cultures need occasions when they can be gay, symbolic, moody, colorful, and yet not be held to it for all time.

The materials of the occasion are even different: they are flowers, paper, ribbons, wire, cloth, smoke, color, air, music. None are asked to hold to the point of shoddiness—they are gone before they die.

It is a tricky problem and a good one for the institute because it seems light but demands a knowledge of prime objectives, demands discipline, demands a concept, demands unity—that is why traditional parades were great and indecisive modern parades just fall to pieces. The Republic Day parade was an example. All the traditional units had some measure of concept and unity (with the exception of the music itself): even the military sections had a discipline that carried it through—but the floats, which had no underlying discipline, turned out to be an unrelated sentimental hash. The floats had none of the conviction or gaiety of their religious counterparts in other parades. (Incidentally, if an elephant is decorated at all on such an occasion he should be beautifully decorated.)

It would do neither the institute nor the image of India any harm to treat an occasion.

4. Aspects of Service

The broadest service would in fact go to the people of India—through the Exhibition, Films, and Literature—and through the fact that there was a group concerned solely with quality and performances of the things they, the people, used every day.

Service to Industry would get more detailed material and would also provide a method by which industry could come to the institute with problems. The institute would not provide a "design" service but would help analyze an approach to industry's problem and familiarize them with just what was happening within the institute. Such an exchange of questions could be of mutual advantage. Some graduate trainees who stay with the institute and become part of the service wing could visit areas where direction in attitude was needed.

Undoubtedly prototypes developed in the institute would find their way into production, but the greatest help would seem to be in triggering similar attitudes and disciplines in industry itself.

Service to Government

We feel that it is very important that the institute invite other branches of Government to avail themselves of the service. It is important to have at government levels some intercourse in the areas of quality, discipline, and image.

The nature of the request for service could take many forms:

—The integration of the design of letterheads, printed material, bulletins—the graphics.
—The study of the approach to a problem of equipment for officers.
—The planning of an exhibition representing some aspects of Indian activity—for local circulation or foreign circulation.
—The planning of details of treating an occasion.
—The design of an international document.
—The selection of a present for a foreign head of state.

—The opportunity to just talk over the problems of national image and of values.

This would be a "design and research" service, but the restrictive aspects would be this—the outside agency or department would have to bear the expenses of the work, and the institute would have the right to final decision on the solution. These restrictions would keep the institute from being overrun by service requests—for a while, that is—until just after the first projects are made public.

5. The Physical Plant

The real introduction of the Board of Governors to each other and to the faculty, and the introduction of the faculty to each other and the first students to life, will come during the analysis and planning of the buildings to house the institute.

One has the feeling that such an institute should either be housed in Fatehpur Sikri or else the most unmonumental, anonymous, pleasant, unpretentious, workable, unshoddy, national buildings possible.

They should face the problems of climatic comfort, both with air-conditioning and without.

Students and some faculty should live within the complex, because much of the development of ideas and individuals would be on a round-the-clock basis—including food, music, conversation, special films and programs, and work.

Source: Charles Eames and Ray Eames, "The India Report," April 1958, National Design Institute, Ahmedabad, India, Container I: 45, Charles and Ray Eames Papers, Manuscript Division, Library of Congress, Washington, D.C.

CHARLES EAMES

"Architecture in Miniature"

ONE OF THE GREATEST FACTORS contributing to the development of furniture design is the concern and participation of architects. Among them: Mies van der Rohe, Alvar Aalto, Marcel Breuer, Le Corbusier, Antonin Raymond, Eero Saarinen, George Nelson, Alexander Girard, Florence Knoll. This list is notable, but incomplete.

The involvement of these architects in problems of furniture is certainly no accident. In addition to their concern with quality of the environment, they find furniture to be a kind of architecture in miniature at a very human scale. Unlike architecture, it is not too far removed from the architect's own hand. Furniture is in many ways a proving ground for architectural hunches and concepts.

Mies van der Rohe's Barcelona chair became the symbol of the elegance of that Pavilion. The Aalto Bentwood chairs had the earthly sophistication of his architecture. Eero Saarinen would probably love to build as simple an architectural statement as his new pedestal chair embodies.

Much of this furniture design has been a function of concept, and recently there has begun real effort to bring to furniture some of the high quality and performance natural to some other products of our time. The next phase will probably be a sober re-evaluation of the objective role of furniture in our lives.

The need to reinvestigate, restudy, and restate old problems is of course as much a part of architecture and planning as it is of furniture. We hope that architects will continue to use the field of furniture as a human-scale proving ground for directions in which they have faith.

Source: Charles Eames, "Architecture in Miniature," *San Francisco Examiner*, Pictorial Living Section, November 1958.

The Solar Toy

Charles Eames to Ian McCallum,
Architectural Review, Westminster, England
November 14, 1958

Dear Ian:

Excuse long winded description but (as Goethe suggested) there was not time to write a short winded one.

Ray sends love, and we miss you.

Charles Eames

November 14, 1958
THE DO-NOTHING MACHINE
A Solar Energy Toy
Invented: January, 1957
Completed: January, 1958

We at first declined to be involved in a promotional project for ALCOA on the grounds that we have too many real projects neglected and unfinished. Then it occurred to us that there are some things worth promoting, and the conservation of natural resources looked like a likely one. A demonstration of solar energy as a practical source of power appeared to be a not uninteresting way of promoting resource conservation.

At this point in the development of solar energy converting techniques it seemed that the best brand of attention could be called by doing an elaborate and delightful NOTHING, rather than a (bound to be meager and apt to be boring) SOMETHING.

So it became a do-nothing machine. First we tried a number of methods of conversion. Steam was attractive because it added to the general do-nothing confusion—however, the transfer to mechanical energy was very inefficient. We tried flash boilers, turbines, and air motors—spectacular in themselves, but low work producers.

The fast growing efficiency of the silicon cells became the determining factor. In one year the energy produced per dollar cost of silicon cells increased over one hundred times.

RESULT:

"Do-Nothing Machine" powered by ten silicon cells (1 inch in diameter), mounted in a reflector. The cells convert light energy into electrical energy, which powers six small motors. Motors then operate the various elements of motion. The motors operate independently of each other by means of a switching device at the foremost part of the plate. The device is a real tour de force in the department of fighting friction and was built entirely in our office of aluminum—cast, cut, turned, brushed, anodized, lacquered, and dyed to the material possibilities.

The problem of a delightful NOTHING, committed to most apparent use of small energy, runs into the trap of eclecticism—because the more eclectic the form and the motion, the more it becomes removed from pure abstract NOTHING.

We optimistically hope that a good look at the Do-Nothing Machine would place the SUN permanently in the viewer's catalogue of practical sources of energy.

The opportunity to view has occurred in publications, on television, at Expositions, and a month's run at New York's Hayden Planetarium.

What Kind of a Nothing? An Exercise in Imagination
Charles Eames and His FORECAST Solar Toy
By Oscar Shefler

Charles Eames's recent contribution to Alcoa's FORECAST Collection is a moving sculpture—a toy powered by sunlight alone. A collector tracks the sun across the horizon, motors respond, wheels turn, pistons rise and recede, colors flash and blend. With the solar toy, Eames has used man's original source of energy to delight the eye and to pique the imagination.

There was first the question of whether to take on the problem at all. Life, said Eames, is too full of real problems to permit introducing hypothetical ones. He began outlining what an ideal hypothetical (or promotional) problem would be. He spoke of something that would have to do with natural resources. He spoke of a means for teaching the younger generation. As he concluded, he found that he had given an outline for a design problem. He agreed to carry it to conclusion.

One thing would have to be understood: if it were done, it would have to be at the highest level. "This is tough," he says. "To make it tougher, we decided to do it within the idiom of the material and the device. We would try to achieve something

elegant." A pause. "What we now have, I think, is not the most unelegant thing in the world."

"And so we decide to make a device that will do nothing. But the answer is not as simple as that. What kind of a nothing? You can do nothing in a baroque way. You can do it in a Gothic way. If you are not careful, you will wind up with a kind of hodge-podge nothing, a big splatter of schmaltz. (I have no objection to schmaltz per se, so long as it is not derivative schmaltz.)"

"We now have a moment in time which is very precious," says Eames, "but this is valid only if the toy does nothing."

"And this, I would say, would be a good test for any design. Does it make somebody aware of something that it is important for him to be aware of? And does it do it in a manner that is delightful (which is the opposite of pedantic)? In fact, this could be a good starting point for somebody wanting to make a design: to think first about what he wanted to make people aware of, and then to move toward the most effective and pleasing way of bringing this about."

Charles Eames to Frederick S. Gilbert, *Time*, October 7, 1958

Dear Frederick S. Gilbert:

. . . The fact is that we feel the Alcoa Program was very good. The relation of the agency to the client was a most interesting one. The account executive, Tom Ross, and his staff took on the role of Alcoa's conscience, searching for the best in long-range values, and building and protecting the company image. I suspect that this situation is not unique, and that there are areas where the agencies demonstrate a kind of perspective that is apt to escape those closer to the business. It is certainly not the work of hucksters, and it makes one hopeful for the future of this form of communication.

Charles Eames

Charles Eames's Sun Machine
By Olga Gueft

In every age, the toy's appearance, action, and motive power (hand-driven key and spring, steam, etc.) reflected the spirit of the age, as well as its mastery of scientific forces. Eames's toy is—esthetically and scientifically—unmistakably today. It also happens to deal directly with a modern problem: the economy of natural resources. Eames's own words best define his approach: " . . . in a way where, let us say, you are not teaching conservation but you are opening the door to the idea of conservation. But if you are going to do that and really involve people and not teach them, you must open the door in an intriguing and fascinating way. All you ask is that you can come up with a demonstration of it that will, for the moment, really absorb their interest. There are relatively few things that you can do it with. But then you look around and you say solar energy—the use of solar energy direct as opposed to the fuels based on vegetation like oil and coal and fairly obvious things."

Sources: Charles Eames to Ian McCallum, November 14, 1958, Part II: Office File series, Charles and Ray Eames Papers, Manuscript Division, Library of Congress, Washington, D.C. Oscar Shefler, "What Kind of a Nothing?" *Design Forecast* 1 (1959): 34–39. Charles Eames to Frederick S. Gilbert, October 7, 1958, Part II: Office File series, Charles and Ray Eames Papers, Manuscript Division, Library of Congress, Washington, D.C. Olga Gueft, "For Alcoa's Forecast Program Eames Creates a Sun Machine That Accomplishes: Nothing?" *Interiors* CXVII, no. 9 (April 1958): 122–23, 182–83.

Aluminum Solar Energy Toy designed and photographed for the Alcoa Collection by Charles Eames, Alcoa Aluminum advertisement, *Life* magazine, 1959.

Glimpses of the U.S.A.

CORRESPONDENCE

In 1958 designer George Nelson was approached by the United States Information Agency to design the American National Exhibition in Moscow for the 1959 U.S.S.R.–U.S.A. exchange in Sokolniki Park, the first cultural exchange between the two countries since the Russian Revolution. His task was to provide a setting for the display of American manufactured products. As a complement to the product exhibition, Nelson and Jack Masey of the United States Information Agency asked the Eameses to produce a film on "a day in the life of the United States" which would serve as an introduction to the exhibition. The Eames Office proposed a multiscreen presentation called Glimpses of the U.S.A.

—Ray Eames and John and Marilyn Neuhart, *Eames Design*

Charles Eames with model of *Glimpses of the U.S.A.* presentation.

Editor's note: *The following letters were written in response to a letter from* Films in Review *editor Henry Hart in which he requested details about* Glimpses of the U.S.A.

Charles Eames to Henry Hart
June 19, 1959

Dear Henry Hart:

We are now doing the final cutting on the Moscow presentation—dubbing next week, so you will understand this is no time to write a story. However, many of the problems were unique and might be of general interest, because they point up other problems always with us. To answer your question, it is only like Circarama in that it is NOT a standard motion picture technique.

1) Our objective was to, in twelve minutes, give the Russian viewers the broadest background of credibility against which to view the rest of the Moscow exhibition. The coverage is broad—the land, the people, the weekday, the weekend.

2) We argued that for this purpose it would be more effective for them to be aware of the existence of many things, rather than to absorb in detail a few things (this is obviously not the only point of view).

3) We soon narrowed the approach to the use of multiple, but related, images—with the general assumption that the international acceptance of picture magazines (*Life* type) had universally trained people to thumb through double page spreads, scanning 6, 8, or 10 images at a time.

4) In some not too thorough tests, we found that it was usually possible to absorb the content of about four related images during a short cut (approximately 3 seconds). When this number of images was increased to 6, 7, or 8, one seemed to be aware of them all, even when not permitted to absorb any in detail. This awareness seemed in keeping with the prime objective—which was credibility.

5) The relation of the pictures of any set to each other is an important factor in the intelligibility of such a set.

EXAMPLE—

We used a series of sets of freeways and overpasses in which the viewer saw about 90 examples in an elapsed time of 13 seconds.

If we mixed long shots with medium shots, the intelligibility of the set dropped. As long as they were related shots of different examples, one became aware of their existence in an extremely short time.

6) The complications of the format forced us into simple means in other aspects—music, mood, continuity. Elmer Bernstein composed and conducted the music, using a concert orchestra and a jazz group.

7) It was shot in 8 perf (VistaVision), will be printed by Technicolor, projected in seven 35mm Simplex projectors on seven screens—each 20 × 30 feet. In twelve minutes, 2,200 scenes are projected.

8) The business of selection of images is a story in itself. While we received unbelievably generous cooperation from some of the national publications, in our search for the *usual* we found ourselves shooting a large percentage of the material. We were always editing horizontally and vertically (across the set, as well as set to set).

We are now in the midst of the lab problems that such a venture compounds. With luck we will carry seven reels under our arms to Moscow.

On the basis of these notes, you might get an idea whether or not there might be a story of interest.

Charles Eames

Charles Eames to Henry Hart
July 13, 1959

Dear Henry Hart:

Yesterday we received the final answer prints of the Moscow show from Technicolor. Tonight we take them under our arms and over the Pole.

1) We missed the Czech Polycran at Brussels—were there the first week. Strangely enough didn't hear of it until we were well into this. Idea developed as we pounded away at the problem of credibility. We had worked with multiple screens, however, in an experiment we have at U.C.L.A called "A Rough Sketch for a Sample Lesson of a Hypothetical Course." This also had synchronized smells.
2) No name for process. It is effective for just this sort of communication problem but doubt it would be an entertainment medium.
3) Both still and motion, but with 2,000 scenes a great majority are still.
4) Essentially color, but b&w was consciously introduced, especially in the tender ending sequences.
5) Minimum narration—only to explain such, to a Moscovite, unrecognizable scenes as air views of shopping centers surrounded by parked cars.
6) Screens stretched flat, but of the shape shown in picture.
7) In a 200-foot geodesic dome of the Buckminster Fuller type, manufactured by Kaiser Aluminum.
8) List of credits and sets of images will follow if possible.

Picture ends with a flute solo by Martin Ruderman. Images are tender goodbyes—mothers, babies, love scenes, old folks. Last picture is a simple picture of forget-me-nots.

(NOTE: In Russia the name for forget-me-nots is forget me not.)

Charles Eames

Charles Eames to Henry Hart
September 4, 1959

Dear Henry Hart:

Back from Moscow, and here are some shots of the crowd. It seems to have set something of a record for the number of people to view a film in a single house—2,250,000 in six weeks.

Many things we could not have planned helped it come off.

Charles Eames

Glimpses of the U.S.A., Moscow.

Charles and Ray Eames boarding
the airplane to Moscow.

Even on seven screens, twelve minutes is too short a time for one nation to tell its story to another. Some of the glimpses we offer will come and go too fast. Many others which we would like to show are completely missing. But we do hope that after these twelve minutes, you will feel that you know us a little better.

When we look at the night sky, these are the stars we see, the same stars that shine down upon Russia each night. We see the same clusters, the same nebula. And from the sky, it would be difficult to distinguish the Russian city from the American city.

This is the land. It has many contrasts. It is rough and it is flat. In places, it is cold. In some, it is hot.

Too much rain falls on some areas and not enough on others. But people live on this land, and as in Russia, they are drawn together into towns and cities. Here is something of the way they live.

A weekday begins.

Adults are off to work. Children to school. Much is to be done, and most of it in a hurry.

So starts a day of working and learning for adults and for children. In the schools, the colleges, and the universities, our youth and our society are being prepared to meet the future years.

In recent times, much of the basic research involved has also been taking place in the laboratories of private industry. These are the laboratories. And these are the industries they serve, surrounded here by the parked automobiles of the workers.

Much of the produce and the manufactured goods are brought to the consumer by way of the planned shopping center, which is often surrounded by a huge parking lot and is, in many ways, today's version of the old marketplace.

The mornings of the American weekend begin quietly. On Saturdays and Sundays, there is time to relax. Time to catch up on the small jobs around the house. There is time to be with friends and relatives, and there is time to be spent in contemplation.

U.S. Family Life Pictures Stir Russian Interest at Moscow Fair
Palisades Exhibitor Reports

A common appreciation for the warmth of family life is shared by Russians and Americans.

This was the feeling expressed today by Charles Eames, Pacific Palisades resident, the first American exhibitor to return from Moscow, where he presented a documentary film on how America lives at the current American National Exhibition.

"Most of the Russians, even Mr. Khrushchev, watch the film unsmilingly until pictures of children on a picnic or mothers with babies are flashed on the screen," Eames said. "It is at this point that one can tell the Russian people feel a close association with the Western world. These scenes are universal—experiences shared by people the world over."

Eames said that apparently the Russians had anticipated that the exhibition would be devoted entirely to American progress in the fields of industry and science.

"Although they ask many questions concerning these areas, they are primarily interested in the social aspects of our life," he said. "They are curious about the segregation problem in the South, the difficulties with labor union strikes, and special problems in education."

According to Eames, the Russians find it hard to believe that Americans are willing to admit their failings and mistakes in social and economic problems.

"Apparently they expected the exhibit to be little more than a propaganda project extolling the wonders of a capitalistic government," he said.

Eames and his wife, Ray, who accompanied him on his six-week stay in Moscow, had several opportunities to discuss the exhibit with Russians.

"One Russian farmer was particularly interested in knowing if there were any people in America who drank heavily, ate a great deal of food, and worked until they had calluses on their hands," Eames explained. "When I told him there were such people, he said, 'You tell those people for me that all we want is peace. We agree with your Mr. Nixon—in the next war there will be no winners, only losers.'"

'Smash Hit'

Eames's exhibit, termed "the smash hit of the fair" by *Time* magazine, is the first thing the Russian visitors see at the exhibition, which closes Friday.

The panorama of American life depicted in the films obviously startles the Russian people. Their reactions run the gamut from cynicism to childish wonder.

"Yet we never encountered anything that could be described as anti-American," Eames said. "Although posters announcing the exhibit and showing the American flag are posted throughout the streets of Moscow, they were never defaced."

An average of 50,000 Russians have visited the exhibit each day.

"They show little interest in American food products and kitchen equipment—their primary interest is in how Americans live," Eames said.

U.S. Life Shown

And that's what the exhibit conducted by Eames, an internationally recognized Los Angeles industrial designer with special interest in communications, does.

Scenes depicting everyday events in the lives of American families are presented to the Russians on a cluster of seven giant screens, 20 by 30 feet each. Seven slides are flashed on simultaneously. The seven screens are hung in a huge aluminum dome.

"We just went out on the street to find our scenes," Eames said.

Pictures of a typical American kitchen were taken in the home of Mrs. William Cunningham, 6 California Ave., Venice, which is located near Eames's studio. Westminster School in Venice was used to depict an American school with children playing in the school yard and studying in class. Pictures of the eastern part of the United States were provided by Mrs. Byron Atwood, of Boxford, Mass., the Eamses' only daughter.

Eames and his wife live at 203 Chautauqua Blvd., Pacific Palisades.

Sources: Ray Eames and John and Marilyn Neuhart, Eames Design (New York: Harry N. Abrams, 1989), 239. Charles Eames to Henry Hart, June 19, 1959, Films in Review folder, Part II: Office File (Pre-1960) series, Charles and Ray Eames Papers, Manuscript Division, Library of Congress, Washington, D.C. Ray Eames and Charles Eames, "Glimpses of the U.S.A." narration, 1959, Eames Office, Venice, California; 12 minutes, 65mm. Donna Walburn, "U.S. Family Life Pictures Stir Russian Interest at Moscow Fair," *Bay Area News Evening Outlook*, September 2, 1959.

Rebus sent by Charles Eames from Moscow to his daughter Lucia and her family.

Industrial Arts Education

CORRESPONDENCE

Editor's note: Richard Hoptner (1921–2002) was a poet and sculptor who expressed through his art the trauma he experienced as a World War II bomber crewman. He taught industrial arts in the public schools of Philadelphia and tried his hand at designing furniture before settling into sculpting full time in the 1960s.

Richard Hoptner, School District of Cheltenham Township,
Elkins Park, Pennsylvania, to Charles Eames
August 28, 1959

Dear Mr. Eames:

Please excuse this intrusion on your busy schedule, but as one who is both familiar with your work as well as your writings, I thought that perhaps you would take a moment to reply to a simple request.

I am a former cabinetmaker, recruited from industry into the teaching profession—a "Johnny-come-lately," so to speak. From my past experiences in the trade with different associates, my teaching philosophy has been strongly influenced by BAUHAUS teaching methods and, therefore, centered around design on all that it entails.

This October 23rd and 24th, the Industrial Arts Teachers' Association of Pennsylvania meets at Hershey for their annual convention, where some six hundred delegates will attend from all over the state. Following a general meeting, the convention will break into meetings of the various areas of the Industrial Arts. As Chairman of the Woodworking Area, my theme shall be "Teaching through Design—Its Importance."

The importance of design in the secondary schools' Industrial Arts program has not yet been fully realized or understood. Some say that the design is the job of the so-called Fine Arts teacher, who, unfortunately, because of his own background, does not understand either materials or tool processes. There are others who consider the teaching of design and all that it entails as something alien to their program and, thus, it is ignored. Every now and then some enlightenment creeps through such thinking, but its degree for effective quantitative or qualitative results are neg-

ligible. Briefly, following are some of the points I intend to bring to the floor for open discussion not only among teachers "on-the-line," but from the very source where changes could be made—the professional educators from the Teachers' Colleges. Any statement you would care to make concerning the following would go a long way in contributing for a better understanding of the importance of design:

1) Combating the incubation of self-propelled copycats. In brief, the horrors of copying from project books, which usually depict pieces representing an era long-passed and thus having no meaning to our present-day society. This is a definite retarding influence in developing the creative capacities of the individual students.

2) Making the present-day Industrial Arts shop an experimental laboratory in which students are encouraged to experiment with both form and structure, thoroughly grounded in understanding the honest use of materials as well as knowledge of tool processes in the medium which is being taught.

3) Encouraging creative inventiveness whereby tool skills become a means to an end and that end being creative inventiveness on the part of the individual student.

4) Developing some degree of design maturity by using fixed criteria for evaluating positive and negative design in all fields of industrial design endeavor. This can be accomplished in

many ways by primarily making use of good visual aids showing all types of products from industry.

5) The importance of architecture. Sad as it is to say, this is an important area of related instruction that is completely ignored. Though industrial time is limited, the importance of architecture beyond the visual should be stressed. Not only is this a job for the Industrial Arts teacher but the teacher of social studies.

Much can be done through an enlightened Industrial Arts program in the secondary schools, no matter how minute; not only in developing the creative capacities of the students but in educating the receptive and perceptive faculties as well.

The need for a better understanding in the secondary schools of what design could do, as "an integral part of our lives" is a slow process long overdue. Changes will not occur overnight, but a beginning must be initiated.

A statement from you on any of the above points or any point you desire to make will be deeply appreciated and may help considerably in clearing the air about the importance of design. Such a statement, as well as others I hope to obtain from leaders such as yourself in the field, will be read to our group.

I trust that I may hear from you prior to the convention.

Respectfully,
Richard Hoptner

Charles Eames to Richard Hoptner
September 25, 1959

Dear Richard Hoptner:

I have a strong feeling that in the secondary school the role of the Fine Arts Department, and the Industrial Arts Department, is not to produce painters or designers, but rather to act in the role of a conscience with discipline to counteract the general tendencies to specialize, point up, develop, and capitalize the relationships of the various disciplines, and to be the constant watchdog of quality at all levels.

You may not be completely happy with all my reactions to the five statements, but if you read them, please read the original statements in each case.

1) Much can be said for and against copycatting, but one thing certain—it is not bad to become familiar with the circumstances surrounding the creation of good things in the past—recent and distant.

2) If you are serious about the words "experiment" and "laboratory," make sure you know just what they mean and do not abandon the strict discipline and control that is implied. An experimental laboratory is *not* apt to be the place for random self-expression.

3) Creative inventiveness I would put quite low on my list of ambitions for the student. I would be more than happy if he only ended up being able to distinguish the prime or basic objectives of a problem from the superficial or apparent objectives. If he knows the real objective and a few possible landmarks, then inventiveness will take care of itself, and he need never hear the word "creativity."

4) One should be highly suspicious of developing any "fixed criteria"—it is an inevitable trap. We live in a rapidly changing world of many facets. Most criteria must now be based on current information, and formed with consideration of the particular reference square within which you happen to be working.

5) The reason architecture becomes so important to instructors is that it is an ideal framework in which to demonstrate the relationship of all the disciplines with which the student is, or should be, concerned. This means *any* student—not the special world of art majors.

Good luck in the convention. I hope it works.
Charles Eames

Sources: Rusty Pray, "Richard Hoptner, 81, Sculptor," *Philadelphia Inquirer*, http://articles.philly.com/2002-06-27/news/25349485_1_industrial-arts-art-in-bloomfield-hills-philadelphia-art-museum. Charles Eames to Richard Hoptner, September 25, 1959, "H" miscellaneous folder, Part II: Office File (Pre-1960) series, Charles and Ray Eames Papers, Manuscript Division, Library of Congress, Washington, D.C.

Charles Eames in his home studio, 1959.
© Vitra AG Photo: Monique Jacot.

CHARLES EAMES

Royal Institute of British Architects 1959 Annual Discourse

EXTRACT:

One of the most penetrating of the changes is that change which makes our society almost completely dependent on current information, that is, information current, and as contrasted to information that is accumulated. In a traditional society, that is a traditionally ORIENTED society, information is mainly accumulated, and almost any action within this pattern calls for a specific reaction. Today there are very few isolated pockets where this could be said to be true.

Ours is a world so threaded with high-frequency interdependence that it acts as one great nervous system. It requires all the feedback controls man has devised to keep from oscillating itself out of existence.

Examples of apparent information vary in complexity and degree. The telephone is a highly personal disorganized complexity. The controls that link airplane traffic and relate operations to weather are only practical to the degree that they are current and disorganized.

In the operation of a processing plant or controls for a rocket, information in the form of signals must come in microseconds in order to be current. In communication even with a computer the speed of light becomes too slow if the light is a bit too low. In problems of inventory and logistics, information can be slower but must remain current. A high percentage of the information possessed in our society would be meaningless if it were not current.

Source: Charles Eames, "Eames Celebration," *Architectural Design* 36, no. 9 (September 1966): 461.

Part Three

1960–1969

"A Prediction: Less Self-Expression for the Designer"

IN GENERAL, I am a sucker for any well turned out page, and often marvel that the work involved could be accomplished at all. There are, of course, special moments of sheer joy. Herbert Matter's ad for Knoll (showing a wrapped Saarinen pedestal chair); the jacket of the recently published *Stones of Florence*—both show no trace of effort, and while the Matter ad was in reality a highly personal expression, neither it nor the *Stones of Florence* jacket makes one actively aware of the personality behind the work.

This cannot be said of much of the graphic art we see. The personality of the designer too often stands as a barrier between the intended message and the viewer. While many a completely boring pitch may have been made less painful by such a personality haze, our real objection arises when such an intrusion of personality fogs subjects of interest and importance. The damage to the message can be accomplished equally well through a self-conscious concern for artistic respectablity, or a desperate drive for originality. In either case, the effort and the personality is apt to show.

The accompanying illustration is from the notebook of a designer who is not apt to be considered weak in character—yet certainly here no evil of personality hangs between the information and the viewer. Da Vinci was completely involved in any subject he attacked. In such a climate of involvement and concern, any drive toward self-conscious originality would quickly disappear. Enthusiasm for the subject is contagious, and information fairly leaps from the page.

A quick broad look at the graphics scene leads one to conclude that we might soon expect a return to more anonymous solutions of design problems in general. When this occurs, one wonders what will happen to those students whose training has been mainly in the direction of developing self-expression, whose study of typography consists mostly of turning type inside out, upside down, printing it through burlap, and whose arrangements seem solely for the sake of the arrangement.

It is reasonable to assume that schools will lay more stress on the disciplines of the art of com-

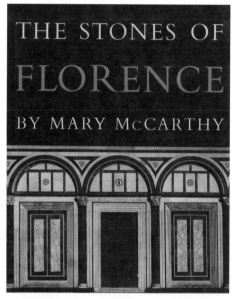

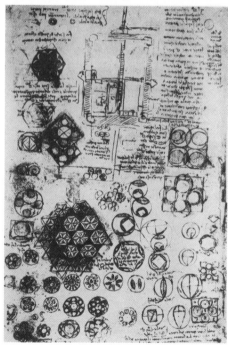

Top: *Stones of Florence.*
Bottom: Page from Leonardo Da Vinci's *Notebooks*.

munication, and the problem of the problem itself. It is a real problem to design a series of problems that will lead to experiences and discoveries upon which the student can continue to build. Here are three general principles which we have used and offer with apologies, realizing that no great teacher is apt to need rules or checklists.

I. That The Objective Be Limited and Specific: The danger in many problems is that limits are so broad that it is impossible for the student to isolate the prime objective and work toward it. This is often responsible for the student seeking originality for its own sake.

II. That The Problem Be Within the Scope of the Student's Understanding: When technological, sociological, or other aspects of a problem

become so complex that they must be ignored, they can create in the beginning student a pattern of irresponsible thinking, a habit of faking. If the conditions can be grasped completely, the student can then bring to bear on that problem the whole of his past experience.

III. That There Be Some Practical Basis for Evaluating Results: To design a problem so that the solution will either stand or fall on some measurable quality is very difficult, but not at all impossible. The great reward is that this approach injects a discipline which prevents evaluations from disintegrating on the level of "I like it—you don't—so what?"

Source: Charles Eames, "A Prediction," *Print* 14, no. 1 (January 1960): 77–79.

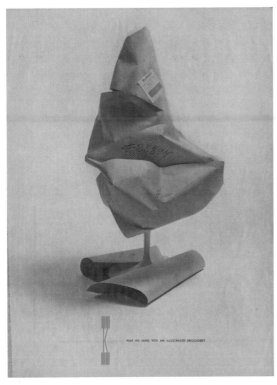

Courtesy Knoll, Inc. Photographs by Herbert Matter.

Architects and Science

LETTER TO REYNER BANHAM FROM CHARLES EAMES

Editor's note: Peter Reyner Banham (1922–1988) was a leading architecture critic, an author, and an educator. His books included Theory and Design in the First Machine Age *(1960) and* Los Angeles: The Architecture of Four Ecologies *(1971). In 1972 he starred in the BBC documentary* Reyner Banham Loves Los Angeles.

Charles Eames to Reyner Banham, *Architectural Review*
June 1, 1960

Dear Peter:

As you can imagine, your series has been of more than a little interest. Architects, collectively, seem to display a feeling of inferiority in the face of science. One suspects that this is because the architecture has gotten to be so bad, and not because science is so incomprehensible or non-architectural. Science shares with architecture the basis of all creative work. Like the architect, the scientist has learned to live and work with the knowledge of his own ignorance. He is not embarrassed by the problems he cannot solve.

In reading the series, I was surprised to find that science was often equated with efficiency, and that meanings of technology and science were freely interchanged. In this connection, I am taking the liberty of briefly restating four of the points I tried (not too successfully) to make in London a year ago.

1. That we have, in recent years, come upon some first rate planning tools—
   Theory of Games of Strategy
   Operations Research
   Linear Programming
   Many aspects of Information Theory
   (the computer or data processor I think of as something else—a piece of very valuable hardware, the development of which has made such theory workable)
2. Much of the nature of these tools would indicate that they belong to the mainstream of the architectural tradition.
3. We can be reasonably sure that these, or similar

tools, will be used to attack some of the architectural problems already upon us.
4. We can hope that the architect will be the one to use these tools.

These are essentially devices for developing a deeper understanding on which decisions can be based. They relieve the architect of no responsibility. They have to do with the restating of the problems of architecture—the rediscovery of the prime objectives. Such avenues could very likely lead to some NON-technical solutions. It has little to do with whether or not technology takes over architecture.

My general apprehension about the state of architecture was not in the least relieved when I read the following in J. M. Richard's article:

It is part of this mystique (of science) to assume, for example, that a new aeroplane which carries you to America a couple of hours faster must be an advance on the last one even if it is noisier, less comfortable and less safe—that makes speed into a race which everyone must try to win. Anyone who questions the actual gain resulting from those two hours of extra speed . . . is regarded as turning his back on progress.

Using this is perhaps not fair to Richard's article, but it represents the kind of fog that spreads when accuracy is ignored in order to make a clever point. The aircraft that carries you to America four hours faster is, in fact, far less noisy, is much more comfortable, is considerably safer, has about half the moving parts of a piston-driven craft, and operates on a more sound economical structure. With these facts, it is still possible to argue the validity of highly developed transportation *or* shelter, but it is hard to understand this architectural pouting, this insistence on being "regarded as stick-in-the-muds wedded to the status quo." I guess everyone has had a dear aunt who, feeling left out during the bustle of preparing for a picnic, would say—You all go to the picnic and have a good time—I'll stay at home with my potato salad."

Professionals, with their increased tendency to specialize, seem to be more and more embarrassed about taking seriously anything outside their specialty. It seems wrong that architects should be included, but apparently they are. There are places in the world today where scientific and sociological and architectural disciplines are starting simultaneously. We doubt if those involved will separate these disciplines into compartments or play science for kicks after office hours (for a while at least).

An awareness of this has perhaps been responsible for the widespread interest in Sir Charles Snow's two cultures. They have already drawn so much comment that I will be bold enough to offer two possible reasons for the apparent division:

1) We may be comparing two unlike things—
   a scientific culture of the twentieth century and
   a humanistic culture of the nineteenth century.
2) We may be looking at the technology and mistaking it for the science.

Charles Eames

Source: Charles Eames to Reyner Banham, June 1, 1960, Container I:218, Folder 2, Charles and Ray Eames Papers, Manuscript Division, Library of Congress, Washington, D.C.

Making Good Designs Better

VENICE, CALIFORNIA—For a man whose designs have had such enormous impact on the furniture industry, Charles Eames has a refreshing attitude toward that industry—he just doesn't pay any attention to it.

The slightly graying, soft-spoken designer described his work as "making designs better—more useful, more comfortable, and more lasting."

Of design piracy, Mr. Eames says, "It would be nice if people improved on a piece of furniture when they set out to copy it. Unfortunately, they are not usually concerned with quality."

"Herman Miller never tells us to do a chair, or a table, or a sofa. We fool around with a lot of things, sometimes for our own houses, or for a commission such as the restaurant of the new Time-Life building. We try very hard to really satisfy ourselves and, if a chair works very well in one dining room, it usually will work in other situations and goes into production at the factory," Mr. Eames explained.

The designer's widespread interests are demonstrated by what he calls "the shambles" of office and work areas. Reading matter ranges from politics, art, and housing to books on witchcraft and magic—"the beginning of mathematics as a science," Mr. Eames explained.

Because his major interest in furniture lies in improving quality and finding new ways to put things together, Mr. Eames has little interest in such widely touted fads as "the return to elegance." He feels design currently is in a stretching, plateau phase and that we can expect no widespread interest in new design until the public reaches a new "consciousness of quality."

Source: Pat Jensen, "Charles Eames Says His Work Is 'Making Designs Better'" *Home Furnishings Daily* (August 2, 1960).

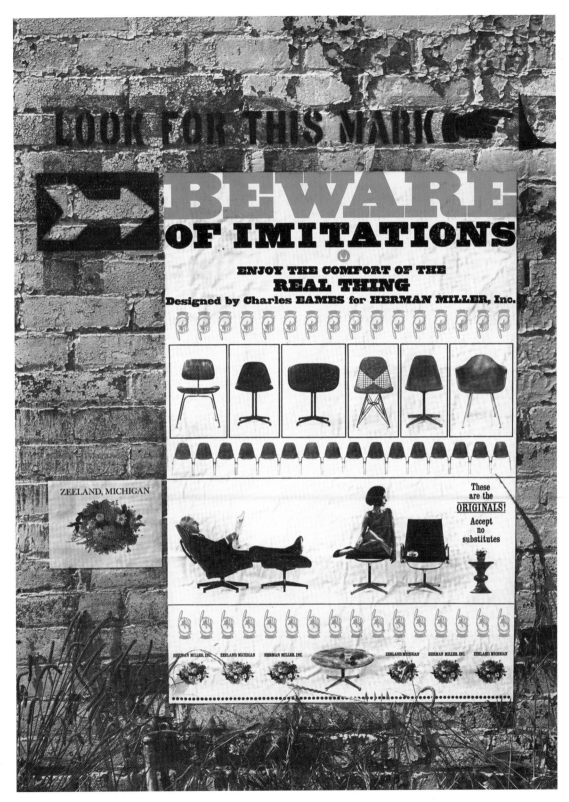

"Beware of Imitations," Eames Office
designed poster for Herman Miller, 1960.

CHARLES EAMES

"The Design of Mathematics"

(SOME NOTES ABOUT DOING A MATHEMATICS EXHIBITION)

Wherein we are thrilled (though not too surprised) to find mathematics an abstract model of relationships by which science (and we) link seemingly unrelated situations, and in which we find some mathematicians, through their handling of relationships, functioning as artists.

For the better part of a year we have been working, trying, building, talking, and battling with mathematics—and with a patient mathematical consultant. It has been much the same harrowing experience that accompanies any design problem, but with the added exhaustion that comes from perpetual excitement peaks.

There were times when we found ourselves at odds with the mathematician—perhaps because he, in terms of his discipline, was committed to proof, while we as designers were committed only to a kind of understanding.

Quite early in the game we heard this surprising general statement: "If mathematics is a mile, what you learned in high school is the first inch." Precollege mathematics one part out of 60,000?! We recovered from the shock gradually, as we began to glimpse a few of the remaining 59,999 parts. Quite a few seemed to be just richer knowledge about the old familiar numbers; but most by far were new concepts, ideas, relationships, and fine abstract bridges.

The exhibition Mathematica became, then, A World of Numbers and Beyond, and in it we try to give some clues to the richness and variety and beauty that make up that mile.

For us the most rewarding experience was to come upon the notion of mathematics as an abstract model of relationships. We had been familiar with this general use to the word "model." In speech, a simile or metaphor is a kind of model.

An architect, for example, may use a shell as an abstract model for many seemingly different buildings, or he may use a skeleton structure as a model in the same way.

A single grammatical diagram can be a model for several sentences with little else in common.

An accounting system can be a model for a shoe business or a bagel factory.

$3 + 2 = 5$ is an abstract model for any number of situations that have this characteristic. $x^2/A^2 + y^2/B^2 = 1$ is the model for the ellipse that forms when we tilt a glass of water, or the ellipse that the earth makes [in] its orbit around the sun.

A computer can be a kind of universal model. In one case, a mathematical model of an airplane being buffeted by a mathematical model of the wind—then by changing the parameters, the same computer can be a model of a community with mathematical models of traffic patterns being affected by mathematical models of traffic crises.

There are men who become so interested in the abstract models themselves that their lives are spent manipulating old ones and investigating new ones with no thought or concern for how they may be applied. These men are pure mathematicians.

A model created in this spirit was the four-dimensional geometry of Riemann. At the time (1859) it must have seemed delightfully useless . . . yet in the next century it was just the model that the physicist, Einstein, needed for further development of his theory of relativity.

In this way it seems that topology, Boolean algebra, calculus, or mathematics in its many other forms becomes the model of those neatly related aspects of a not so obviously related world.

CHECK WITH REDHEFFER: Geometry of Riemann —4 dimension?

BOOLEAN

Ray and Charles Eames working with
an early model for Mathematica.

Source: Charles Eames, "The Design of Mathematics,"
February 20, 1961, Container I:218, Folder 10, Charles
and Ray Eames Papers, Manuscript Division, Library
of Congress, Washington, D.C.

What Must a Drumstick Do?

CORRESPONDENCE

**Colin Low, National Film Board of Canada, Montreal,
to Charles Eames
December 15, 1960**

Dear Charles,

Herewith a new upgraded and, we hope, richer storyboard for DESIGN. We decided to change the center chunk entirely by using characters. The action in that important part takes place within the thought-world of the designer. The drum player incidentally in the thought sequence is the same guy as the one in the Concert Hall.

We are geared up now to push the project into production and we hope the sponsor will go along with the new idea. What do *you* think? Are we onto it?

Congratulations incidentally on that fabulous award, you had quite a write-up in the local "papier." Bob and I tried everything to wangle carrying the storyboard down ourselves, but Strube alas, did not come up with the aluminum airplane he promised.

Christmas greetings from us all and a fabulous year of good mental planning to you and yours.

Best regards,
Colin Low

**Glen Fleck, Office of Charles Eames, to Mr. Colin Low
March 1, 1961**

Dear Colin Low:

Sorry that Charles was called out of town before he was able to finish his letter regarding your storyboard. He did, however, leave his notes, and I thought I might send them on to you in the hope that they will be of some help until the time when Charles is able to write you in more detail. . . .

Sincerely yours,
Glen Fleck
Office of Charles Eames

Designer has been asked to design a drumstick. His question is:

"WHAT MUST A DRUMSTICK DO?"

Make music—by beating—a drum

Mm mm mm mm

What is the best way to beat a drum—

The best thing to make drum music with— the musician present at the ball and stick testing does not seem right. Could he have a quick analyst couch-type interview with designer (musician on couch)?

It is then logical for the designer to say as he does in effect—"how would one beat a drum if one had never heard of drumsticks?"

This notion would perhaps be cinched if he could make more than one quick try at how to beat a drum.

The air pressure machine and some Rube Goldberg pellet-shooting device—perhaps mechanical arms.

NEXT—he would normally want to review all drum beating devices from the past to see how it *has* been done.

After this research into fantasy and history, he is convinced that the ball and stick method is pretty good—so he addresses himself to the problem of getting the best possible ball, and the best possible stick.

The last of the history pieces may have been decorated with feathers and be a natural lead to his decoration attempt—failure of which brings him back to concentrating on selecting the best possible ball and stick testing (without musician present . . . could be aided by machines).

I am not so sure about the ever-present musician. It gets to be a sort of "Twenty Questions" game, which is perhaps not the point you really want to make. The inner desires of the drummer could perhaps be explored by having him questioned on an analyst's-type couch. Judging the texture, the material, the weight, etc., etc., is really the designer's job, but maybe he could be assisted by texture testing, weight testing machines.

Ending

It carries with it a very good point—THE SUCCESS OF ONE THING GENERATES THE NEED FOR ANOTHER.

The idea of the cycle is there. Could be strengthened if the first time he answered the phone he performed some action (for example: sharpening a pencil), then that action repeated at the end to complete the loop.

It is possible that it should end on—"A DRUM-PROOF CONCERT HALL"—then repeat a small action leaving out the last few storyboard frames.

Source: Charles Eames, notes on a storyboard sent by Colin Low, March 1, 1961, Canadian National Film Board folder, Part II: Office File (1960–1969) series, Charles and Ray Eames Papers, Manuscript Division, Library of Congress, Washington, D.C.

Design Education

CORRESPONDENCE

Mrs. Paul Tornheim, San Diego, to Charles Eames
February 21, 1961

Dear Sir:

As you are considered by many to be one of the outstanding designers of modern furniture, I thought you would be in a better position to offer some advice to my son who hopes to become a furniture designer.

Knowing you are busy, I'll try to keep this letter brief. My son had shown some talent in redesigning auto, boat, and plane models; and so when he started college, I suggested he major in subjects relating to Industrial Design. Very little is being offered at San Diego State College where my son attends; but they did offer furniture design, which he took. At the end of the first semester, his instructor suggested he keep attending his classes all through his school years as he considered him an outstanding craftsman [who] showed a flair for furniture design.

That my son is an outstanding craftsman is no surprise to me. His dad, who used to teach crafts years ago and whose hobby is working with woods, has just about every hand tool there is and has taught our son how to use these tools expertly and with pride in his work.

I gave you this background to show you that he has possibilities. However, in order to be a good designer, he needs a much wider background. I would appreciate it if you would answer the questions I have listed on a second sheet of paper with a brief comment. Enclosed is a self-addressed stamped envelope.

I am sure your comments would help set my son on the right path. Please accept my sincere thanks for your kind helpfulness.

Sincerely,
Mrs. Paul Tornheim

Charles Eames to Mrs. Paul Tornheim
March 7, 1961

Dear Mrs. Tornheim:

I wish I could answer your questions by suggesting a design school so perfect that it would take care of everything. It is not as simple as that, but here are a few suggestions. If he is really interested in design, there is no particular need in rushing into specialized design education. Looking, reading, drawing, and drawing, and drawing, and working in the summer if he can.

There are certain things, however, that he can only get in school. Physics is perhaps on the top of the list, then mathematics—especially the geometries. English literature and composition, then at least one foreign language—French, German, or Russian. If he does take any art courses, they should be in history and appreciation. He can

paint if he wants to, but there is no point in wasting good school time doing it. Parallel to this education, he can develop the tools of his craft if he wants to. After this education, he can go to a design school and learn something about the specialties.

There are a thousand different ways to prepare oneself for a career in design. This may or may not be the one best suited to your son, but I hope it is of some little help.

Charles Eames

Source: Charles Eames to Mrs. Paul Tornheim, March 7, 1961, "T" miscellaneous folder, Part II: Office File (1960–1969) series, Charles and Ray Eames Papers, Manuscript Division, Library of Congress, Washington, D.C.

CHARLES EAMES

"Architecture and Science"

ICA SPEECH

WITH THIS broad picture of architecture in mind—I would like to do the following:

First: Give some clues to the creative process that goes on in architecture and suggest that they are not unlike the ones that go on in science.

Second: Indicate that the tremendous change taking place in problems of architecture and environment are related to another change—the shift from a dependence upon accumulated information to a dependence on current information.

Third: To show that science has developed some interesting tools for handling current information.

Fourth: To suggest that the architect-planner had better get hep to the use of such tools.

Fifth: To hint that the use of such tools will not interfere with the architect's creative genius.

If we consider science in such a broad way that it becomes almost a state of mind—the result of a particular kind of consistent attitude applied in many, many areas—then we should think of architecture in much the same way. We can think of it as concepts and structure applied to our physical environment—not the buildings alone—but the fences and the sidewalks, the streets, the parks, the communities, the freeways, the cities and their relation to other cities. The plumbing fixtures, the outlets, the furniture, the dishes, the ashtrays, the wallpaper, and much of the visual communication we receive.

There are some architects—and people—who have always though of architecture in this de-limited way.

In starting to work on a problem, the architect—or the scientist—may face what looks, at the moment, like pure chaos. As he becomes familiar with this chaos—steeps himself in it—explores it—he may find that one element bears a relation to another—and then find that some aspect of one part depends on an aspect of another part. He may even determine the *degree* to which one thing depends on another, and finally with a few such ideas of the functions, he can start to give the problem a structure. Even if the first structure is not right it can still be helpful in determining the next.

It is this concept of structure and method of developing it that characterizes much of the creativity of our time.

Hypothesis is the counterpart of structure—it need not be the only hypothesis. How much help it is in enabling you to organize your idea.

Source: Charles Eames, "Architecture and Science," speech, Institute of Contemporary Arts Third Congress of Artists and Writers, Washington, D.C., April 1961, Part II: Speeches and Writings series, Charles and Ray Eames Papers, Manuscript Division, Library of Congress, Washington, D.C.

JAMES B. O'CONNELL

"A Visit with Charles Eames"

WE CALL ON the noted designer-toymaker-educator in his California studio and get an inside view of the special mathematics display he has just created.

The latest achievement in the Eames career is a program of exhibitions, films, and other devices called Mathematica, A World of Numbers and Beyond. Its first section, a huge and brilliant display, opened March 24, 1961, in a new wing of the California Museum of Science and Industry, Los Angeles. An expected 1,000,000 people each year will visit this cooperative venture, which fuses Eames's imaginative design, IBM sponsorship, and the museum's experienced services.

He and his crew, 16 young jacks-of-all-skills, work in a plain one-story, white-painted brick building about three blocks from the Pacific Ocean—a converted garage. There is no sign or nameplate on the front, only the street number. The building's anonymity is deliberate. Eames likes to protect his privacy from those who might take to dropping in. "It is not entirely an accident that all our clients are east of the Mississippi," he says.

Eames then enters. He speaks in a soft voice, slowly; smiles light his face easily and frequently. A bow tie, a Madras shirt, tan corduroy trousers, close-cropped hair indicate a casual but collected personality. As the day goes on we see his most common moods are amiability and enthusiasm.

We asked him to tell us the purpose of the mathematics exhibit, on which he and his crew had been working for more than a year. "To suggest," says Eames, "the richness and variety of mathematics, so that visitors will forget any preconceived notion of mathematics as a dry, boring subject, limited to the manipulation of complex numbers, we want to free people's minds to see mathematics as the art of building relationships, the art of constructing abstract models of situations."

Mathematica exhibition entrance.

"If the whole of mathematics were a mile, what you learned in high school would only be the first inch. We will be happy if we can give a few clues to the excitement and beauty that make up the rest of that mile."

The exhibit's means to do this were taking shape under the high-peaked ceiling of the shop spaces. On one table was a model of the whole exhibition as it would be installed in the museum. All around were full-scale mock-ups of individual exhibits, entire equations in three-dimensional form. A large wall panel was devoted to examples of basic mathematical concepts, shown in the regular patterns of snowflakes or crystals and precise graphic devices developed by mathematicians. A collection of five active, colorful machines is devoted to as many major areas of mathematical activity; by simple operations a visitor to the show will be able to demonstrate each basic kind of activity to himself.

Spread around the studio, in every stage of development, were machines, electronic devices, optical setups, scale models, photo blowups, motion picture sets, and a full-size mock-up of an 11-foot-high, 50-foot-long History Wall—words and pictures devoted to the mathematician in modern times.

The History Wall reveals Eames's way of working. Before developing any displays, he dug deeply into the history of math, consulting mathematicians and studying a wealth of available explanatory material. He and his staff spent months choosing basic ideas—suggesting many, discarding many. For his own guidance, as he went along, he began to organize the mass of documentation into a large wall chart, which showed, from left to right in chronological arrangement, the great mathematicians, their important ideas and their dates, from the 12th century to the present.

"With each mathematician's portrait," said Eames, "we put down a professional description of his ideas and biographical notes about the man. Soon, in order to keep relationships clear in our minds, we began to fill in information about the world each man lived in, the great events around him. It ended up being much more than a tool for us. It became one of the biggest and most useful features of the show."

Another large, odd shape proved to be a famous mathematical curiosity, becoming more and more valuable in today's scientific research, the Moebius ring. This closed, twisted band has only one continuous surface, a fact that seems to defy logic. In Eames's model, a traveling arrow runs around the strip, magically proving to even a casual observer that the ring really has only one surface. "If it makes one wrong turn," Eames says, "it will disappear forever—into the fourth dimension."

Many devices Eames wanted to use didn't exist when he started building the show; he was forced to invent them. In the course of solving larger problems, Eames and his staff have invented some ingenious gadgets such as a sound-motion-picture projector that fits, screen and all, into a case about the size of a portable typewriter. When we asked Eames if he had patents on his inventions, he brushed aside the idea. "Energy spent on patent routine is like energy spent trying to get money from foundations. . . . If you put the same energy into work on the project itself you'll be way ahead."

Eames enjoys nothing more than the challenge of solving communications problems crisply and dramatically. One such problem was: how to give a museum visitor maximum mathematical information with minimum distraction. His solution: peep shows. The six, two-minute peep shows continue the presentation of basic math areas begun in the work-it-yourself models. "Two minutes," says Eames, "is a delightfully short time in which to state a mathematical notion—from a standing start. We hope that it is short enough for the viewer to push the button again if he didn't get it the first time."

The notion had been growing on us, as we inspected the displays, that what Eames was building here, out of basic concepts and do-it-yourself devices, was a collection of serious toys. We asked if it was fair to call them toys.

"Well, toys are really not as innocent as they look," he said. "Toys and games are the preludes to serious ideas. Electricity was a game first, before it became a source of power. There would be no dynamos today if people hadn't once been fascinated by playing with pith balls and glass rods."

"Much of mathematics has the appeal of magic," Eames said, "and some of it really is—pure magic." He hopes that a traveling show of magic acts, displays, and peep shows will follow up the big museum display, reaching an even wider audience.

Source: James B. O'Connell, "A Visit with Charles Eames," *Think* 27, no. 4 (April 1961): 7–9.

"There is a certain relationship between playfulness and art, and there is a relation between playfulness and science, too. When we go from one extreme to another, play or playthings can form a transition or sort of decompression chamber—you need it to change intellectual levels without getting a stomach-ache." Photograph of a Mathematica exhibition display.

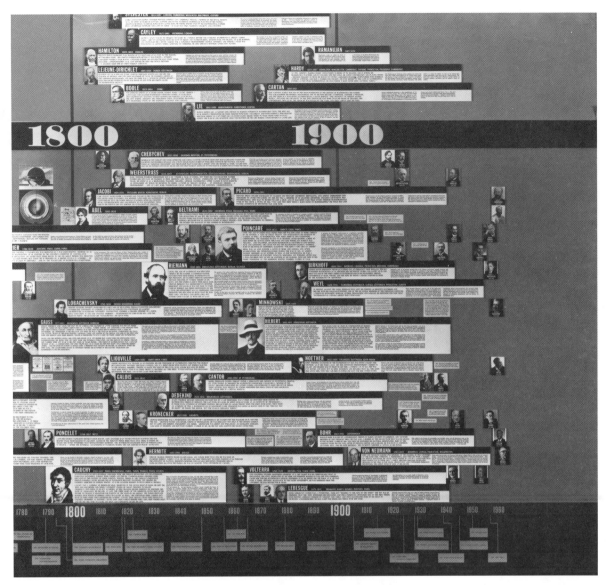

History Wall.

In Eames's model of the Moebius
ring a traveling arrow runs around
the strip. "If it makes one wrong turn,"
he says, "it will disappear forever—
into the fourth dimension."

Eames Contract Storage

Editor's note: Film script as recorded May 21, 1961.

For a long time we have been haunted by problems of storage—storage of clothes, of books and the like, all those things that collect in the average home, the bedroom, the dressing room, the kid's room, the guest's room.

But this so-called average home has so many variations that the real objectives of the problem are rather hard to pin down.

Designers have methods by which to clarify such problems. One method is to study an extreme case for tender care and sensitive use.

One such extreme appears to be the dormitory—men's dormitories—and women's—in colleges and universities. The concern that these privileged young people display makes the problem a challenge to any designer and manufacturer.

If the designer, the manufacturer, and the system can survive this extreme . . . we will be confident that the normal unusually rugged use should prove no problem.

Let's look at our system—it is secured by two of these structural sections which are either applied to an existing wall or built into a new one at approximately the one foot and seven foot levels. These receive the basic divider panels which separate the different units. The horizontal shelves are used to give the necessary lateral bracing—and then enclosure is provided by hanging hollow core doors on the divider panels.

The facilities that the system provides are:

One—A long hanging unit with shelf hooks and shoe storage.

Two—A short hanging unit with three shelves—and a dressing mirror and laundry basket on the back of the door.

Three—A dressing unit with four shelves. A counter and five drawers—mirror and towel bar on the door.

Four—A study unit with desk, tack board, book shelves, drawer, and light.

Five—A bed that folds—complete with shelf and reading light.

It should be of interest to housekeepers to note that the panels of the system do not touch the walls or the ceiling or the floor.

Department of Sanitation please note—heavy mesh drawers and shelves permit constant ventilation through the accumulation of old socks, sweat shirts, etc.

Comptrollers please note—Some of the most significant economies of such a system occur in the construction and planning of the building—the efficient arrangement of the space—and the benefits derived per square foot per person.

The details are not details—they make the product just like details make the architecture—the gauge of the wire, the selection of the wood—the finish of the castings—the connections, the connections, the connections. It will be in the end these details that provide service to the customers—and give the product its life.

Sources: *ECS* film script, 1961, Part II: Projects series, Charles and Ray Eames Papers, Manuscript Division, Library of Congress, Washington, D.C. "Eames Contract Storage," Private collection, Los Angeles.

ECS product page, front and back,
designed by the Eames Office.

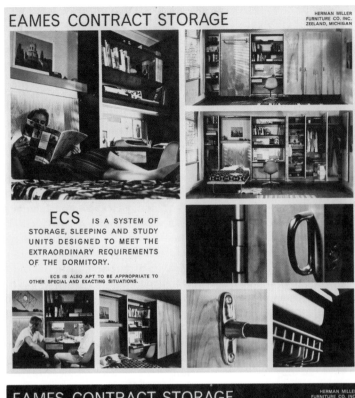

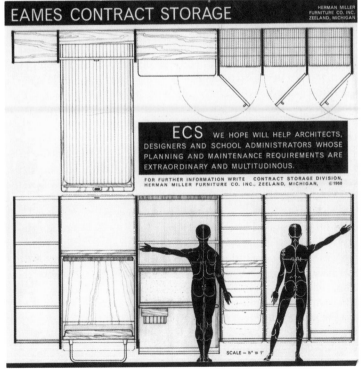

CHARLES EAMES

U.S. State Department

I. DECISIONS

I assume that the concern for the cultural aspects of our programs for the underdeveloped countries includes a concern for quality of the environment and the attributes of living.

If this is true, then some sober and immediate thought and energy should be given this subject for our own sakes as well as theirs—any experience gained abroad can be well used at home.

High on the list of helpful hints is the habit of making *decisions* about quality. The FACT that decisions should be arrived at through consideration of relevant data would seem to be much more important than whether the decision itself is right or wrong.

It is a good habit because it encourages including the *consideration* of the other person's point of view and the effect of the decision on his values.

It encourages awareness of long range effects whether this awareness is acted on or not.

Example

The nightmare of litter that can be seen on the Santa Monica Beach each Monday morning is *not* the result of *decision*. It is the result of no decision. Had any of those who dropped a beer bottle made a decision, chances are about 75% they would have dropped it in a can.

The reason that the City of Los Angeles is such a horror is the case of each building—NO decision was made in relation to the effect on the whole— the "next larger thing" was simply not considered.

The same holds true for the appearance of children's homework on a page—

This has something to do with the respect for "things" (which have little intrinsic value) that we, as a nation, seem to have lost in the flurry. It has also something to do with the pleasure we feel when we see some French fields meet some French roads—or some German paving meeting the curbing which meets the Platz—or the way some coffee is still brought to the table.

II. RUSSIAN BREAD

There is some evidence to indicate that one can judge the state of culture in a country by the quality of the bread and soup. I hope this is not completely true, because every restaurant in Moscow serves the equivalent of Pepperidge Farm or better— which far outclasses the laundry-flavored paste that is served as bread under the average U.S. hot beef sandwich. With the Russian borscht there is also no contest—but the surprise comes in the excellence of the Moscovite ice cream. It is possibly the best citywide standard in the world—but I understand they do it in a sneaky way—they use real ingredients. *How* can you trust a nation that makes ice cream with real cream?

While reviewing Moscow's cultural pulses—we should mention the circus, of course, and the way the parks and gardens are used, the open-air reading of poetry, the not-so-ridiculous subway, and the strange fact that we saw no guns or military toys in any of the toy stores. The enthusiasm with which they keep *all* the streets of Moscow clean makes one think that they think that they own the place, and finally, the way in which they speak of almost any problem in terms of its future—they put themselves in what C. P. Snow has called the "jam tomorrow" class.

The above are small but important elements which, if retained, can form the base of a future culture (the predominant "Stalin Gothic" architecture is even more boring than its photos).

I was very surprised to hear Robert Frost and Edward Steichen broadcast a report on their Russian visit without any hint of the warm and positive human qualities that do at least in instances exist. In the face of our experiences the report they gave seemed so *unlike* these two great men—perhaps they didn't leave the circle of officialdom, which is maybe another story—

III. ON EXPORTS

In India we were often and prematurely plagued by the question of what to export. The question was premature because while we were directing our energy toward something that would affect the quality of the objects in their own environment—they wanted to know immediately what they could successfully sell—

One answer came in an experience at Fatehpur, Sikar, the abandoned Moslem capital of Northern India. The place drew tourists, mostly Indian but also many Europeans.

There were the persistent sellers of impossible objects typical of which were the enlarged brass slipper ash tray, and the cigarette box with the cobra that reached in and got you a cigarette, which was punctured in the process. This object would under no circumstance be used or enjoyed by the maker or the seller—it would be quite useless to any real smoker. The only possible objective in making such a contraption was the immediate gain from the sale.

The vendors themselves were insistent and creepy, the day was hot, so when I rounded a corner and saw a dotty figure approach with outstretched hand, I thought, here it comes again.

As the man got closer he plucked something from the object he was holding, crushed it between his fingers, and held it to his nostrils—then offered it to me—and I plucked, crushed, and smelled. It was exhilarating and refreshing. I bought his lemon verbena leaves and urged others to do the same.

If he were refreshed it stood to reason I would be. The opposite situation from the cobra cigarette box.

The successful export of consumer goods by Germany and the Scandinavian countries stems from an attitude that is much like the lemon-verbena man. They export things that have served them well and that they, as a rule, really hope will serve the final buyer.

This is a difficult role for the exporter in an underdeveloped country to take, but it is a necessary one for long-term success in consumer goods export.

In some cases the effect of the American-style expert is as bad as the cobra cigarette box. The myopic expert comes to India and, based on some idea of fashion he specifies some purse or scarf or whatnot—a pilot run goes well on Fifth Avenue [and] the manufacturer in India tools up a product, only to find that the fad has passed. In the meantime, traditional styles and techniques have been altered for the production—never to be the same again.

IV. CARDBOARD COMPUTER

During a meeting with Mrs. Gandhi and the Minister of Commerce and Industry, we found ourselves making a proposal that India build some cardboard replicas of the IBM 704 Data Processor. The proposal was only about 2½% joke, and was under the following conditions:

There had been a lengthy discussion of the difficulty in handling some of the complicated problems of logistics that occur in India.

Someone suggested that a large computer could help but that cost of the equipment made it impractical.

I had seen earlier in the day some very skilled craftsmen working on some models and suggested that they be put to work on a full-size cardboard model of an IBM 704. The model to be so perfect, that for all intents, it IS a 704.

Now, having such a computer, it would be foolish not to use it, so naturally a programmer would be hired and put to work on programming the logistics problem for the computer.

It is a fairly well established fact that, in doing the work of organizing and relating data, and preparing instructions and sequences of operations for the use of the computer, much of the problem is solved.

If, for example, 70% of the problem is solved during the exacting period of preparation for computer, we suggested settling for that 60 or 70% and moving on to the next problem.

This is essentially the task of completely restating old problems in the light of the most current information—especially under conditions such as those in India, the restated problem is hardly recognizable as the old one.

Source: Charles Eames, Statement to the State Department, June 1961, Part II: Speeches and Writings series, Charles and Ray Eames Papers, Manuscript Division, Library of Congress, Washington, D.C.

CHARLES DAVENPORT

"Chairs, Fairs, and Films"

CHARLES EAMES is turning to the last rush to deadline on still another major and significant project, this one for the Century 21 fair, which opens in Seattle in April. The U.S. government is spending several million dollars for a vast scientific exhibit. What the visitor will see first, orienting him for all that is to follow, is a picture presentation by Eames. For it, Eames will use a modified version of a technique that proved enormously successful at the Moscow Fair in 1959. . . . Eames will use six screens and project motion pictures as well as still pictures. "Our job," he says, "is to de-limit science, to suggest its infinities, not its specifics. . . . Instead of showing one man and saying, "This is a scientist,' and maybe *all* scientists," Eames says, "we'll show a lot of scientists—men, women, all ages, shapes, postures—and we'll perhaps say, 'These are a few scientists,' and establish the fact that these are a few of a great many." Eames has been deep in consultation with ranking scientists at UCLA and elsewhere, having at his subject with the intensity (and the intellectual rigor) of a Ph.D. candidate in the throes of preparing a thesis. "We found that there were some cultures we wanted to photograph that we couldn't buy anyplace, so we're growing our own," Eames says, gesturing toward a window full of bottles, jars, and glass dishes. . . .

One of his associates, Glen Fleck, is working up a four-minute animated sequence that will trace the accelerating rise of science, from tinkering caveman to orbiting astronaut, in terms of what Eames calls "a super-architectural allegory." This is to say, very roughly indeed, that it will show men building a house which changes in style and grows in size and complexity along a constant time-scale of one second of viewing time per century. "I think you'll get a nice picture of the speed of the acceleration and complexity of science," Eames says happily.

He was born in St. Louis in 1907 (three years after the World's Fair ended). "Now that was a fair," he says. "Colossal. They had savages there, and they lived in the compound. None of this going back to the hotel at night. And they sacrificed dogs for breakfast, dinner, and supper. Quite a thing.

And the Ferris wheel, 250 feet in diameter! Each cage held 30 people, they were big as trolley cars. When the fair was over they dynamited it down and buried it right where it was. During the second World War they thought seriously of digging it up for scrap metal. It was much bigger, that fair, than this thing in 1964 will be. Robert Moses could learn a lot from it. He ought to learn a lot from it." . . .

It was in 1941 that Eames moved west to Los Angeles, and from that year also he dates his professional collaboration with his Sacramento-born sculptress wife, Ray Kaiser Eames. That collaboration was, and is, real, lively, stimulating, creative. The Eameses share the credit as co-producers on many of their first-rate films (e.g., "Toccata for Toy Trains" and the one on their Pacific Palisades house), but it would in fact be very nearly impossible to sort out projects which should not carry joint credit, so complementary is their thinking and so constant their working association. The usual arbitrary and unfortunate division of life into Home and Office ceases to have meaning in their case. What exists instead is an enviable continuity of interest in good design, new ideas, and unexpected beauty. Their friend Billy Wilder has said, "They are *one*." . . .

The Eames workshop for 18 years has been an unmarked, one-story, white and sprawling building in Venice. Thoughtfully cluttered, the shop is also well equipped. (Most of the royalties from the chairs have been poured back into the shop.) Here, with less than a dozen associates—young, talented, familialy attuned to the proprietors—the Eameses forge their considerable achievements. "The formula is the same for everything," Eames says. "You work your way through the objectives as they appear and you find the prime objective, which is often entirely different. The superficial objective may be completely misleading. . . . We become totally involved in a problem. . . . Sometimes she works on a project and then I criticize it and she makes changes. Sometimes I work on a design and she criticizes it and I change it."

The Eameses live in a steel and glass house amid a towering grove of eucalyptus trees on Santa

Monica canyon overlooking the bay. Nearby, connecting by a walkway of railroad ties set in pebbles, is a studio of similar steel and glass design. The severity of the lines and materials is softened by the play of sunlight through the eucalypti and by the disparate "stuff" with which both house and studio are furnished. At various times this has included: Chinese kites, pre-Columbian pottery, a bowl of eggs, a golden egg (hung from the ceiling), pilings from a wrecked pier, photo-murals of wooden planks and a huge mouse-trap, desert plants, Indian blankets, a basket of artificial flowers, Japanese newspapers (their characters making a pleasant pattern) folded to form a border for a room, abstract paintings, primitive paintings, straw mats, Eames furniture, machinery parts with oddly graceful shapes. "If people would only realize," Eames once said, "that they have the real stuff right in their hand, in their backyards, their lives

could be richer. They are afraid to get involved. That's why they call in decorators, because they are afraid. To do their own decorating they have to get themselves involved in thinking and feeling."

"We all have some preconceived ideas. We can't help it, but it is the degree to which we have them that counts." At that, Eames does not regard the ability to think clear of preconceptions as either a panacea or a mark of genius. "The genius baloney is just a lot of work. An incredible amount of things go wrong all the way." Of his own achievements: "It's just work, and the best part of it are accidentals, the things we never anticipated. . . . So often things start out as an extracurricular interest with us, and the first thing we know it's curricular."

Source: Charles Davenport, "Designer Charles Eames: Chairs, Fairs, and Films," *Los Angeles* 3, no. 1 (January 1962): 24–27.

Lobby of the Eames Office,
901 Washington Boulevard,
Venice, California, circa 1962.

Films on Architecture

CORRESPONDENCE

Charles Eames to Robert R. Denny, Henry J. Kaufman & Associates, Washington, D.C.
May 4, 1962

Dear Robert Denny:

It was good to see you and talk about your favorite subject—a film on architecture.

It is correct to start with the assumption that the first film the AIA makes will be just one statement on many; otherwise the burden of the single film becomes too heavy.

The subject of the first film is not too important. It is much more important that it be great. One thing it should not be is a sales pitch for the AIA.

Someday the Institute may want to do a film—the primary mission of which is to promote the services of its members—but such a film would certainly not be at the head of the list.

When asked about the deplorable state of our cities, Mies said, in effect, the following:

If our surroundings are to be improved, it is necessary that many more people come to want good things.

There have been times when more people were concerned with the quality of their environment—on the works of the culture reflect this concern.

The prime objective of a series of films might well be to heighten the general interest and concern with the quality of our surroundings. The need to generate such concern is as great among the architects as it is among the general public. It would seem that such films should be addressed as much to the needs and pleasures of the architects as to those of anyone else.

Films showing the "good versus bad" are hopeless. The selection itself is precarious, but the most discouraging thing is the beautiful way in which much of the so-called "bad" architecture photographs.

So much for the motivation and objective talk. The fact remains that one of the factors affecting the quality of the film is the degree to which the filmmaker is involved in the subject and wants to make it. Here are some single subjects that could intrigue a filmmaker who was also interested in architecture.

The Individual Architect
There are, I believe, no films dealing with industrial architects comparable to the marvelous one on Picasso. This should be of some interest to the Institute.

The Connections
The story of architecture—"moment of truth"—when one material is made to meet another.

Space
Some of the experience of space in architecture inside and outside.

World's Fair
The Columbian Exposition at Chicago and the St. Louis Fair of 1904. The Paris Exposition of 1925 and its influence on the architecture that followed.

Townscapes
"A la" *Architectural Review* or otherwise.

The Chicago School
Before it is all gone—

The City
Viewed from the various points of view of the cast of characters that make up a city.

The Unsophisticated Arts
Lettering on architecture, carnival, and festival architecture, the great temporary triumphal arches, etc.

The Monumental
Honoring the idea, the occasion honoring the dead—

Paolo Soleri's Notebook
One of the few "honest to God" notebooks kept by an architect today.

Architecture to Keep Things In
Grain elevators, silos, warehouses, hangars—

Add to this list subjects based on structure, on history, on style, something of the teachers, the pedant, and the scholar, and here you have a beginning.

The important thing, I believe, is to keep to limited subjects that can be attacked with enthusiasm—then hold the enthusiasm within bounds by limiting the films to one reel (11 minutes) each. Longer films are easier to make, but that is only one of the troubles with them.

Charles Eames

Source: Charles Eames to Robert Denny, May 4, 1962, American Institute of Architects, proposed architecture film, folder, Part II: Office File (1960–1969) series, Charles and Ray Eames Papers, Manuscript Division, Library of Congress, Washington, D.C.

"Evolution of a Design"

EAMES TANDEM SEATING

IN JANUARY of this year, two new terminal buildings were opened at Chicago's O'Hare International Airport. At present, O'Hare handles about 1000 operations every day (a scheduled landing or take-off every 83 seconds); traffic totals nearly 33,000 passengers daily. It is estimated that by the end of the year 10 million people will have used O'Hare and that it will be the "world's busiest airport."

C. F. Murphy Associates (formerly Naess & Murphy), the architects of the terminal buildings, were as concerned with interior details as they were with the larger considerations of airport planning and design. One of the interior elements they carefully explored and defined was public seating. Through a collaboration with Charles Eames and the Special Products Division of Herman Miller, Inc., the architects achieved a unique new design that may alter the accepted standards for comfort and appearance in public seating.

P/A presents the background of this three-way collaboration in the words of the design team— the architects, the consultant specializing in furniture design, and the manufacturer—as a further illustration of the questions raised concerning special furniture in the Symposium on Interior Design [October 1962 P/A]. Function, aesthetics, budget, testing, maintenance, and replacement are discussed to show how careful collaboration can enhance the quality of architectural performance.

CARTER H. MANNY, JR. *(Partner-in-Charge of the O'Hare Project for C. F. Murphy Associates)* From our analysis of traffic, we knew that O'Hare had a passenger service problem unlike any other terminal in the country. More than 25 percent of all passengers who deplane at O'Hare continue their trips on flights with other airlines. Quite often, many passengers must wait up to two and three hours between planes. This pointed up the necessity for soft seating; comfort became an objective of prime importance.

Having spent countless hours ourselves waiting in airline terminals, it was obvious to us that most of the public seating used in such places was inconsistent with the image of comfort and

service that the airlines attempted to portray. In a final presentation to executives of the several airlines using O'Hare, we emphasized that their responsibility of providing comfort and service to the passenger did not end with the termination of a flight: it included the furnishing of comfortable seating for the traveler who might have to wait several hours in the terminal between flights. Too often the advantages of jet travel end as soon as the plane touches down on the runway.

We knew also that cost would play a major role in presenting any new ideas to our clients—not only the initial cost, which had to be within a range experienced at other airports, but maintenance and replacement costs as well. We therefore evolved objectives for the structural strength of the seating, its durability, resistance to wear, and the ease of replacing parts.

As architects, we were concerned with the beauty of the seating when used individually and in groups. We were also concerned with the aesthetics of relating blocks of seating units to interior spaces. Like most architects, we rebel at the thought of cluttering up building interiors with a lot of furniture. In our planning of the interior spaces at O'Hare, we wanted to keep the furniture as anonymous as possible.

At one time, our own staff considered developing the new design but concluded that it would be better to draw on the experience of firms who made a full-time profession of seating design and manufacture.

HARVEY STUBSJOEN *(Project Designer of the O'Hare interiors for C. F. Murphy Associates)* After we had established the program for the seating and determined quantity and placement, we were ready to examine designs themselves. We approached several suppliers, were in turn sought out by others, and, in the end, conferred with seven different manufacturers. To our surprise, we found most of them very co-operative and willing to modify their present designs to answer the specific requirements we had laid down. We felt, however, that the problem called for more than simply a variation on an existing design.

Close-up photos by Charles Eames
of the seating in finished form.

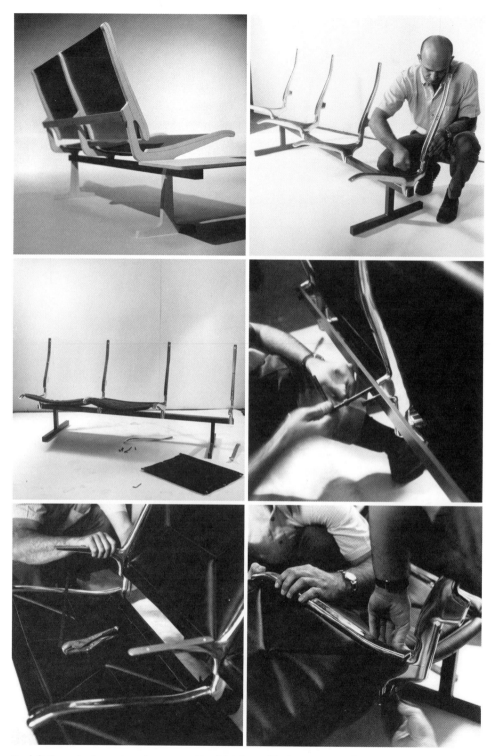

Top left: Eames's plywood mock-up.
Center left: Installation of seat pads.
Bottom left: Addition of arm supports.

Top right: Assembly: frames secured
to tee beam. Center right: Back
spreader attached with Allen screws.

Bottom right: Seat pads secured
by seat caps.

One of the suppliers to submit samples was Herman Miller. We were familiar with the Eames Aluminum Group and suggested that the construction and scale of these pieces might be applied to a new multiple unit for public seating.

As it turned out, Eames had been thinking along the lines of developing public seating based on the concept of suspended upholstery and was happy to continue in this direction.

CHARLES EAMES Occasionally we work on a piece of furniture without any specific application in mind—but that is the exception. Usually the development of a design is triggered by some real and immediate need—a need of our own, or that of a friend, or a building or a situation. In the case of Tandem Seating, C. F. Murphy Associates, via O'Hare, provided the trigger. Our response could not, however, be completely impersonal—not with the amount of air travel we do these days.

Specific applications, such as O'Hare, have deadlines, and deadlines require definite statements to be made by a definite time. This is one of the things that makes product design different from research in the same field. It also makes such design a kind of architecture in miniature—sometimes hair-raising, but not without its pleasures.

The role of the manufacturer in such an endeavor is interesting. In the early stages of development, Herman Miller kept a flow of information going between the architects and our office, and vice versa.

HUGH DE PREE *(president, Herman Miller, Inc.)* Upon completing a mock-up, then a prototype, the Eames office put the seating through basic tests. Herman Miller's Technical Center subjected this prototype to the following tests: a 100-lb. padded weight was dropped in a 5-in. freefall onto a seat pad 15,000 times; arm, seat, and back-pad materials were subjected to 100,000 cycles on a Wyzenbeek abrasive test machine; seat and back-pad material was chilled at -15F for 30 minutes, then folded and run through a wringer; seat and back-pad material was exposed to 120 hours of ultraviolet light, 65–70 per cent relative humidity, and to 105F ambient temperature.

CARTER H. MANNY, JR. The exhaustive, accelerated testing the Eames design was given indicated that it was very durable and would require little maintenance over the years of hard wear that lie ahead.

CHARLES EAMES As the project progressed, Herman Miller began treating the complete O'Hare installations as a prototype, working to raise all the values that could be built into the seating. As for concern about appearance, their hope and ours was that the seating would become a part of the overall unity that is characteristic of the O'Hare architecture.

HUGH DE PREE Herman Miller did not analyze the market for public seating before deciding to produce this new seating group. To be sure, we were interested in market response, but the real impetus came from a desire to see the new design become a reality. We are depending on the validity of the design and on the quality of its manufacture to create a demand for Tandem Seating.

CHARLES EAMES Two gratifying things about the project can be directly attributed to the architects: the architectural background within which the seating worked was sound and consistent; and the architects were content to consider black as a color.

CARTER H. MANNY, JR. Eames Tandem Seating was finally selected over the other submissions because it met our requirements more than any other design. It was easily as comfortable, perhaps even more comfortable, than units with conventionally upholstered seats and backs, yet the black back and seat in this Eames design are simple reinforced pads, identical, interchangeable, and capable of quick, low-cost replacement. This replacement factor was also constant for the polished cast aluminum legs and frames, which are assembled with mechanical joints. It was a key factor in deciding on the Eames unit. None of the other designs submitted had such a feature.

HARVEY STUBSJOEN We enjoyed a thorough understanding of our objectives on the part of Eames, and the feedback worked constructively both ways during the course of development.

Before we had come to grips with the specific design of public seating, we had determined the functional and visual considerations relating to the placement of seating in the waiting lobbies. The basic configuration of the terminal buildings at O'Hare is a direct result of ticket-counter requirements and distances between concourses. Together, the two buildings constitute well over a quarter of a mile of continuously enclosed space, not including the links, the restaurant, or any portion of the concourse buildings.

The rectangular buildings are divided into three basic zones that extend through this entire distance at the concourse level. These zones are:

(1) A long, central core containing concessions on one side and ticketing offices on the other. (2) An open space devoted entirely to airlines' ticketing functions between the entrance side of the building and ticket-office side of the core. (3) An open space devoted to merchandising, advertising, and public waiting on the concession side of the core.

Since the scale of the interior space of the waiting lobbies makes it difficult, if not impossible, to perceive an entire building from a single vantage point, we had to rely on the organization of elements within the space to orient the traveler as he moves about in the buildings.

To produce meaningful relationships between the elements used in these spaces, and to determine the exact nature of these relationships, we studied the building and its parts in model form. From these studies we decided the following: (1) Separate groups of elements should be kept at a minimum in order to relate well to one another and to the whole. (2) Each group should be easily and quickly recognizable as a group. (3) Groups at the ends of the terminal units should be as low as possible so that the passenger could see into each unit. (In the end, this consideration had to be modified, and the taller concession units were placed in the areas of greatest traffic.) (4) Each terminal unit should be developed exactly alike in order that it be recognizable as one of several independent entities within the whole.

Each half of each building is organized very much alike (seating groups, rest rooms, and other services) to facilitate visual recall for the passenger. We considered the basic unit of space to be one half of a building and arranged the interior so that the traveler can easily perceive this spatial unit at once. This technique is an effective aid for the traveler in orienting himself as he walks from building to building.

Although some seating was arranged in single rows, it was primarily planned in block form, in units of threes, so as to count well in the large space with the other major elements and to provide the maximum number of individual units. This created an aesthetic problem in that it was necessary for the seating to present an attractive appearance when used back-to-back as well as side-by-side. Eames's final solution satisfied our requirements in a most direct and outstanding manner.

CARTER H. MANNY, JR. We think the aspect of this story that other architects should know is that out of this three-way collaboration (architect, industrial designer, and manufacturer) came something good. This is especially laudable since the price had to be competitive and the specifications had to be approved by several groups with diverse interests. Our experience in specifying seating units for O'Hare again illustrates how important it is for the architect to know exactly what he wants in product design and how to define its required characteristics.

DATA: Legs: Cast aluminum/polished; nylon glides. Support beam: steel tee/epoxy painted/black; available in combinations of from 2 to 10 individual seats; maximum number of seats between legs is 5. Seat frames: cast aluminum/polished; height 33¾'; depth 28'; width of seat 23¼'. Back spreader: steel/epoxy painted/black. Upholstery: seat pads, backs/black Naugahyde/reinforced by nylon Fiberthin and vulcanized fiber strips/heat sealed. Armrests: Royalite/black.

Source: "Evolution of a Design," *Progressive Architecture* 43, no. 11 (November 1962): 140–44.

Cartoon of Herman Miller Technical Center by Glen Fleck of the Eames Office.

Photos of seating with passengers at
O'Hare International Airport, Chicago.

At the University of Georgia: "A Rough
Sketch for a Sample Lesson for a
Hypothetical Course."

CHARLES EAMES

Industry Film Producers Association Speech

WE HAVE NEVER thought of ourselves as motion picture producers. We have never been involved in a theory of multiple projection. Rather, we came upon it out of desperation, more as a tool to get across ideas and to relate ideas of importance.

The first showing of this was at UCLA. We called it "A Rough Sketch for a Sample Lesson for a Hypothetical Course." My wife, Ray, George Nelson, Sandro Girard, and myself had been investigating educational problems at the University of Georgia —a sort of Rockefeller study. When it came time to make a report we decided to put it in the form of a film.

Having seen the stuff that goes on in classrooms, the talk and going over material and inadequate presentation of material where students doze off, etc., we thought we'd try to concoct an hour's program in which we would cram just as much stuff, just as many notions related to a subject as we possibly could. We wanted to make maximum use of that hour. It had nothing to do with taking the place of the teacher, we were simply trying to give out material which was essentially background material from which an educator could then take off and build a hypothesis and follow it.

At the time it was quite a production. It involved some six still projectors, two motion picture projectors, three tape recorder units, and a ventilating system, because we had figured some smells into the thing. It was part of the total thing, since the subject of the hypothetical course was on communication. We started with a single-screen projection building up certain cases in the communications area, and then we began to talk about the sort of experiences in the communications area. We were talking about the difference between what, say, a bit of archaeology communicated to those of us at the present and what it communicated to those who were there at the time. We were going on with the usual travelogue of some cathedrals in Europe and all on a single screen. But then it began to spread out all the way around the classroom, and as it developed, we got into the interior of the cathedral where the sound of the music got louder and

louder and gradually got into the interiors, with the stained glass, which spread on all the screens. And as this was happening, a medieval incense was being pumped into the room, and you had to look through this smoke at the stained-glass windows all around you. And the sound got to be up in the room and this vibrated the seats. Now, this may not have been a realistic re-creation of what went on in Chartres Cathedral in the middle ages, but to some Southern Baptist who had never been in Chartres or had a religious experience quite of this caliber, it might have been—I mean, the likelihood of his going out of this room and forgetting it forever is extremely small.

So this was a single point that was made, and we then went on to more of a monotone. We picked it up again, naturally giving time for the room to clear of smells, with what was actually an epilogue to the whole thing. It was supposedly a teaser for the next lesson (which, of course, was nonexistent, therefore, namely the teaser) and we chose to have the subject for that lesson bread. There was a great film on bread. And the whole vocabulary of bread smells, going all the way from yeast to burnt toast, came into the room, circulated, and by that time had everyone in hysterics. They were drooling, et cetera.

An interesting thing happened. In the published reports of this . . . people described smells we know darn well weren't there. They described relationships because, in a way, they were in a mood to believe it. Not only did they fill in with these things, but any criticism which was leveled at this hour was not leveled on an hour's lesson. If they felt something was missing in the course, they said something was missing in the whole semester's course. In other words, they were subconsciously convinced that they had seen the whole semester and not one lesson. Now, for this, we had used for the material any possible device. We would have used anything to get an idea across. We were not doing it as filmmakers. We were convinced of an idea and we were just trying to do it. Now, I think even filmmakers can trick themselves into this attitude and work well within the medium.

One thing to consider, which is fairly important when you later go to judge the validity of the thing, is the experience in space. In other words, you cannot reproduce or attempt to measure the validity or effectiveness of a multiple-image technique by reproducing it, whether on one screen or on pieces of paper, and judge from that. You have got to look at the room in which this thing takes place very much with the same attitude as those of you who study the problems of display of information in a classroom. In a sense, you are creating an environment. For example, if you look at a single picture, whether it is in a magazine or on a screen—and assuming that your night vision is up to par—you're aware of all kinds of things going on. So that you are really taking information in from the picture and you are taking it in from all this peripheral stuff.

When we go to a multiple-image technique we are, in a sense, making use of this peripheral stuff, and using it as peripheral. And, if you attempt to then take all of this, put it on a screen, measure the results, you have not only compounded the complexity of the single image, but in addition to that, you have peripheral stuff. This is just one thing one has to consider when 1) making any sort of evaluation, or 2) reproducing the phenomena. In other words, you're going into the experience, and you're taking advantage of the fact that your eyes are not focused on this, but you're still pulling in information.

Now, at the Moscow Exhibition it was entirely different. We were taking a message to a group of people who had not heard from this country at all. There had been no communication before us. There was an exhibition that showed a tremendous amount of gear: toasters, pancake mix, and all those things that make life worthwhile. There was a lot said, and we knew these people were propaganda-receiving-tuning-out experts. They had been hearing words for many years, and words are a very unconvincing thing. Pictures are more convincing, but still we had a feeling that if, for example, we did put a great picture of a freeway cloverleaf on the screen, let them absorb it or become involved in it, the chances are that they would say, "A freeway, so we've got one planned for Minsk, three for Schmalynck, we'll have four, they've got one." So it was how to make the message credible—how to make the information they were going to receive and in the rest of the exhibition seem absolutely credible to them.

Now the problem was just as simple as that. We were not saying, "How can we use the gadget called the multiple-image technique?" We were really saying, "How can we make this notion credible?" Well, we argued several ways. What is a universal method of communication today? One is the picture magazine, of which *Time*, *Life*, *Sports*, *Look*, Who, What—all those things. They exist in Russian, in many languages in the world, and people use them in gathering up information. It is an absolute demonstrable fact that you can take, not to be critical of *Life*, you can take an issue of *Life*, you can thumb through it in fifteen seconds and have a darn good idea of what's in it. In other words, the creditability of its contents has been established. You don't get as involved in the details, but what is there is the main credit. You can look at four pages of *Jane's Fighting Ships* and have a pretty good idea of what the general strength of the Bolivian Navy is. It has been made credible to you.

You can absorb an awful lot of information from a book. So what we figured was, we wanted enough images going at the same time that it would completely discourage being absorbed in a single one. But not so many that you would be absolutely confused. However, we found that if you had more than you could really take in, the effect of information was one that was greater than you had actually experienced—even with seven. And in a sense this was no lie. Because even if we were using seven, we were only choosing from an infinitely greater number of examples. So in effect, you had another layer of truth there, if you will.

Now, an example is that in about twelve seconds we had on the screen some seventy separate overlanes and overpasses. There was no question as to whether these things were different, but in that time, I swear, you could not have spotted any two that were alike. The levels of information that are communicated are phenomenal. There is another thing. There were some guys in the audience who were no dopes. They could look at this and they would say: "Any country who has to handle their traffic this way has really got problems!" So, the creditability was the problem at Moscow, and this is the way we used it.

At Seattle, it was something else. We set out to complete the introduction to an exhibition on science. Now the thing that we were confronted with there, in the form of an introduction, was to delimit the viewer's notion of what science was—

to push back the limits. There is today a sort of a narrow band of the spectrum that the public is beginning to regard as science. You know, if it isn't "take use of the solid state" or "go off and make it," it's not science.

What we tried to do with this introduction was to show the complete spectrum, and sort of delimit the notion of what the role of tools and instruments was, delimit what the notion of what a scientist was, etc., and we begin with the idea of broadening it out. When we were talking about astronomy or a telescope, for example, we found that if we were working with a number of these at the time, you wouldn't say, "Oh, yes, a telescope looks like this." Rather, you would say, "It looks like this, this and this—" . . .

You know, we have clients for whom we do, for example, furniture; where a film becomes part of extracurricular activities in servicing that client. And when you're sort of interlocked in an idea like that, then again, it's the notion of using the technique any way to sort of accomplish a fact. The next little thing, which runs about a minute and a half, is the sort of problem which might be in almost any one of your institutions. We were being interviewed with Arlene Francis on that morning show, and we were introducing a new piece of furniture. Now you know when they put a live television camera on a piece of furniture, or any object, it's just mush, zero, nothing—the product can look like hell. So what do you do? You sort of make a little piece of film, arrive at the interview with this film in your pocket, and you say, "It just so happens that I have with me this little thing." People in a situation like this just reach for the stuff; they love it. They put it on, run it through, see that it's nothing obscene or anything, and we then had this device. And as Arlene began to talk about this item—"How do you put these things together?"— we said, "It just so happens we have here in the studio . . ." I find that they hesitate to cut film there at the last minute. This is the way, directly serving an idea. It's not that we were filmmakers, it's just that this was a handy device.

Now, we have been doing some work for IBM for quite a few years. I think our job description is "Design Consultants" or something. We haven't drawn a line for IBM, I should say, but we have done films and things. As part of a series—we were not setting out to do a film, we were doing an exhibition—now within the exhibition it became very handy to have some device. We set out to do a series of what we later called "Mathematical Peep Shows." The object was to experiment and see how condensed we could make the mathematical notion. So we limited ourselves to two minutes. You know, we have a feeling about films, that even though it's much harder, it's much better to make a one-reel film than a two-reel film. And we charge more for one-reel films than we do for two-reel films for that reason. It's infinitely more difficult than a two-reel, but it's really worthwhile. They get shown about four times as often and people sleep through a much shorter percentage. So to cover this now, we tried a two-minute one.

FILMS ARE SHOWN[:]
   "Toy Trains"
   "St. Louis"
   "The Fabulous Fifties"

What that is is a depiction of the people who died in the fifties. . . . It runs about four and one half minutes. What happened was, this was part of a thing we did for Leland Hayward. We were doing the Fifties, the Fabulous Fifties, and we were talking on the phone and I said, "Look, you know, all this good stuff that happened in the Fifties, it would be nice to really look at some of the negative side." And Leland, you know, he said, "But you mean sit for five minutes and look at dead people?" We had a nice relationship on this. The "Fabulous Fifties" footage was not being previewed by anyone at CBS or an agency or by the producer before. It went out on the air, and this is partly because we had been working here for some twenty years in the Los Angeles area and we've never had a client west of the Mississippi. It is a very handy thing.

Source: "Industry Film Producers Association Speech by Charles Eames," June 16, 1962, Private collection, Los Angeles.

Note: From the organization's letterhead, on a letter sent to Charles thanking him for his speech: "IFPA: The Association of the Film Communications Profession" and "Official Magazine: Business Screen."

CHARLES EAMES

"Design: Its Freedoms and Its Restraints"

RECENT YEARS have shown a growing preoccupation with the circumstances surrounding the creative act and a search for the ingredients that promote creativity. This preoccupation in itself suggests that we are in a special kind of trouble—and indeed we are.

The group headed by Dr. MacKinnon at the University of California at Berkeley has conducted a series of tests involving characteristics of creative persons. Among the groups invited for testing was a selected set of architects. The response was high. They were suspicious but curious—some had imagined themselves being asked interesting questions about their sex life, philosophies, etc. Such was not the case. A group which included most of the outstanding architects in the country found themselves answering some pretty boring questions, true and false, etc.—their personal experiences and observations largely being ignored.

They were given one problem, however, involving a collection of one-inch-square tiles of many different colors. They were asked to create from these tiles a design one foot square. Each was done in secrecy. After the test was over, several of the participants were describing their efforts. One asked Philip Johnson what his solution had been. Philip answered, "I used only black and white, what else?" He then turned to Eero Saarinen and said, "Eero, what did you use?" To which Eero replied, "All white."

This incident gives a clue to how far the sophisticated architect—or artist—will go to define the restraints of the problem he attacks. If limitations are not apparent, he will search for them or he will create them. This is no trick and no accident. It is one of the few ways that a concept of unity and structure can be maintained in the face of the unrestricted choices and the foggy or nonexistent limitations that are characteristic of our time.

The problem of defining restraints is one that our whole society will have to face. In the meantime, the responsibility for making choices that involve the forms and structures of our environment have been half-heartedly delegated to the creative individual, the architect and the designer. Education in these fields has felt that effect of the preoccupation with creativity. Some of the schools of architecture and design seem much more concerned with the freedoms of design than the restraints. They seem at times to be more interested in the self-expression of the student than in putting an edge of sensitivity on his disciplines. It is hard to reconcile self-expression with the creative act. It seems more natural to identify the artist with his restraints than to identify him with his freedoms.

For example, consider on one hand, the architect (if there was one) of the Summit Hotel on Lexington Avenue—and on the other hand an architect like Richard Neutra. If you were to apply the attribute of restraint to one of these two—it would not be apt to be the designer of the Summit Hotel, where design freedom seems to cross the line of irresponsibility. The attribute of restraint *would* apply to Neutra, or to Mies or Corbu, or to Eakins, Ryder, or Giacometti—or Paul Rand or to Calder.

A fairly good example of how a limitation or restraint works in a creative process occurs when a sculptor attacks granite with hand tools. Granite resists such attack violently. It is a hard material—so hard, that in granite it is very difficult to do something bad. It is not easy to do something good, but it is extremely difficult to do something bad—in granite, that is.

In plastilene it is a different matter. In this spineless material it is extraordinarily easy to do something bad—one can do any imaginable variety of bad without half trying. The material puts up no resistance, and whatever discipline there is—the artist himself must be strong enough to provide.

I feel much about plastilene as the ancient Aztecs felt about drunkenness. They had the drinks—but intoxication in anyone under fifty was punishable by death. They felt, you see, that only with maturity, a man of fifty had earned the right to let his spirit go free—give vent to self-expression. Plastilene, airbrush—should be reserved for artists over fifty.

Historically, self-expression has never fared well. Although the primitive artist is often pictured as an unfettered spirit expressing itself in a natural atmosphere, free from restraint, a moment's reflection would suggest that such a description is something less than accurate.

When a Hopi Kachina maker carves and paints the rat-catching Kachina, the particular result may be great, fair, or poor. The quality may vary, but not the concept or the idiom. If he were to change the prescribed costume, the color, or the attributes, or any of a thousand more subtle things that make up Hopi Kachina tradition—he would be drummed out of the corps. I doubt if any other aspect of his life—his labors or his pleasures—were less restrained. The sculptors that carved the figures on the south portal of Chartres were as tightly bound by the traditions of their time and their guild as was the Kachina maker or the stained-glass maker or the armourer. And I doubt that any of these were concerned about creating an art form.

It would appear that we have always been tradition-oriented creatures, in our art, our social patterns, our clothing, or our wars. Our societies have all had tradition-governed cultures—in which most every action by an individual called for prescribed subsequent action. There was never a real free choice involved. Changes came slowly. Today man not only has the opportunity to make choices, but he indeed *must* make them—and he must make them at an increasing rate.

Ray and I were in India at the same time that the young Aga Kahn went through the public ceremony which elevated him to the position of religious head of all Mussuldom. It was in Bombay—a very colorful occasion—huge, festive, and quite sober. After witnessing the ceremony, I returned to the hotel and wrote a note to Elmer Bernstein. It described the occasion and asked—"If you were to score such a sequence in a film, and were to do it in a very realistic way, what kind of music would you use?" I enclosed a smaller envelope which contained in order of their appearance—the actual pieces played—

1) On leaving the official car and entering the enclosure: "Marching Through Georgia"
2) On the trip down the heavily carpeted aisle: "How You Gonna Keep 'Em Down on the Farm"
3) As he approached the dais and mounted the steps to the throne: "You're In the Army Now, You're Not Behind the Plow"

The example is more amusing than it is horrible—but there are many more just the other way around. Man is totally unprepared for the role of free choicemaker. Historically he has absolutely no experience in the art of making such choices. Then it started—the steady advance of communication techniques and plumbing.

Considering the general level of sophistication in the average person today—and comparing it with that of other times, and the objects that those times have produced, most of the stuff that we are making and using is bad. And most of the relationships in which we put this stuff is worse.

California, and particularly Los Angeles, is a very special example. If it were as good a lesson as it is an example it would be exceptionally helpful.

This is what happened. People in large numbers from many different cultures came together to form a community—leaving all their traditions, social mores, inherited land responsibilities, and restraints behind. The form the community has taken is more a product of its freedoms than of its restraints. And the result is frightening.

It is not that we have thrown away our sense of values, we are just up against a kind of problem that has never existed before. A very large community has been forced to make many decisions large and small—without the restraining effects of a common cultural tradition, or limitations that come with isolation, or social responsibilities of long standing, or a lore of materials and their appropriate use—

Assuming for a moment that the unrestricted freedoms of choice did largely contribute to this mess, I would like to review some of the restraints that may have helped shape some of the older and more handsome communities we have known.

First the material restraints. These have a strong effect on the visual character of a community. The adobe of the Indian pueblos, the crisp wood structures of the New England fishing village, the grass huts of the Watusi, the stone walls and cottages of the rugged Irish countryside. In each case, the abundance of one material or the poverty of others—combined with the climate to develop a traditional idiom. This idiom gave the whole community a visual unity.

Second, the social restraints. Whether they were the tribal mores and taboos of the primitive villages or the more complicated entwinings of civic, business, and family responsibilities of the European small town, the social restraints were there. No individual was in a position to make a free choice. Anything he did to his property or his buildings had to enhance the total community and preserve its unity. The position of any violator could be made very uncomfortable.

Third, the pleasures. In the same way that the individual had to relate his home and his business to the community as a whole, so his pleasures and his ceremonies had to be those of the larger group, and nothing that he built or made could be allowed to detract from their performance—processions, promenades, bowling on the green, war dances, harvest dances, public executions.

In a city like Los Angeles, almost none of these restraints exist. As far as building materials are concerned, you name it—and you can have it. If not the real thing, at least a substitute that resembles it. The result is a hash of countless combinations of materials in varying degrees of inappropriateness.

As an aside, it is interesting to speculate on taking any single idiom from the collection and repeating it throughout the community. Whether it were clapboard, fake Spanish tile, or corrugated metal, if handled with a consistent attitude, the resulting character and unity would be impressive.

The absence of the social restraints is perhaps the most serious—the planning and building that take place without consideration or responsibility for its effect on the next larger relationship. There are no indignant groups of influential solid citizens to protest the flouting of tradition, no networks of family, business, and political ties on which each action might have effect—no strong religious or patriotic tradition—no restraints. Each is free to burden the whole community with his own mistakes, as long as it is sanitary and it is properly designed to resist an earthquake.

Of those positive restraints that go with a community's concerted enthusiasm for pleasures or ceremony, we have almost none. There isn't even enough collective awareness of what pleasure could be to move the citizens to demand a real park system.

The aesthetic nightmare that is Los Angeles has not happened because Los Angelenos are a less sensitive group than any other in the world. This would happen in the hands of any group freed from the restraints of tradition, and with no new restraints to take their place. (Such as might exist in a community built on a space platform or underground.) This is happening in varying, but increasing, degrees all over the world. The problem of which Los Angeles is such a dramatic example will soon be a universal one. It would pose an interesting question to the university of the state that has become the most populous of the united ones.

What can be done in a society where it can be said, "Man's highest ambition is to say first what is about to be said—and do first what is about to be done." We cannot revive old traditions any more than we can invent new ones—but there is much

to be learned about the way traditions grow and the way they function. The tradition, or lore of an art, helps the artisan bridge those gaps where he lacks sufficient current information upon which to base a decision. Innovation which usually takes place outside the restraints and assets of tradition often suffers from the lack of many obscure bits of seemingly unrelated information, small but vital bits of information which accumulate slowly in the development of a tradition.

For example: a plastic cup seems like a very reasonable thing. Who would guess that one would actually miss feeling the heat of the coffee or the coldness of the drink—or that the constant neutral temperature of the material would give some of the disoriented feeling of novocaine in the lip. Who would guess that one would be disappointed in not hearing it clink when set down or feel slightly cheated at the thought of its bouncing if dropped.

A more dramatic example of how subtle the true restraints of a problem can be concerns the Navajo in Arizona. When their allotted grazing land was cut and the flocks of sheep had to be reduced, the agencies involved decided that the logical thing to do was to ship the sheep to Chicago, can the lean meat, and send it back to the Navajo for food. This they did, and as a result many Navajos died of malnutrition. The traditional Navajo stew is made from nothing but sheep. However, except for wool, hide, and hoofs, it is the whole sheep—the eyes, the brains, the tongue, the bones, and all the insides.

We too will die of malnutrition if we mistake a part for the whole. The lean meat for the whole sheep. The new tradition which we expect might well turn out to be a tradition rooted in the search for restraints—a tradition of problem structuring—not a tradition of finished form. The forms developed in such a tradition may have to relinquish some of the visual uniformity we seem to cherish.

In the meantime, with the limited restraints we can muster, we find it much more possible to design an elegant flywheel for a gyrostablizer than it is to design an elegant hubcap for an automobile. We find it much simpler to build a beautiful oil refinery than it is to build a beautiful city hall or a healthy city.

Source: Charles Eames, "Design: Its Freedoms and Its Restraints," speech, New York Art Directors' Conference, New York, April 1963, Part II: Speeches and Writings series, Charles and Ray Eames Papers, Manuscript Division, Library of Congress, Washington, D.C.

RAY EAMES

Handwritten Notes on Design

C.E.:
The idea of design as a development of a series of
progressive sketches is romantic and not very true.

It is more an optimizing process that is apt to
start from a series of hunches which are either
developed or discarded by purely intellectual
means long before any sketch or model is made.

When these hunches finally begin to combine in
such a way that they seem to satisfy more aspects
of the problem than any one has a right to expect,
then this is the beginning of a concept.

When the concept is formed it represents about 5
percent of the design effort—the remaining 95 percent of the effort being used to keep the concept
from falling apart.

Source: Ray Eames, handwritten notes, dated July 1964,
"Undated or unidentified notes and transcript" folder,
Part II: Speeches and Writings series, Charles and Ray
Eames Papers, Manuscript Division, Library of Congress,
Washington, D.C.

Graphex Speech

Editor's note: The International Publishing Corporation sponsored IPC Graphex 65, an exhibition of their combined printing, creative, and allied services, along with three days of lectures and a design forum. The following lecture was presented in London on October 14, 1965.

DAVID COLE *Good afternoon, ladies and gentlemen. As you all probably know, these two lectures today were originally going to be given by Saul Bass. A couple of days before the IPC Graphex Exhibition was due to open I had a cable from Saul Bass in which he said that unfortunately he had to go into the hospital for an operation; fortunately only a minor one, but it did prevent him coming here today.*

Now, this placed us in a terrible situation. We had got all you good people coming along and we thought who is there . . . who is as good as, if not better than, Saul Bass, and I immediately thought of my good friend Charles Eames, who has helped me out on several occasions before.

I telephoned Charles at this office in California. He was busy at the time with the Nehru Exhibition in Washington, which, as you know, has already been at the Festival Hall here, and Charles was responsible for designing it. And that brings me to another little story. He was nearly responsible for the fall of the Labour Government a few weeks ago when they were called for a division and there were not enough Labour MPs available. The reason was Charles was entertaining them! [Laughter] Anyway, Charles Eames. [Applause]

CHARLES EAMES Thank you, David. We may even turn on lights, because this is not going to be a one-way operation, and I can see what I am dealing with.

It was much simpler this time. First of all, the last-minute things are always the best because you have a sort of way out—that is not about the date but also you have a reasonable excuse for not being prepared. Also, I had come back from a tremendous amount of work and had been away from my office and had not read any mail at all for at least two months. I had just settled down to read this mail when the call came, and I would have gone

any place to get out of reading that mail. [Laughter] That is the reason.

I do not have too clear of an idea of who you are as a group, but many of you have [something] to do with Graphex ad art direction—they call it?

[AUDIENCE] *Communications.*

CE Communications and both in a graphic sort of way. I am just quickly trying to think of some of the things which have just been happening in the last few weeks or so, and one is the closing of the New York World's Fair. I do not know how many of you visited the World's Fair, but it is a great lesson especially to see it in its closing days, when the fair stands as a shambles and you see in the raw all the mistakes that communicators can make these days when they are right up against communication.

There is a way of remembering about the date of a great exhibition, which, of course, is very simple. All you have to do is remember how long the Crystal Palace was in feet, which was 1,851 feet long, and that gives you the date. [Laughter] So that explains why I know the date.

There was something happening in 1851 in that exhibition which contrasts with what is going on in New York and it is quite important, and that is the involvement of the people in that they had things to show. One of the most significant things about the New York fair was that there was almost no relation between those involved with the nation's products, countries, or enterprise and the front that they were putting on at the fair. The line of communication had been drawn so thin as to be nonexistent. You had a situation at the Great Exhibition and also the following ones in our country, at Chicago and Louisiana where those involved, whether it be on the scientific fronts or the philosophical fronts, those involved in the act itself were involved in the exhibition. The shoe manufacturer

was there, telling of his wares, and, more important at that time, the guys who were manufacturing
stationery, engines, metallurgy, or whatever it was,
had a direct communication; and that was before
the rise of the art director, the Graphex personnel
and those people, who, in a sense, represent communications today.

But out there you had a different kind of thing.
You had a show being put on to impress a public
about the goodness of an abstract company, in a
way through motherhood or something, which had
nothing to do with the product or the inference or
the significance of the product or the enterprise
itself.

I cannot really believe that this is because
people are insensitive to the ideas that are going
around, but really something almost more sober-
ing than that, and that is that the implications of
advances on all these fronts and the implications
of the situations of large companies, corporations,
vis-à-vis the sort of social structure of the country
today. The implications in many ways sort of out-
reach or out-step . . . the symbolism that we had
evolved to talk about it, and we then have no way
to talk about it. Then when you even take that idea
second-hand and you hire a company to front for
you to talk about it, then it really degenerates.

This means, of course, a couple of things. On
the one hand, it means involvement of people right
at the front of ideas in these organizations or these
groups. The academic world is no exception. They
are worse. They don't even talk to each other, so
that you get a discrepancy between the kind of a
front that is put on. This would not be so bad if
the implications of the work that the people were
doing weren't so important to us and important
to life in general.

You have, at the same time, a preoccupation
with certain symbols of culture; certain aspects
of this that really mean the state of culture of the
country is completely good. But the symbols of
culture get the big play. There is a guy, a sort of
television personality, Alexander King. He is a character and you catch him on these interview shows
late at night. I turned on [the television] before
going to bed and there was Alexander King. By this
time he was facing the audience and he was saying,
"Before I leave I want to say something directly to
the audience." So he got the camera in and said,
"You out there in the big audience, I want to warn
you about one thing, I want you to be prepared, for
some day, sometime, somebody is going to knock

at your door and," he said, "they are going to bring
up a subject which is terribly important to you and
to your community. What they are going to do is in
some way lead in to the subject—a very vital one—
the organization, the building, the creation of a
cultural center in your town. Now is the time for
you to really act. Stand up and be proud, and when
they ask for your participation say no, absolutely
no. Have nothing to do with it." [Laughter] Then
he went on, you know, "Take Lincoln Center, for
example," and you can have it—[laughter]—with
the exception of the repertory theatre. Alexander
King went on to point out, "In almost every case
the acoustics have been worse, the problem of
fewer seats, the prices of the seats are higher,"
etc., etc. He went on to say, "You take Philip
Johnson, anybody that paraded in the rain in front
of Pennsylvania Station cannot be all wrong." Of
course Philip had done the ballet theatre.

But the point is that the thing is very real to us
in the United States, that the symbols of culture
sort of get this attention in the name of culture
while these real things which make the culture, the
quality of the soup that you get in the restaurant
or bread or what you walk on underfoot, or those
thousands of things that really stand for the true
measure of the culture are being neglected.

There is this sort of aspect to the fair, and this
holds almost to the graphics, which becomes a sort
of nightmare. You are sort of sure that when you
see a graphic panel that at some moment in the
evolution of this panel explaining nuclear physics
or heredity or something that there was a meeting
of the minds between the scientists and the graphics person, and you have seen it happen very often
where a scientist will explain an idea to someone
who is capable of handling the graphics and he
will have a solution to it and the scientist will say,
"Yes, it does symbolize it; it explains it," except that
a third party is brought in, presumably another
graphics-oriented person, and he looks at it and he
says, "What is this? I can't tell this from anything."
The scientist says, "You don't understand it?" And
he says, "No." He goes on to explain the principle,
and now the third person, the second graphics
person, says, "Oh, that is what you mean." He says,
"You do it so and so; this is the obvious way to do
it." Then the fourth person, the third graphics person, he does not see it, and so it goes. But at some
time they stop and build it. [Laughter] And so it
goes on.

Billy Wilder is a motion picture director in

Hollywood, and he has got what I call a keen sense of the phony. It is one of his really great talents, I think, of many, to smell out what is phony about a situation and eliminate it. I was working on a picture with Billy, and we were just going to shoot a scene which was going to be shot near some docks and some ships—it involved some ships and an airplane—and the photographer was a romantic sort of guy. He had been working with Cezanne, and Cezanne had brought out the romance in him, except that Cezanne could control it in a certain way. He was the photographer on things like *East of Eden* and *Johnny Belinda*. But what Billy was worried about was not that the shots would not turn out to be pretty, but they would turn out to be too pretty, because it was a dramatic situation. How could he get the photographer to really not pretty this shot up? And so the three of us rode out together, the cameraman, Billy, and myself in the back. Billy said, "You know, you did a masterful job in *Johnny Belinda*." And he went on, "When Dorothy McGuire, the deaf mute, was under the root of the tree, the result was a tremendous situation. There were a lot of beautiful things in the picture, but that was one of the most beautiful shots in the whole picture, except that the beauty of this great

stump, this great root of a tree, sort of detracted from the horror of the situation and you were so struck by the beauty that you could not really feel the horror. You have to be careful," he said. "You want to watch that, because Goethe once said," and he quoted Goethe in German. He said, "You see the effect and you suspect the intent." The cameraman, whose name I will not mention, turned round and said, "If your friend Goethe did not like the picture, he can go and take a flying such and such." [Laughter]

This really is a thing to remember. When you are aware of the effect, you have every right in the world of suspecting the intent, and in a world, not only the graphics world but the architectural world, when we have, in a sense, freed ourselves, quote "freed," of so many of the restraints that have, in past generations, sort of made us really heel to the line, and then you suddenly get this freedom—you know, witness this freedom, the architecture along the street. I do not know how many materials are in the façade of this new building, but I doubt if I could count them on both hands. In the efforts to make something free of restraint, it is a terribly tough job and it is something we have to learn. It is awfully hard to do something where the ideal is

Antony Armstrong-Jones (Lord Snowden) at the Eames Office with model of the IBM World's Fair Pavilion.

to do a building that you pass by and didn't realize it was there because people can suspect less of the intent.

It is always a real job, and one of the great jobs of our time, to sort of build our own restraints, among painters, sculptors, or even architects. An example of how the creative person will try in the face of no restraint to build them can be seen at the University of California where they were attempting to make some measures of creativity. They were a bunch of people doing research, and certainly their immediate answers were answers that could draw a lot of criticism, but you could not deny them the attempt. They got a lot of architects together, and the architects came because they thought they were going to be asked questions about their sex life. [Laughter] But not at all, they were given terribly boring things to check off, and at one time they gave them a whole bunch of colored squares. The idea was to put these colored squares together to form a pattern and then they would photograph these. They did these in secret so no one else knew what the other was going and they hoped to learn something by the way geniuses worked. After it was all over everybody got together and asked, "What did you do, what did you do?" One of them said, "I only used the three primary colors." Philip Johnson—this happens to be a true story; he keeps getting involved in these situations—Philip Johnson said, "I used black and white, what else?" And Philip, who is the real gamesman, game-lifemanship of all time, turned to Eero Saarinen and said, "Eero, what did you use?" and Eero said, "All white, what else?" [Laughter] This is an example of really the extent to which people will go.

There is a lot more to learn from this World's Fair than I am saying. There is the tremendous cost—it ran to something like a billion dollars, which is an awful lot of money. We count a billion as a thousand million; I do not know how you do it, but it is an awful lot. It is about two magnitudes or a hundred times more costly than almost any other fair per square foot; and the change of one magnitude, which is ten times, a very dramatic change, from the cost, say, of the World's Fair in St. Louis in 1904 is a tremendous figure. One of the things that it indicates, a special object or a special thing, is that in the meantime an Emery Roth skyscraper in New York is going down really in cost of service per square foot, and even the service of the mammoth automobiles that we make, in a sense

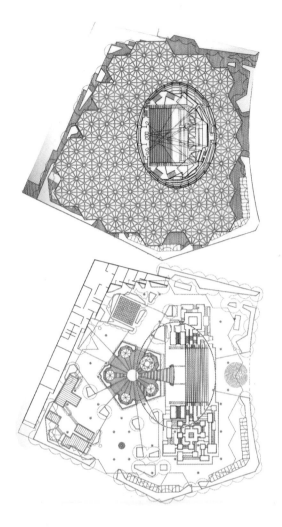

Plans for the IBM World's Fair Pavilion.

per cost, per erg of service or whatever it gives begins to level off and, in some cases, to go down. In the case of special things like World's Fairs, wars and stuff like that, they get terribly expensive, and you wonder whether somehow or other our lives are leveling out to eliminate such extravagances as those.

I think that the World's Fair will probably be the last one—I thought that the Brussels fair would probably be the last one, and Brussels had less reason to be the last one than the New York World's Fair has. In 1967, everyone sort of expected a fair in Russia for the 50th anniversary of the Revolution. If they had not just carried the banner and acclaimed the idea of World's Fair to its logical conclusion, or if anybody would, we would have a central theme—

that is a fair starting whether it is London, New York, Moscow, you name it; but it starts here, for example, and simultaneous with it, because almost anything that can go into a World's Fair is both reproducible, 90% of it is reproducible, but what is important is that about 90% of it is applicable in any continent or subcontinent that you can name. This is the real difference between 1851 and 1960— whatever it is, it is all applicable. And not only that, there are parts of the same entities in all these subcontinents, and it is as vital to any one of these groups, and you can imagine a central statement being made, simultaneous statements being made all over, and in truth, having a World's Fair, which would be a network. I think it would make a kind of sense, and I do not know [but] maybe the *Mirror* might do it. It is just their scope of operation, a World's Fair on that basis.

At this fair which I am giving such a hard time, they lost a lot of money, not counting this fortune—it was really immoral the amount of money that was lost—but had the people attended that would have made—nothing could have justified that—but it would have helped justify it, there would have been so many people there that they could not have taken care of them. I mean, it would have been the point of no return—that is not it, I mean that other cliché that has to do with when you carry a thing so far that it ceases to be practical.

Our relationship with IBM has been a reasonably good one from our standpoint for some time, and when IBM asked us if they should go in the fair, we disagreed. We said, "Do not go into the fair," because we felt it was a bad thing. By the way, there was a concept at the beginning, a concept of a huge bagel with a big hole, like a doughnut. Do you know what a bagel is? [Cries of "Yes"] It is

Kiosk at the IBM World's Fair Pavilion.

a classic example of a circular clock in the United States. It was a building about a mile and a half in diameter, which would have housed the whole exhibit and would have made an awful lot of sense. Had it gone through we would have recommended that IBM go in. We [advised] them not to, and they said for other reasons they had to.

So that the next position we took as consultants to IBM was, "If you do, just don't do anything that you would not have done in any of that. Just carry on in the line of direction that the company is proceeding. Don't do it, especially for the fair. Let us do a thing which would be a natural thing in the general line of the development of the company and then put it in the fair and let the public in on it." In a sense at this moment in time, we really cannot make great statements about the significance of a computer in today's society, but the second best thing we can do is to really let someone in on an honest segment. We will do something, which is important for the development of the concept of the company. We will put it in a form that can go into a pavilion, and we will indeed let the public in on it.

At first it sounds like you are writing the prescription for a death by boredom. But this is not true and this does not necessarily eliminate the fun because, in fact, one of the best-kept secrets of our whole time is the amount of fun, real fun, that scientists and mathematicians have at their work. If you can sort of break through that one, well you have already made something. So this is the way we proceed.

Now, we have always worked this way, and there is a way of working with clients where we have an area of interest, which is an area of interest of our own, the client has an area of interest, and there is a place where these two areas genuinely overlap. What we have done is to take those general overlaps and work like hell in the overlap and, as you work in this overlap, both their areas and ours tend to expand and it becomes a genuine thing and you are not doing the client a disservice by half-heartedly doing something he wants to do or forcing upon him something that you want to do.

Now, it sounds simple as anything, but I think there is a basis for a lot of good. Our office is like, you know, "design or architecture as she is talked about is different than as she is practiced," and our office is no exception. It is a small office, and we are away once in a while. We take on a commission for just the regular, the standard reasons. We look at something and say it is a thing that we want to do, but that is only one thing. You see as many mistakes that we have made and the many bad things we have done, [but] it has never been because it was something we did not want to do at the time. Sometimes we did not succeed in doing what we had hoped to do, but it has always been our own fault.

But we take on a thing and we say, "Well, there is a chance this time to do something good and still something that will be profitable, that will bring some returns to the office." It is a nice job; it is something that is interesting and we can sort of recoup something of what we lost on this job. We start to work on it and we get halfway through and find we are on the wrong track and realize that this dream of recouping has gone and now you say to yourself, "We can't make any money on this one but at least we will make a statement which is valuable to us that we can build on and will be really interesting for the client."

You go on and on and pretty soon we find that we were entirely up the wrong tree. First, we decided that we would break even and then you go past this and you decide well, it is not working after all, if we can just succeed even though we put some money into it, maybe it will not be embarrassing—[laughter]—and we will have a reasonably good solution. You work on that for a while and then you begin to think, "If at the end of this job anybody in the world will ever speak to us again we will be happy," and we start work and pretty soon, you know, the desperation of just this thing that started out as a beautiful idea that you wanted to do, if only you can survive, if you can just survive it and keep your head up and that you won't do something that you will be completely ashamed of, it is about that time that you start looking for the lifeboat.

My lifeboat is a sort of little obscure college out in Arizona, some place where they probably have never heard of you, and I like to go there and teach a course, a little course. And to keep myself from staying awake all night, I begin to invent lessons in this course, and pretty soon the course gets to be so great that when you realize that the project is not a complete failure but is somewhat of a disappointment you are longing for the place to give that course.

I want to try to show a couple of examples of things we have done, where you take an idea, because as we have worked in film, none of them

has really been with any thoughts that it is experimental film. That is a complete misconception. We have only used films in one way and that is as a tool to get across an idea. It happens that as a result we have had different solutions, but in this case it is not a film at all, it is a series of puppet shows.

In doing the puppet show, or the film, or the drawing, or the cartoon, one of the great traps is when one either makes jokes or uses colors, which are not intimately related with the concept of the thing itself. . . . There is so much information to be got across in this growing society and culture of ours that you are just going to have to face it. You are going to have to face the job of really transmitting meaning and all the tricks, and every joke, every color; every tear is sort of pertinent to the meaning. . . .

So what this is is a record of a puppet show. The puppet show has to do with the subject of solving problems on a sort of "yes" or "no" basis, and thereby is related to the computer. What you are going to see now is a film of the puppet show. Remember it is not to be seen as a film, but as a puppet show. It really works better even as a sound track than as a film. [The film was then shown.]

This was one of a series of puppet shows that we did. One, the story of the stealing of the train, was written exactly four weeks before the actual train was stolen in England. Now, this caused quite a bit of comment, because the plot had already been outlined here. Yang, who was a member of the team Lee & Yang, who upset the whole theory of the perfect symmetry of the universe, happened to be in our office at the time that the news of the real train robbery had taken place, and he just pointed out that it was an example of hemispherical symmetry that existed in the world, thereby getting us off the hook. [Laughter]

The little patter, the sort of Gilbert & Sullivanish patter where he goes through the development of the logic. The logic holds up. In a case like this it naturally goes so fast, but it is the essence of it that is all that you want to get. Then you have to have faith that it will actually hold up. We have got 500 analyses from experts that have seen this and have tried to break it down, and they will every time. . . .

We have been concerned recently, in relation to this general thing I am talking about, with problems having to deal with early learning. Early learning is what they call "the law of the instrument," which sort of pervades everything. It is best illustrated by the fact that if you give a child a hammer, he will invariably find out that everything he encounters needs to be pounded. [Laughter]

So if you give a sociologist a new tool, like the problems of early learning, every problem in our society can be traced to problems of early learning, and I am convinced that it can. You know, a victim of the law of the instrument. But we have been interested in this, and Bob Speck, who is one of the chief mathematicians at the Rand Corporation at Santa Monica—Rand is a group, a team, like an operations research team, that works on game theory . . . ; it is a government-subsidized thing.

But we are sort of trying to argue how you can teach mathematics with proof, because one of the problems is that you can teach an idea, but once you introduce the proof, immediately everything goes blank. The proof is usually so complicated that it completely destroys everything.

He said: "Look, I can set brilliant geometry and have an angle here." To demonstrate that these angles are the same he put in a mirror down the line. "And to a child," he says, "as everybody knows, in a mirror it would be true symmetry, so the angles have to be the same, unless the little bastards happen to hear of Lee & Yang, who have just disproved symmetry." We have to have faith like Albert Einstein, who, when it was put to him that maybe out in the far reaches of space, the laws of relativity may not hold because the laws may change as you are way out, answered with a sweet answer. He said, "God may be subtle, but he is not malicious." [Laughter; film featuring the IBM Pavilion at the New York World's Fair was then shown.]

Shall we show something else, or would you like to indulge in some questions? The one thing that I was going to do—I do not know whether the pictures are sort of miserable for you—but one of the things that comes to the forefront in this whole problem of attacking design problems is that building of our own restraints. We find ourselves in the situation where as a society it is much easier for us to build a magnificent flywheel on a gyrostabilizer than it is to build the wheel of an automobile. Well, it is certainly easier to build a beautiful cracking plant than it is to build a city hall or a healthy city. This is not that we have an interest in those things, but the defining of these problems, the defining of these restraints has got so out of hand that those things that we can define, those things that we can build the perimeters for, we have to solve fairly well.

This isn't because people don't care, although not caring is one of the most nightmarish things we have to face today, but it is because as a race, as a culture, we have never been up against the problem of making a free choice. In each case in our own histories why each act calls for a prescribed subsequent act and now not only do we have the opportunity to make a choice but we are forced to make choices, and we are just plain not prepared to make them. So in many respects this is the problem before us. To sort of build a pattern, a structure, by which we can build our own restraints.

With that as a taking off point, I was going to show a whole series of images, which was built around the beauty of a single kind of discipline. . . . We have a choice of two tapes here. One is an Indian Rajah and the other is Walton's Façade, but while we are waiting for the tape there must be something you are dying to know about the New York World's Fair.

SPEAKER *Yes, the last picture there, everybody rushing around, was absolutely fascinating. I take it that it was the IBM exhibition in the New York World's Fair, was it?*

CHARLES EAMES Yes.

SPEAKER *And the public was taken up on lifts?*

CE The reason for it is that we expect to make the real film from some such material like that which will in itself eventually just show the spirit of the thing. Very often a pavilion is made and then one could make a very serious, very long, and very boring picture after the fact that no one particularly wants to see because it is in the past. Instead of doing that we are going to make a record of it in several parts.

One is greatly condensed and should run for about ten minutes, and through a lot of motion and images it gives a little bit of the feeling of the space because what it was was essentially a garden. It was something like the Tivoli Garden in Copenhagen except that instead of being puppet shows in one sense, they were all things which had to do with mathematical ideas, some of them directly related to the computer, like the Holmes thing. This was the typical way of Holmes arriving at a solution, but it was also typical of the way that a computer really comes to its solution—that is, to break things down to simple statements. This seemed to be a valid statement.

Then we have another one on the random walk, or the drunk's walk, which is quite a probability

Top: Master of Ceremonies welcomes
visitors to the "Information Machine."

Bottom: The Scholars Walk, IBM
World's Fair Pavilion.

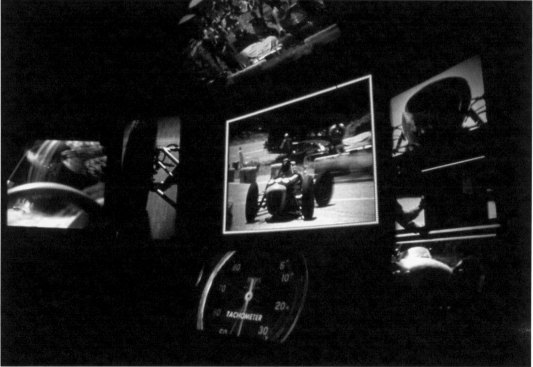

Top: The multiple screens.
Bottom: "Think" on screen.

problem, and then we have some that we call projected geometry related really to computers because you cannot feed into a computer a point in space; it has no way of handling that information. However, a computer can handle the data on the projection of this.

SPEAKER *Why did you have a number of screens, all the different pictures?*

CE I am so glad you asked. We have done multi-screen pictures before. We started with the very large one we did of Moscow. The purpose of the film was by showing multi-images. We were talking about a freeway and an overpass which showed seven. There were four on the top and three on the bottom, and the four measured half the length of a football field. So that, in a sense, it reinforced the statement. There were very few words because we felt that whatever the Russians had received, words they had received plenty, and images might be a better route to go, especially since by reinforcing it with many, you gave it a kind of credibility. We played the game straight. That is, we used real things in a real way. If someone could see all this traffic, any Russian in his right mind would say, "If our ambition was to have a car for every man, woman, and child—forget it!" [Laughter] A lot of rather negative things like this came through if you were quick enough.

Now I said that we are going to do something for IBM which IBM would logically do for itself and that is to create a device which combated the concept of a thin line of communication, the words becoming a thin line of communication which my words, so far from occupying your receptive channels, if you are not falling asleep it is a wonder, because, you now, you people have a tendency— and this is the way they brainwash people; that is, to cut our communication so that they begin to hallucinate and they feed in information. Reading in a lecture is a classic example, because the communication is so thin that even though you are fascinated with the subject, you often, or I often fall asleep.

So we were trying to combat this by giving simultaneously information on many of these screens.

Now the information is related, although it did not always seem to be, but at one point one thing would relate to the other and that relationship would form the essence of the idea.

SPEAKER *It kept the audience visually on their toes?*

CE It kept them visually on their toes because it was like when you drive down the street, you think you only look at one thing at a time, but it would be suicide if you did. No doubt you are aware of all this.

But ideas are built by these relationships, and the thing was that we took a World's Fair audience and held them. I do not know if at the end they applauded because they were relieved or what, but they were responsive. We held them with one subject and that was the concept of an abstract market, and this was a fair-going audience. But we kept building the ideas by these related images so that it was not really a trick.

Now, the next step was to take the idea, and in the IBM laboratory the same concept is being used for theoretical mathematicians having to present a certain concept to another group, and we use this technique to present some fairly sophisticated

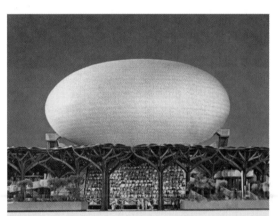

Soar 50 feet into a fascinating new world at the IBM Pavilion

WHAT goes on inside that huge dome atop the IBM Pavilion? Come and find out. Awaiting you is one of the Fair's *most talked about experiences.*

1. You enter a shaded garden with paths suspended in space. You arrive at the "People Wall," and soon you are soaring into a fantastic new world called the "Information Machine."

2. Here, a new kind of living picture entertainment comes to you from nine separate screens. It puts you inside the mind of a racing car driver at 120 miles an hour. You will explore the mysteries of a woman's mind as she plans the seating of a dinner party. Don't be surprised if your *own* mind stretches a bit, as you see how computers use your own everyday way of

reasoning to solve some of the universe's most mystifying riddles.

3. Then, return to earth for fascinating puppet shows. Visit Scholar's Walk. Give a computer the date of your birth. Instantly, it will print out the news headlines of the day you were born—a souvenir to take home.

4. Why are you sometimes lucky, and other times unlucky? The Probability Machine will explain it.

5. There's much, much more that will keep you talking and *thinking.* Continuous shows. Everything's free. Look for the IBM Pavilion. It's just to the left of the main entrance.

IBM

IBM Pavilion advertisement, *Popular Science*, 1964. Private collection, Los Angeles.

ideas. So that little thing you saw a flash of was the beginning of not just of an entertainment device, but a way of communicating information within a company, and the thing worked pretty well.

The device, the big gimmick, was to have an audience—this room holds not more than 200 and there were 500 people on that thing, and "whoom" they went up into this egg.

Now, the beauty of this was that surely it was a device which in showbiz you call a marquee, but the people became the marquee and they entertained the people that were looking at them and they felt as though they were part of it because they were indeed being looked at and then they rose into the auditorium and they never had to walk in.

Sometimes in delivering an idea, a notion, you almost have to build a false world, and if you can build a world that is not the ordinary world in which the person lives, he becomes less distracted. This we did by bringing him up into a going show and then, of course, they left the same way.

That is the 5,000-word explanation to a 10-word question. [Laughter] But I appreciate your asking because the notion was a little bit more serious than it seemed.

SPEAKER *I suppose your biggest task was to decide what you would show on these screens all the time?*

CE This is again the thing. I would point out that we were not setting out to entertain or to please, because this is a trap if there ever was one. It is a trap every time, because then you start to build in an anxiety which can only lead to kinds of, you know, originality for its own sake. So we did not fall into this trap mainly because it is tough enough to think just how do you explain a concept like this. So then you begin to build up and talk about details of it. . . . [Slides were then shown.]

I do not know if you could see any of the pictures, but it is interesting that on the sets and sometimes making the lousiest picture you can imagine, the most beautiful things will happen, and you just regret the fact that nobody sees them. . . . There is a saying that after they have shot the fifteenth take and everything is going wrong and everybody is sort of crippled and you are just about to start again, somebody will say, "The blood will never show." And so it is with the work that we do. I hope that too much of the blood did not show on this performance and thank you very much.

Sources: Charles Eames, "Thoughts on Design," speech, IPC Graphex '65, London, October 1965, Part II: Speeches and Writings series, Charles and Ray Eames Papers, Manuscript Division, Library of Congress, Washington, D.C. *Design Journal* 202 (October 1965): 71.

A Twenty-Five-Year Appraisal

To celebrate *Interiors*'s twenty-fifth birthday, the magazine has invited the nation's most influential design figures to take a substantive look at the field today: Where does it stand, where is it heading.

CHARLES EAMES Any questions—thus any answers—are tempered by the time of life they are asked—whatever cycle you are in at the time . . . after a decade of neat, beautiful rectilinear drawings and somebody shows you squiggles, you fall upon squiggles as the answer to the world.

But as to your question about the effect of affluence . . .

It turns the design field into a field of cultural boobytraps unparalleled in the history of man. For the insensitive consumer, it all but rules out any possibility of acquiring a sensitivity or any lasting enjoyment. For the sensitive one, it is a satiating experience to the point of panic.

Amounts of current information are greater and more difficult to cope with but somehow not as satiating. Example—Beautifully printed art books that would have become a treasured part of our lives thirty years ago are now so commonplace that unless we are attacking a specific research problem with high resolve, a visit to an art bookstore can be a dizzy and disorienting experience. Another example—I visited a good toy store this morning— satiated? It was sick-making. I longed for the desert—even though quite a few of the things in other times could have been treasures. Among the great and elegant design exceptions is a toy produced this year that has swept the country. What is it? A small bouncing ball—Superball.

Affluence offers the kind of freedom I am deeply suspicious of. It offers freedom from restraint, and virtually it is impossible to do something without restraints. If you look through history at the great things, of all times, the greatest were produced where the conditions of restraint were so great that there was relatively little choice—like the obsidian knife of the Aztec, a play of Euripides.

Available dollars open up choices. We as a society are not prepared for the problem of choice . . . few painters know how to cover a very great space.

Increasingly, technology is a lessening limitation. You don't think this offers a new freedom?

We seem to be indiscriminately trying it on everything, and from many standpoints it works— from other standpoints it makes havoc. From a sociological standpoint, I suppose, we are on the verge of starting to learn how to use it. From the cultural standpoint, the freedom is like a hurricane. It becomes not a question of what we are doing with "this new freedom"—it is the appalling fact of what *it* is doing with us.

What is the designer's responsibility in influencing our society towards better design?

A design specialist certainly has no greater responsibility than his counterpart in other responsible walks of life.

With the hair-raising build-up of communications into a technology and into apparent affluence, the resulting hurricane demands (for survival's sake) some sweeping design changes across the whole scene—a redesign of our structure of education, our philosophies, our views of nature and conservation, and the ideas and environment that might make for a rich life. . . . The problem is to build in the kind of understanding that will find security in change; the large number of choices available requires a more secure person to make value judgments. The question will become not "How do we do it?" but "Should we do it?" The responsibility, stated as a design responsibility, may be much the same in all these cases. As much as possible, it is our responsibility to restudy and restate each aspect of the problem in the light of all available past and current information. If one adds to this, the responsibility of considering the next larger (or smaller) aspect of the problem, there is a chance of avoiding the traps that lie in blind substitution of new materials (or ideas) for old—and surprises that come from too hasty innovation.

The mass speed and frequency of innovation in our time make it an entirely new phenomenon. Its surprises can be funny or tragic, become apparent immediately or not for generations. Effects of detergents on waterways are an example—and the foam plastic cup that seems a great innovation for coffee time—until its nonheat-conducting nature causes us to scald our throats.

What are and what should be the individual and collective goals of the profession?

Some time ago when Richard Feynman (recent Nobel physicist) was talking about what the individual scientist could hope to accomplish in the world of science, he had no grand illusion. He said the best one could hope for was to select an area and then some little piece of that area and with all his heart pick away at it.

It is much the same with design but perhaps the greatest lesson to be learned from the good individual scientist or architect or teacher is in the capacity they have for *really caring*. This is the lesson.

Whatever the *collective* goal of the design profession is, it is probably very wholesome. But the collective task of the profession is more specific. In the world of freedom and affluence which the first two questions suggest, the task will be to work toward finding operational constraints that will make meaningful design programs possible.

Freedom and affluence usually mean freedom to do any imaginable amount of ugliness because they are seldom accompanied by clues as to what is appropriate enough to result in beauty. Example: The problem for designing either an oil cracking plant or jet transport would consist of a great list of functional and economic restraints—and the probability of a good and handsome result would be high. The program for designing a monument or a World's Fair pavilion which would reflect freedom and affluence would have a low probability of a great solution. The great cities and great objects of the past came into being under great restraints—social, technical, and economic. How much freedom for innovation did the builders of the Taos pueblos enjoy—or the builders of Cuzco—or the makers of Chartres' stained glass? Los Angeles is an example of a city built without restraints, either traditional or material. The collective goal of the design profession might be to find the guideline of restraint that exists in all this so-called freedom.

Whom do we try to influence? The young? The elite? Government? Industry?

If you substitute thinkers for elite, we are and want to be influenced as much as influence—and when we work with any of these groups or combinations of them, we do so by finding some area where our interests genuinely overlap and then work on these areas. If the overlap is a genuine one, the influences on each other will most likely cause the area of mutual interest to grow.

There is a kind of machine that we could build that would approach having one hundred percent influence and could provide much in the way of the restraints we need. Of course, it would take about thirty-five years to get it going, but if we could survive that long it would be worth it. The machine I am suggesting is the unit of a human generation. The trouble is that many of the tools and the really raw material for building this new force of citizens have been tragically neglected.

Jerome Bruner has said that some relevant aspect of any great idea can be taught at any age. I believe this to be true, and I believe it to include those rare and precious qualities that give some people the capacity for caring. This naturally focuses attention on the very early years of life and this in turn highlights qualities that may only be built in those few years after birth. When we think of those people we have met who might be capable of leading a rich life regardless of the circumstances of affluence and deprivation in which they might find themselves, I suspect we are recognizing one of those qualities rarely acquired except in those early years, a quality that will be in rapidly increasing demand for some years to come.

When you are morally committed as you obviously are to bettering the human condition, how do you give ordinal importance to the clients and projects you become involved with?

My ideas and behavior have not changed since the mid-thirties. Affluence, or having a wide choice of projects, has nothing to do with them. I get involved in things of value to me, as I have always done, and don't get involved in things I do not value.

What are some of the projects you are currently involved with?

Well, I am working with IBM on establishing a communications center, which will primarily be concerned with films as educational devices . . . and for the sisters from the Convent of the Immaculate Heart in Hollywood (California), we are examining the role of a small college. This involves a study of both program and buildings. Lots of mistakes have been made in small colleges, with buildings that end up as monuments when they should be as open and fluid as possible. . . . Traditionally, we don't drive nails in the classroom wall. Well, it may well serve the function of a classroom to do so. That's what we'll look for.

For the Smithsonian, I have done a bicentennial film and will be doing some other things—the study of methods of diffusion of knowledge. It is a terrible problem, how to make ideas meaningful.

I am also working on some school furniture, upgrading and refining and consolidating dormitory furniture.

Source: Priscilla Dunhill, "25 Years of Appraisal: Charles Eames," *Interiors* 125, no. 4 (November 1965): 129–132.

Charles Eames and Sister Corita Kent of
Immaculate Heart College. Photograph
by Bob Specht.

CHARLES EAMES

Immaculate Heart

Editor's note: This was written in response to an announcement that Immaculate Heart College of Los Angeles needed a new campus. It was later published in a community calendar given away by the Los Angeles Times.

The Sisters of the Immaculate Heart occupy a peculiar place in the heart of the community in which they work.

The uniqueness of this place in our hearts becomes evident when we know that they will be torn from (what we on the outside have considered) their comfortable quarters.

The significance of the move and the potentials in the new relationship to the other colleges at Claremont have all the dramatic expectancy and risk that we have learned to expect from immaculate hearts.

However, a new college means buildings and buildings mean architecture and architecture means architects and it all makes us break out in a cold sweat.

If only they were moving into an evacuated army barrack or an abandoned monastery or some really great old warehouse—then we would have complete faith.

But architecture on order is a different thing, and those architects who could subjugate themselves to the real and evolving needs of such a community maintaining a relentless concern for quality— would be very rare.

What we, who love Immaculate Heart, want for the college is easier to taste than it is to say—

We guard ourselves against wants that could be hazardous—such as expressions of form or structure or monumentality or even an over-emphasis on beauty—

We want a college that will shelter those within it on the sad days as well as the gay days—

A system of buildings that will not be embarrassed by complete changes of program—

A structure that can be scotch taped, nailed into, thumb tacked, and still not lose its dignity—

Spaces that will welcome and enhance teaching machines as well as celebrations and pageants—

Materials that will not tend to become shoddy and will still show a response to care.

One would hope that the experience of the buildings would seem so natural that the question of their having been designed could never come up.

We want these buildings to demand something of those who enter them and to enrich and shelter those who remain within.

We now know why gurus choose caves.

Source: Charles Eames, statement, Immaculate Heart College, February 14, 1967, Part II: Office File (1960–1969) series, Charles and Ray Eames Papers, Manuscript Division, Library of Congress, Washington, D.C.

CHARLES EAMES AND RAY EAMES

"Excellence"

Editor's note: "Excellence, G.E.M., or Government, Education, and Management" was a 345-image, 3-screen (115-pass) slide show.

ONE CAN BE SURE that in the past when a man would rise to the point of producing work of great quality, it was not through any conscious attempt to excel but rather because he *cared* about what he was doing—he was committed to his work.

This has become something rare—because being committed means becoming involved and to become involved means giving something of one-self. It is only the rare ones today who seem to care that much.

Yet, that quality that makes for excellence—that commitment—is more important to us *today* on a daily operational basis than perhaps ever before.

At least one of the reasons this is true is quite simple.

The nature of the problems we face changes even as we work with them. We cannot tell from what disciplines or from what art the preparation for the next step will come.

We cannot fall back on the lore of the art because that lore does not yet exist.

There is, however, a tradition that is held in common by natural philosophers, explorers, pioneer woodsmen—anyone who in his daily life has been compelled to face new problems. That is a tradition of respect and concern for the properties and the quality of everything in the world around them.

To excel in the structuring of a problem we must be committed to a concern for quality in everything around us. We must learn to care deeply.

Sometimes it is also good to be reminded of the many areas where concerns for quality have been felt and of the worlds around us where quality and excellence can be perceived. In some cases they are quite sophisticated and in some they are simple and even naive—but in each case someone cared.

Source: Charles Eames and Ray Eames, narration, "G.E.M. (Government, Education, and Management)" slide show (originally titled "Excellence"), IBM sales convention, Miami, March 18, 1967, Part II: Projects series, Charles and Ray Eames Papers, Manuscript Division, Library of Congress, Washington, D.C.

A selection of "Excellence" slides.

Gio Ponti

PONTI IS one of the rare ones—an architect who considers everything as architecture and has practiced architecture in all his work. He has both the skills and the lore of the art—perhaps a superabundance of the lore, but his concern with lore grows naturally from his willingness and need to become completely involved in anything he does. His masteries of skill are those that seem to come automatically to the special few who have the capacity for really caring. Perhaps what strikes us most is Ponti's remarkable ability to live and relive every aspect of every experience that each possible person will have in any situation he constructs. Have him introduce you to a project on which he is working—a model or an object or an idea—and you will find yourself experiencing, through Ponti, the reactions, the pulls, the needs, and the pleasures of many different people. Your own notions of function will have broadened considerably, and you will feel that somehow the project itself has developed a little farther. You know that every drawing, every costume, every object he has built, every loving action has gone much the same route—the examination of spaces, of the city, at home, working in theatre, with exhibitions, with machines, and in the freedom and the discipline of producing "DOMUS," and in instilling the same love and the same eye in his daughter, Lisa. In this process of design, or growth, where he anticipates and relives the experiences that others will have—in this enthusiasm—he surely thinks of all people as rich human beings possessing those same capabilities and sensitiveness to experience that are his own. This is the only way—and this is the secret.

Source: Charles Eames, "Foreword: The Expression of Gio Ponti," *Design Quarterly*, no. 69/70 (1967): 3.

"Gio Ponti," *Design Quarterly*. no. 69/70.

CHARLES EAMES

"Art and Science" Speech

I THINK of our work as essentially that of tradesmen: the tools we use are often connected with the arts, but we use them to solve very specific problems which we or others may define. In this same way I think of architects as tradesmen—and it doesn't seem an unflattering idea.

I would hold "artist" as title to be earned—one that can be earned in any field. Being trained in the arts doesn't make one an artist any more than the study of philosophy makes one a philosopher or science a scientist.

One of the questions of our time that will not be answered for perhaps another thirty or forty years is "Who are the artists of our time?" The chances that they would happen to be the products of our art schools would seem exceedingly low. There is just no way to tell.

Therefore, to hear anyone refer to himself as an *artist* immediately gives rise to great suspicions. As a group, painters and sculptors tend to use the term "artist" loosely—though of course there are artists among them. I suppose that most painters and sculptors are also tradesmen—some entertainers, and some talented ones clowns, acting the role of clown with all the pleasure-giving mixed emotions, satire, and artistry that the role of clown can provide.

There seems to be a growing conspiracy to bring painters and sculptors together with good people now working in scientific and technical fields—somehow, with the hope that the former will gain new media with which to express themselves and the latter will gain some sense of aesthetic values from which their work will profit.

The conspirators may have the best intentions, but to anyone familiar with both the groups involved, it is a frightening idea—and the reasons for apprehension are real.

The world we think of when we think of science and technology includes a vast amount of information handling and problem structuring that is also largely based on particular sets of restraints—real and difficult to define.

We have every right to hope that out of this rich mixture of facility and need will, in time, come clues to values and aesthetics appropriate to our changing world. We expect these values to come as a logical extension to the disciplines employed.

We might also expect this to be a long time, because, with few expections, scientists, technicians, mathematicians are culturally an innocent lot. At the sound of the word "art" they are most apt to completely abandon the disciplines that serve them so well and adopt a sentimental and romantic attitude. Putting an unnatural mystique around anything having to do with form or color—the danger is one of bringing a serious infection into this fertile but innocent atmosphere before it has a chance to produce.

The painter and sculptor are for the most part uneducated. Even when they are pretty skillful in setting up their own restraints, they are likely to lack sufficient education in the scientific disciplines to work at all meaningfully within them—and the innocents will possibly mistake the lack of meaning for part of the mystique of art.

The more serious cause of infection comes from the preoccupation that dominates the work and training of painters and sculptors. Freedom to express and originality for its own sake have been strangely included as part of the idea of creativity itself.

This has never been a part of the things of great aesthetic value—of beauty—that have come out of the past, and there is little reason to believe that it will have much part in producing the things that those in the future will hold beautiful.

If the role of the painter and sculptor is tradesman, more urgently needed work can be done if the base of his education is broadened. If the role is clown, a highly valued though not always recognized service can be performed in the pleasure it gives, in the irritant it provides, in the insights it reveals, and the reflection it holds up.

But please don't louse up the innocents from whom we need so much. "Who are the artists of our time?" more parallels the question "What are the restraints?" than it does "What are the freedoms?"

Source: Charles Eames, "Art and Science," speech, U.S. Embassy, London, March 1968, Part II: Speeches and Writings series, Charles and Ray Eames Papers, Manuscript Division, Library of Congress, Washington, D.C.

100 Words on Symptoms of Creativity

Charles Eames to A. C. Spectorsky, *Playboy*, Chicago
June 20, 1968

Dear Mr. Spectorsky:

Here are the one hundred words on sources or symptoms of creativity—I've often suspected that it must take a good case of the guilts to keep the creative types going at the rate they do—but one thing is certain—the really creative ones are much more at home with the restraints that surround their work than they are with the freedoms. Even when the restraints are not apparent they are apt to concoct some special ones as a guide.

They are also absolute whizzes at finding neat relationships between what might seem to be extremely dissimilar events—an art which punsters, poets, painters, and scientists appear to have in common.

If by any chance you publish, please pay directly to NOW, Inc., Neighbors of Watts, Suite 208A, 9229 Sunset Blvd., Los Angeles 90069, California.

Thanks again for the best in airplane reading—
Charles Eames

Source: Charles Eames to A. C. Spectorsky, June 20, 1968, Private collection, Los Angeles.

"The Eames Design"

EDWARD P. MORGAN *It is Sunday evening, April 6th [1969]. And this is* PBL*'s second season.* The Public Broadcast Laboratory, *an experiment in public television. Tonight, "The Eames Design." Chief correspondent Edward P. Morgan visits Charles Eames, architect, designer, filmmaker, and exception to most rules. . . .*

CHARLES EAMES You ask great questions. And yet sometimes I feel that my answers sound like the talk on a David Susskind show.

The result of being asked questions or actually any form of an interview is a kind of a metamorphosis in which it turns me from a sort of a simple, unassuming guy into a monster full of great bits of—of wisdom, Mr. Know-It-All of the Century. With Ray it's—it's no less violent, but it's simpler. It's pure paralysis. With me it's a running off of the mouth and a sort of sweaty palm and an animated gesture.

EPM *Charles, where did the classic Eames chair come from? Did it come to you in a flash as you were shaving one morning, or how did the thing develop?*

CE It sort of came to me in a 30-year flash. I hope you're thinking of the same chair I'm thinking of.

EPM *Yes, I'm sure I am.*

CE I'm thinking of the molded plywood chair with—

EPM *Exactly.*

CE That came over a—came over a long period of time. And it's no break from the rectilinear. God, if you think of what Mies had been doing, as well as Aalto, and certainly chairs in the past . . . it was very, very fluid.

If it formed any kind of a break, it was one, of course, which we weren't conscious at the time, although we were intent on doing a piece of furniture which, when you looked at it, if you got anything from it visually, that what you got had a direct relation to the way that it was made.

EPM *The late, great Eero Saarinen and his work are bound up with much of Eames's work. Washington's Dulles airport has special warmth for Charles Eames, not just because he designed its furniture, but also because his friend Eero designed Dulles.*

CE Eero, at the time he did Dulles, was an amateur airport designer. And I think that there's a thing when an architect does the thing too many times, he loses his amateur standing and no longer has the ability to even look at a problem in a fresh way. So that when Eero did Dulles, he was looking at airports for the first time, not as a professional airport designer. I think that has a lot to do with the way it turned out.

Eero's notion was to completely remove the aircraft from the terminal itself so that in sense they could put all the services in line and, through the mobile lounge, go out and service the aircraft, which would mean that the second, third, fourth generation jets—no matter what form they took—they could be serviced.

We did the film for Eero on Dulles Airport. Eero was having really a tough time with the official groups involved, including the presidents of airlines—Smith, Rickenbacker—getting them together to listen to the idea. And he said, "You know, it takes three hours. And they just can't sit still for it." And he said, "There's going to be another meeting in a month."

"And if we had a film that could state the concept of the Dulles Airport—the thing we have in mind—if we could state it in 15 minutes, God, it would be great." And so we spent a whole day with Eero before he left. And then we went back to the coast and, using his notions, put together in a sense what was this concept film. It happened to run 10 minutes because you can get 10 minutes on one reel.

EPM *Aren't you using the medium and the techniques of the film to crowd into it lucidly a whole lot—a whole flock of ideas—forms and definitions—that otherwise would take you all night to explain?*

CE It may end up this way. I think maybe one of the things that causes it to come about is that audiences scare the hell out of me. And the thought of holding them for an extra second is so—it's so terrifying that we do, I think, in that spirit work to sort of hone things and sort of get them done. If I walk into a theatre and there's a group that's going to look at a film, I quick add up in my mind the number of man hours, how long it took them to get from home and—and this is the major—the responsibility. And it scares you. One of the reasons we arrived at those mathematical peep shows where you can try to get a significant idea across in two minutes, not so much as a tour de force, but we thought, well, if it's two minutes, maybe they won't mind seeing it again because sometimes it's good to see things twice.

EPM *In a tiny office swirling with an unbelievable blizzard of things, she sat concentrating on a sweep of subjects, which would seemingly choke a computer. Ray Eames's stamp is on every film, every exhibition, every piece of furniture conceived in the shop.*

CE In the office here that's composed of a lot of—a lot of people, everybody doubling in brass, looking at problems—Ray, you know, really usually looks at a problem, and the contribution doesn't have to do with the juxtaposition of colors. It usually has to do with the consistency of structure. And I think that this kind of function is not only appropriate to the function of a real painter, but it sort of tells the kind of training and instincts that she has.

RAY EAMES And I don't consider that I've ever left painting. I'm also so thankful to have been interested at an early age in many things which one draws upon actually as a painter and which we draw on every day.

EPM *Charles Eames is his own severest critic. Recently he had an exhibition at the Smithsonian on cities. It was fascinating—too fascinating. People were gripped by a blown-up photograph of an earthquake in Santiago, beguiled by a balloon nudging the ceiling, intrigued by a 19th century shot of Manhattan. But they missed the point. Through the medium of still photography, Eames had wanted to bring the city and its problems into focus. His own verdict: he failed. So now he is translating the whole thing to film, hoping this time to deliver a clearer message.*

CE How do you create images that make the problems of the city seem real and dynamic—I mean, not static images, but images in time? What can you do to really make the problems seem real so that you can sense some function or get an idea of how to even attack them? . . .

One of the things that seems to be common among those who tend to not be miserable is the ability to have concern, get pleasure from, and respect things—objects, people, things—that are not of immediate value to them—respect for the thing that isn't going to pay off tomorrow because

tomorrow's problems are going to be different. And the things that come to your rescue are often the things you learn to respect when you had no idea they were going to be of value. If you want to take a real look at this pleasure, you take the job to do a film—let's say a film we're now doing for the Smithsonian, which is under the sponsorship of Westinghouse. It seemed like a very interesting project. And we thought, "Well, maybe even we might make some money on it this time, you know, because we've done a lot of basic work, and this is pulling it together."

We began to get into it and got more and more done, and said, "Well, maybe we won't make any money, but it'll be a good film because we . . . [now] know it's going to cost more than we thought to do it." And then we realized the material isn't quite so good. We say, "God, maybe it's not a good piece of film. Maybe it won't make any money. But, you know, at least it'll be a respectable statement."

At the moment we're wondering whether it's going to be a respectable statement. And if it goes the normal course, tomorrow we're worrying whether we'll be run out of town on a rail. And this is sort of a real picture of what the fun is like. And it is tremendous pleasure. But, boy, you're laying it on the line every time. It could just be a colossal bomb.

EPM *Do you get the feeling sometimes that you're really working in a rarefied atmosphere, well-paced though the discipline may be, and sensitive though you are, that you are sort of inured to the problems that society is making for itself? Or do you relate directly, at least in the way you think?*

CE Well, we live in the society. We are concerned about society. And we may not know what good is. But we see in some cases what bad is. And we assume that good is the kind of order that we have known. And in that we may be in error.

But I think that this is true of anything that you do. The aquarium project is an example where we're not essentially marine biologists, but we see in the building of a national aquarium another opportunity to get past the more superficial aspects of a society into some of the disciplines because in many respects, the young people are right.

The values are to be questioned, particularly those things having to do with physical stuff—the intrinsic values of things because first place, if those are the only values, there's not enough to go around. And a lot of people aren't going to share them. But in the case of the—the pleasures and the concepts of a discipline like marine biology, it's like the fishes and the loaves.

EPM *What is a 10-year-old boy or a 50-year-old mother going to get out of watching these animals in this environment that they wouldn't get in the old-fashioned type aquarium?*

CE Well, naturally you can't look at an octopus without getting a little bit of the "Gee whiz." I mean it's built into an octopus.

On the other hand, and a guy that is functioning like this, if you back it up in such a way as to say all right, let's now look at all these strange creatures in the way they propel themselves, the way they move through the water. Now you're beginning to sneak up on the attitude that a scientist might take by isolating a little function. And if you look, this fellow propels himself this way; then the next step is to find that there's a relation to the way he moves to the way he has to make his living, his peculiarities.

So that then the next step is, well, God, these strange attributes of these creatures is not a capricious thing on the part of nature. But it's part of the system of development that supports this particular kind of life. And once you're down that road, why, the riches are endless. It's a big deal.

EPM *Eames himself philosophizes with a self-effacing grin.*

CE Much of our energy is like the guy in vaudeville that has the plates going. And—and he's intent on getting 30 plates spinning at one time. But part of the process is quickly being aware of the ones that are winding down, keeping them spinning, and going to put another one and it's spinning and—and keeping these all in the air at once. And in a sense, this is—this is what's happening because we are concerned about some of the toys that we did some time ago, the furniture, and certain introduction of films, and keeping up certain intensities and validity in these all at the same time. And one begins to sort of die down. And you go and work at it. Now, it's the concern about the computer techniques, and methods of even stating problems in relation to modern techniques is a concern that came out of architecture.

I think that the common denominator is structure.

Source: Charles Eames and Ray Eames, interview by Edward P. Morgan, "The Eames Design," *The Public Broadcast Laboratory*, PBS, April 6, 1969.

"The Eames Design"

.

John Benson to Charles Eames, Coyote, California
April 7, 1969

Dear Mr. and Mrs. Eames,

Seven minutes ago I just finished watching a documentary on *Public Broadcast Laboratory* on your work. I think that I tuned in about halfway through the program, but the half I did see scrambled my concepts almost completely.

Perhaps I shouldn't say scrambled, since now I realize that most of them were pretty muddled in the first place. What I loved about the program was that it articulated and altered a few of my concepts so beautifully and clearly that I would very much like to do it again. Because of this, I would like it very much if you would send a catalog of your works (be they math, computers, cities, people, *anything*) and information on how to get them if possible for the school I go to. I know a few teachers and students that would probably learn a lot from them (as I want to) if we could just pry the funds loose from the school district.

Now that the humble request part is over, I want to ask you a few questions—

I. Are you crazy? Hardly any people I know look at things the way you did in the films I saw. Beautiful thinking—concepts like that have been extremely hard to come by, at least for me, indicating that most people don't do that. Because you did it so well, and because I like it a lot, I want to know how you learned to think like that; i.e., how you went crazy—how you can look at the real nitty gritty without getting bogged down in the conceptual superstructure like most of us.

II. How do you make a computer part of a man? I'm just a beginner at computers and I feel like part of the computer, not vice versa. At the teletype end I feel more like the world's slowest input/output device than the new renaissance man that thinks and learns with his computer. How do you fit in with yours?

III. Do you think your general line of attack is somewhat the same as Marshall McLuhan's, even if the content is different? I mean your attacking previously unquestioned ideas afresh with a different view intimately interrelated with the media complications you find in communicating it.

IV. What do you think about Computer Aided Instruction? Multi-Image, Multi-Media approaches? Do there exist any fairly developed curricula in these areas ready to test on real, live kids?

If you have time to answer, please send it to:
John Benson
Box 288
Coyote, California 95013
God bless and keep you full of beautiful concepts.
John Benson

Charles Eames to John Benson
April 21, 1969

Dear John Benson:

Many thanks for your immediate and interesting response to the PBL show.

The nature of your questions should lead one to believe you are well down the road to answering them yourself in a pretty satisfactory way.

I am mailing you a history chart that shows the lives of great mathematicians in relationship to some peripheral events in history, and one of the things we have done for IBM in printed form for Mathematica in Los Angeles, Chicago, and Seattle.

Many of the films we have done are for IBM, and enclosed is a list of those as well as some others that your school (you did not say which one?) could obtain, providing they have an experienced projectionist and projector in good condition.

You no doubt have read Norbert Wiener's *The Human Use of Human Beings*. It is now old, I suppose, by some standards, but it gives you an idea of the perspective that such a guy can have.

Computer instruction will be really great when it arrives, and at the moment there are not many programs that can do what they could do.

Charles Eames

Source: John Benson to Charles Eames, April 7, 1969; Charles Eames to John Benson, April 21, 1969, Container I:11, Folder 13, Charles and Ray Eames Papers, Manuscript Division, Library of Congress, Washington, D.C.

"Eames"

AN INTERVIEW

CHARLES EAMES IS an architect, but he became world famous because of some chairs. Though he travels all the time, he is seldom in the Netherlands. But on Friday, the 30th of May, he showed some of his famous movies to the architectural students of Delft and to an audience in Amsterdam, in the municipal museum. He makes many movies, together with his wife, Ray, principally in the educational field.

Eames, who lives under the smoke of Los Angeles, is the prototype of the modern, all-around designer. Thanks to the fact that IBM is one of his oldest and most important clients, he has a computer connection in his office, which he can switch on any time and connect to some computers stationed in New York and use them to solve certain problems that could present themselves in his work. (He can do this at any time necessary.) Our contributor Simon M. Pruys had a talk with Mr. Eames.

Seldom one meets a man who is so unpretentious. My question, if one can talk about something as an "Eames-aesthetics," should really not be asked anymore. But he does answer it:

"If one compares my chairs with those of Rietveld, then mine are much more naive. Rietveld started out from intellectual conceptions to which he subordinated the facts and the reality. We, on the other hand, were completely taken in by the facts, by the immediate reality, for example, that a chair in the first place is something (a gadget) to sit on and therefore should be comfortable. Aesthetical considerations did not come first with us. To mention the so-called Eames-aesthetics, you should not forget that Ray and I on purpose withdrew from the so-called New York aesthetical climate. We really wanted to turn our backs on the artistic centre of New York. We went to the West Coast. Just because nobody knew us over there! And this was a very important decision. Since that time we really have never had a client close to home, closer than 3000 kilometers."

ALGEMEEN HANDELSBLAD I suppose, Mr. Eames, that you really never had the intention of being revolutionary in aesthetics.

CHARLES EAMES No...

AH *Did you ever have some design philosophy?*

CE Yes, but I do want to describe that. I am all for maintaining the natural situation; designing is really nothing else than reacting to unnatural situations. Only when one experiences something unnatural one reacts. The great difference with earlier times is that we are now forced to make choices. In reality it is unnatural for man to make choices. In traditional society man never had to make a choice, as everything was mapped out beforehand. Actually you were not able to do anything wrong; you could only go in one direction with everything you undertook. Nowadays we have to choose every moment from many alternatives, and it is very easy to make a wrong choice. That is why Los Angeles is such a mess. The people were not prepared to have to make a free choice in determining their environment....

This problem would have been unthinkable fifty years ago. What we lack is a more or less consequent and stable set of standards on which we can test our eventual decision. The possibility of making a choice has become too large. Some years ago they made an investigation in California to try and measure creativity. A lot of important designers were involved in this. They were given, amongst other things, a large amount of tiles in all kinds of colors. The assignment was to make a design with a limited amount of tiles—I believe twelve. Each man had to work on his own, without knowing what the others were doing. The story goes that Vernon DeMars came proudly forward with the information that he had limited himself to the use of the three basic colors. The somewhat affected and self-confident Philip Johnson thought this already too much and presented a black-white design, but he was scored off by Eero Saarinen, who wiped everything off the table with the remark: "All white, what else...?" The moral of this story is that man creates his own limitations.

AH *So we can say that there are two kinds of aesthetics: one for the in crowd, the trained eye, and one for the taste of the public. Is it necessary that the public is educated in this designer's aesthetics, or is it the designer who has to be educated?*

CE The designer has to be educated. Imagine that the public had been educated in the aesthetics of the thirties, then we would have had to re-educate them now to get rid of it. Aesthetical education of the public does not interest me at all. I don't like crusades. . . .

The only thing the public has to learn is to have respect for the objects even if they do not always bring profit.

AH *Are there standards to judge these objects by, to see if they are designed well or not?*

CE When you think about design as the bringing together of a number of materials and parts, letting them interact—and not as the expressions of your own personality—the demand must be made that it answers the purpose, no matter how complex. This can also mean that a couch, on which you sit, should be able to satisfy your sense of feeling, and so it has to be soft and supple.

There is also a psychological function present in the object, but we as yet do not know much about this. In any case an object should never betray its user. A chair that radiates an ostentatious cheerfulness and gaiety could let you down when you are depressed. This I call a betrayal.

AH *What do you think of engaging of more rational methods, such as the usage of computers [in] designing . . . in contrast with the traditional intuitive method?*

CE This contrast does not evoke the slightest conflict with me. You have to use the rational methods as far as possible. You must be a fool to decide in favor of less information instead of more.

Source: Simon M. Pruys, "Eames," trans. Jordan Sowle, *Algemeen Handelsblad*, Amsterdam (June 14, 1969).

"Sitting Back with Charles Eames"

EAMES CHAISE

CHARLES EAMES has never found the innovative aspects of his furniture design particularly interesting.

"The structure of the thing, and the use to which it will be put, make innovation seem very incidental. If a piece of furniture goes into a good room or surroundings, it would more or less disappear. It serves its purpose best when it is not the subject of attention in a room. I flatter myself in feeling this has already come about in some of my designs. . . .

"I don't think you'll see any design breakthroughs. I hope we might have a performance breakthrough. One of the problems is to attempt to use metal in an honest way. I've always looked at Oriental lacquers as an integral part of the piece, whereas paints and enamels are more of an applied thing. Lacquers are great to look at and feel. Now we will either cross the threshold or not. We may find a finish that works in the same way with metal. Don't ask me about new lines and curves. I'm more interested in performance and the way things act in the room. . . .

"If there is any underlying theme to my work— whether in film, furniture, or graphics—it comes through as one begins to question any specific aspect of the problem, and it usually comes out in architectural terms."

Eames says too the day-to-day and year-to-year life at his design studio in Venice, Calif., is "absolutely mixed up. The guys making drawings for a chair will be exactly the same guys that work on film. There is no such thing as a furniture department. Our approach is no different, whether we're dealing in furniture or with the National Aquarium in Washington."

The Eames office is doing the general format and display of the aquarium, which will open in 1972. "We're doing all the pedagogy that goes with it, all the films." . . .

Films remain an abiding interest, starting with Eames's early interest in the work of René Clair and coming to modern times with his friendship to director Billy Wilder.

"Billy's influence shows as much in my architecture and furniture as it shows on film. He has a sense of quality and a natural smell of what is phony, and the ability to avoid it. Anyone can learn a lot of lessons from that. Being with him on a set is a naturally invigorating experience. I directed a second unit for him for *The Spirit of St. Louis*. I dug out the research and directed all the events having to do with the building of the original Spirit.

"But there are an awful lot of guys in the world who influenced me: Eliel and Eero Saarinen, Frank Lloyd Wright, Mies van der Rohe, Alvar Aalto, Le Corbusier.

"All were great architects first. They happened to have done furniture secondarily. Most architects have found it gratifying to build furniture. It's frustrating to do buildings, and in furniture they think it's at least at a scale they can control."

Eames, though describing the catchy wordphrases on environmental design as recurring "ad nauseum, and I react to some of it with some nausea," nevertheless finds the idea very encouraging.

"I'm getting to a point where I'm getting hypersensitive to the use of the catch phrase. I suspect the intent to which it's used. But environmental technology is terribly important. The entire aquarium project is based on that, in the way of raising the level of the conversation by involving concern in the balances of ecology. And computer technologies are the only way to make out the rash of information."

Eames is continuing his consulting work for IBM and praises the symbiotic relationship of the computer company with Herman Miller. "Herman Miller was one of the first furniture producers to make extensive use of computing equipment. IBM has established an identity in its use of Herman Miller furniture."

Miller has reacted as the liaison-catalyst. "I really enjoy doing furniture, and I look at it as kind of an unfinished business. When pieces have had the life these pieces have had, they deserve a hell of a lot of attention. The first molded plywood chair in 1946 was one of the longest-lived. It's the only piece that has gotten the attention it deserved. I don't feel the lounge chair did. With the plywood

The production models of the Eames chaise have the finish that Charles Eames describes in this interview.

chair, we designed it over a period of time, doing 50 models, and designed the tools on which it was built. We manufactured the first 5,000 chairs in our studio. I'd like to go back to redo and refine it. Eero had a way of talking about the unsolved problem. He thought nature had never solved the problem of the armpit. He'd look at a piece of architecture, look at its weak point and call it the armpit.

"We continue learning. You can't have lived through the last decade of the growing expres-

sion of youth and retain the same attitudes about the learning process. It has nothing to do with condescending or making youth fully happy. It's a change in a point of view. It's a great pleasure, and it doesn't come as a shock, for it's a pleasure to discover you were wrong. Just think. You may never have discovered it."

Source: Hector Arce, "Sitting Back with Eames," *Home Furnishings Daily* 41, no. 143 (July 20, 1969): 4–5.

Charles and Ray Eames with Richard
Donges examining a model of the
chaise during its development.

Eames Office staff members Richard
Donges and Sam Passalaqua working
on a model of the chaise.

National Aquarium

CORRESPONDENCE

Editor's note: Jerome Seymour Bruner (b. October 1, 1915) is a psychologist who has made significant contributions to human cognitive psychology and cognitive learning theory as well as to history and to the general philosophy of education.

Charles Eames to Jerome Bruner, Cambridge, Massachusetts
October 25, 1969

Dear Jerry:

A note like yours activates a hair-trigger response in the Aquarium Report Department.

The Nixon freeze came just as the finished drawings for the building were going out for bid, however, we are still working on notions for presentation and pedagogy.

I am sending you a report in film form (10 minutes)—I believe you would be interested in seeing how such material can be presented in ten minutes. This was the initial report presented to the secretary, then Stewart Udall.

Among all our reasons for pushing the Aquarium, I will mention two:

It would seem that one of the most sound ways to get a feeling for the delicate balance of a natural ecology is to get to know something of the process of natural selection, and the aquatic life seems a good place to start.

In a time in our world society when those who may covet are increasing fast—and the covetables seem to be getting more and more sparse, it looks as though in twenty years or so, it will be the mastery of concepts, ideas, and disciplines that will be the new covetables.

The coin of that realm is the willingness to give of oneself. Everyone has it, if they are willing to spend it—furthermore, the product divides like the fishes and the loaves, with no degeneration.

As a small (maybe significant) demonstration of the preceding, we are sending you the *Whole Earth Catalog*—is this old stuff in Cambridge?

I will be in New York all next week—sorry not in Cambridge, as it would be nice to get a glimpse of you both. We have just opened an exhibit at the Louvre in Paris and are working on an interesting problem for the U.N.

Charles Eames

Source: Charles Eames to Jerome Bruner, October 25, 1969, Container I:11, Folder 8, Charles and Ray Eames Papers, Manuscript Division, Library of Congress, Washington, D.C.

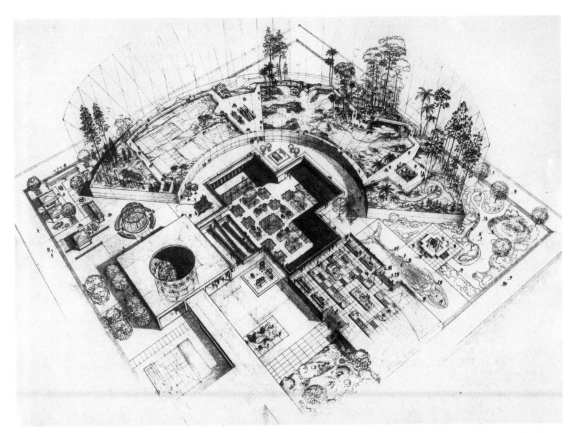

Drawing for the proposed National
Aquarium in Washington, D.C. Designed
by Eames Office and Roche Dinkeloo.

"What Is Design?"

AN EXHIBITION AT THE LOUVRE

In the exhibit, we are trying to show something about a decision that the designer must make when he starts to work for a client. We have found it a very helpful strategy to restrict our own work to subjects that are of genuine and immediate interest to us—and are of equal interest to the client. If we were to work on things or in ways that we knew were not of legitimate concern to both of us, we probably would not be serving our clients, or ourselves, very well.

Throughout the work for the various clients, the unifying force is this common interest, plus a preoccupation with structure which comes from looking at all problems as architectural ones.

The enclosed diagram also includes a critical and changing area that represents the concerns of society as a whole. None of these areas are static. As client and designer get to know each other, they influence each other. As society's needs become more apparent, both client and designer expand their own personal concerns to meet these needs.

(Paragraphs to be used as captions sent to Amic for Louvre catalog—8/29/69)

I. The problems of protecting the natural ecology, and the pleasures of inquiring into the biological process, have made our work on the aquarium a natural extension of this interest.

II. Our involvement in the man-made environment has been largely concentrated on furniture because it is still at the human scale. The problems are still in the details, but at least one can hold them in one's hand.

III. For many years we have used photography as an information tool. As the information we needed to communicate developed greater urgency and complexity, we got more and more involved in the medium of motion picture—multi-image—collections of stills.

IV. Mathematics has the fascination of games and the discipline of philosophy. For both our client and ourselves, it provides a rewarding base from which to attack other problems—particularly those problems where proper structuring and computer technology may help society respond to the special needs of individuals.

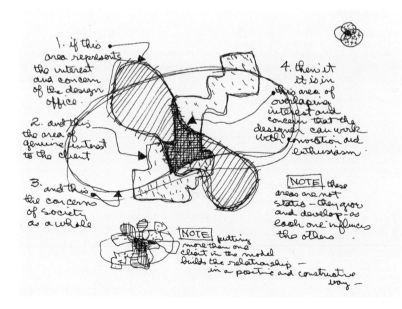

Charles Eames drawing of the design process.

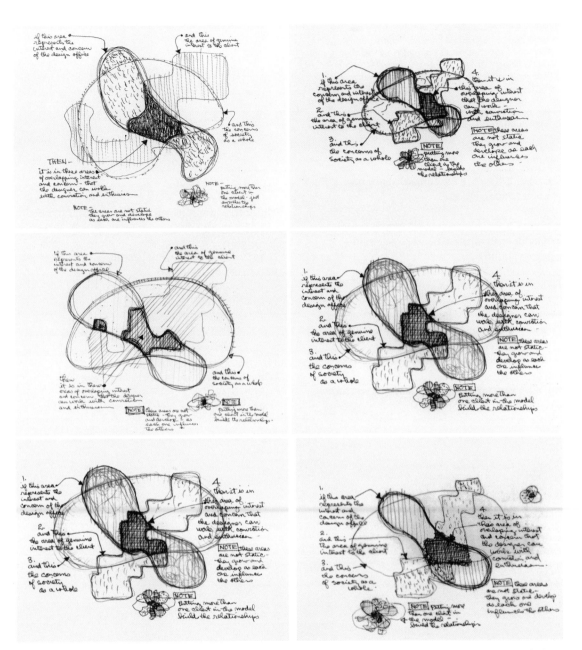

Charles Eames drawings of the design process.

Editor's note: These questions—answered by Joe Colombo, Charles Eames, Fritz Eichler, Verner Panton, and Roger Tallon—were the conceptual basis of the exhibition "Qu'est ce que la design?" at the Musée des Arts Décoratifs, Palais de Louvre. In a film by Charles and Ray Eames made in 1972, "Design Q & A," the questions and the Eames answers are read aloud, and although no spoken answer is provided to the last question, a bouquet of wildflowers is shown. Questions by Madame L. Amic, answers read by Charles Eames.

MADAME L. AMIC: *What is your definition of "Design," Monsieur Eames?*

CHARLES EAMES: One could describe Design as a plan for arranging elements to accomplish a particular purpose.

Is Design an expression of art?

I would rather say it's an expression of purpose. It may, if it is good enough, later be judged as art.

Is Design a craft for industrial purposes?

No, but Design may be a solution to some industrial problems.

What are the boundaries of Design?

What are the boundaries of problems?

Is Design a discipline that concerns itself with only one part of the environment?

No.

Is it a method of general expression?

No. It is a method of action.

Is Design a creation of an individual?

No, because to be realistic, one must always recognize the influence of those that have gone before.

Is Design a creation of a group?

Very often.

Is there a Design ethic?

There are always Design constraints, and these often imply an ethic.

Does Design imply the idea of products that are necessarily useful?

Yes, even though the use might be very subtle.

Is it able to cooperate in the creation of works reserved solely for pleasure?

Who would say that pleasure is not useful?

Ought form to derive from the analysis of function?

The great risk here is that the analysis may be incomplete.

Can the computer substitute for the Designer?

Probably, in some special cases, but usually the computer is an aid to the Designer.

Does Design imply industrial manufacture?

Not necessarily.

Is Design used to modify an old object through new techniques?

This is one kind of Design problem.

Is Design used to fit up an existing model so that it is more attractive?

One doesn't usually think of Design in this way.

Is Design an element of industrial policy?

If Design constraints imply an ethic, and if industrial policy includes ethical principles, then yes—design is an element in an industrial policy.

Does the creation of Design admit constraint?

Design depends largely on constraints.

What constraints?

The sum of all constraints. Here is one of the few effective keys to the Design problem: the ability of the Designer to recognize as many of the constraints as possible; his willingness and enthusiasm for working within these constraints. Constraints of price, of size, of strength, of balance, of surface, of time, and so forth. Each problem has its own peculiar list.

Does Design obey laws?

Aren't constraints enough?

Are there tendencies and schools in Design?

Yes, but these are more a measure of human limitations than of ideals.

Is Design ephemeral?

Some needs are ephemeral. Most designs are ephemeral.

Ought Design to tend towards the ephemeral or towards permanence?

Those needs and Designs that have a more universal quality tend toward relative permanence.

How would you define yourself with respect to a decorator? An interior architect? A stylist?

I wouldn't.

To whom does Design address itself: to the greatest number? To the specialists or the enlightened amateur? To a privileged social class?

Design addresses itself to the need.

After having answered all these questions, do you feel you have been able to practice the profession of "Design" under satisfactory conditions, or even optimum conditions?

Yes.

Have you been forced to accept compromises?

I don't remember ever being forced to accept compromises, but I have willingly accepted constraints.

What do you feel is the primary condition for the practice of Design and for its propagation?

A recognition of need.

What is the future of Design?

Source: Charles Eames, design drawings and statement for "What Is Design?" August 29, 1969, Eames Office, LLC Archives, Santa Monica, California.

Puerto Rico Advisory Council on Natural Resources

CORRESPONDENCE

Editor's note: In a newspaper interview Charles Eames explained, "I'm on a council to advise the Puerto Rican government on the use and protection of their land and environment now that American companies are getting into strip mining there. As an isolated island, it's an opportunity to show how a balance between industry and nature can be worked out."

Charles Eames to Cruz A. Matos, Under-Secretary, Commonwealth of Puerto Rico, Department of Public Works, San Juan, Puerto Rico, April 17, 1970

Dear Cruz:

We have just returned from some work in India, which took us home via Australia, the Great Barrier Reef, and Hawaii. It gave me a quick review of Western man's desecration of other lands and other cultures.

It was fascinating how continuously Puerto Rico was brought to mind. Because of its being an island, and because of its size and the nature of the land and the people, Puerto Rico could become a model or testing ground for many lands.

As we talked with Indira Gandhi about some of the alternatives that India faces, the possibility of the success of Puerto Rico as such a model seemed more and more feasible, even in the light of those serious and valid concerns voiced by Maximo Cerame-Vivas and Antonio Santiago Vazquez.

Here are some of the notions from our San Juan talks that kept coming back to mind—from half way around the world, they seemed pretty plausible.

1. A program of educating the young—and the old.
   a. In those disciplines and pleasures that would prepare them to participate in a low-energy, semi-industrial society.
   b. To develop a passion for preserving the natural surroundings so they will have it to enjoy after they have won the other battles.
2. To make a particular effort to protect and preserve the natural perimeter of the island, carefully selecting less ecologically vulnerable sites, inland, for the planning of housing and the development of light industry.

3. A determination to avoid such gross spoilers as strip mines and mass production farming that could cause the ruin of an island the size of Puerto Rico.
4. To avoid those traditional heavy industries that tend to exploit the limited land rather than develop it; but to encourage low energy industries in which skillful people can work profitably and where the landscape has a chance to come to livable terms with the development.
5. Through a carefully planned relationship to light industry, develop small farms dedicated to extremely high quality perishable produce.

This civilized idea would enrich the landscape, but it would also contribute greatly to the enjoyment, the living standard, and the culture of the island.

Such a combination of light industry, small-scale, high-quality agriculture, concern for the natural landscape, and an intelligently educated people could actually happen on this island, and perhaps in a surprisingly short time.

The low energy aspect must be more important than one at first suspects—the climate itself does not make great power demands, and there is no apparent need for a heavy industry that can be easily switched to armament production. On the other hand, with present technology, most all cultural, educational, health, and recreational activities can be satisfied by low energy means (television, computer, radio, electronics). This also broadens the area over which these commodities can be spread.

I hope you can forgive this oversimplification of a distant view. I have been grateful to you for the experience of the visit.

Charles Eames

Sources: Charles Eames to Cruz Matos, April 1970, Puerto Rico Advisory Council on Natural Resources, Container I:89, Folder 9, Charles and Ray Eames Papers, Manuscript Division, Library of Congress, Washington, D.C. Susan Rogers, "Charles Eames: The Designer Is a Poet," *New York Post* 52, May 6, 1970.

PAUL SCHRADER

"Poetry of Ideas: The Films of Charles Eames"

They're not experimental films, they're not really films. They're just attempts to get across an idea.
    Charles Eames

Charles Eames was baffled by the fact that anyone would want to write an article about his films. "When asked a question like that, about 'my approach to film,'" Eames said, "I would almost reply, 'Who me, film?' I don't think of it that way. I view film a little bit as a cheat; I'm sort of using a tool someone else has developed."

Because of his casual attitude toward "Film"— his debunking of the romantic myth of the "artist personality" and his concept of film as a primarily informational medium—Charles Eames has been able, in his recent films, to give "Film" what it needs most: a new way of perceiving ideas. As films move away from a period in which they were content to only show what they felt, and attempt little by little to also tell what they think, many of the most talented filmmakers, young and old, are trying to graft onto movies the cerebral sensibility they have so long resisted. Eames personifies this sensibility, a sensibility so synonymous with his life and work that he cannot conceive of himself as only a "filmmaker."

The Eames films commenced in 1950, and over the next fifteen years they won awards at Edinburgh, Melbourne, San Francisco, American, Mannheim, Montreal, and London film festivals. "A Rough Sketch for a Sample Lesson for a Hypothetical Course," presented by Charles and Ray Eames (with George Nelson and Alexander Girard) in 1953 at the University of Georgia and UCLA, was the first public presentation of multimedia techniques. In 1960 Eames's rapid cutting experiments in the CBS "Fabulous Fifties" special won him an Emmy for graphic design. During this period Eames designed a series of World's Fair presentations: in 1959 the multi-screen presentation for the U.S. exhibit at Moscow, in 1962 a multi-screen introduction to the U.S. Science Exhibit at Seattle (where it is still shown), in 1964 the IBM Ovoid Pavilion and the film presentations in it, at the New York Fair. Over the years Eames has pre-

pared courses and lectured across the world and will this fall hold the Charles Eliot Norton Chair of Poetry at Harvard.

Although Eames rarely rhapsodizes about anything, his most "emotional" prose is saved for a description of the problem-solving process:

"The ability to make decisions is a proper function of problem solving. Computer problems, philosophical problems, homely ones: the steps in solving each are essentially the same, some methods being elaborate variations of others. But homely or complex, the specific answers we get are not the only rewards or even the greatest. It is in preparing the problem for solution, in the necessary steps of simplification, that we often gain the richest rewards. It is in this process that we are apt to get a true insight into the nature of the problem. Such insight is of great and lasting value to us as individuals and to us as a society."—from "Think," the IBM New York Fair presentation

For Eames, problem solving is one of the answers to the problem of contemporary civilization. Not only does his problem-solving process provide beauty and order, but it constitutes the only optimistic approach to the future. He is currently working for the Head Start program, a task he feels vital because "you have to teach children to have a genuine respect for a large number of events and objects which are not of immediate gain to them. It is the only thing that puts a human being in a situation where he can promptly assess the next step. Whether it is in the ghetto or Appalachia, kids get their beginning having respect only for things which have an immediate payoff, and this is no way to run a railroad, particularly when you don't know what the next problem will be." Eames will not indulge in the despair of a complete overview, not because it is illegitimate, but because it can't solve the problems. "You can't take too broad a perspective," he says, quoting Nobel Prize–winning physicist Richard Feynman. "You have to find a corner and pick away at it."

Charles Eames is, in the broadest sense of the word, a scientist. In his film introduction to the U.S. Science Exhibit at the Seattle Fair, Eames prescribed what the rare creature, the true scientist, should be, and it is a description of Charles Eames:

"Science is essentially an artistic or philosophical enterprise carried on for its own sake. In this it is more akin to play than to work. But it is quite a sophisticated play in which the scientist views nature as a system of interlocking puzzles. He assumes that the puzzles have a solution, that they will be fair. He holds to a faith in the underlying order of the universe. His motivation is his fascination with the puzzle itself—his method a curious interplay between idea and experiment. His pleasures are those of any artist. High on the list of prerequisites for being a scientist is a quality that defines the rich human being as much as it does the man of science, that is, his ability and his desire to reach out with his mind and his imagination to something outside himself."—from "House of Science"

. . . His statement about the designing of a chair is not only a remarkable account of the creative process, but also a pioneering approach to art in a society in which the individual has become progressively functionalized and collectivized:

"How do you design a chair for acceptance by another person? By not thinking of what the other guy wants, but by coming to terms with the fact that while we may think we are different from other people in some ways at some moments, the fact of the matter is that we're a hell of a lot more like each other than we're different, and that we're certainly more like each other than we're like a tree or a stone. So then you relax back into the position of trying to satisfy yourself—except for a real trap, that is, what part of yourself do you try to satisfy? The trap is that if you try to satisfy your idiosyncrasies, those little things on the surface, you're dead, because it is in those idiosyncrasies that you're different from other people. And in a sense what gives a work of craft its personal style is usually where it failed to solve the problem rather than where it solved it. That's what gives it the Noguchi

touch, or whatever. What you try to do is satisfy your real gut instincts and work your way through your idiosyncrasies, as we have tried in the stuff we've done, the furniture of the ideas. You know it's tough enough to make the first step of understanding without trying to introduce our personality or trying to outguess what the other guy's thinking." . . .

Eames's films give the viewer more data than he can possibly process. The host at the IBM Pavilion succinctly forewarned his audience:

"Ladies and gentlemen, welcome to the IBM information machine. And the information machine is just that—a machine designed to help me give you a lot of information in a very short time."—from "Think"

Eames's information machine dispenses a lot of data, but only one idea. All the data must pertain directly to the fundamental idea; the data are not superfluous, simply superabundant. Eames's innovation, it seems to me, is a hypothesis about audience perception, which, so far, is only proved by the effectiveness of his films. His films pursue an Idea (Time, Space, Symmetry, Topology), which in the final accounting must stand alone, apart from any psychological, social, or moral implications. The viewer must rapidly sort out and prune the superabundant data if he is to follow the swift progression of thought. This process of elimination continues until the viewer has pruned away everything but the disembodied Idea. By giving the viewer more information than he can assimilate, information-overload short-circuits the normal conduits of inductive reasoning. The classic movie staple is the chase, and Eames's films present a new kind of chase, a chase through a set of information in search of an Idea. . . .

The films of Charles and Ray Eames fall into two categories. The first, the "toy films," primarily use the first Eames contribution, object-integrity; the second, the "idea films," use the second Eames contribution, information-overload.

Through precise, visual, non-narrative examination, the toy films reveal the definitive characteristics of commonplace objects. The toy films were the natural place for the Eameses to begin in film, for they found in simple photographed objects—soap-water running over blacktop, toy towns and soldiers, bread—the characteristics they were trying to bring out in the furniture design:

Charles and Ray Eames at work
in their home studio on "Toccata
for Toy Trains."

"In a good old toy there is apt to be nothing self-conscious about the use of materials—what is wood is wood; what is tin is tin; and what is cast is beautifully cast."—from "Toccata for Toy Trains"

Eames feels that the toy films are as essential as the idea films. "I don't think it's an overstatement," he remarked, "to say that without a film like 'Tops' there would be no idea films. It's all part of the same process, and I think I could convince IBM of that, if necessary."

From the outset of their filmmaking, the Eameses were also making another sort of film, a film that dealt with objects with cerebral integrity. Eames's first idea film, "A Communications Primer," resulted from a problem Eames realized he had to state before he could solve. He says, "I had the feeling that in the world of architecture they were going to get nowhere unless the process of information was going to come and enter city planning in general. You could not really anticipate a strategy that would solve the increase in population or the social changes, which were going on unless you had some way of handling this information. And so help me, this was the reason for making the first film, because we looked for some material on communications. We went to Bell Labs and they showed us pictures of a man with a beard and somebody says, 'You will invent the telephone,' or something. And this is about all you get. So we made a film called 'A Communications Primer,' essentially for architects."

Innovation is often a by-product of Eames's problem solving, as when Charles and Ray developed a lamination process for wood veneers to permit mass manufacture of their chairs. Similarly, Eames, in his desire to solve the complex, nonimmediate problems of the city, and in his desire to bring integrity to the computer, developed a revolutionary method of information presentation. In 1953 Charles and Ray presented "A Rough Sketch for a Sample Lesson for a Hypothetical Course," the first multimedia demonstration. "A Rough Sketch" not only featured three concurrent images, but also a live narrator, a long board of printed visual information, and complementary smells piped through the ventilation system.

Eames's technique of information-overload has progressed just as his toy film technique has, and some of the first "revolutionary" films look rather primitive compared to his recent work. Eames has developed several methods of information-

overload. The most basic, of course, is fast cutting ("Two Baroque Churches" has 296 still shots, roughly one every two seconds). He often has several screens (the most being twenty-two at the New York Fair, although not all the images were projected simultaneously) but has realized that a multiplicity of action on one screen can often have more impact than a single action on several separate screens. He has often used animation to simplify data, so that it can be delivered faster with clarity. One of Eames's most successful techniques is to split the screen between live action and animation, each of which affects the mental process differently. Eames also counterpoints narration, sound effects, music, and images to present several related bits of data simultaneously.

Two of Eames's recent films, "Powers of Ten" and "National Aquarium Presentation," are refinements of the idea-film technique, just as "Tops" is a refinement of the toy films. These two films represent the two sorts of ideas Eames designs, the single or the environmental concepts, and are more universal than Eames's earlier computer ideas. Because of the richness of the aesthetic Eames brings to these films, the ideas they portray inevitably strike deeper than originally intended.

"Powers of Ten" was a "sketch film" to be presented at an assembly of one thousand of America's top physicists. The sketch should, Eames decided, appeal to a ten-year-old as well as a physicist; it should contain a "gut feeling" about dimensions in time and space as well as a sound theoretical approach to those dimensions. The solution was a continuous zoom from the farthest known point in space to the nucleus of a carbon atom resting in a man's wrist lying on Miami Beach. The camera zooms from the man's wrist to a hypothetical point in space and zooms back again, going through the man's wrist to the frontier of the inner atom.

Eames approached the problem in universal terms (to please the ten-year-old as well as the nuclear physicist) and, as in designing a chair, sought to find what was most common to their experience. Sophisticated scientific data was not the denominator (although the film had to handle such matters with complete accuracy to maintain credibility), but it was that inchoate "gut feeling" of new physics, which even the most jaded scientist, as Eames says, "had never quite seen in this way before." . . .

"National Aquarium Presentation" resulted from a more earthly problem. "Aquarium" is, simply enough, a report to the Department of Interior on a proposed national aquarium. After two years of research and design, the Eames office presented the Department of the Interior not a voluminous sheath of blueprints, but a ten-minute color film and an illustrative booklet. The problem was not only to develop the design and rationale for the aquarium, but also to persuade an economy-minded Congress to lay out the cash for such a project. When dealing with the government, film is the petitioner's ideal medium: "I've discovered," says Eames, "that not even a senator dares to stand up and interrupt a film."

Again Eames had to state the problem before he could solve it: "'Aquarium' wasn't a selling job, it was a report. Mike Kerwin, a venerable member of Congress, was interested in this, and this was to be Mike Kerwin's monument. But Mike Kerwin didn't have any idea really of what an aquarium should be. As he or someone else said, 'Anything to keep those little children from peeing in the Capitol.' This is about the level these projects get started. The only thing you can do is try to create a level someone else should be embarrassed to fall below."

"National Aquarium" presentation constructs the aquarium in ten minutes, from overall conception to minute detail. Step by rapid step the film discusses the rationale, decides on a location, landscapes the environment, constructs the building, details the departments, and takes the viewer on a guided tour of the finished institution. Diverse methods of information presentation are used: graphs, animation, models, live-action, narration, music.

The guiding principles of the aquarium are not simply aquatic curiosity or research. Like all of Eames's creations, the aquarium is founded on organization, practicality, intelligence, and enjoyment. "Aquarium" makes sure that the viewer doesn't mistake those fish for something inessential to man. One who wishes to attack the aquarium must attack the principles it is based on. The true function of the aquarium is stated in the concluding lines of narration:

> "Still the greatest souvenirs of the Aquarium may be the beauty and intellectual stimulation it holds. The principal goal is much the same as science, to give the visitor some understanding of the natural world. If the National Aquarium is as good as it can be, it will do just that."
> —from "National Aquarium Presentation"

Even though Congress has yet to give final approval, the National Aquarium exists. It exists not only to the architects, to whom it always exists, but also to those who have seen Eames's film. After seeing the film, viewers speak of the aquarium in the present; the fact that they cannot go to Washington and experience the aquarium tactilely is only a chronological misfortune. The viewer has already experienced the full delights of the aquarium, its beauty and intellectual stimulation. . . .

Eames returns to film in a limited and exploratory manner what Cubism took from it in the early 1900s. What Sypher wrote of the cubist art of Cézanne, Eliot, Pirandello, and Gide, is now true of Eames's films:

> "Have we not been misled by the nineteenth-century romantic belief that the imagination means either emotional power or the concrete image, the metaphor alone? We have not supposed there is a poetry of ideas."

Interview

I spoke with Charles Eames on several occasions during January 1970, and the quotes in the preceding article are excerpted from those conversations. Afterward, I posed written questions to Eames, intended to capsulize and explore many of the discussions we had had, to which he responded in writing.

PAUL SCHRADER *Your career has seen many permutations. At times you have been an architect, a furniture designer, a craftsman, an inventor, a filmmaker, and a professor. Do you see a sense of design in your own career, or does it appear to be more accidental or haphazard?*

CHARLES EAMES Looking back on our work, I see no design—certainly nothing haphazard, and not much that could really be called accidental. What I think I see is a natural, though not predictable, growth toward a goal that has not ever been specified.

Given an empty blank, say, about the size of an IBM card, how would you characterize your current occupation?

I am occupied mostly by things that I have to fight my way through in order to get some work done.

How does an Eames film originate? What do the

discussions with the producer(s) entail? What determines whether you and Ray will accept or reject a proposed film?

A film comes as a result of one of two situations. It is either a logical extension of some immediate problem we are working on, or it is something we have been wanting to do for a long time and can't put off any longer.

On several occasions you have stated that you regard film simply as the medium through which you solve problems and explain concepts. What, for you, has made film so uniquely suited to this task?

We have fallen for the illusion that film is a perfectly controlled medium; that after the mess of production, when it is all in the can, nothing can erode it—the image, the color, the timing, the sound, everything is under control. It is just an illusion—thoughtless reproduction, projection, and presentation turn it into a mess again. Still, putting an idea on film provides the ideal discipline for whittling that idea down to size.

One of the most consistent techniques in your films is information-overload, that is, you habitually give more data than the mind can assimilate. What do you think is the effect of this cascading level of information on the viewer? Do you think this effect can be conditioning, that it can expand the ability to perceive? In other words, will a viewer learn more from the fifth Eames film he sees than the first, assuming they are of equal complexity?

I don't really believe we overload, but if that is what it is, we try to use it in a way that heightens the reality of the subject, and where, if the viewer is reduced to only a sampling, that sampling will be true to the spirit of the subject. Maybe after seeing one or two the viewer learns to relax.

Concerning "Day of the Dead" and "Two Baroque Churches in Germany," films which utilize a rapid succession of still views, Michael Brawne wrote in Architectural Design *that "the interesting point about this method of film making is not only that it is relatively simple to produce and that rather more information can be conveyed than when there is movement on the screen, but that it corresponds surprisingly closely with the way in which the brain normally records the images it receives." Do you feel this is actually the way the brain works, and is that why you used that technique?*

Because the viewer is being led at the cutter's pace, it can, over a long period, be exhausting. But this technique can deliver a great amount of information in much the same way we naturally perceive it—we did this pretty consciously.

Alison Smithson, another British critic, has written of your furniture, "The influence of the West Coast comes to us through Eames." To what extent do you think Mrs. Smithson is correct? This question may imply that Los Angeles is the prototype for America, as some city-planners have said, and I certainly wouldn't hold you responsible for that.

Los Angeles is the prototype for any city built by any people from anywhere who have been removed from their native constraints. We have perhaps carried with us a few more constraints than most, and this may be what the Smithsons choose to recognize.

You have never handled a fictional situation in your films, and I assume this is by choice rather than accident. I would like to ask if there might arise a problem, which you felt could best be solved in a fictional manner—but this is incumbent upon an understanding of what is "fiction." The IBM Puppet Shows segment "Sherlock Holmes in 'The Singular Case of the Plural Green Mustache'" would seem to be a fiction in conventional terms, yet its plot is nothing but an exercise in Boolean Logic. The outstanding feature of "National Aquarium Presentation" is that it seems to be a fiction more real—more immediate—than the object it portrays. Perhaps it would be more accurate to ask what you would consider a "fiction" in the framework of your films, and if you feel or have felt any aspects of fictionality creeping into your work.

I think the meaning of fiction that you ascribed to the aquarium is quite accurate. Fiction in this case is used as a model of simulation against which to try out possible reactions. I suppose it is true that none of our films has had any trace of plot; in most of them it is structure that takes the place of plot.

Our definition of fiction, which might be applied to your films, is anything that violates the scientific verities of the universe. Yet one of the thrusts of modern science is the truth that science considered from any one perspective is in itself a fiction. Would you consider making a fiction of science, that is, either criticizing a particular theory-fiction because it is too limited, or positing a multi-faceted conception of perceiving the universe, just as you posited the aquarium?

I believe it would be possible to build in film a conception/a fiction of science—but it would probably be bound by the same constraints as any scientific hypothesis.

Relevant to this discussion is the fact that you have never explicated philosophical or psychological prob-

lems, only scientific ones. You have never attempted a film like, say, an adaptation of Cassirer's "Philosophy of the Enlightenment," although such a film made in your style could be extraordinary. A philosophical theory cannot be extraordinary. A philosophical theory cannot be empirically limited in the way a scientific one can, yet I think your best "science" film, "Powers of Ten," works in that area where modern science and philosophy converge in outer space. You once mentioned the possibility of making a film illustration of one of Richard Feynman's lectures. Would not such a project bring you even further away from the comfortable ground of computer logic and into the nebulous sphere of modern philosophy?

I have never looked upon any of our films as being scientific, but at the same time I have never considered them less philosophical than scientific.

When dealing with some fairly elaborate problems, such as the computer, the city, the aquarium, etc., we have usually tried to reduce the general problem to a series of small simple units that even we could really understand, and pass something of this particular understanding on. Some special combination of units may give the whole piece a smell of science or of philosophy.

Several years ago, C. P. Snow's Two Cultures revived the science-art debate in England, and to a lesser extent in this country. Are there two cultures in the way Snow describes, and is this necessarily dangerous? Science and art seem to have merged completely in the lives of yourself and Ray, but others have a difficulty integrating these spheres.

If there are two cultures, as Snow suggests, it is probably no more or less dangerous than the ignorance that goes with polarized training and thinking ever was—but, at this time in particular, it seems unnecessary.

You once expressed concern over Feynman's involvement with local artists. You said the tendency for a collision with a sculptor or a painter who is preoccupied with certain personality idiosyncrasies could derail him (Feynman) and you want to protect him because something great could happen. Is this statement simply altruistic, or perhaps are you reacting to a certain voguishness or lack of thought on the part of the artists, or even that scientists shouldn't truck with "idiosyncratic" methods of expression?

Naturally, I would not think that any exposure to the art types would really derail Feynman. I am super-impatient with those, who, with the object of somehow heightening the aesthetic values of the community, seek to bring painters and sculptors together with scientists in a conscious effort to affect the aesthetic climate.

I have a conviction, no matter how unlikely it sometimes seems, that somehow, sometime, out of the world engaged in problem-structuring and scientific pursuits, will come a sharpening and a new awareness of aesthetic values.

The danger is that this world can be prematurely contaminated by a virus that results in preoccupation with self-expression. When a scientist, engineer, mathematician (with natural resistance less than that of Feynman) collide with the painter, sculptor, they catch the bug to which the painter, sculptor have developed an immunity. Little moves toward self-expression, a self-conscious attitude toward "Art," and a numbing of the sense that would allow them to recognize aesthetics as an extension of their own discipline.

In "House of Science," the scientist is defined as one who "assumes that the puzzles have a solution, that they will be fair." What would your scientist say if someone countered that the puzzles had no solution, and weren't fair?

He could give one scientist's reaction, Einstein's. When asked a question similar to that, he replied, "God may be subtle, but he's not malicious."

Filmography

This filmography was compiled with the assistance of the Charles Eames Workshop. Information about many of the films is sketchy, inadequate, or unknown. Eames has written descriptions of some of the films, and I have supplied others. All of the films were conceived and directed by Charles and Ray Eames, and photographed by Charles Eames.

Glen Fleck, a vital part of the Eames filmmaking process, is not mentioned in the filmography because his contribution to individual films is difficult to assess. "Up to very recently," Eames said, "he [Glen Fleck] is the only one in the office with whom we have talked about concept or form." Eames wrote the following description of Fleck's role and credits: "Glen came to the office during the development of the first Mathematica (1960). He did the drawings on three of the peep shows then later organized the material and did the animation on the prologue to the "House of Science." Recently, he also did the organization and animation on "Computer Glossary" and worked on the IBM fair show. At the moment most of his work is computer concepts, and he is masterminding that big history of data processing. Glen is one of the very few people who has a sense of what it is to communicate meaning. What is more, he has a sense of when he has not communicated it, and a sense of when he has not understood it in the first place—very rare."

"Traveling Boy." 1950. Color. A journey through the world of toys, with a mechanical boy as tour guide.

"Parade, or Here They Come Down the Street." 1952. 6 minutes. Color. "Filmed entirely with mechanical toys as actors moving against a background of children's drawing of a city street. Band music, Sousa's "Stars and Stripes Forever," accompanies the toy elephants and tigers and horses while brilliant Japanese paper flowers and balloons burst in the air over their heads. Drawings by Sansi Girard at age 5." Winner of Edinburgh International Film Festival Award, 1954.

"Blacktop." 1952. 11 minutes. Color. "An exercise in musical and visual Variations on a Theme, 'Blacktop' is the image of water and foam generated in the washing of a blacktopped school yard viewed against the music of Landowska playing Bach's Goldberg Variations." Winner of Edinburgh International Film Festival Award, 1954.

"Bread." 1953. 6 minutes, 30 seconds. Color. Study of bread made for Eames's "A Rough Sketch for a Sample Lesson for a Hypothetical Course."

"Calligraphy." 1953. Study of calligraphy for "A Rough Sketch."

"Communications Primer." 1953. 22 minutes, 30 seconds. Color. "An early attempt to make a popular presentation of communications theory—while a few of the techniques and words seem dated, most of it holds up quite well. The original motivation was to encourage such disciplines in the worlds of architecture and planning."

"Sofa Compact." 1954. 11 minutes. Color. Traces the design and development of a product and its uses.

"Two Baroque Churches in Germany." 1955. 10 minutes, 30 seconds. "These two churches, Vierzehnheiligen and Ottobeuren, are rich examples of mid-18th Century German Baroque, a time when music, literature, architecture and philosophy were unified. The film, rather than explaining the structure, attempts to give in one reel, with 296 stills, the feeling of what German Baroque was and what gave it such great style. Music by Georg Muffat played by Walter Korner on the organ at Vierzehnheiligen."

"House." 1955. 11 minutes. Color. "Largely because of Elmer Bernstein's fine score this becomes a rather poetic view of the Eames house in Pacific Palisades, California. It is full of details of everything but is now a bit dated except for those with a historical interest." Winner of Festival International du Film Montreal Award, 1961.

"Textiles and Ornamental Arts of India." 1955. 11 minutes, 30 seconds. Color. Film record of an exhibition, designed and installed by Alexander Girard of material selected by Alexander Girard and Edgar Kaufmann.

"Eames Lounge Chair." 1956. 2 minutes, 15 seconds. B&W. "A stylized and sped-up scene of the assembling of the Eames leather lounge chair and ottoman, with music improvised by Elmer Bernstein."

Aerial sequences in *The Spirit of St. Louis*. 1956. Color. *St. Louis* was directed for Warner Brothers by Billy Wilder, a lifelong friend of the Eameses.

"Day of the Dead." 1957. [14 minutes, 59 seconds.] Color. A portrayal of the Mexican Day of the Dead consisting of still shots and narration. Winner of San Francisco International Film Festival Award, 1958.

"Toccata for Toy Trains." 1957. 14 minutes. Color. "Toy trains in toccata form is a nostalgic and historical record of great old toys from the world of trains. The characters, the objects with which the scenes were built, were all somewhere, at some time, manufactured and sold. Music score by Elmer Bernstein." Winner of Edinburgh International Film Festival Award, 1957. Seventh Melbourne Film Festival Award, 1958. American Film Festival Award, 1959. Scholastic Teachers' 11th Annual Film Award, 1960.

"The Information Machine." 1957. 10 minutes. Color. "An animated film made in 1957 for use in the IBM Pavilion at the Brussels World's Fair. Because it deals mostly in the general principles surrounding man's problems and the electronic computer, the points made in the film do not yet seem too dated. Music by Elmer Bernstein. Drawings by Dolores Cannata." Winner of Edinburgh International Film Festival Award, 1958. Melbourne Film Festival Award, 1963.

"The Expanding Airport." 1958. 10 minutes. Color. Presents Eero Saarinen's concept for Dulles Airport.

"Herman Miller at the Brussels Fair." 1958. 4 minutes, 30 seconds. Color. A film for the American Pavilion at the 1958 Brussels World's Fair.

"Glimpses of the U.S.A." 1959. 12 minutes. Color. "Glimpses of the U.S.A." was commissioned by the State Department to introduce the United States Exhibit at the Moscow World's Fair. A rapid succession of still photos depicting various aspects of American life were projected on seven 32-foot screens enclosed within a geodesic dome designed by Buckmister Fuller. "Glimpses of the U.S.A." was never shown in its original form outside of the Moscow Fair presentations.

"De Gaulle Sketch." 1960. 1 minute, 30 seconds. B&W. "An at-the-moment attempt to put together all the images that appeared in the press on the De Gaulle crisis in a one-and-one-half-minute resume. Later, in January of 1960, Eric Sevareid used it on CBS in his recapping of events of the fifties."

"Jazz Chair." 1960. 6 minutes, 30 seconds.

"Introduction to Feedback." 1960. 11 minutes. Color. "By using a large variety of familiar examples that all have the feedback principle in common, this film presents a broad view of the phenomena present in control mechanism and social situations. Musical score by Elmer Bernstein." Winner of Festival International du Film de Montreal Award, 1961. Internationale Filmwoche, Mannheim, Germany, Award, 1961. Melbourne Film Festival Award, 1963.

Sequences in the CBS special "Fabulous Fifties," including "Music Sequence," "Dead Sequence," "De Gaulle," "Gift from the Sea," "The Comics," "Where Did You Go—Out?" 1960. B&W. Eames described the "Music Sequence": "This introduced what later became a fashionable quick-cut technique in television. It was a resume of the popular music of the fifties, for Leland Hayward's 'Fabulous Fifties.'" Winner of Emmy Award for Graphics, 1960.

"IBM Mathematics Peep Show." 1961. 11 minutes. Color. "Produced originally to support the mathematical exhibition designed for IBM, this film is composed of five individual segments—each about 2 minutes long and each demonstrating a particular mathematical concept. Music by Elmer Bernstein." Winner of Festival International du Film de Montreal Award, 1961. London Film Festival Award, 1963.

["Kaleidoscope Jazz Chair."] 1961. [7 minutes.]

"Kaleidoscope Shop." 1961. 3 minutes, 30 seconds. A tour around the Eames workshop through a kaleidoscope.

"ECS" (Eames Contract Storage). 1962. 7 minutes. Color. A training and sales film for Herman Miller.

"House of Science." 1962. 15 minutes, 30 seconds. Color. Six-screen presentation commissioned by the U.S. Government for Seattle World's Fair. It has become a permanent exhibit called "Eames Theatre." Eames has described a single-screen version: "A single-screen version of the multi-screen introduction to the United States Science Exhibit in Seattle. The 'House of Science' draws attention to the role of men, their environment, ideas, and achievements in our world—a view of science and how it got that way."

"Before the Fair." 1962. 8 minutes. Color. "This film, made for Herman Miller, shows the very last-minute hustle, bustle, painting and clean up on the days just before opening the 1962 Seattle World's Fair—also some Herman Miller furniture."

IBM Fair Presentation Film I and II. 1962, revised 1963. Made for the IBM presentation at the Seattle Fair, and later revised for the New York World's Fair.

Sequences in the CBS special "The Good Years," including "Meet Me in St. Louis," "San Francisco Fire," "Panic on Wall Street." 1962. B&W.

"Think." 1964, revised 1965. 13 minutes, 30 seconds. Color. A multi-screen presentation at the Ovoid Theater of the IBM Pavilion of the New York World's Fair. "Think" was projected on 22 separate screens (shaped in circles, squares, triangles, and rectangles), and included a live host. The 22 images were not projected simultaneously, and included live and still motion and animation. The IBM Pavilion, including the Ovoid Theater, was designed by Eames. "Think" is available in a single screen version titled "View from the People Wall": A single screen condensation of the elaborate multi-image show at the IBM Pavilion in New York, aimed at showing that the complex problems of our times are solved in the same way as the simple problems, they are just more complicated. Musical score by Elmer Bernstein.

IBM Puppet Shows. 1965. 9 minutes. Color. Two puppet shows titled "Sherlock Holmes in 'The Singular Case of the Plural Green Mustache'" and "Computer Day at Midvale." "A film version of two electronically controlled puppet shows on display at the IBM Pavilion at the New York World's Fair. In one, Sherlock Holmes solves a crime by his usual method (and the computer method)—Boolean Algebra. In the second, then, the town of Midvale celebrates the installation of its first computer. The mayor jumps to some conclusions which the computer expert has a difficult time correcting."

"IBM at the Fair." 1965. 7 minutes, 30 seconds. A fast-paced montage of the IBM Pavilion. Music by Elmer Bernstein.

"Westinghouse ABC." 1965. 12 minutes. Color. Pictures some quick glimpses of current Westinghouse products—in alphabetical order. Music by Elmer Bernstein.

"The Smithsonian Institution." 1965. 36 minutes. B&W. "A film produced at the time of the 200th anniversary of [James Smithson's] birth. It describes events leading up to the founding of the Institute and the work of those men that set the character of the Smithsonian. Music by Elmer Bernstein."

"Horizontes." 1966. Opening and end titles for a series of Latin-American films for USIA.

"Boeing: The Leading Edge." 1966. 11 minutes. Color. "A film designed to illustrate the degree to which computer control is used to support, insure, and extend development, design, and production in a modern aero-space manufacturing facility."

"IBM Museum." 1967. 10 minutes.

"A Computer Glossary." 1967. 10 minutes, 47 seconds. Color. "With a live-action prologue that gives an intimate view of a computer data path, this animated film presents, through computer terminology, some revealing and characteristic aspects of the electronic problem-solving art. Used in the IBM Pavilion at the San Antonio World's Fair. Music by Elmer Bernstein."

"National Aquarium Presentation." 1967. 10 minutes, 34 seconds. Color. "A film report to the Secretary of the Interior showing what the architecture and the program of the new National Aquarium will be, something of what it would contain and general philosophies and discipline that would be involved. Musical score by Buddy Collette."

"Schuetz Machine." 1967. 7 minutes, 15 seconds. Color. Visual study of the Schuetz calculating machine.

"Lick Observatory." 1968. 10 minutes. Color. "A somewhat nostalgic view of an astronomer's environment in an observatory on a mountain—made to give students who have not seen a large instrument something of the smell and sentiment of these surroundings."

"Babbage." 1968. 3 min, 50 seconds. A visual study of the calculating machine or difference engine.

"Powers of Ten." 1968. 7 minutes, 53 seconds. Color. "A linear view of our universe from the human scale to the sea of galaxies, then directly down to the nucleus of a carbon atom. With an image, a narration, and a dashboard, it gives a clue to the relative size of things and what it means to add another zero to any number."

"The Smithsonian Newsreel." 1968. 20 minutes.

"Photography and the City." 1969. 15 minutes. Color. "A film about the influence photography has had in the shaping of cities and the solving of urban problems. The first part is a historic review of some of the photographs that for the most part, by intent, have had an influence on the city. The last part is essentially a catalogue of those images from which a wide variety of information about the city can be derived."

"Tops." 1969. 7 minutes, 15 seconds. Color. A visual study of tops.

Films in Progress

"The UN Information Center." Another "fiction of reality," proposing a communications hub for the United Nations. "In this film we really go beyond our ourselves," Eames said. "What we really end up doing is making a case for the U.N."

"Man's View of Himself." A study of "man's changing notion of what makes him unique, and a realization that only when man stops worrying about what makes him unique can he solve the problems his uniqueness poses." Commissioned by IBM.

"Memory." Commissioned by IBM.

"The Perry Expedition." Commodore Perry's 1853 "Opening of Asia," as seen through Japanese documents of the times. Commissioned by the Smithsonian Institution.

Two films for the National Aquarium. One on shellfish, and another on the introduction of exotic species into an environment. The latter will consist of 25 rapid, consecutive examples.

Source: Paul Schrader, "Poetry of Ideas: The Films of Charles Eames," *Film Quarterly* 23, no. 3 (Spring 1970): 2–19.

MIT Report

**A report to President Howard Johnson from Charles Eames
as one member of the 1969–1970 Arts Commission**

THE CHARGE TO THE COMMISSION

"Suggested
Functions
of the
Commission"

The Suggested Functions of the Arts Commission (May 1969) were
framed with reference to "the several arts"; Theatre and Dance, Music
and Poetry, Film and Photography, Painting, Sculpture, Graphics (and
Electronics) were specifically mentioned in the Agenda for the Initial
Meeting. The implication was that the "several arts" have not been sufficiently represented in the institutional experience of the MIT student,
and that this constitutes an important deficiency in his education.

Is this really it?

I cannot believe that the deficiency of which MIT is conscious, however, really depends on insufficient representation of the several arts
as such. It seems that the diagnosis implicit—partially explicit—in the
"Suggested Functions" is mistaken in its emphasis.

I believe that this mistaken emphasis is a result of the present confusion around the terms "Art" and "arts."

> (I think that the confusion has come about because of a widespread,
> nostalgic desire to extend to current artistic activities a set of atti-
> tudes and criteria, which were established for application to the
> art of the past. The functions and motives of artistic activity are *not*
> constant; and even if they were, categories and criteria appropri-
> ate for retrospective operation are not appropriate for helping us to
> organize our interaction with current phenomena.)

I don't believe we will lose anything, in fact, we may stay closer to the
purpose of the charge given to this commission, if we skip these questions altogether.

INTERPRETATION OF THE CHARGE

The objective

MIT's objective in setting up this commission, as I read it, was to look
for ways of enlarging the experience offered to the student; of helping
him to enrich his perceptions and sharpen his discrimination; of making him more sensitive to the cultural and esthetic aspects of his own
discipline, and extending this sensitivity to interaction with other disciplines, and the wider community.

298

Dangers in emphasizing "the several arts"	There seems to be in many schools (particularly technical schools) a nervous preoccupation with the "arts" as a kind of dietary supplement, an esthetic vitamin concentrate. This tendency works directly against the objective as I interpret it. The "arts" tend to become tokens of cultural and esthetic concern, which with few exceptions are cut off from the effective culture of the community. Much of the present trouble stems from the feeling that esthetic inclinations are to be satisfied within the "several arts." Scientists and technicians already show a peculiar susceptibility to this view, and it would be a shame to do anything to foster it. Further, with an abrupt and limited introduction to the arts, there often comes a preoccupation with a largely artificial idea of "self-expression," which has nothing to do with a sense of quality and is a less than appropriate partner for the mental disciplines of science.
The burden of the commission	The burden of the commission, then, is to suggest ways in which MIT can build an environment and a program calculated to produce people sensitive to the quality of things in general—of their own activities and surroundings; people with an extended sense of responsibility and perhaps a widened concept of payoff.

THE PHYSICAL ENVIRONMENT OF MIT

In such matter as sensitivity to the quality of things in general, we can assess the degree of realism of the institution's intent by our impression of the character of the physical surroundings—the walks, the courts, the corridors, the lighting, the acoustics, the basements, the signs . . .

A technical institute should have a highly sensitive notion of function.	1. If a college of arts and sciences lets its environment go to pot, it suggests that it has somehow lost touch with some of the elements that make for a rich and spiritual rewarding life. But, if MIT lets its environment go to pot, it suggests that MIT doesn't know its business and will produce people who don't know theirs. The decisions that produce a really functional environment are no different from those that set the esthetics of that environment; unless one has an extremely limited or brutal view of function.
Problem not *lack of art* but *lack of decision*.	2. On too much of the campus, the impression now is of things going by default—of not caring, or of caring not being brought to bear. In the light of our present concerns, this *lack of decision* is much worse than is any *lack of art*. If the student learns from the institution the *habit* of treating the seemingly peripheral elements with lack of decision, he is in real trouble.
	3. The layout of the campus and the architecture of the buildings, all being inherited, are found objects. However, given these found objects, the institution is responsible for how they are handled—for making the best of them.
	4. In terms of the broader, surrounding environment that the institution and the people in it somehow produce, it is interesting to compare the bookshops, coffee shops, stores, etc., around MIT with (for example) the same services around Harvard.

RECOMMENDATION ONE

The first suggestion is a pragmatic present day extension of an idea that Gyorgy Kepes introduced 26 years ago in *The Language of Vision*. What we would propose is the following:

"Language of Vision" in each department

1. That each of the twenty-five or so departments—biology, chemical engineering, political science, meteorology, etc.—have working within it a unit of 2 or 3 teaching assistants; people whose first allegiance is to the particular discipline, but who have skill and initiative in photography, film, sound, graphics, the use of the English language, and so on.

Information packets, insight-motivated

2. The work that each such unit performs within its department should be "insight-motivated"; arriving at as well as conveying insight. The responsibility—to produce packets of current information on film, slides, tapes, holograms, anything to let the entire department in on key developments that occur within parts of the department. In this climate a kind of visual shorthand will collect on walls and corridors that will be informative for those without as well as within.

The diffusion of the product

3. The obvious next step would be to have the most prized of the information packets available to other departments, and other disciplines; and the prized ones among these available to other institutions and to the mass media. Still, the first responsibility would be to convey insights through the languages of vision and sound within the particular department.

A service center as a technical back-up

4. The media work being done in the various departments would hasten the need for a Media Service Center providing technical back up. Unlike many media centers now coming into being, there would be nothing vague about this center's function—not with some twenty-five or so teams of professionals all calling on it urgently for specific services.

In the communications that this recommendation calls for, esthetic considerations are not separable from functional ones. At this point, visual (or linguistic) discrimination presents itself as *needed*, for effective communication, and not just as an amenity.

RECOMMENDATION TWO

The second recommendation does not depend on the first—or vice versa—but each would gain from the other. It has to do with the building of a relationship between the student—his discipline—the institution—the larger community—and his own developing powers of discrimination. It goes something like this:

1. At a particular point, somewhere near the end of his career at MIT, each student would join a team with one or two other students. Each team would have the responsibility of teaching one class in an elementary school of the Boston area, half a day, twice a week, for an entire semester—then maybe give the same course the next semester to another class.

2. The material for each such course would be drawn from the particular interests and disciplines of members of the team. The ideas presented would be so completely familiar to the team that they would be free to interpret them in films, demonstrations, words, experiences, pictures, plays, models—anything that would help the central idea have meaning to the children.
3. The MIT student would have to face the realities, the pain, and the esthetic experience, of drawing some neat concept through the eye of the needle necessary to make that concept meaningful to children. This process has in it the essence of the creative act; if the MIT student is going to learn anything about art, he will learn it here.

To be a link between institution and community, the scale must be such that the impact is more than symbolic. If, for example, 2500 students formed some 1000 teams, then that would come to some 2000 elementary classes. The effect on the elementary school faculty would certainly be something; and the feedback from the community to the institution would be of a kind that has been sadly lacking.

Source: Charles Eames, report to Howard W. Johnson,
president, Massachusetts Institute of Technology,
Container I:218, Folder 6, Charles and Ray Eames Papers,
Manuscript Division, Library of Congress, Washington, D.C.

Part Four

1970–1979

Eames to Fehlbaum

CORRESPONDENCE

Charles Eames to Rolf Fehlbaum, Munich
November 9, 1970

Dear Rolf:

Everyone is insecure about how to use film in education. The reason is simple.

If Francis Galton were to do a film on probability (or a dozen other subjects), you could be sure it would be great. If Galton were to ask a filmmaker to do it, you could be sure it would be bad. A mathematician would not hire an essayist to write a mathematical paper.

I am doing the "Charles Eliot Norton" lectures at Harvard this year—and in them I use much visual material. Several good people at Harvard are into the problem, but are mostly struggling (real computer instruction is much the same).

Naturally, I feel that if you really faced the problem you could do it, but like Galton, you would have to do it—not someone else.

When you know your plans, let us know immediately—we might help with some people to talk with.

Charles Eames

Charles Eames and Rolf Fehlbaum.

Source: Charles Eames to Rolf Felhbaum, November 9, 1970, Container I:110, Folder 7, Charles and Ray Eames Papers, Manuscript Division, Library of Congress, Washington, D.C.

RALPH B. CAPLAN

Eero Saarinen's Trick

Because Charles Eames and the architect Eero Saarinen had launched their design careers as collaborators in a furniture competition which they won, Charles was asked about the trick of winning competitions. He admitted there was a trick.

"It's really Eero's trick," he said, "but I'm going to break a rule and reveal it. This is the trick, I give it to you, you can use it. We looked at the program and divided it into the essential elements which turned out to be about thirty odd. And we proceeded methodically to make one hundred studies of each element. At the end of the hundred studies we tried to get the solution for that element that suited the thing best, and then set that up as a standard below which we would not fall in the final scheme. Then we proceeded to break down all logical combinations of these elements, and this turned out to be quite a few, and we made one hundred studies of all combinations of these elements, trying to not erode the quality that we had gained in the best of the hundred single elements; and then we took those elements and began to search for the logical combinations of the combinations, and several of such stages before we even began to consider a plan. And at that point, when we felt we'd gone far enough to consider a plan, worked out study after study and on into the other aspects of the detail and the presentation.

It went on, it was sort of a brutal thing, and at the end of this period, it was a two-stage competition and sure enough we were in the second stage. Now you have to start; what do you do? We reorganized all elements, but this time, with a little bit more experience, chose the elements in a different way (still had about 26, 28, or 30) and proceeded: we made 100 studies of every element; we took every logical group of elements and studied those together in a way that would not fall below the standard that we had set. And went right on down the procedure. And at the end of the time, before the second competition drawings went in, we really wept, it looked so idiotically simple that we thought we'd sort of blown the whole bit. And won the competition. This is the secret and you can apply it."

Source: Ralph B. Caplan, *By Design* (New York: Fairchild, 2005), 208–10. Copyright © Ralph Caplan, 2005, *By Design*, and Fairchild Publications, an imprint of Bloomsbury Publishing, Inc.

Eero Saarinen at the Eames House.

"Banana Leaf" Parable

There is an unfinished Eames film called "Banana Leaf," based on a kind of parable that Charles developed in his talks. Abridged, the story (as told by Charles) goes like this.

In India, those without and the lowest in caste, eat very often—particularly in southern India—they eat off of a banana leaf. And those a little bit up the scale eat off of a sort of low-fired ceramic dish.

And a little bit higher, why, they have a glaze on—a thing they call a "tali"—they use a banana leaf and then the ceramic as a tali upon which they put all the food. And there get to be some fairly elegant glazed talis, but it graduates to—if you're up the scale a little bit more—why, a brass tali, and a bell-bronze tali is absolutely marvelous, it has a sort of a ring to it.

And then things get to be a little questionable. There are things like silver-plated talis and there are solid silver talis and I suppose some nut has had a gold tali that he's eaten off of, but I've never seen one.

But you can go beyond that, and the guys that have not only means but a certain amount of knowledge and understanding, go the next step, and they eat off of a banana leaf.

I'm not prepared to say that the banana leaf that one eats off of is the same as the other eats off of, but it's that process that has happened within the man that changes the banana leaf.

Source: Eames Demetrios, *An Eames Primer* (New York: Universe, 2007), 79.

RAY EAMES

"Goods"

Editor's note: Charles and Ray Eames created a three-screen slide show of 33 images for one of the lectures given by Charles during his tenure as the Charles Eliot Norton Professor of Poetry at Harvard, 1970–71. In 1981, Ray Eames transferred these slides, along with the narration recorded at Harvard, to a film entitled "Goods." The narration follows.

This one is going to have something to do with what I think of as "The New Covetables."

Ray, who is my wife and not my brother (she was here last time), about a month ago had her car broken in. And Ray's car invites breaking in, because it's usually loaded with presents to and from grandchildren—beautifully wrapped flowers, things to put flowers in, things of food for picnics and stuff. We have a picnic every day at the office.

And so any passerby that looks—he'd be invited to break in. And it happened. They broke in.

Well, we usually leave the office about eleven o'clock every night, so . . . they had plenty of time for this maneuver. But everybody in the office (soon it was found out) everything in Ray's car had been strewn all over the lot.

There wasn't much missing. I think a beautifully wrapped broken alarm clock that was being sent to a grandchild for further dismantling was the most important thing lost, and I regretted this very much.

But while going around and picking these things up I came upon a bolt of cloth. And this was really distressing, because it was that kind of a bolt of cloth—it was a bolt of wool. When you take hold of it; why you can feel the animal wax and oil in it somehow or other. A great bolt of cloth.

What was shocking about it was that the guy hadn't thought enough of it to take it . . . That somehow or other, he had not a sufficient respect for a bolt of cloth to take it to his girl, his wife, mother, or whatever it is.

This is really a shocking experience, because somehow or another a bolt of cloth comes under that heading of goods—the kind of goods that people lay great store in. The kind of things that you have a feeling of tremendous security about. And I don't know if you remember quite what goods are, but this is the way a bolt of cloth looks. It's fascinating because it is goods.

There are things about cloth—it reminds me of Mrs. Manly of the Manly party crossing the desert, Death Valley, when they were abandoned and going to face the Indians. She dressed up with every shred of cloth that she had, because she couldn't afford to leave it. . . .

But the way cloth itself looks and packs and feels— it's not just what you do with it, and what you sew with it. The cloth, it takes the place of a hank of rope. We don't see ropes often in hanks anymore. I think clothesline comes in hanks, and it comes in hanks that are sort of linked one to the other. And even that makes a perfect—you don't want to break into it. You want to keep a hank as it is.

Or a reel of line. Line is marvelous. We haven't some of the halyard line here, but it's great stuff. The way it comes in the package from the haberdasher, or from the ship chandler . . . the way it wraps; sort of the detail.

These are goods. A ball of twine. Who would throw away a ball of twine? Because there is something special about that ball of twine before the moment that it's opened up and gotten into. Because as long as it's somewhat of a seal, why it's an object to hold onto. Even the way that marvelous iron thing that the twine goes in so that the string comes down, and in a sense you think it's going on forever.

A keg of nails. A keg of nails. When anything was broken into while in the house somebody would always refer to it as "breaking into the keg of nails." Boxes of candy are thought of as kegs of nails. But once into it, the beautiful mass of stuff, which like a barrel of apples or a bushel of apples you think is going to last forever. Because once you open a keg of nails, how can you run through it?

Reams of paper. Haven't you dreamed of reams of paper? It's absolutely beautiful, beautiful, beautiful stuff. What you do with a ream of paper can never quite come up to what the paper offers in itself. There's something about that broken package, you know, where the corner is torn, and it invites you to

come in it. And there's something about taking out that first sheet that sort of changes it.

Boxes of chalk. Now chalk is never so wonderful as when it lays in there, the boxes. The boxes. It wasn't easy to find a box of chalk these days— tell you, sawdust and all.

A cord of wood is one of the most covetable things that you can imagine at certain times. And again, there was always that moment when somebody'd eat first—eat into the cord of wood. The first one to take the piece out and it would start to tumble, and before you knew it, the cord of wood was gone.

Source: Ray Eames, "Goods," slide show narration read by Charles Eames, Eames Office LLC, 1981, Santa Monica, California. 3 minutes.

Slides used in "Goods."

CHARLES EAMES

"General Motors Revisited"

Introductory note: The first phase of Eero Saarinen's plan for the General Motors Technical Center was completed in 1951, and subsequently published in this magazine [Architectural Forum]. *This month, Charles Eames, one of Saarinen's closest friends, revisits* GMTC.

TWENTY-FIVE years ago, the electronic computer was just emerging as the tool we know today; the systematic problem-solving strategies developed in World War II were being reapplied in peacetime science and production; and—for these and other reasons—large-scale industry was beginning to shed its brute-force, Industrial Revolution image in favor of a more sophisticated and responsive one.

A major industrial company, for the first time, was setting out to build a campus-type complex of technical buildings whose high architectural quality was to express a promise about the company's role in the future.

Alfred P. Sloane was Chairman of the Board, Charles Kettering was Director Emeritus of Research, and Harley Earle was Director of Styling when General Motors commissioned Eliel Saarinen as architect of its Technical Center. Eliel, in association with his son Eero, did design a first version; but the second version—three years later—and its subsequent development were the work of Eero, with the critical support and stringent conscience of his father.

In the course of the General Motors job, Eero learned to smoke cigars, but he learned a great deal more besides. He had already a practical instinct for problem-solving methods of a kind which in a formal version would be called operations research. He had an intuitive grasp of the branching structure of alternative strategies; if instinct or evidence suggested, he wouldn't hesitate to go back down the tree and start along another route—keeping the effort invested up to that point only as background and experience.

Much of this can be traced back to the fact that he was perhaps the most natural architectural *competitor* that ever lived; he spent his childhood in an atmosphere of disciplined architectural

competition, he was educated in competitions. He formalized his competition-winning methods to the point of inventing his own matrix schema, based on exhaustive lists of variables, which he would apply to decisions of all departments of life; the desire to carry off the prize was giving way to a passion for finding the best of all possible solutions.

In this intense optimizing mode, Eero's interaction with a generous mix of systems-oriented engineers produced a remarkable architectural result and had a lasting effect on the work of the Saarinen office.

Industrial research vocabulary and procedures accorded in many ways with Eero's fondness for testing by models, both abstract and concrete; innovative building elements were tested at full scale, in real conditions, over time. Energy and experience from each stage of construction were fed back to the successive ones, to upgrade the details and materials. Surface finishes were changed and changed again; aluminum glazing strips gave way to precisely detailed neoprene gaskets as the same new techniques were incorporated in GM's assembly lines. From the beginning, the 5-foot grid governed not only the plan and structure but the mechanical services, lighting, and movable fittings as well; the modular principle, so often taken only as an esthetic guideline, was applied with unprecedented operational thoroughness.

By the time the center was completed, Eero had become a master of the feedback principle; he had found confirmation of his natural commitment to systems, but he didn't narrow it to technical applications. He retained from then on the capacity to sit down and really communicate with engineers and businessmen.

In the work that followed, Eero intensified his pursuit of the concept and the structure peculiarly appropriate to each particular problem. It is this consistent attitude that gives continuity to Eero's architecture; each building is in effect a model of the particular problem it seeks to answer. Both Kevin Roche and John Dinkeloo joined the

Saarinen office just at the time that the first of the GM buildings was going into construction. They have succeeded in carrying on this continuity—perhaps because it is a legacy of concept and procedure, rather than of form.

If you consider the buildings together—

GM Technical Center
Kresge Auditorium at MIT
St. Louis Gateway Arch
TWA Terminal
Dulles Airport
John Deere & Company Center
Bell Telephone Laboratories
CBS Building
Oakland Museum
Ford Foundation
Knights of Columbus
New Haven Coliseum

—what they have in common becomes apparent. Each building is a model of its special problem; and Eero's "shortcut" to the model was simply that he put more energy and time into clarifying the unique nature of each problem than anyone else had even thought of doing. And the process was remarkably free from preconceptions; he was always open to new concepts, yet constantly on guard to protect existing concepts from erosion.

It isn't an approach that makes the practice of architecture any easier; but in a time when the latitude of choice threatens to overwhelm us, it seems to be our best bet for improving the state of things.

Source: Charles Eames, "General Motors Revisited," *Architectural Forum* 134, no. 5 (June 1971): 21–28.

THE ARCHITECTURAL FORUM / JUNE 1971

FORUM

Architectural Forum 134, no. 5.
Photograph of General Motors Technical Center by Richard Nickel.

ANTHONY G. BOWMAN

"Renaissance Man"

Editor's note: This article was published in the USIA magazine Ameryka (no. 161), published for distribution in Poland by Press and Publications Service, United States Information Agency, in June 1972.

EXPLAINING THE VARIETY of his interests, Charles Eames notes that it is the "structure" of each thing that attracts him, whether it be furniture, architecture, a toy, a film, a photograph, or whatever. Why, then, his passionate interest in mathematics and science?

"What grabs you about anything?" he answers. "It is like good music or a dance or a painting. It has in it some little surprises that come to you along with the realization that the surprises have followed the rules. It is also the essence of the puzzle, the pun, the well-chosen metaphor."

Today, he frequently works in conjunction with his wife out of their studio in Santa Monica, California, and, although he has worked on whole buildings, concentrates on smaller projects or details of larger ones.

"I guess I'm a cop-out," he says. "Designing a whole building is just too demanding of attention to keep the basic concept from disintegrating. Builders, prices, materials, so many things work toward lousing it up.

"I've chosen to do things which one can attack and better control as an individual. Furniture design or a film, for example, is a small piece of architecture one man can handle.

"It's like the difference between a writer who takes something toward its logical conclusion and the poet who takes it to its ultimate conclusion." . . .

In an article by reporter Saul Pett which appeared in the *Washington Star* and which is excerpted below, Eames summed up his approach to modern life and his own work.

"Our problems," he says, "do not stem from a degeneration of human beings but from changes for which people were not prepared. We are at least aware of the problem. For almost the first time, we view gigantic problems for which we have no villains, problems which are universally shared."

"The scary fact is that many of our dreams have come true. We wanted a more efficient technology and we got pesticides in the soil. We wanted cars and television sets and appliances and each of us thought he was the only one wanting that. Our dreams have come true at the expense of Lake Michigan. That doesn't mean that the dreams were all wrong. It means that there was an error somewhere in the wish and we have to fix it."

On a broader visual scale, he attributes the "aesthetic nightmare" of Los Angeles and other cities to an absence of restraints that used to be imposed on communities by available materials, common traditions, and needs. Such restraints once produced "the adobe of the Indian Pueblo, the crisp wood structures of the New England fishing village, the grass huts of the Watusi, the stone walls and cottages of the rugged Irish countryside," all of which had a unity that was more than visual.

The absence of such restraint, he says, produces in Los Angeles and elsewhere a "hash of countless combinations of materials in varying degrees of appropriateness."

"With the limited restraints we can muster, we find it much more possible to design an elegant flywheel for a gyrostabilizer than an elegant hubcap for an automobile. We find it much simpler to build a beautiful oil refinery than it is to build a beautiful city hall or a healthy city."

What the quality of life in America today needs, Eames says, is a long, slow, noninstitutional education of children, beginning before they are three, in which they develop the "habit of immediate respect for objects which have no immediate value or payoff." He cites the case of the Navajo mother who sits with her small child in the dust and forms lines and circles out of pebbles.

"I think we might have a decent world if it were universally recognized that to make a hideous lampshade, for example, is to torture helpless metals. And that every time we make a nuclear weapon, we corrupt the morals of a host of innocent neutrons below the age of consent."

Definition of design: "A plan for arranging elements in such a way as to best accomplish a particular purpose."

Profession: "I think of myself officially as an architect; I look at the problems around us as problems of structure. The tools we use are often connected with the arts, but we use them to solve very specific problems. . . . I think of architects as tradesmen—and it doesn't seem an unflattering idea. Anyone who calls himself an artist is suspect to me because an artist is a title you sort of earn, you don't gain it by choosing a line of work."

Method: "As a rule, several of us work together on a project. We start gradually, like most love affairs. We only begin to ignite when every living moment is dedicated to the search. (We contact all people who might possibly provide even a drop of information.)"

Training for a career in design: "The best preparation is a general education. I've never found a good mind that allowed techniques to stand in its way. By education I do not mean schooling— I mean the development of a sensitivity to the forces that give structure to life."

The Eames chair: "In our chairs, we have not attempted to solve the problem of how people should sit. Instead, we accept the way people do sit and operate within that framework."

Traditional design: "I love old things, for there is a richness about them—in relation to the life and time that made them."

International Business Machines' History Wall collage: "We expect this to be meaningful at almost any level. A schoolchild can look at the wall and see that the history of computers comes from getting on with the processes of life. Specialists will find inside jokes and rare memorabilia that only they will recognize. (In between, of course, there is the great lay public.)"

Approach: "I think the search for rewarding experience comes directly from the business of getting on with daily life. When we planned the IBM wall, we weren't immediately worrying about communicating with the public. We were simply trying to understand the computer ourselves. I feel that if we can genuinely satisfy ourselves, we have a fair chance of reaching other people. Never for one moment did we think of the exhibition as a marriage of art and science; we always viewed it as a part of life."

Play: "One of the things that seems to be common among those who tend to not be miserable is the ability to have concern [for], get pleasure from, and respect objects, people, and things that are of no immediate value to them. Respect for the thing that isn't going to pay off tomorrow. Because tomorrow's problems are going to be different, and the things that come to your rescue are often the things you learn to respect when you had no idea they were going to be of value."

Source: Anthony G. Bowman, "The Designer as Renaissance Man," translation October 19, 1971, *Ameryka*, Eames Office LLC. archives.

DIGBY DIEHL

"Q & A: Charles Eames"

Consistent with their philosophy, [Ray and Charles] Eames live in one of their most beautifully innovative creations, a house built in [Pacific Palisades] in 1949, which is still considered a classic of architectural design. In those comfortable surroundings, I talked with the Eameses on a Saturday evening after they had put in their usual seven-day work week. Although initially reluctant to be interviewed, Eames relaxed and explained his ideas about modern design with a charm and clarity that is the trademark of his work.

DIGBY DIEHL *You've worked in so many fields— films, toys, architecture, furniture, displays—that I wonder how you define your main function. As designer?*

CHARLES EAMES I think of myself functionally as an architect; I can't help but look at the problems around us as problems of structure—and structure is architecture. A good film needs structure as much as a good front page does.

DD *But is "structuring" what we think of as innovative work?*

CE We do seem to be trapped in some drive to be original or innovative. That's deadly, I think. The preoccupation with self-expression is probably no more appropriate to the world of art than it is to the world of surgery. That doesn't mean I would reduce self-expression in surgery to zero, because, indeed, I'm sure that the really great surgeons operate on the edge of intuition. But the tremendous, rigorous constraints in surgery—those are what are important in any art.

DD *And yet you're credited with being such an innovator. That seems something of a paradox.*

CE To court innovation, I think, is really dangerous, because if you were to take a long view of the development of artifacts in our environment, innovation would follow the same rule as mutation in the process of natural selection. There are nine hundred and ninety-nine failures to every thousand mutations. It is the exception that enters the mainstream of development. And I think that is also true of social innovation. If anything, I'm an innovation avoider whenever possible.

DD *Still, you've worked with many new materials and processes—multiple screen projection, for example.*

CE When we first worked on multiple screen projection in 1952, we were not attempting to innovate. We used it for a thing called "A Rough Sketch for a Sample Lesson for a Hypothetical Course"— which we did in the East and then here at UCLA— and the absolute, down-to-earth question was: "How do you express such information in a short period of time?" And we discovered that the use of multiple images was an answer.

Then, later on, at the Moscow Exhibit in 1959— when we used seven screens over an area that was over half the length of a football field—that was just a desperate attempt to make a credible statement to a group of people in Moscow when words had almost ceased to have meaning. We were telling the story straight, and we wanted to do it in twelve minutes, with images; but we found that we couldn't really give credibility to it in a linear way. However, when we could put fifty images on the screen for a certain subject in a matter of ten seconds, we got a kind of breadth which we felt we couldn't get any other way. Now, naturally, having come upon the use of multiple images in 1951, we exhibited a tendency to find new uses for it. There is the Law of Hammer: If you give a young boy a hammer, he'll find that everything he encounters needs hammering. We found that everything we encountered needed the multiple image technique. But we were reasonably rigorous about the use of constraint with our process.

I did use little vignettes with triple slides in the Norton Lectures at Harvard, in order to give a depth of view to subjects. In each lecture I would talk about five minutes and then show about three minutes of imagery, and then talk seven minutes more. So in all, I had about six of these vignettes in every lecture. But each collection of imagery backed up a certain point I was making.

DD *Aren't the Norton Lectures usually given by a literary figure?*

CE Yes. It is literary, a chair of poetry. But I think about every three years they give it to an off-beat fellow. Among the offbeats were Ben Shahn, and later Stravinsky—who were actually pretty poetic now that I think of it. The theme of my lectures—which will eventually be published by Harvard U. Press—was that the rewarding experiences, the aesthetic pleasures of our lives should not be dependent solely upon the classic fine arts, but should be, rather, a natural product of the business of life itself. As we look around us, we find many people making decisions easily when they handle any subject having to do with efficiency and things of a factual nature. But when they're up against questions having anything vaguely to do with the area of aesthetics, they immediately abandon their own disciplines and turn the responsibilities of pleasure over to the fine arts. The lectures were sort of an argument against the discontinuity that now exists between the areas which we measure and the areas which we feel.

DD *That idea was central to the whole generation of architects and designers that you came out of, wasn't it?*

CE Yes. Certainly I was closest to Eero Saarinen—a great architect—and we both learned from his famous father, Eliel, to consider any specific problem in the light of the next larger and the next smaller thing. That led you to a kind of natural continuity—once you have a concept.

DD *Can you explain what you mean by "concept" in this context?*

CE Well, it is an idea practiced by two men as seemingly different as Le Corbusier and Frank Lloyd Wright. Wright contended that the building and the landscape should be one. Le Corbusier held to the opposite, that what is built by man is man's and what is Nature's is Nature's; he thought these things should have a natural separation. But the thing about the two men together is that they were both strong concept men: the battle they fought was to keep the concept from disintegrating.

DD *Have you always been conscious of fighting that same battle in your own work?*

CE Naturally, compared with those of really strong people like Mies van der Rohe or Le Corbusier, or even Wright, our success at sticking to a concept is sometimes frustratingly limited, despite effort. But, sure, that's the problem—to keep the concept from disintegrating. An example of it in another field is Edwin Land of Polaroid. He's a very strong concept man, an inventor not in the sense that one ordinarily thinks of an inventor—as a tinkerer—but more an inventor of systems. His job involves that same feel for the concept. Also Edison. Edison was often thought of as a tinkerer, but the electric light was just part of a systems concept—the concept of generating and using power. He's sometimes shortchanged on that.

DD *When did you begin your own career as an architect?*

CE I opened my office in 1930. If you think about it, it will occur to you that the year before that was 1929—a great time for a young guy to open an office. But when you practiced architecture then, you did everything. For churches and schools we painted murals; we did wood and stone sculptures for the office building; we built lighting fixtures; we did most all the furniture; we designed and supervised the making of vestments and fabrics and rugs. You had to put an awful lot of energy into the few jobs you could get, to help people do something that they didn't have the means to do, really. But it was real training for any kid in architecture. It laid the groundwork for everything we've done since.

In 1938, I was asked to do some work at Cranbrook Academy of Art in Michigan. I guess all schools have vintage years, and this happened to be a vintage year at Cranbrook. There was Eero, of course, and Lily Swann. Florence Knoll was there, and Ed Bacon, who's done city planning in Philadelphia, and Harry Bertoia, and Harry Weese, who's a very strong architect, and Marianne Strengel, the weaver, Jack Spaeth, who's doing city planning in Seattle, Ben Baldwin and Ralph Rapson, who now heads the School of Architecture at Minnesota. It was a very hard-working group. And it just so happened that Eero was attacking architecture in the same way I had been. He was doing ceramics, he was doing the fountains, he was designing fabrics. One day we were talking about what the quality is that really makes an architect, and one of the things we hit upon was the quality of a host. That is, the role of the architect or the designer is that of a very good, thoughtful host, all of whose energy goes into trying to anticipate the needs of his guests—those who would enter the building and use the objects later. We decided that this was a very essential ingredient in the design of a building or a useful object. Those years of the Depression helped revive much of the tradition that had belonged to earlier architects. Whether it be Brunelleschi in the fifteenth century, or

Stanford White in the late nineteenth century—their concerns were very much the same. And now, when anyone works on a project in our office, it's with that sense of a host.

DD *Of all the people you've spoken of, however, you're the only one who's continued doing a multiplicity of things. Why?*

CE Well, that is partially the result of my chickening out. Practicing architecture is a super-frustrating business. You work on the idea, but then standing between you and the event itself are many, many traps to dilute it. The finance committee, the contractor, the subcontractor, the engineer, the facilities guys, the political situation—all of them can really degenerate the concept. Going into furniture or film is a deviation of a sort, but at least we have a more direct relationship with the end product—better chance to keep the concept from degenerating.

DD *But why do architects design furniture?*

CE So you can design a piece of architecture you can hold in your hand, that won't get away from you—in concept.

DD *What were the origins of your own first venture into furniture, the molded plywood chair? Was it to be part of some larger environment?*

CE No, it wasn't a part of a larger scheme; it was the scheme. The concept was to do a piece of furniture which had a certain minimum of means, but a cushion chair, austere only in that it would be of a hard substance, which would be really comfortable. It must be, we decided, a chair which was a product of mass production, and mass production would not have anything but a positive influence on it; it would not be a substitute for handicraft. It would have in its appearance the essence of the method that produced it; it would have an inherent rightness about it, and it would be produced by people working in a dignified way. That sounds a little pompous, but at that time in the development of things, it was a perfectly legitimate thing to strive to do.

DD *Where were the chairs first produced?*

CE Of course, when we were doing our first pieces of furniture, we were not only designing them, but as we still do, we were designing most of the tooling, too. With the earliest pieces, we built all of the tooling. We even manufactured the first five thousand chairs in our office. We shipped the tools to Herman Miller in Zeeland, Michigan, and they have been producing them ever since.

DD *I know that by this time you had moved to California. What were the reasons for the move?*

CE We really came out to California in 1942 with the purpose of just finding a quiet place to work where we didn't know anybody and we could concentrate on our work. Just being by the ocean here is comfortable. The climate is nice to us, and we enjoy the house. But, in a sense, our work is directly with people three thousand miles away. All the time we've been in Los Angeles, we've never had a client living west of the Mississippi. Oh, we've done one or two things with people out here. I worked with Billy Wilder on *The Spirit of St. Louis*. But essentially, we've never had a client west of the Mississippi.

DD *What projects are you working on now?*

CE At the present time we're continuing to do things for IBM, and they're things we would like to do anyway, if we had the wherewithal to do anything we wanted. In furniture, we're not trying to invent new systems or produce innovations. We're just trying to make the furniture we do now turn out to be as good as we thought it was in the first place years ago. It's kind of an interesting thing to do, you know, in your old age. We've tried to avoid doing any really large projects, because there are some very interesting small things we want to do, such as a series of two-, four-, and five-minute films—capsules that have a bearing on some simple, cogent ideas. But we did accept an offer from the USIA to do an exhibitional life of Jefferson, which will open in the Grand Palais in Paris in 1972 and come to this country in 1976, I think. It's a little more of a project than we should be doing at the moment, I suppose, but again, it's pretty interesting to re-examine the life of an old hero.

Then we met Edwin Land, and he wanted a film explaining the concept of his new camera—his attitude toward it, the development he's put into it, and the particular kind of involvement he has with it—so we are doing this introductory film. And right now, it's a lot of fun. Then, next year is the five hundredth anniversary of the birth of Copernicus, right? So in Cracow, where Copernicus was born, we spent three days researching and shooting, and then spent three days in Uppsala, where along with some astronomers and astrophysicists we shot some material for this celebration.

We also have a habit of becoming involved in projects like the National Aquarium, which never seem to end. When the aquarium was dumped from its position of priority last year due to administrative decisions, we were left with some thoroughly interesting marine biological studies in our studio. In the last two weeks, in fact, we've given birth to two sharks, which we incubated for twelve months or so. So, we're making some little concept films with things in the tank, because who could kill off their pet octopi and sharks?

DD *Are you at all optimistic about ever seeing the National Aquarium created as you conceive it now?*

CE Well, I think it's in the nature of large governmental projects that if they ever come to a halt, part of the spirit of reviving them is to change the cast of characters. So I think it would be an unnatural act for them to revive this one with us. We hope that at least we made a statement about aquaria in general, and that the next aquarium proposed cannot fall honorably below that standard. Anyway, we went into it knowing that the mortality rate was incredible.

DD *How did you first begin working with IBM? Did they come to you with a specific project in mind?*

CE Eliot Noyes brought us in as consultants to the Design Program, but with the advent of the Brussels World's Fair we drifted into the area of communications. In the case of Mathematica, IBM came to us with a problem. "We feel that we should do something in the Los Angeles area, and most probably at the Museum of Science and Industry, that has some of the ideals and principles and feelings of the company, and that will be able to help the community in a way that is appropriate to IBM's interests." Instead of having an exhibition based on binary arithmetic, which would be directly related to computers, with Ray Redheffer, a theoretical mathematician from UCLA, we suggested that we could deal with the broader aspects of mathematics, beyond the world of numbers— that is, theories, and principles, and mathematical insights. That way, they could maintain a much broader interest than simply that of those members of the community particularly involved with computers. It seemed to work, and the exhibit at the Museum of Science and Industry is still there. I'm even a bit embarrassed about its being there so long. A graduate student in mathematics at Cal Tech was visiting me, and he said that, as a child, he first learned about some mathematical ideas as a result of that exhibit.

DD *And how did you first become involved with film?*

CE Well, first of all, I'd been taking an awful lot of pictures for a long time. My father was an elaborate amateur photographer. But he was a much older guy; he died when I was only about twelve years old, and he was well into his seventies then. So it wasn't until later that I came upon a cache of his photographic equipment. Then, being an avid instructions reader, I mixed the emulsions, and for a year I was photographing my friends with wet emulsions on glass plates before I found that film had already been invented. So photography had been an old thing, and we had made a few films, including two, "Blacktop" and "Parade," that immediately joined the Museum of Modern Art. Our first real try, though, came when we wanted to make a statement about communications theory for architects. We did a film called "The Communications Primer," which became involved in that 1951 multimedia show at UCLA. Few architects ever saw it, but the Department of Agriculture bought two blocks of fifty prints each.

DD *Did your involvement with film also signal the beginning of what seems to have been a long love affair with scientific subjects?*

CE No, I think there's always a certain amount of curiosity about scientific phenomena and scientific discovery among architects, and also an enjoyment of a certain rationale in things. I don't know to what degree you'd find it in architectural schools now, but it does seem to be the case that there is always a running love affair being carried on by architects with mathematical games, and with the contradictions that appear in history and archaeology, and with a kind of general detective story approach to history and scientific investigation. Because architects should be able to concentrate and attack a puzzle. I think that is a part of architecture. Engineers have it, too—certainly good ones do—and of course scientists use it as their mainstay. It's the element that brings a scientist close to a poet—the ability to take a situation, which is essentially a mess, and try to find good, solid, meaningful relationships in it.

DD *What prompted you to begin designing toys?*

CE Well, the "House of Cards" was something we wanted to make for our grandchildren and our friends, so we figured the best thing was to find somebody to manufacture it. It's just as simple as that. "The Toy" came about more or less the same way. It was the first of that whole family of toys based essentially on triangles and squares, and we did it with paper triangles fitted for wooden dowels with slip-on sleeves, which made a very large, colorful thing out of a small package. I suppose we were thinking of Bucky Fuller.

The motivation behind most of the things we've done was either that we wanted them or we wanted to give them to someone else. And the way to make that practical is to have whatever it is manufactured. I think that's a natural motivation. The lounge chair, for example, and, later, the chaise were really done as presents to a friend, Billy Wilder, and have since been reproduced.

DD *How did a present like the chaise come about?*

CE Well, Billy put it succinctly: he wanted something he could take a nap on in his office that wouldn't be mistaken for a casting couch. So we talked about it, but then he and I were together in a lighthouse in Newfoundland, and we saw that the lighthouse keeper had a very thin, narrow napping bench. It took a few years but we finally made the chaise.

DD *Why is all this beautiful furniture so expensive?*

CE Indeed, the lounge chair is expensive. But it wasn't designed as a high production item. On the other end of the scale, however, we've got that whole world of molded plywood chairs, and I think the stacking chair is the most economical, serviceable chair that an institution hard put to it for money can get. If you go into the waiting room of an airport, or into quite a few restaurants and schools and commissaries, you'll find that chair. We've done some office furniture since then, too, using a technique by which the soft support of the chair is sort of foamed in place between the leather and the shell. It has a certain capability in terms of contour and comfort, along with an economy of production, and, you know, I think if you can now get a good-sized, upholstered, comfortable chair for a hundred dollars—and that's about what they cost—then that's quite a good thing.

DD *There seem to have been many shoddy copies of your designs on the market lately. Does that distress you?*

CE I think that in any work, whether it's in film or chairs or whatever, you hope that somebody will come along and just take the central idea and improve on it. That you don't mind. But what you do mind is somebody who copies the most miserable aspects of it. You see exaggerated some of the misery that you built into it. A copier will emphasize that area in which the designer failed to solve the problem, rather than where he succeeded in solving the problem.

Take an ax handle, for example. You wouldn't say that an ax handle has style to it. It has beauty, and appropriateness of form, and a "this-is-how-it-should-be-ness." But it has no style because it has no mistakes. Style reflects one's idiosyncrasies. Your personality is apt to show more to the degree that you did not solve the problems than to the degree that you did.

Source: Digby Diehl, "Q & A: Charles Eames," *West Magazine/Los Angeles Times* (October 8, 1972): 14–17.

"Eames on Eames"

IN FURNITURE, photography, and beyond, the art of Charles Eames aims at simplicity, abstraction, and a quality of rightness.

"If you start out in architecture, then go on to furniture and then to toys and films, essentially it's the same problem. You don't set out to invent something, you just want to make whatever you're working on right. Look at an ax handle—it's a beautiful thing because it's the way it should be. And when you set out to do a chair, you're not setting out to do something that will floor somebody. You just want to do it the way it should be, so that it's appropriate and reflects the way it's made."

Does he see abstraction in the chairs he makes, the picture he takes?

"Well, it doesn't scare me. I think it's obvious what abstraction might mean in a single photograph—you come upon a situation, and out of a very complicated situation you try to abstract some simple relationship that you can hold on to. In that sense you are constantly abstracting.

"I should warn you, there might be a tendency to romanticize what we're doing. To me it's just like a shoemaker building shoes.

"Eero Saarinen had a gallstone and was about to be operated on when the surgeon said, 'Eero, did it ever occur to you that the average surgeon is as good at his work as the average architect?' And Eero said, 'Let me out of here.'

"I like to think of myself as an architect, and I like to think of all those things we work on as aspects of architecture. They all have structure—Did you see the Copernicus exhibit downstairs?

"In some ways we're probably better equipped to do an exhibit as long as we're working with somebody who will keep us from doing anything booby, because we have an exuberance about passing on newfound knowledge. The catch is never attempt to present something you don't feel you really understand.

"I would say that Salem in its heyday had certain drawbacks. People were being publicly burned at the stake. But at the same time it was a pretty beautiful city. So if you look at some of the rewarding things of the past, they have taken place as a result of built-in structure. Not that the people had good taste. But there was really just one way to build a house. You only had certain materials. And even the choices you would normally have were limited because you could not offend the large critical body of Salem. In other words, there weren't a lot of choices, but a lot of structure built in by tradition. And I think it's very helpful to have a structure in life, except that today it's a structure where, more and more, we have a collective choice."

Eames dates the beginning of his work from 1930, the year he opened his own office.

"In those days the clients that a young architect could get were few and far between, and when you got a job you did the furniture, the drapes, sculpture, everything."

During the Depression he did a Catholic church for an Italian neighbourhood in Helena, Arkansas.

"It was kind of a miserable situation, because in Arkansas at that time, the Catholics were being persecuted by the Ku Klux Klan. We designed all the vestments. And we got fabrics and showed the women of the community how to sew the vestments. We did the murals, the sculpture, and then all the fabrics in the church. And there was no money to speak of. I went down there and worked, and in a sense it was doing everything. I just want to point out that I wasn't alone. There were a lot of young architects doing that."

Any favorites in his past?

"It's very much like children—the things you have the greatest affection for are not always the best or the most successful. I think that in terms of chairs, very few pieces of work that you do end up having the attention they deserve. The molded plywood chair, the molded plywood seat and back, is probably one of the few pieces that got all the attention it deserved. When we did that piece a lot of things were established that we fed from later. We also made several multi-image film shows—six or seven pictures going at a time—very early in the game. The first was called 'A Rough Sketch of a Sample Lesson for a Hypothetical Course.' We did it along with Alexander Girard and George Nelson. That has a soft spot in my heart because it set some of the basic rules of handling multi-images. You feed off these for a while, you work on something very intensely, and then the product of that work comes out over a period of years. Those are the things you remember.

"Does the name Eric Gill mean anything to you? He was a great graphics guy, and he had a lot of insight into those things. He said you look after goodness and truth, and beauty will look after itself. Naturally I enjoy beauty in a lot of old things, other things, new things, but I'm never conscious of really going after it."

And what about his childhood, or anybody's childhood?

"You see a Navaho woman with a papoose board doing her work, arranging little stones, and the child watches that. In a Jewish family, whether it's the hamantaschen [a Purim cake] or the lighting of the candles, a myriad of small things commands the respect of the very young child, things that in themselves have no payoff. I think this is really the secret—if a child can get in the habit of respecting what will not yield him instant reward, whether it's a little ceremony, pebbles laid in a row, some crazy cookie, or the lighting of a candle. There are kids in Los Angeles who have never sat down to a table that has been set. You start going though life looking for the instant payoff, which is an impoverished situation. In design, you rely on stuff you didn't even know was going to be of value. You may solve a spatial problem out of a love of dance. But you didn't love dance in order to solve the problem."

Eames, who grew up in his mother's French family in St. Louis, Missouri, remembers how his grandmother insisted he drink a glass of claret before lunch.

"As a little kid, because my father died when I was very young and all the rest of the men in the family were gone, little things were expected. It didn't matter if you were seven years old, you had to perform those things. Then, around the Fourth of July you had boiled salmon and blueberries. You had those things—a hem or a patch on a sock was sewn a certain way. Today a properly darned sock is a luxury. It was a necessity then, but there was a ritual about it. I had a tremendous respect for well-darned socks, and today I'm fortunate. My wife and I work together all the time and so we have a housekeeper, Maria. And she darns my socks, turns my collars, turns my shirtsleeves—and goddamn it, if I want the pleasures of growing old, I'd like to include having properly darned socks."

Source: Harriet Shapiro, "Eames on Eames," *Intellectual Digest* 3, no. 2 104 (August 1973): 34–37.

The wake of a powerboat photographed by Eames curves as roundly as his 1969 soft-pad aluminum chair.

Eames's experimental 1944–45 molded plywood chair has some of the layered unfolding quality of a growing plant.

Eames, chairmaker and photographer
—this time of a butterfly—always finds
the simplest shapes. That simplicity
shows in this fiberglass version of his
classic 1946 plywood dining chair.

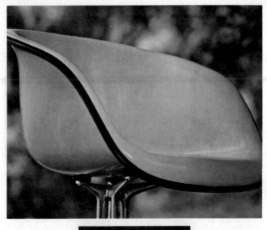

Eames named the curving La Fonda
armchair after the restaurant he did
it for in 1960. Like the eggs in the bowl
below, the La Fonda has a rounded
fullness about it.

"Disciplines of the Circus"

Editor's note: The transcript of Charles Eames's speech to the American Philosophical Association has not turned up. These are the note cards Charles took with him, as indicated by this handwritten note by Jehane Burns of the Eames Office: "Duplicate of lecture cards as sent with CE to Philadelphia, April 17, 1974." On the first card, Charles wrote an outline for his speech, including notes on timing and the films and slide shows he would present. The numbers represent the number of minutes Eames planned to devote to each section of his presentation.

TOPS 5
Personal background
CHINESE LIST 5
Intro to "Callot"

CALLOT 3
Note: This film, "Callot," an array of carefully photographed details from the circus etchings of Jacques Callot, the baroque printmaker, was made expressly for this talk.

Forbidden Games
VEILED PROPHET 5
Intro Circus Slides

CIRCUS SLIDES 7
Watusi
Canvas Boss
NOMADIC SOCIETY-CONSTRAINTS 10
History
Clowns

CLOWN FACE 4
Note: An Eames movie shot as a teaching tool for aspiring clowns, detailing the process by which experienced clowns apply their makeup.

Vulnerability

TEARDOWN 3
THIS-IS-AS-IT-SHOULD-BE-NESS 5

MOVIES 6
Note: A slide show presentation of Eames photos taken behind the scenes on movie sets.

MORAL 10

TOPS
perhaps establishes my credentials as a table-top physicist and hints at a relationship between this audience, this speaker, and the subject of the CIRCUS [a relationship which gets stated more explicitly in the MORAL].

A PERSONAL VIEW of circus
how it relates to my own work and interests
the core of the relationship—taking pleasure *seriously*, using it as a basis and a touchstone.
My profession, and (I believe) yours too.

As an introduction, a bit of personal history:
born St. Louis 3 years after Great Louisiana Purchase Exhibition (aunts still reliving it)
first exposure to SCIENCE not as part of schooling

MYSTIFICATION, SHOWMANSHIP,
astonish-your-friends
parlor séances, magic lantern shows, charades, marketable skills
(portraits of Kaiser Wilhelm)
Howard Thurston's conjuring tricks

EXPERIMENTAL SCIENCE—Cleveland
Hopkins—1871
instruction-reading in all languages
math through magic squares
wet-plate camera
shocking machine (meant for therapy)
cat's whisker radios
St. Nicholas Magazine
The Book of Knowledge

PERSONAL HISTORY CONTINUED
public spectacles and marvels
prodigies in Nature like Halley's Comet
great human enterprises—Great Eastern Titanic
[that seemed to fly in the face of Nature]

... INTO ARCHITECTURE
It seemed completely natural that most all the
sophisticated ARTS and SCIENCES had had their
origin in [playfulness, magic, and showmanship]
gunpowder—fireworks before cannon
static electricity—toys before understanding
pneumatics and hydraulics—miracles and wonders
in temples and at courts
(Mexico—wheels on toy carts for gods long before
"practical" use)

Phil Morrison the other day brought to our attention a page in Joseph Needham's *Science and
Civilization in China*

"Perhaps the passage of jugglers and acrobats
to and fro merits more attention in the history of
science than it has yet received, when we remember how much of the early mechanics of such men
as Heron of Alexandria (+1st), and also of their
Chinese counterparts, was occupied with mechanical toys for palace entertainments, devices of
illusion, stage play machinery, and the like. The
jugglers appear right at the beginning of Chinese-
Western relations. [Those of +120 could "conjure,
spit fire, bind and release their limbs without assistance, interchange the heads of cows and horses,
and dance cleverly with up to a thousand balls."
Similarly, we read in the later *Sou Shen Chi* (Reports
on Spiritual Manifestations) of +350 about wander-
ing magicians and conjurors from India.] This is
a point which seems well worth further investigation. For ancient and medieval people there was
not much difference between jugglers, alchemists,
mechanicians, leeches, star-clerks, and all dealers
in magic and gramarye."

(Obviously the maker of the Antikythera machine
falls into this category)

In any fairly stable society there's a NEED which
is met by strange visiting groups
    gypsies
    strolling players
    mountebanks of all kinds

The earmark is not just that they're TRANSIENTS—
they DO THINGS THAT AREN'T DONE
Different freedoms and different constraints
the audience responds to the freedoms
[children's suspicion that the rules ain't necessarily so] but tonight the subject is the special
CONSTRAINTS

COMMEDIA DELL'ARTE intro
The circus as a nomadic group of popular, extrava-
gant entertainers has many PREDECESSORS
I want to show a view of one highly stylized
example
Italian Commedia dell'Arte, 16th, 17th, 18th
centuries

Closely knit traveling troupe, actors and actresses,
with a portable stage and a repertoire of scenario
sketches nailed up behind the scenes; a small set
of stock types—Harlequin, Pantaloon, the Doctor,
the young lovers; survived into stage pantomime in
this century; traces of them among modern clown
types, and clear back to Greek comedy.

"Travelled by boat; 12 actors and actresses with a
prompter, a stage carpenter, a property-man, eight
men-servants, four maids, nurses, children of all
ages, dogs, cats, monkeys, parrots, birds, pigeons,
a lamb . . . it was a Noah's Ark." —Goldoni's
Memoirs

COMMEDIA DELL'ARTE Discipline

What the connoisseurs in the audience looked for:
— The smoothness and inventiveness of the *improvised dialogues*
— Long, arduous training: "It was easier to train
  10 actors for the regular theatre than one for the
  Italian Comedy."
— Self-discipline and consideration in improvis-
  ing; one actor couldn't shine at the exposure of
  another.
— Many of them (Harlequin especially) had to be
  trained in acrobatics and the ladies were usually
  required to sing.

DISCIPLINE OF THE COMMEDIA DELL'ARTE
From the memoirs of an 18th-century playwright:
"The success of even the best actor depends upon
his partner in the dialogue. If he has to act with a
colleague who fails to reply at the right moment
or who interrupts him in the wrong place, his own

discourse falters and the liveliness of his wit is extinguished."

"These plays are never withdrawn on account of illness among the actors or because of newly recruited talent. An impromptu parley before going on stage, about the plot and how to play it, is enough to insure a smooth performance."

"I have often heard these improvisers reproach themselves for having 'planted' the scene badly, and then they build it up again by excellent arguments so as to give it a [motive] and so prepare the ground for a new attempt."

CALLOT view
Jacques Callot's engravings (published 1622 as a kind of coffee-table portfolio) probably not the most faithful view. Copied by Inigo Jones among his costume sketches for entertainments at the court of Charles 1st. Copied by us [in the same tradition].

AFTER CALLOT
The indecency—part of the popular stock-in-trade
Catherine de' Medici invited a Commedia dell'Arte
    troupe to France
They had COURT and POPULAR patronage
Civic authorities tried to get rid of them
Uneasy response of stable societies—fascinated/
    threatened

FORBIDDEN GAMES
Presenting the unpresentable—padding in strange places, ladies scantily dressed, bottom-showing, enormous codpieces, low body-English, slapstick of the lowest kind.
Plenty of this in Greek vase painting (BURLESKS of the GODS), still
a token element in clowning today.
    things that aren't done [against Nature]
    jugglers, tumblers, escape artists, fortune-
    tellers, mind-readers
people *don't* . . . people putting their heads in tiger's mouths.

VEILED PROPHET; a different phenomenon some of the same motifs
once-a-year special behavior
magical-religious: mystery plays with comic devils kept some of the motifs from Ancient Greek comedy
regular members of the community—guilds, businessmen

HOPI Kachina clown
Aside: Church in middle ages
    civic authorities in Renaissance France
    Cromwell as against "Popish Showes"
    tendency to *outlaw* professionals
    excommunicate

INITIATION
parents took their children to circus
a limited exposure to a kind of reality
they will never live with but *ought*, somehow, to get a taste of

THE CIRCUS OF DR. LAO

INTRO TO CIRCUS SLIDES places the time the nomadic circus at *this level of organization* lasted from 1871 (first [three rings] under canvas) until RINGLING BROS. First tour 1884 first three ring circus under canvas (copied from Hippodromes) was P. T. Barnum's in 1871.
CIRCUS SLIDES

SAM ZIMBALIST—*King Solomon's Mines*

LLOYD MORGAN lot boss in a sulky counting the paces and throwing down markers entrance side— 8th Av 49th St (Short Side)

EARLY MORNING
Cook tent already up
Harness makers, blacksmith, cobbler
Side show and banner line so they could get ready for day time business
Menagerie, horse tent, dressing tent
Big Top (last to come down) last to go up

BIG TOP GOING UP
Entire canvas crew
No. 1 Pole—center poles 62½ feet
Inner quarter poles
take drivers (Ford axles?)
rope caller of the guying out crew

STATISTICS OF BIG TOP (1947)
544' 6" long, 244' 1" wide.
Canvas weighed 20 tons when dry (3½ times that when wet)
6 center poles (62')
20 inner quarter poles (47')
34 outer quarter poles (37')

Charles Eames, photographs of circus
aerialists.

122 side wall poles (17')
600 guy ropes
60–70 miles of rope, all kinds, on the whole lot
1,400 employees
10,000 customers at each performance

THE ORDER IN WHICH THESE EVENTS TAKE
PLACE FOLLOWS A STRICT RITUAL
What does not vary
In case of emergency or panic a minimum of deci-
sions have to be made
Rigorous discipline and established priorities
ensure the survival of the group
All nomadic societies (Navajo, Gypsies) have had
such constraints built into them

CONSTRAINTS
In the Circus—Each person allowed one trunk
placed in same position each day [other belongings
in sleeping quarters on train—Ringling people *still*
sleep on train]
To move it . . .
Each had 2 buckets of cold water—wash basin—
bath—do laundry
Places in cook tent and dressing tent fixed by
tradition
HORSEBACK RIDERS AND EQUESTRIAN
PERFORMERS
Best light closest to back door

FAMILIES
Franconi—equestrians, liberty horses
Chiarini—acrobats
Christiani—equestrians
Hanneford—equestrians
Wallenda—aerialists
Costello—aerialists
Colleano—aerialists
Zacchini—aerialists—fired from cannon
Silbon—aerialists

CONSTRAINTS, continued
then in descending order:
    great stars other than equestrians
    aerialists and acrobats
    and so on in a complicated hierarchy
    Never (by changing roles) *descend* in privilege
    Whoever is in center ring chooses music all
    3 work to
    High status of equestrians in traditional
    Director of show is not the ringmaster but
    the Equestrian Director

HISTORY
The priority of the equestrians goes back to the
ORIGINS of modern circus.
PHILLIP ASTLEY, earlier, the Spanish Riding School
in Vienna 1572.
London 1770s, ex-cavalry, started a display of
trained horses in a circular ring (tumblers and
clown interludes) later added a pantomime 1780s
this kind of stationary show multiplied.
1785 Bill Ricketts' Philadelphia circus "frequented
assiduously" by President Washington.
1800–60 bulky wooden slow-traveleing structures
still primarily equestrian.
Around 1850 large tents begin; quicker moves;
increased value of parade, midway, menagerie for
instant daytime publicity; performance gets more
various.
1871 P. T. Barnum put 3 rings under canvas
1884 Ringling Bros. first wagon tour
1890 Ringling changed to railroad transport

INTRODUCTION TO CLOWNFACE
CLOWNS
Early
Grimaldi
Debaru (Pierrot—Enfante der Paradis)
Muriol
Dan Rice (1850)
Early 20th C.
Gijon Polidor (mimicked other acts)
Silvers Oakley (1911 about)
Poodles Hannaford (equestrian began 1911)
Polidor C. Mortier (Chesty)
Albert Flo White
Hamlyn
Paul Jung
Duffy
Ernie Birch
Bob Kellog
Paul Jerome
Bones Brown—Flier
Rose Alexander
Otto Griebling
Felix Adler
Lou Jacobs
Emmett Kelly (Weary Willy)
recent—Nimmo
Pio Nock (wire act)
Dutch
Paul Wenzel
Coco
Al Bruce

Buck Baker
John Reilly
Harry Nelson (stilt)

VULNERABILITY
Imagine all that stuff *wet*

CIRCUS TRAGEDIES
May 17, 1892—Ringling Circus, train was derailed
by swollen river en route to Washington, Kansas;
26 horses and one man were killed outright and
many others injured. The show missed only its
Washington shows and went on to play Concordia,
Kansas, the following day.

The Ringling Bros. circus has had blowdowns
in Niagara Falls, Ellsworth, Kansas, and Crookston,
Minnesota. In 1945, in Dallas, wind took down the
horse tent and others, but the big top withstood
the storm and after it passed the show went on
with a 20 minute delay.

Cleveland, August 4, 1942, a disgruntled
employee who had been fired started a fire in a pile
of straw next to the animal tent; within minutes 65
animals had burned to death or shot to put them
out of their misery. No people or horses were hurt,
the afternoon show was canceled, but the evening
show went on.

In June 1938, during the labor strike, the
Ringling circus was in Scranton, Pa., stuck in a
mire of mud and water when the mayor of the city
ordered the circus to move out of town. After 5
days of haggling with the union leaders the circus
people managed to load their equipment onto railroad cars and head back to Winter Quarters for the
remainder of the season.

The worst tragedy of the Ringling circus
occurred July 6, 1944, in Hartford, Conn. During the
afternoon show the big tent caught fire, the circus
band began to play "Stars and Stripes Forever"; the
signal to circus employees to clear the tent. The
audience, however, panicked, and 168 people died
and many more were injured. Five circus employees were indicted for involuntary manslaughter,
convicted, and eventually pardoned. The circus was
sued for $4 million in damages which it paid off in
10 years by not taking a profit from its earnings. It
was later learned that the fire was started by pyro-
maniac. The circus returned to Winter Quarters
after the fire and within four weeks was ready to
travel again to earn the money to pay the damages.
They did not play under canvas for the rest of the
season and had to develop new rigging for the acts

that could stand without the tent.

FRED J. DOCKSTADER
The pure fun-making aspect of the cult should not
be minimized.

A people who are as prone to laughter as the
Hopis would never flourish under a fearsome, dole-
ful, Calvinist religion. Therefore the Kachinas who
enact the roles of funmakers and clowns, playing
tricks, acting out absurd pantomines, or cleverly
mimicking spectators, have as important a function in Kachinas' religious activity as joy and laughter do in Hopi daily life. Further the Burlesque
drama and impersonations are opportunities to
strike back at oppressors, for example the white
man.

This affords a psychological release that is
important for a people such as the Hopis who have
a strong inclination for peaceful living.

The limited opportunity in Hopi life for individual expression or for the attainment of personal
eminence, has often been mentioned. A person
who achieves prominence in the village through
expression of his own abilities or talents may be
criticized by his neighbors or in extreme cases
may even be accused of being a witch. Likewise,
teachers have found that one sure way to failure in
dealing with the Hopi students is to praise an individual highly, or to select one (or a few) and elevate
him to a prominent position as exemplary to the
balance of the class. This almost never succeeds,
and usually results in unhappiness for the selected
student.

TEARDOWN 1947
When the evening show gets under way, the cook-
house, with its crew of 130 men and fourteen
wagons, has already left the lot. The harness,
blacksmith and service tents are being loaded on
the trains; the menagerie tent is coming down and
the lot is filled with the sound of tractors and the
light of flares. During the performance the banner
line and sideshow have dispersed. After their last
appearance the elephants walk straight out of the
ring and off tail trunking to the railroad station.

By 10:45 the show is ending—as the audience is
encouraged to move out quickly, work elephants
start pulling wagons inside the tent to be loaded.

Six hundred men work on the teardown—
including ticket takers and clowns and midway
concession men. It takes about seven noisy minutes to fold all the ten thousand chairs.

All the electric wiring has to be dismantled—
four miles of cable—and stored systematically;
performers' rigging is packed into canvas bags;
the side-walls are unlaced and folded away. At
the end of the first hour, the big top is completely
empty, and the quarter poles have been pulled
out.

The canvas boss gives the order, "let 'er go."
Simultaneously, the last hitch that holds the canvas
at the top of each center pole is pulled loose, and
the bases of all the smaller poles are knocked free.
The canvas subsides slowly, like a balloon; and
by the time it's all the way down the canvas men
on the outside have run up the slope, and started
unlacing the 18 sections; performers and crew fold
and roll them into bundles.

The six main poles are still held up by their own
guying; after the canvas is away, five of them are
lowered one by one and the tractor that pulls the
stakes starts it round. The finale is the lowering
of the last main pole. Its weight and its leverage
is now on one rope that weaves through a bunch
of stake smoking and steaming from the water
poured on to cool it down.

The poles and canvas of the big top are the last
to leave the lot; and they go off on the third section of the circus train. The performers and the top
circus executives, in their sleeping coaches, are the
last section to leave the railroad siding; the only
person left in town is the "twenty-four-hour-man"
who has to pay local tradesmen's bills and see the
lot is clean.

THIS-IS-AS-IT-SHOULD-BE-NESS
A group of people and equipment brought together
for a fairly demanding purpose
the way they stand and wait—tuning themselves
(von Stroheim on the set)
discarding things not needed
    Julia Child
    surgical theater
    some lab situations

MORAL, Stage One (after Movie Sets) the circus
as an example of TAKING PLEASURE SERIOUSLY
in one's everyday work. For the circus and for architecture, this is a PROFESSIONAL NECESSITY; many
of the rigors of the discipline come from consideration, anticipation of how things will affect people.
AND: you can't do this successfully from cold:

you have to have serious attention and respect
for your own pleasures/loves/preferences. There's
nothing frivolous about a high-flier's pleasure in
his work (or an architect's appetite for a space to
be just so).
SCIENTIST—not my mission to point out to this
company that scientists do have a lot of fun but—
by analogy with the circus, and with architecture—to suggest very strongly (EXHORTATION) that
pleasure is (and ought to be) the thing to take most
seriously and to build on.

William Wordsworth, Preface to the "Lyrical
Ballads," 1845: "We have no knowledge, that is, no
general principles drawn from the contemplation
of particular facts, but what has been built up by
pleasure, and exists in us by pleasure alone. The
Man of Science, the Chemist and Mathematician,
whatever difficulties and disgusts they may have
had to struggle with, know and feel this."

MORAL, Stage Two
the current problem of CELEBRATIONS
the last great American celebration for my money
was the WPA—adversity and limited resources.
The idea of celebrating by committing the community to attacking a major need—only Gerry
Piel's proposal to put Library of Congress on-line
REGENERATION OF VOCABULARY—"Festival"—
how often does an actual festival live up to the
flavor of the word?

The same failure to TAKE PLEASURE SERIOUSLY,
transferred from day-to-day life to the exceptional
event. DISCONTINUITY has set in between the
solemnity of a celebration and the festivity and
neither is healthy without the other. And the festive side gets to be just another competing piece
of CULTURE or ENTERTAINMENT and the solemn
side gets left to the speechwriters.

(a conclusion to the moral: not much hope for
public bodies to be more vigorous about this
unless individuals allow themselves to entertain
real respect for their own pleasures)

Source: Charles Eames, lecture notes, Penrose Memorial
Lecture, American Philosophical Society, Philadelphia,
April 1974, Part II: Speeches and Writings series, Charles
and Ray Eames Papers, Manuscript Division, Library of
Congress, Washington, D.C.

CHARLES EAMES

"The Language of Vision: The Nuts and Bolts"

The following communication was delivered by
Mr. Eames at a Stated Meeting held last spring under
the auspices of the Western Center of the American
Academy. The lecture was illustrated with several
of his films and slide shows.

UNFORTUNATELY, universities today are becoming discontinuity headquarters, with each department avoiding communication with the others and with the rest of the world. Used as it could be, the language of vision is a real threat to this discontinuity, and so it is avoided at all costs. The film department is usually located in the drama or in the art department and caters for the most part to people's creative idiosyncrasies rather than to the development of basic, current, working ideas of science and the humanities. The danger is that film will be prematurely contaminated by a virus of self-expression. When a scientist, engineer, or mathematician collides with a painter or sculptor, he often catches the bug to which the painter or sculptor has already developed immunity. Instead, the scientist should recognize aesthetics as an extension of his own discipline. For instance, if a mathematician is writing a paper on mathematics, he would not particularly improve his work by hiring an essayist to do the job. On the other hand, if the mathematician were part essayist, he could make his point more accessible to his colleagues, his students, and perhaps an even wider audience. The film department can support the university's charter for promoting intellectual inquiry only if it is able to serve all departments from a central position within the school.

I believe that universities should establish a visual service unit open to every department to assist the faculty in learning to use the language of vision effectively. Some time ago, we made a proposal, as part of a program at MIT, whereby a person knowledgeable about the nuts and bolts of the language of vision (the making and use of film, records, tapes, etc.) would be assigned to each class, whether it be history, biochemistry, small particle physics, or chemistry.

In the future, intellectual, political, and technical people are going to need ways of communicating complex ideas; MIT seemed a very good place to test the possibilities of the language of vision.

In a film which we made about Copernicus, we tried to communicate an overview of his life, the time in which he lived, and the development of his ideas. The film is the record of an exhibition honoring the five hundredth anniversary of Copernicus.

Because exhibitions are usually dismantled and never seen again, we made this film as a history of the event. The film shows landscapes, artifacts, buildings, and astronomical imagery of Copernicus' time, as well as original manuscripts of his work. A narrator describes Copernicus' work and quotes from his writings and those of his peers. We hear Copernicus' description of his early thoughts on the place of the sun in the universe: "I began to be annoyed that the philosophers had discovered no sure scheme for the movements of the machinery of the world; therefore I also began to meditate on the mobility of the earth." Complementary to this quote, we see his own simple drawing of "Sol" as a small circle with a larger concentric circle indicating the course of the earth about it.

As far as possible, Copernicus and his world speak for themselves. The accompanying music, put together by Elmer Bernstein, captures the spirit of the sixteenth century. The imagery and the narrative are chosen to decrease the distance between a modern audience and the world of the past. A film of ours comes into being because it is either a logical extension of an immediate problem we are working on or it is something we have been wanting to do for a long time and cannot put off any longer.

The film "House of Science," which was made as an introduction to the United States science exhibit at the Seattle World's Fair, seeks to provide a rough but real feeling of how science came to be the way it is. The first section is, in effect, a time-model that has a scale: every two and one-half seconds is equal to a decade. The various disciplines of science are represented as buildings. The growth of the buildings is an architectural allegory approximating the number of people in each field at any given time. In the opening of the film, the "House of Science" is shown as a small building, which then begins to change and grow. For example, it soon adds the "House of Anatomy"; the "Science of Alchemy" appears temporarily as a tent and is then subsumed under the "Science of Chemistry." Near the end of the sequence, branches of science appear very rapidly spreading over six screens, and finally the entire screen area is filled with all of the sciences, which have developed by 1962.

For the body of the "House of Science" film, of which this clip is just the introduction, and also for a presentation called "Glimpses of the U.S.A.," prepared for the United States exhibit at Moscow in 1959, we used a multi-screen technique. This was not a capricious method but rather a way of establishing credibility and avoiding superlatives. At the time of the Cold War, when this exhibit was prepared and shown, the citizens of the Soviet Union had heard much about the United States but had little concrete imagery on which to base a belief in what they heard. We wanted to present not an editorial statement but a comprehensive, fair picture of this diverse country. With seven screens we were able to show simultaneously a whole range of examples of various subjects—say, families eating. In the same way, in "House of Science" we showed simultaneously many different examples of the category "microscope." The audience recognizes an open set, and this somehow raises the level of truthfulness.

Some of the same technique is again used in our "Circus" slide show. The circus is a nomadic society, which is very rich and colorful but which shows apparent license on the surface. Parents tend to take their children to the circus as a kind of ritual, a kind of initiation into a world which is just not allowed and which cannot be. Everything in the circus is pushing the possible beyond the limit— bears do not really ride on bicycles, people do not really execute three-and-a-half-turn somersaults in the air from a board to a ball, and until recently no one dressed the way fliers do. Yet within this apparent freewheeling license we find a discipline which is almost unbelievable. There is a strict hierarchy of events, and an elimination of choice under stress, so that one event can automatically follow another.

The layout of the circus under canvas is more like the plan of the Acropolis than anything else; it is a beautiful organic arrangement established by

the boss canvas man and the lot boss. Upon arrival at a circus site, the lot boss used to drive a horse-drawn cart around the entire lot to make his preliminary investigation. Then he began again and, by counting the horse's hoof beats, marked out the appropriate spots for the boss canvas man to place the quarter-poles. In this activity, and others of the circus people, one can see the precise arrangements of people in relation to one another. The lot boss knows exactly what his relationship is to the boss canvas man because the mutual objective and the method of accomplishing it are clear to both.

In the actions of circus people waiting or rehearsing or preparing to perform, there is a quality of beauty, which comes from appropriateness to a given situation. There is a recognized mission for everyone involved. In a crisis there can be no question as to what needs to be done. The circus may look like the epitome of pleasure, but the person flying on a high wire, or executing a balancing act, or being shot from a cannon must take his pleasure very, very seriously.

In the same vein, the scientist, in his laboratory, is pushing the possible beyond the current limit, and he too must take his pleasure very seriously. The concept of "appropriateness," this "how-it-should-be-ness," has equal value in the circus, in the making of a work of art, and in science. It often turns out, however, that scientists, engineers, or mathematicians abandon their own disciplined approach to problems when they face questions that concern pleasure. They tend to think of the aesthetic level and the scientific level as discontinuous, whereas both actually involve this quality of appropriateness and exhaustive definition of the problem. They fail to take pleasure seriously.

I was raised in a nineteenth-century mode, where my first experiences with science involved minor physics experiments done almost as parlor tricks, mathematics through magic squares and electricity by way of a "shocking machine" which was reputed to have some therapeutic value. All this had an aura of magic about it; by the time I became an architect I was not at all surprised that our understanding of electricity grew out of toying around with pith balls, or that pneumatics and hydraulics were first used to impress the populace by magically opening doors and raising fountains.
. . .

Cable television, as a means of promoting the language of vision, offers a special opportunity for improving communication between groups, but its potential has not been fully realized. I think that cable television could be of great benefit to a small university or college. Once a school purchases a franchise, it faces the problem of reducing the contents of the college into a form that can be transmitted on several channels and made available to the public. . . .

Think what the universities could do if they were to take their own best offering and transmit it on a "found education" basis. Of course, it is important for the university to have good projection facilities so that the viewer can gain a feeling for the quality of projected images. The sloppy use of images can erode the sensibilities in a way that many of the people who tout sensibility fail to recognize. Universities—and everyone who purports to carry on the sacred flame—have a responsibility to the details of communication. . . .

Since I have been urging scientists and mathematicians to use the language of vision in their work, I would like to point to an able exponent of this effort, Raymond Redheffer, a distinguished mathematician at UCLA who has acted as a consultant to us in many of our exhibitions and films. Redheffer takes his pleasure seriously; after collaborating with us for some time, he decided that he wanted to be in more direct touch with film. We set up a camera for him and, using direct animation, he created a film of his own dealing with equations. His art was rigorous enough so that he was able to make jokes on film, which were not peripheral to his topic but actually furthered understanding of his concepts.

As we said in the "House of Science," "science is essentially an artistic or philosophical enterprise carried on for its own sake. In this it is more akin to play than to work. But it is quite sophisticated play, in which the scientist views nature as a system of interlocking puzzles." In Redheffer's film, we see a mathematician involved in very serious, sophisticated play. . . .

The choice of a title for this evening—"The Language of Vision: The Nuts and Bolts"—was intended primarily as a warning. We have sometimes found ourselves presented under a title such as "bridging the two cultures." To me this is a non-issue and a counterproductive one. If the media people truly had the confidence of their craft they would be ready to assume the task of conveying those ideas that individuals have a need to convey with a minimum of added art. And if the scientists and engineers had not somehow browbeaten themselves, they would recognize that they have no need for extra aesthetics. What is required to bring these two groups together is nothing exalted—just the nuts and bolts of the subject.

Source: Charles Eames, "The Language of Vision: The Nuts and Bolts," *Bulletin of the American Academy of Arts and Sciences* 28, no. 1 (October 1974): 13–25.

Design Process at Herman Miller

Editor's note: Curators Mildred (Mickey) Friedman and Dean Swanson conducted this interview with Charles Eames (CE) and Ray Eames (RE) as preparation for the 1975 exhibition The Design Process at Herman Miller *at the Walker Art Center, Minneapolis. Also present and participating was Jehane Burns, a writer and scholar who worked at the Eames Office from 1966 to 1978.*

FRIEDMAN *Could you characterize . . . the difference, let's say, between the De Prees [founding family of Herman Miller] and their approach to the problems of furniture design, and, let's say, Hans Knoll, who had a very different background and a different attitude? . . .*

CE There was a great competition at the New York show and, of course, we were strongly influenced by Eero. And Eero had a built-in internationalism, which made him, sort of, be able to enjoy and appreciate certain aspects of Hans that were sort of based in international intrigue and fashion and a certain kind of momentary panic that goes with that kind of a pressure that he was sort of under. And Eero rolled with that and enjoyed it, and I think Florence saw it as almost one of the few ways of putting this whole thing to work. She saw it as an immediate outlet for instincts and convictions that she had, and it's very close to ours, because we were all at Cranbrook together in the old days.

FRIEDMAN *How did it happen that you started to consult for Herman Miller rather than for Knoll? [I ask] because of your previous association with Saarinen and Florence Knoll, and so forth.*

CE Well, I didn't ever confuse my loyalty and love for Eero with a general ability to evaluate a climate in which I would be at home. This was never a case. I was just plain not at home in such a fast-moving set. First of all, I was not that sure about what we were doing.

FRIEDMAN *In other words, . . . you saw the Knoll development as a kind of sophisticated international sort of thing, unlike the Miller, which was more indigenous to what was available here or how do you . . . ?*

RE No, that's a backward view of the situation. It really wasn't the pressure of Hans. I think, more

than anything, it was the pressure on him—it was so intense and so crucial for him to make things work that I could hardly stand the thought of that operation. We had developed the things and continued; we never thought that it was a finished thing, and we had just sort of come to a point in development and that seemed to be a totally different operation.

FRIEDMAN *Was [D. J.] De Pree very relaxed in a different sense, in some sense, and not as demanding?*

CE No. D. J. was never relaxed about an investment, but on the other hand, you see, the situation Hans presented was one where you're, prematurely, viewing yourself as from the outside. It's a play in which you're taking part where you're also the viewer and the audience and you're sort of part of this thing, and that did not occur with D. J. D. J. was in there and he had all his own personal prejudices, biases, devotions, and they were all working. And not only were they working there, but they were alive and working in this extraordinary character, who was indeed the whole sales force, which was Jim Eppinger. And George had already not only made this contact, and you've heard George describe the scene I'm sure . . .

FRIEDMAN *But he adores D. J. I mean, he thinks he's a saint, in contrast, perhaps, to some of the younger people. You know, he feels that that was the great period.*

CE It was a great period. Because he was a saint.

RE And George was working with everything he had all the time.

CE Saints have a very strong vein of bigotry in them, and they have all these other things, but, nevertheless, he was a saint. And yet it was George, who was one of the few people who could really enjoy the saint with complete ease, out saving him.

FRIEDMAN *You'll have to tell me what that is.*

CE OK, let's consider, George is now a young designer, who has just been given the post of director of design for the Herman Miller Furniture Company. He is now making studies—he really hasn't produced anything to speak of yet, because he hasn't gotten into motion. Among the first, big significant acts he does is to pick up his patron, D.J., . . . invites him to the [MoMA] show in New York, and suggests that he take on, to put into production, the work of somebody who is, in D.J.'s terms, a competitor of his. Me. Boy, when you're from . . .

FRIEDMAN *Now, this was the Organic show in New York?*

CE No, not the Organic show but the personal show in '46.

FRIEDMAN *The Eames (MoMA) show in '46, OK.*

CE Now, boy, to a Zeeland Dutchman, their view of such risks and competitions that you can't much top that in sainthood, if you wonder what is it, what's happening here that this person should in any way risk his own position. This is very hard to come to terms with. Now that's only one example; there are a lot of examples through the whole thing having to do with truth in advertising, having to do with . . .

RE Material treatment.

CE Treatment of material, but also having to do with politics and the view on the political scene, because I'm sure you can write the script in terms of someone like George having a kind of ability to look at something rationally and without bias that no saint would ever be equipped to do.

FRIEDMAN *OK. That's a point. Now, in addition to that point about both George Nelson and De Pree, De Pree bought this obviously, and decided that if he was going to do this, that there had to be darn good reason because it was such a great sacrifice on his part.*

RE He said he bought it after spending the night, previously, on his knees praying.

FRIEDMAN *Oh, wow! That's a bit much. Anyway, assuming he did that, then after he decided that, yes, he needed to have Eames, as well as Nelson, did he suggest projects to you or did you say, all right, we're doing the chair now and the next thing we want to do is something else? How was that done? How were the projects decided?*

CE Let's see now. You've talked to George.

FRIEDMAN *But George didn't tell me about you.*

CE Are you making up this question?

FRIEDMAN *Yeah, no, yeah. Of course I'm making*

it up, because he didn't tell me about how you worked with him, how the project that you worked on happened, because I asked him that and he said, "I don't know." You'll see when you get the transcript.

CE No, he didn't really ever ask for anything.

FRIEDMAN *So then, how was it decided that something would be made?*

RE It was never decided.

BURNS *Did you ever bring him anything he didn't make?*

CE Nothing that we ever felt was either worth making or logical to make. There was nothing that we felt was really logical to make that I think we didn't make. That is, in that period, the developments came, but . . . this is largely true of most everything we've done for IBM.

FRIEDMAN *For example, let's take IBM. You've had the project for many years of doing exhibitions for the space on Madison and the content of those exhibitions, and so forth, has been left, more or less, up to you.*

BURNS *Was it ever even made explicit, in other words, the role of putting things into it?*

CE It's just that the space was still there and we would think of things to put into the space, and it was never made explicit that we were responsible for this space, nor has it been even in the films that we've done for them, with the exception of certain key things like the film for the Brussels World's Fair.

But you have to face the fact that we knew, we had a fair idea what their problems were, and we had a fair idea what we could do to fill the problem. Like we knew, nobody had to spell it out that Herman Miller has to manufacture furniture and sell it in order to stay in business. Now any elaboration . . .

FRIEDMAN *But the kind, Charles, you know, what direction that furniture would take was something the designers gave to the company, as I understand it, rather than having the company give direction to the designer.*

SWANSON *Right, saying we need a new chair in this year's line or . . .*

CE Well, yes, they said we need a new chair for this line or new pieces for this market, the coming summer market, but, in discussion, we said look, is that a logical way to develop furniture? They said no, it certainly doesn't seem to be, but there have always been markets. Well, instead of doing new furniture, maybe we can do this, and then we began to take part in the showroom design. And George did the same thing and so that, by and large, . . . at this point we were keeping somebody like Jim Eppinger in touch with what was developing because he was a salesman (and he was really the whole part of the company in sales) and then Jim would have an idea that we felt was good. He would, maybe, sell it before it had even been made. Now you could do that in the company now, and it was largely the pressures of then having committed yourself to a sale, and you'd really have to do it. And it would be saying something, an idea that we wanted developed.

FRIEDMAN *George Nelson said that the company was so small in the early days that he felt that that was one of the advantages, that it was possible to do these things that were not standard ways to respond to the problem of design and production because of the fact that it was not really mass production. Things were made in . . . quantities, it was somewhere between handmade and mass production, but the quantities were very small at that point.*

RE I don't think so; mass production was the basis of the design—to produce them.

FRIEDMAN *. . . The uses of your designs moved out of the domestic market into the commercial market, into the office market, into the industrial market, etc. Now, why did that happen?*

CE Very simply and clearly. We were doing some chairs, which we felt you would use in a home, and, for example, even a swivel or tilt chair seemed to be a very natural thing to have in a living room, as you shift your weight you're comfortable in the evening, and so what happened was Herman Miller had, I can remember it well, in Chicago where we set up the sample rooms, which we viewed as great rooms, for all children, people, and people in business came in and looked. "Ah, this is just the thing we need for the office, this lecture hall, this so and so." . . . This changed the whole direction of the business. . . . Then George went on; I'd have to look at the map to see what time and where, but George's, those Executive situations, these things fell right into that, so that the whole mass, the whole trend shifted, and now we have some things which were done as part of the office program. . . .

FRIEDMAN *. . I noticed in reading the early material about your devotion to Frank Lloyd Wright, when you were a young student and so forth, and the fact . . . that your interest in Wright was not acceptable to the people with whom you were studying, and, therefore, you just stopped studying.*

CE It was a Beaux-Arts School.

FRIEDMAN *Right. And so has this Wrightian inter-*

From left: George Nelson, Ray Eames, Charles Eames, and Alexander Girard, circa 1951.

est, you know, affected your later things, or how has architecture played a role, let's say, after the house? There hasn't been really much architecture, except maybe your work with Kevin Roche on the Aquarium Project. Was there a lot of architecture there on your part? How has architecture played a role, in other words, in succeeding years?

CE Well, I don't think it would be any exaggeration to say that we couldn't have the things that we have done recently, or the things that we have done long ago and recently, . . . if we weren't architects. I think Ray has gotten her degree in between time. So I think, for example, like Jehane, she comes on, Jehane attacks these problems, not just as though they were architecture, attacks them largely as an architect would and Ray has, for some time. I don't mean that Jehane started to do that after she came here, because that's not true, but she came with this relationship. But, certainly, the things would be very different if they weren't architects.

FRIEDMAN *But you haven't, except in the sense that exhibition design is architectural, which it is to a great degree, architecture, as such. As people think about architecture, building, structure, shelter, okay. That has not really been something you have been involved in.*

CE Well, we haven't been building shelters.

RE Otherwise, everything is architecture.

FRIEDMAN *How do you feel about Wright in 1974—as strongly as you did as a student?*

CE I suppose more strongly in some ways.

FRIEDMAN *I mean, what did you like about Wright?*

CE Oh, I liked the description of building that windmill. Well, see, a few years before he'd written, he was in general disrepute in the whole country; it wasn't just in the Beaux-Arts Schools. He wrote this autobiography, and I believe that it more or less starts with, after he's into it, [that] he was raised with Froebel and Froebel's system of blocks, and so was I. Except that he was raised when they were sort of real avant-garde and I was raised with them as they were a hang-on in the St. Louis Kindergarten School. But none of that; the Froebel blocks could care less. They were operating just the same both ways, and then he described, he went through that. . . . I felt we were on the same wavelength because I liked Froebel's blocks, and then he described the building of this windmill. And he was on the farm, his aunt's or uncle's farm, or something, and this was the first piece of architecture that he did, and it was an essay having to do

with the interplay of materials, the paint, and the function. And it was a very nice thing. The reason I mention that is that the affection for Wright has always been based more on this kind of an idea, this attitude, rather than forms. I must say, my pulse certainly quickens when I see a Frank Lloyd Wright stained-glass window or a piece of furniture and things like that. So it's not entirely true that it's just the ideas. But that's what it really is.

FRIEDMAN *I see a strong relationship between his caring and interest in detail in your work. You know, that same kind of concern about what you were talking about earlier, about craftsmanship.*

RE Of the consideration of everything.

FRIEDMAN *That sort of totality of his design.*

RE This marvelous thing between Eliel Saarinen and Wright. You know they had all violent arguments but underneath, the work is basic, really . . .

CE And, also . . . Antonin Raymond. But there (were) a lot—Raymond, Eliel, Wright—and I have seen them together, they all cared about these things. But when I said, oh, yes, this was unacceptable because it was a Beaux-Arts school, I don't mean anything negative about the Beaux-Arts school. I still thought it was the best possible training. Eero was trained in the Beaux-Arts, too.

FRIEDMAN *But wasn't everyone at that time? I mean, was there a school that was not a Beaux-Arts school at that point?*

CE Yes, there were.

RE There were sort of not—rather than something else.

CE Yes, it's more that they were not Beaux-Arts. Yale was a Beaux-Arts School.

FRIEDMAN *That's for sure. I think it was much later that the Bauhaus influence came over with Gropius at Harvard and so forth. That was much, much later.*

CE I went to Europe. I was in Europe in 1929, and had not really heard of the Bauhaus. I was in touch with a lot of things, but it just plain wasn't known about, and then I came onto it full-blown at the Weissenhof exposition in Stuttgart in 1929.

FRIEDMAN *And I guess at this same period of time Nelson was in Europe, also.*

CE Yeah. He was on the Prix De Rome. It was a little bit later.

FRIEDMAN *Maybe a little bit later, but then was introduced to Mies and Corbu and so forth and so on, as you know, much the same time, and was writing these wonderful articles for, what was it,* Pencil Points?

CE *Pencil Points. . . .*

RE By the way, did you ever read his introduction to *How To Wrap Five Eggs*, the Japanese book by Hideyuki Oka?

FRIEDMAN *No, but I hear that it must be read.*

RE It's so beautiful. It's so good, so good.

FRIEDMAN *I guess what is the most difficult and, also, interesting thing about your work over the years is that it has so many facets. Unlike most people, I mean most people are, let's say, they're architects and they build structures, or they're furniture makers and they make furniture, or they're this or that or the other and they don't do half a dozen things. If you try to analyze what makes these various things happen and how they relate and obviously they do . . .*

SWANSON *What is common to all of them?*

FRIEDMAN *Right.*

BURNS *As you ask your questions, you're sort of working on a baseline of the visual because of the nature of your own task. You're working on a visual baseline.*

FRIEDMAN *Yeah, I guess we are.*

BURNS *In a way, you seem to be sort of resisting that. I don't know how you could characterize a baseline other than the visual one.*

CE Well, I naturally, to begin with, characterized it as architecture. That was because I hadn't put it exactly that way. But that would be a common answer to that in terms of characterization. And it's absolutely true. As soon as you start to pin it on the visual, you begin to react exactly the same way as if you were talking about architecture. And that's certainly true in furniture.

BURNS *But, if you say the baseline is architecture, then you have to define it in a generic enough way.*

CE You see, without thinking of defining architecture, why, you think of it as a process of looking at a collection of elements that on the surface seem chaotic, and finding some relationship between the parts. And finally, homing in on functional relationships between the parts. With that clue of relationships, why, giving the whole a kind of structure makes sense.

FRIEDMAN *What you're saying, essentially, Charles, is that those clues are not really visual?*

CE No, not visual.

Source: Ray Eames and Charles Eames, interview by Mickey Friedman, November 6, 1974, transcript, Herman Miller, Inc., Archives, Zeeland, Michigan.

Photograph taken at the time of this exhibition. From left, Glen Walters (Herman Miller, Inc.), D. J. De Pree (Herman Miller, Inc.), George Nelson, Alexander Girard, Ray Eames, and Charles Eames.

An Eames Celebration:

PBS, February 3,
Special of the Week,
8-9:30 p.m. EST
(Please check local
listings)

The Several Worlds of Charles and Ray Eames

Made possible
through grants by
IBM and the
National Science
Foundation

"An Eames Celebration," advertising
flier, PBS, 1975, Private Collection,
Los Angeles.

An Eames Celebration: The Several Worlds of Charles and Ray Eames

Editor's note: From the website of Perry Miller Adato, the filmmaker: "In 1973, on the occasion of a large retrospective of their achievement in furniture design at the Museum of Modern Art in New York, Charles and Ray consented to be filmed and interviewed at MoMA and to be filmed within their latest exhibition on the history and future of the computer at the IBM building in Manhattan. Later, Charles reluctantly agreed to a biography of their lives and work as well while protesting that it was too soon for a summing up. Yet once filming began, his cooperation was unstinted. The filmmakers were given free access to the whole remarkable range of their activities, to excerpts from their films, and to their vast photographic archives." The following excerpt is from the initial interview, at the Museum of Modern Art.

CHARLES EAMES There's a thing that you can't lose sight of, even, aside from the technique of production. That is, in the general concept in design. You can do a piece of furniture or you can do almost any object, and you can look at it and it can seem to be quite satisfying. But there are often, there are several questions, questions we've usually asked ourselves. First of all we'd say, you know, "What would Mies van der Rohe have said if he'd looked at it?" Then, "What would Bucky Fuller say about it?" Then you'd ask yourself another question, that was: "You can stand it now, but could you stand it if you saw 50 in a row?" This is a very brutal question. Because very often you can do a thing which will stand up as one of a kind, but God help you if you do more than five or six."

RAY EAMES Any one making one thing . . . that's very nice, to make one thing. But to be able to keep the quality in mass production is the only reason we've been working so hard—because we could easily turn out a nice thing and another and another—but to figure a way that the hundredth and the five hundredth and the thousandth would have the original character.

CHARLES EAMES [Speaking of the molded plywood chair] the general misconception about the shape, because when people say shape—why immediately afterwards there was a rise of seating in a soft material and make a casting of your behind as if that's the work, and that isn't true. Because that is a non-architectural solution of the problem. What the solution really depended on, you've got a certain amount of bulk in your physiology, but there are also a lot of points to take, certain points to take stresses. What it really depended on was the recognition of this in the molding of the plywood so it was really a form that would support, not a form that would completely conform.

Source: Charles Eames and Ray Eames, interview by Perry Miller Adato, *An Eames Celebration: The Several Worlds of Charles and Ray Eames*, PBS, 1975.

KEITH COLQUHOUN

"Innovator in Earth Shoes"

A lot has been written about American designer Charles Eames since he first began surprising and charming the world nearly 40 years ago: about his furniture and his film sets and his toys and his exhibitions. But this may be the first time there has been a reference in print to his shoes. They are a good deal broader than the conventional shoe, and there is no instep, simply a flat surface that spreads your weight and allows you to stay on your feet for a long time without getting tired.

Eames says they are called Earth shoes. He calls over his wife, Ray, who is also wearing Earth shoes, and she affirms, "They are life-saving." Eames didn't design the shoes; he thinks they are Swedish. But choice is a form of design too. "Every time I lay a table I am designing something."

Eames is also wearing a single-breasted lightweight four-buttoned suit, a style of the 1960s that looks remarkably discreet when compared with today's men's fashions, and his greying hair is cut short, almost in the style of a wartime crewcut. At 68 his appearance strides the central years of the century. And so does his influence as an innovator.

He and Ray have recently been in London watching over the installation in the British Museum of the exhibition they have designed called The World of Franklin and Jefferson. This is the main effort by America (supported by private enterprise money from IBM) to acknowledge the bicentennial of the Revolution, and before coming here had been seen in Warsaw and Paris. After closing in London on 15 November it will go on a tour of America.

The London exhibition is clear, exciting, and informative. It has the qualities of a good feature in a color magazine, with the additional advantage that you can walk round the items. If, in the mid-1970s, it does not seem particularly new, this is because many of the Eames ideas—blown-up pictures, coloured mounts, and well-written captions—have been copied so widely that now nearly every exhibition put on has a bit of Eames in it. One of the perils of being an innovator is that your ideas become commonplace. Years ago, in an interview, Eames said that one of the best bits of design

he had seen in Britain was the London taxi. Since then it has become a cliché in design talk. But Charles Eames was the one who said it first.

Eames says he has been a Jefferson buff since he was a child. "There is an expression in music, 'doubling in brass.' You play in the strings but you can double in the brass section. Jefferson could double in brass. In the Jeffersonian sense, everything is architecture: his design for the University of Virginia not only concerned the building but the curriculum, the professors, the faculty. His Land Ordinance for the settlement of the West was the grandest conception of land use America has seen—and to Jefferson it was pure architecture." Eames was trained as an architect, and he has a Jeffersonian inquisitiveness. In the British Museum he often slipped away from his exhibition and spent hours "looking at little odds and ends of Roman and Egyptian domestic stuff."

The most famous item designed by Eames is an easy chair in moulded plywood with leather upholstery. It is elegant and comfortable and right, and whenever there is a new book or exhibit about design, this chair, Chair 670, usually has a place, summing up all that is good about twentieth-century design as precisely as Hepplewhite spoke for the eighteenth. Although it first went on sale 20 years ago it has that curiously dateless look characteristic of a classic.

Wherever in the world Eames goes, for whatever enterprise he and Ray are engaged on, people mention the chair, and a slightly weary look comes into his face as this celebrated ghost of the past intrudes into his current enthusiasm. It isn't the chair he liked best: he mentions another chair on slender steel legs designed in 1945. He didn't originally intend the easy chair to go into production.

"I made it as a present for Billy Wilder. Billy had made a picture in East Germany and had found a Marcel Breuer chair and brought it back to me, and this was a return present."

Charles Eames speaks affectionately about Britain in an unsentimental way. "The greatest thing for the world would be for Britain to become the communications center for the world."

Communications? Satellites and so on? No, not that, Eames says, but a place where all the information anyone needed would be available. A sort of world superlibrary? Something like that. He says we have a headstart that comes from our heritage, from being concentrated in an island and being in the right place. Of all the roles offered for Britain, isn't this the most unusual? "I don't put it forward in the spirit of pity. We really need your help."

Source: Keith Colquhoun, "Innovator in Earth Shoes," *Observer* (November 2, 1975): 16.

Charles and Ray Eames in London. Photograph by Ian Cook.

RAY EAMES

Arts, Education, and the Americas

*Editor's note: Ray Eames delivered these remarks at
the David Rockefeller Symposium of Arts, Education,
and Americas.*

THIS PANEL MEMBER—*in the context* of our original assignment: "reviewing the field, and preparing
recommendations for new directions in national
policy" *bearing in mind* David Rockefeller's words,
in his letter of invitation:

> There have been many claims made for the arts
> in education. We will expect to look critically
> at all of them. For example, it is said that the
> arts are a humanizing force in education and
> that they help us to overcome cultural barriers;
> that instruction in the arts has spillover benefits
> into the cognitive fields, including math and
> reading . . .

welcoming the clear priority expressed by Michael
Straight: "to raise the general level of aesthetic
awareness in the nation, and thus, to create
a society within which the great artists of the
future may grow"

fearing a tendency to reverse this priority, and to
assume—uncritically—that the first step is to
increase the quantity of Art, and that good con-
sequences for the "quality of life" will follow

recalling Charles Eames's insistence (when pro-
voked) that "art is a quality, not a product"

convinced that, in a time of low aesthetic demand-
ingness on the part of society, the teaching of
fine art, in practice, often does not do enough
to bridge the gap between quality in the fine arts
and quality and appropriateness in the circumstances of daily life

endorsing some things said at the last meeting:

Frank Oppenheimer: too many, not enough time
(4,000,000 children; 30,000 teachers)

Peggy Cooper: the problem is the quality of
teachers;
overtaxed
not well taught
lack of knowledge

Frank Stanton: it's the writing that counts, not
the lighting effects. (And our chairman's
uncle: "Participate; and get the best damn
people you can get.")

recognizing the beginning of "artist-in-residence"
programs, and believing that ideally the function of the artist-in-residence would be to
uncover qualities, values and pleasures in every
discipline taught in the school—sciences as well
as humanities

concludes (short of instantly calling into being
tens of thousands of dedicated and brilliant
teachers) that what has to be done, in order to
improve the quality and pertinence of teaching,
is immediately to begin to capture the very best
in every field, that already exists, using film and
all other appropriate technologies; and—in preserving the special quality of the best teaching—
to ensure that the product is at least as good as
a good commercial; so that these units become
a network of top-level thought and feeling, expo-
nentially available as a concentrated vitamin
supplement for a malnourished country. (And
so that ideally, as a result of such a network,
and of a broadened and heightened artist-in-
residence program, another level of projects
might develop in the schools themselves: projects in which students would *use* the "language
of vision," not for its own sake but as a tool in
relation to *every* subject.)

Source: Ray Eames, statement to Arts, Education, and
the Americas, December 4, 1975, Container I:218:13,
Charles and Ray Eames Papers, Manuscript Division,
Library of Congress, Washington, D.C.

Library of Congress

CORRESPONDENCE

Editor's note: In 1981, Daniel Boorstein presided over the acquisition by the Library of Congress of the Charles and Ray Eames Papers and working materials.

Charles Eames to Daniel J. Boorstein, Library of Congress, Washington, D.C.
January 9, 1976

Dear Dan:

Congratulations and best wishes to you both—wear it in good health.

It was good to get the piece on the induction and read your to-the-point response.

I went through this pre-bicentennial period touting a celebration idea that came from Gerry Piel—that is—put the entire Library of Congress on line in the computer. It would cost a bit more than the moon shot, but combined with the stationary satellites, it would have been a real celebration, and most every stage would have some instant value to the community.

I spent some time last night in a lab with some young guys working with image enhancement and advanced computer graphics—a pure visual language that was difficult to accommodate.

Hope that this new job won't keep you completely out of circulation.

Charles Eames

Source: Charles Eames to Daniel Boorstin, January 9, 1976, Container I:10, Folder 5, Charles and Ray Eames Papers, Manuscript Division, Library of Congress, Washington, D.C.

Note: Gerard Piel was credited with revitalizing *Scientific American* magazine, and was the author of many books on science including the two-volume *The Age of Science: What Scientists Learned in the Twentieth Century.*

Eero Saarinen

THE WHOLE RELATIONSHIP with Eero started at Cranbrook. Schools have vintage years like wine or anything else. Those years Florence Schust, Harry Weese, and Harry Bertoia were there. It was a good, good, group, a very interesting and lively group of people. There was a closeness. Ray and I were there. Eero and I had done the competition for the Museum of Modern Art. Ray worked on that too. The result was announced in 1941. The furniture thing, while very stimulating, was disappointing in techniques and manufacturing costs; and we were interested in pursuing it. We came out here to pursue the problem of low cost in furniture.

We—Eero, Ray, and I—would all sort of work together on these things. We were working together and we remained very close. It was simply at Cranbrook, a tremendous amount of time and energy had begun to be spent, but there was a tendency towards people coming in as visitors. As it became an attractive place, less concentration and work could be done. At that point, Cranbrook, as an atelier, began to cease to function. There were also pressures on Eero's time, and he began to withdraw from the Cranbrook activity. This largely had to do with the fact that the Booths began to come back into the picture, and they viewed Cranbrook more as an atelier in which the craftsmen and the artists are to serve the will of the patron than the development of an idea itself. They seemed to ask Eero to leave the Academy because he was too strong a force. That's the turn things took then. It marked the end of Cranbrook as a free-flowing atelier with the forces coming from the people within it. Eliel was very open to that kind of work.

Bertoia wasn't involved in sculpture. He was making cream pitchers and things like that. He hadn't even touched sculpture or furniture, and, actually, had no experience in metal work other than the working in silver. That hadn't occurred to him.

Eero had a very competitive nature, and he would call up—his time early morning, my time the middle of the night—and start to describe an idea for a chair, which we would lay out for patent application in every possible usage. This was the general spirit of staking out your claim.

Eero used to come out here to work when his office would get very demanding. We'd give him an office or a room here. There was a very successful office chair he did that Knoll produced. It was a very good chair. It's the one that sort of wrapped around, the hole in the back, the balance was good. I think it was the best functional piece he did. Eero came out here and we had a lot of molded parts around. He would pick up all these parts and take them back into his office. He would make models with little pieces of tin, metal, and wood parts. Finally, again, he showed these things and began his spiel about patents and whatnot. He designed the chair right here in the office, the parts and all the things. It was not only the most successful but also it was one of the most serviceable pieces of furniture, and they're still making a lot of them.

During the war years we went on to the use of molded plywood; we turned to splints. We developed the pieces of furniture that were in the 1946 exhibition at the Museum of Modern Art. Elliot Noyes was involved at that point too. This was right after the war, 1946. Edgar Kaufmann was involved in the Organic show. That's the point when the merchandisers, the people in the know, predicted that any kind of furniture like this would have a six-month fashion life. George Nelson brought the Herman Millers over; and, of course, Hans and Shu were married. We all knew each other, and Eero was very close to Shu. When that started and Herman Miller became interested in the furniture at the '46 exhibition, Hans, of course, was interested in it too.

There was this sort of competition to do it. At the moment, it didn't seem like doing a sure thing. It was all very risky and it wasn't as though you were sitting on top of something of great value and trying to auction it off. It was more the willingness of two people to take this kind of risk. It didn't have the view that you have in retrospect. At that point, Hans was risking a lot in everything he did. He had some very good products. Eero hadn't done any furniture at this point, but he had some things in mind. Hans was very interested in the pieces and wanted very much to do them. Ray and I were sympathetic. Hans was sort of an international character. He acted it. Shu was the same, she wore it very well. When she was at Cranbrook, Eliel adored her. She was an orphan, her parents had died. I don't know what her guardianship had been. Eliel and Loja adored her and regarded her almost as a child of theirs. That is quite a thing, because they were reserved people. They saw the qualities which Shu had. Of course, Eero and Shu were very close, and she had marvelous taste and was terribly attractive.

They came out of the Midwest, Herman Miller. I think I am somewhat of a rube myself. Ray is less of a rube; she was born closer to San Francisco than I was. I think we both felt more comfortable with this Midwest bumbling rather than a relatively fast-moving, sophisticated, international set-up. I think we felt pressures in Knoll. Hans' sell was passionate and came with feeling.

My own feeling, and I think Ray's, was that what we had been developing hadn't really quite matured yet. If you exposed it instantly at too fast a level, it never would have had a chance to mature. The slow-going, Midwest, unsophisticated surroundings might give it a better chance. I think this speed was somehow out of our league. The Herman Millers were Midwest compared to Hans in their attitudes. Although they had this success, it was not as sophisticated as we look at it now. Gilbert Rohde had just died, and George Nelson had just come on as director of design. It was George who brought the Herman Millers and D. J. De Pree, who is the president of the company, to the Museum of Modern Art to see the exhibition. De Pree, of course, was a little surprised that the guy he had just hired as director of design was touting somebody else. I suppose as head of the Gideon Bible Society he viewed this as a kind of Golden Rule's application that he did not expect to find among architects and designers.

Photograph of Eero Saarinen and Charles Eames at Cranbrook, copyright Cranbrook Archives, Benjamin Baldwin papers.

I've had tremendous admiration for what Knoll had done. I have regretted not having some of the sense of class that Shu brought to the situation. I think of the sophistication connected with Knoll, particularly at the time when they had Herbert Matter. Herbert came and had sense enough to let him take off in some of his ads—set a kind of pace and a mood. If we had any regrets, it was that we didn't have some of that class to go with it. I didn't ever know Hans as well as I would have liked to. I'm sure that I am overstating some of his high pressure, his anxieties. He certainly developed a good thing.

Eero and I kept this thing going back and forth, and we were always comparing notes. I remember when he did the first pedestal chair. That one was an idea he developed completely on his own. There was a situation in which he had a full-size drawing on the back of a door, and he gave me a tenth of a second view of it. It was in the dark and he turned the light on—pop, pop. Then he asked me to describe the whole situation. As far as he was concerned, that tenth of a second was all you needed.

I remember, with the first models of the womb chair, he would criticize, criticize, and criticize. Eero was a concept man. The womb chair was an idea and a concept. The name is very typical of Eero—to take a word that doesn't particularly sound like a decorator's vocabulary. A simple concept like that was very close to him; so was the pedestal. He referred to the slum of the legs. This was an attempt to clean it up, and he did.

In moments of remorse he would castigate himself and say he only thought of these big forms while we were concerned about the details and all

that. He carried this into his architecture, and in many respects this is where greatness lies. While many people talked about form and traditions of form, he built an architecture which gained its strength only after you saw many, many solutions together. The thing that they had in common certainly didn't turn out to be their form. That is, the vocabulary of form was apt to change drastically from one piece to another. The thing that they did have in common was the fact that, to a remarkable degree, each building turned out to be in itself the model of what the problem was.

His furniture was similar to that; but people very often, at least earlier, missed it. The remarkable thing about it is that a vocabulary of form is an almost impossible thing to hand on from one to the other. We are all familiar with second generations of architectural firms who have attempted to do that.

I think the solutions still have that characteristic of modeling the problem. We used to talk with Eero, in terms of the designs, that his paws were showing. We looked at some of Eero's things as having the beauty of a puppy. There was an early idea and the paws, the bigness of some of the parts. It has to do with a kind of ugliness, if one uses the word. I use it in connection with a lot of our own things. As Alice B. Toklas said about Picasso, "If anything is new, really new and really original, it can't immediately be beautiful. It has to go through a period of ugliness."

Source: Richard Saul Wurman interview with Charles Eames, January 2, 1977, Container I:118, Folder 1, Charles and Ray Eames Papers, Manuscript Division, Library of Congress, Washington, D.C.

CHARLES EAMES

"Education as a Found Object"

Editor's note: The marginalia, presented here in italics,
appears in Charles's own transcript of this speech.

"However if you are going to lecture and to write the lecture before
hand you have to read it out loud. And it is not possible not to write
it before hand because in that case it is not written and what is spoken
is never written and as spoken it is not really interesting."
—Gertrude Stein

- *Model before the fact: say an architect's proposal, showing how*
  something might be structured, if we chose,
- *Model after the fact: say, a scientist's model of a giant molecule,*
  showing how something may be structured, according to the evidence.

Most any time I'm asked to talk about a general subject, I find I can
only go through with it if I can relate it in some way with actual current
work that's going on in our office.

For those who don't know the office—I would be at a loss to know just
how to describe it.

We think of ourselves as *tradesmen*. Mostly a kind of custom trade;
people come to us for things. And mostly, what they come to us for
are *models*, in one sense or another: models before the fact, or models
after the fact.

For thirty-five years now we have been working on the West Coast,
while our clients are all east of the Mississippi.

But we also have a group of loyal stringers, with various specialties,
who send us choice material from time to time from the civilized
world.

For instance: in an editorial in the Winter (76–77) issue of *American
Scholar*, there was a quote from David Hume, which quickened some
pulses around the office.

I cannot but conceive myself as a kind of . . . ambassador from the
dominions of learning to those of conversation; and shall think it
my constant duty to promote a good correspondence betwixt two
states, which have so great a dependence on each other.

Hume is about five years younger than Benjamin Franklin.

Two centuries later, there are all kinds of barriers within the world of learning that are not too easy to surmount for even very well-informed people. And outside—there's a world of theater, of sports, of painting, of business, of engineering—they may overlap in individuals, but not in conversation.

It's a question whether there is a "dominion of conversation" anymore, except at a trivial level [of short-term gossip and catastrophe].

There's a particular problem that sets in when even responsible people are invited to speak on television about some current topic. Because the audience is so vast, the speaker feels committed to stick to his (or his party's) side of the case, and to show no *hesitation or uncertainty*; which means in effect that he can't afford to stop and think on the spot. Which is obviously very bad indeed for conversation. Just occasionally you see someone crusty enough to stop and think on camera. Averill Harriman has this rare quality. And yet almost anyone in his audience, I believe, responds with something like gratitude when they do see a politician stop and think.

Still, our own trade depends on keeping up the assumption that there is a market for non-trivial, non-departmentalized conversation.

In a high-flown moment, we might think of ourselves as merchant venturers, making forays into the world of learning, and bringing back—with the help of friends and sympathizers—miscellaneous goods for the world of conversation.

When a question comes up about what *audiences* our projects are intended for, the answer is almost always about the same. Whether it's a film or an exhibition, we want it to convey some—not incorrect—meaning to an alert child; but at the same time we want it to be not trivial or embarrassing for a broadly informed specialist in the subject—or a broadly informed nonspecialist.

CLIENTS: OVERLAP OF INTEREST

And when we're considering a new project, the first question is: Is there a real, workable *overlap* between the client's interests, our own interests, and our view of the interests of the community at large? If there is, then it's in this area of overlapping interest that we can work comfortably. You can get into as much trouble by not thinking in advance about the client's interests as you can by not thinking enough about your own.

It turns out that we have three main categories of clients: *business concerns*, with a certain amount of complexity and enlightenment; *teaching institutions*, public and private; and a *third category* which is really our main subject this evening.

348

Although we constantly turn to *individuals* in the academic world—as resources, consultants, admonishers—we've usually found ourselves to be on rather firmer ground with our business clients than with the keepers of the sacred flame.

For one thing, inside most businesses there are strong, practical incentives to keep the frontiers open between one discipline and another (even though there are also the usual pressures to keep them apart). In a university, *all* external incentives seem to be on the side of discontinuity, so that personal interdisciplinary excursions seem more and more quixotic.

"The circumstances that intellectuals mostly have to do with intellectuals, should not deceive them into believing their own kind still more base than the rest of mankind. For they get to know each other in the most shameful and degrading of all situations, that of competing supplicants."
—*Theodor Adorno*, Minima Moralia

Then again, a business is relatively used to measuring its actions against definite goals: negative feedback has some chance of finding its way upward. By the same token, a business firm contracting for a product can usually recognize, without too much fuss, whether the product offered in fact meets the firm's needs, and if not, why not.

In the nature of things, it's quite difficult for a university to be as straightforward as this. Perhaps one reason is that universities fall into that special category of service institutions where the beneficiary is expected to meet the requirements of the supplier, rather than the other way about (like some governments, and many churches).

Which brings us to our third category of client, of which the Smithsonian is an eminent example. (And I suppose Doubleday and Co. is another.)

INSTITUTIONS NOT COMMITTED TO TEACHING

This is the category of institutions, whether profit-making or not, which are *not committed to teaching* but whose stock in trade is a great amount of cogent information, and whose customers are the public at large.

Museums; libraries; public television; some government agencies, like the Parks Service; information-handling companies like IBM; book and periodical publishers. The great thing about all these is that they have no captive audience; as suppliers, they have a history of needing to meet the requirements of their customers, which in most cases has kept them on their toes. And they tend to be relatively unselfconscious about getting the word out to non-initiates.

In the last few years, our convictions and hopes about this whole category of institutions have been accumulating until they almost amount to an argument. In November 1976, talking to the American Academy of Arts and Sciences in Boston, I tried to state a first approximation to this argument, which went something like this:

"FOUND EDUCATION"

First, that there is an urgent national need, not for more teaching but for more "found education."

Second, that more emphasis on "found education"—on learning rather than on being taught—would mean a shift of opportunity towards our Institutions-Not-Committed-to-Teaching— whose business is to leave good things around to be found.

Third, that this would also mean an erosion of the barrier between "recreational" and "educational"—an erosion which has already begun.

And fourth, that these changes would also mean a sharp increase in demand for the skills involved in putting together cogent models (higher demands than either "educational" or "recreational" programs make as long as they stay apart).

A found education is one that is come upon, not prescribed.

Like a good collection of found objects, it isn't come upon casually, by any means—not without effort and even sacrifice. It's sought after, piece by piece, and probably through a lifetime.

SOME NEW INITIATIVES

In the months since we first made this case, it's happened that several prominent institutions in this category have taken major new initiatives—with some strikingly recurrent elements. Consider, as examples, the Library of Congress—IBM's new building in midtown Manhattan— the Metropolitan Museum in New York—and the Smithsonian itself.

synthesis   . . . Each recognizes the need to work out legible models of itself— for its own use, and for the use of its users. In other words, to make a synthesis of the institution's own functions; to improve understanding and access; to let people know what commodities are available.

"language of vision"   Each recognizes the need to come to grips with the informative uses of the "language of vision."

Words, well used, can tell everything, given time. But current, highly structured data (especially data about process) often cries out to be modeled by quickly changing visual images.

distribution   They need this language to build up a repertoire of "samplings of ground truth"—that special kind of contact with literal, local reality that keeps statistical models honest—and alive.

These samplings are likely to be, not great surveys of a whole field of knowledge, but small, independent, informative modules—film or videotape.

interconnectivity   Each of these institutions also recognizes the importance of systems which will make their services available in places far distant from headquarters:
— regional storefronts,
—tape and video libraries,
— on-line "congenial" terminals,
— cable TV picking up programs by satellite.

And lastly, each recognizes the need for all of them to have on-line access to some at least of each other's data.

Now—if you extrapolate and imagine a real campaign along these lines—you would begin to have a real enrichment of the available materials, across the country, for a found education.

And if the universities were to get into the act, and start producing learning materials good enough to make their own way as a commodity, independent of curriculum and credit . . .

I wanted to draw attention to what's already happening all at about the same time, a number of institutions of long standing are attempting (as a health or even a survival measure) to get a fresh grasp on their own functions and nature.

And all, at about the same time, taking a fresh look at their *accountability* to a broader section of the community than heretofore—in response (maybe belated) to the boom in "universal expectations."

UNIVERSAL EXPECTATIONS

With television in every home, everyone grows up feeling pretty much entitled to what everyone else has. But as things stand, one can't help feeling that if everybody had what everybody else has, they'd already be short-changed. The goods aren't good enough. What goods are good enough to be truly covetable, when the condition is that we "include nobody out"?

Ownership of property, in general, is not what it used to be. The last stronghold of the old-style covetables seems to be portable equipment. A cameraman's trusted repertoire of lenses, Julia Child's knives . . .

NEW COVETABLES

One finds oneself looking for covetables where individual ownership
is not the point. What are the conditions that "new covetables" would
have to meet? If you have equity in a shared network—access to a valued facility, a source of information of experience—that's a commodity
that isn't diminished by being shared with others. On the other hand, a
"new covetable" mustn't be too easy to acquire; one must want it badly
enough to pay a real price. If the price is self-involvement—attention—
giving of oneself—then the conditions would be satisfied by such treasures as
  • the mastery of a new language;
  • or of a musical instrument;
  • acquaintance with the classics in any field;
  • personal skills of all kinds
  • insights into history, "natural philosophy"
These are getting to sound like pretty old covetables.

NEW SUBJECT: THE WORLD OF FRANKLIN AND JEFFERSON

It happens that in our office we're just emerging from four years of
fairly intense involvement with an exhibition about Benjamin Franklin,
Thomas Jefferson, and their world. Planning it, researching, writing the
story (40,600 words). Photographing (1,000 prints, finally), laying it out,
and building it, caring for it through French, Polish, and now Spanish
translations—and living with it through installations and openings in
seven cities.

We began the show with an introduction to some of Franklin and
Jefferson's circle; "friends, associates, and a few adversaries." We
started out bound and determined *not* to be biased in favor of our two
heroes and their friends; not to gloss over Jefferson's slave owning
or Franklin's land speculations. And the show does try to spell those
things out fairly.

But overall, what happened was that as we knew more, we got more
impressed with these people rather than less. With what someone like
James Madison, for example, actually managed to pull off.

*"We know that on two very different planes Franklin and Jefferson
managed to span the whole way from a living, and in some cases even
practicing interest in science to the world of affairs. And we know how
full their writings are of the illumination which one sheds on the other."*
—J. Robert Oppenheimer

You get the feeling that these were educated people—in a way that
made a practical difference to what happened around them.
  • they took their pleasures seriously
  • they were not afraid of trial and error

352

- they were quick to hand on newfound knowledge to others—
- there was no discontinuity between their interests, their work, their passions and their actions . . .
- and they "acted as if they owned the place."

In the nature of things, there was only a limited amount of high-quality *teaching* available. And yet you have this impression of a really high level of *learning* going on—of people finding out about things piece by piece, in pursuit of their own needs, loves, and curiosities. It was a kind of learning that went on throughout their lives. John Bartram, finding a neighboring schoolmaster to teach him "enough Latin to read Linnaeus"—or the exuberant mode in which Charles Willson Peale conducted his extraordinary museum enterprise.

There's a kind of reliable texture about this kind of "found education." The background fills up with accidental discoveries that become cherished landmarks—some cul-de-sacs, some unexpected connections—but all of them things that you turn to in time of need.

MORE TEACHING THAN LEARNING

Two hundred years later, the balance seems to have shifted the other way: as a society, we now put much more of our total energy into teaching than into learning.

In many ways, a found education is much harder to come by than it was when Franklin was a boy in Boston, and his father took him to see all the trades of the city at their work.

Now, a child doesn't get to sit for hours in the corner or the black-smith's shop—exposure to actual work comes later and later.

In practice now, most work's *invisible* to the average observant kid-around-town.

And, conversely, if your car breaks down, well, if *my* car breaks down, that's likely to be, for me, not a mechanical problem but a people problem, in finance and logistics.

Children know about *purchasing*—they go to the market with their mother—but purchasing is a kind of magic. "To pay is not to learn," somebody said.

My friend Eero Saarinen, on the other hand, used to recall sitting as a child in his parents' living room before they left Finland. It was all so interesting; his dream then was to grow up and have some fun. (Then he did grow up and came to Michigan, where he found most people took the opposite view.)

The point about Eero's childhood is not so much that it was socially exceptional but that it was rich in tradition and ceremony.

But the tendency of our present circumstances is to *slow down* the transmission of useful information—of lore, of models; maybe it's even approaching danger point.

BACKUP MATERIALS

Under these conditions, you'd want young people to have available, as part of their education, the richest possible supporting materials: *sources* for comparison; access to classic examples in the arts and sciences; a much enriched culture of *cogent models*.

The "Problem" Our Society Faces is not so much a lack of scientific, or technical, or even sociological knowledge. It's a lack of ways of transmitting existing knowledge to people, as they "need it," in forms they can readily grasp and use.

Our accumulation of data has outstripped our capacity to model it.

MODELS

What's a model? It's a human artifact. It may be the characteristic human artifact. Phil Morrison points out that though ants build arches, they aren't architects because they don't build to a plan but to a rigid algorithm.

Some would think first
  • of an architectural maquette (a model before the fact);
  • or a brass clockwork orrery (a model of the solar system, after the fact);
  • or an explanatory hypothesis—like Ptolemy's earth-centered model of the universe;
  • or a concrete model of a mathematical abstraction— say a rosewood hypersphere;
  • or a computer model of a traffic-flow problem.

Still—leaving aside for the moment the *Vogue* model, the artist's model, the model child—all the senses of "model" have strong family resemblances.

A model is an abstraction from raw data—for experiment, contemplation, and/or communication.

The thing about a model is that you can play with it; you can test things out, in the model, that it would be laborious, dangerous, or costly—or just plain impossible—to test in "reality."

You use models to report to your colleagues, to get their feedback, or for them to take away and work with.

Language is a model-building kit—which goes together only certain ways. You can describe anything with it, *if* you have no restrictions or scale. (=time)

Models are what science is made of, and much of art: (I don't know if music is a model of something—some composers say it is—certainly a musical score is a model of sound in time.)

A film can be a model; our aquarium film, and the film we made on Dulles airport, were architectural models before the fact—describing a possible experience—inviting feedback from interested parties.

We also made a film (called "Powers of Ten") that was a sketchy but rigorous model of the relative sizes of things in the universe. We wanted to see how it would look.

In the end, models are what you hand on to the next generation (besides the physical plant, that is—preferably in not worse shape than you received it). The "culture" of a time is the sum of its models.

REPRISE: A SERIOUS CALL FOR MODELS

Now—to go back to our statement that "our data have outstripped our models."

It's true that there is already a spectacular renaissance of models *within* disciplines of science and technology, largely based on the computer.

What's lacking is the *next level* of interpretation, clearly legible and applicable beyond the local discipline. Contributions to the "world of conversation."

Naturally—it's easier to delegate data gathering than to delegate model making. It's easier to fund, easier to verify, easier to write a research proposal for.

[In the case of city management, for instance; in 1968 an exhibition and film called "Photography and the City"; we collected a lot of examples of existing modeling techniques. The crying need was (and still is) for the people involved in decisions to have access to all that material—not higgledy-piggledy but brought together into a synthesis, in such a way that relationships are clear:
  • what's a trade-off with what,
  • what's dependent on what,
  • what predictions and projections really mean
  • and what assumptions went into them.

For any large agency that's answerable to the community, the effort towards this kind of modeling has to be now, an integral part of its business.]

PARENTHESIS: MODEL-MAKING IN TEACHING INSTITUTIONS

A few years ago, in one of MIT's periodic bouts of genuine concern about humanenness and aesthetics in technical education, we were asked for some recommendations.

The important thing seemed to be not for MIT to import someone else's humanity or aesthetics—or to let every engineer in on the pleasures of self-expression—but to encourage nondiscontinuity in the institute's approach to its own subjects.

So the first recommendation was that each graduate student take one quarter out of a year and develop one fairly advanced notion in his chosen discipline—work it up into a form good and clear enough so he could give it to a 5th- or 6th-grade class in Boston.

The second recommendation was to assign to each department of the institute—geology, microbiology, statistics, cosmology, architecture —2 or 3 teaching assistants, with considerable skills in photography, video, audio, editing—and a sense of reportage—but whose first loyalties would be to the discipline itself, plasma physics or whatever, not to the techniques of communication—and put them to producing short film segments on the forward edge of development in each department—not without some perspective of history or local lore.

These [modules] would be used first within the department, then intramurally, then as grist for a cable channel connecting MIT with the community at large—casting on the waters some more elements of a found education.

NEEDLESS TO SAY—

nothing can replace the treasures that can only come from being at ease with written words—

just as *nothing can replace* a great deal of looking at real paintings, if painting is the subject—or walking through a great many real buildings, if you want to be a good architect

and *nothing can replace* personal contact and study with a more experienced person,

and *nothing can replace* supervised practice in skills.

I'm not concerned here with a defense of particular kinds of *hardware*; the hardware is here and working.

356

The fact is, there are now two generations trained by television and cinema to take in fast-paced information and coordinated sound— a vehicle which is quite efficient at describing *processes* and *systems*.

These people find it hard to slow down to read solid print.

For better or for worse, television is educating these generations.

ANOTHER DISCONTINUITY

The hard and fast line between "entertainment" and "education" holds things back in a way we can't afford.

Producers of entertainment—with some notable exceptions—feel little or no pressure to take on informative description of real, complex situations;

and producers of "educational material"—with some notable exceptions—feel little pressure to make their products *really* rhetorically, poetically, aesthetically informative. Or don't know how.

Separately, that is, neither side makes the high demands on its practitioners that would be obviously appropriate if there was continuity . . . between them.

The disciplines of cogent reporting *on real knowledge and experience*, on the one hand, and the technical and poetic skills *of the language of vision*, on the other, have hardly begun to come together.

But they need each other desperately. Our powerful information carriers are short on substantial content; and on the other hand, treasures of knowledge, at every level, are locked up in forms where only a minority will ever come upon them, or recognize them as alive.

SOME PITFALLS

This problem is still in its infancy (though it's been in its infancy a long time)—with skirmishes, misreadings, and self-protectiveness accordingly.

Some bearers of the sacred flame feel free to assume a priori that new techniques mean "slickness," compromise, inauthenticity, packaging.

Some individuals trying to make the transition go overboard into effects and devices that clarify nothing.

And some carry over into film an ex cathedra manner that leaves you with little more than the feeling that you've had a glimpse of significant matters [and failed to get the point], and that it's probably . . . your fault.

But the hopeful thing is that when someone does a good job—when some biologist is such a nut about frog genetics that he forgets he isn't a "creative type" (or forgets that he would like to be one) and simply sticks with his film collaborators and *makes sure* that everything in his frog genetics movie is clear and pertinent, and aesthetically up to his feeling for the subject—then anybody seeing the final product can tell the difference; suddenly frog genetics is breathtaking.

And that's a very important payoff. Not because the citizenry at large urgently need to know about frog genetics; but they *do* need to know that the structural excitement in the scientist's work is something directly recognizable—continuous with anybody's pleasures.

[That's valuable information about science; but it's also valuable information about oneself.] I think this has to do with a phrase Jerry Wiesner used about "making the country whole again."

I suspect the real "two cultures" split—the one that hurts—is not between science and the humanities; it's between the people in charge of current substantial ideas and knowledge in general, and the people in charge of current effective *methods for conveying* knowledge and ideas.

A LAME CONCLUSION

In default of a super–Public Broadcasting Corporation in the sky operating a continental cable-and-satellite network of 20–40 channels— And a major federal commitment to gather and produce high-quality programming for it—which would mean, in practice, something on the order of the Manhattan Project multiplied by the WPA and threaded through liberally with Head Start—the next step would be . . . what *is* the next step?

We've been talking here about great institutions. But when it comes down to it, the only thing is for each of us (clients, vendors, customers in the trade of Found Education) to make every place we work, and everything we work on, a corner in which to keep picking away at this problem.

Source: Charles Eames, Frank Nelson Doubleday Lecture, Smithsonian Institution, May 1977, Part II: Speeches and Writings series, Charles and Ray Eames Papers, Manuscript Division, Library of Congress, Washington, D.C.

OWEN GINGERICH

"A Conversation with Charles Eames"

OWEN GINGERICH *Most people, I believe, think of you in terms of chairs. I remember so well how, when we were starting on the Copernicus show, we arrived at the Arlanda Airport in Sweden and you looked around and said, "These are all my chairs."*

CHARLES EAMES I probably said, "These are all our chairs."

OG *Never mind.*

CE But it's unlike me to say "my chairs."

OG *But nevertheless they were from your designs. Were they Scandinavian copies, or were they really imported?*

CE By that time there were licensed manufacturers in Europe. But honestly, it's a disappointment to walk into a Swedish airport and not see good Swedish chairs. It's sort of like walking into a European restaurant and being offered a Kansas City steak. Particularly in Scandinavia, as a traveler you should be allowed to enjoy some indigenous quality, and some exotic experience.

OG *Most people would call you a designer, but I know you prefer to think of yourself as an architect. How do the chairs fit into that?*

CE I think I've mentioned to you that we consider this all as architecture: the chairs are architecture, the films—they have structure, just as the front page of a newspaper has structure. The chairs are literally like architecture in miniature. For an architect who has difficulty controlling a building because of the contractor and the various forces brought to bear on anything that costs that much money, a chair is almost handleable on a human scale, and so you find great architects turning to chairs: Frank Lloyd Wright, Mies van der Rohe, Le Corbusier, Alvar Aalto, Eero Saarinen—any number of them doing it, because this is architecture you can get your hands on.

OG *Do you have an objection to the word "designer"?*

CE It is not that I'm embarrassed about "designer" so much as the degree to which I prefer the word "architect" and what it implies. It implies structure, a kind of analysis, as well as a kind of tradition behind it. I was put on the spot by some students at Oxford (University) because of things I

had said about the world of painting and sculpture, and they said, "How do you think of yourself?" I said I really think of myself as a tradesman, and I'm a little taken aback by anyone calling himself an artist because of my feeling that that's the kind of designation other people should give. You can *be* an artist in any field, but getting a degree to *call* yourself an artist would be like getting a diploma to call yourself a genius.

I call myself a tradesman, but any good tradesman should work only on problems that come within his genuine interest, and you solve a problem for your client where your two interests overlap. You should do an injustice to both yourself and your client to work on a problem of interest to the client but not to you—it just wouldn't work. In that spirit, we are tradesmen. If your work is good enough it can be art, but art isn't a product. It's a quality. Sometimes that's lost sight of. Quality can be in anything.

OG *Concerning the chairs, I've heard that you've never patented any of them. Is that correct?*

CE No, it's not. In the late thirties and early forties we were working on molded plywood techniques, and this was a very expensive procedure that could be used only for airplanes. We were terribly concerned about being able to make compound curves in a way that would be less expensive. Because of the general state of affairs, we had to take out patents on six or eight things related to the technology, and along with them, as demonstrations, were some of the early chairs. One of the things we had committed ourselves to was trying to do a chair with a hard surface that was as comfortable as it could be in relation to the human body and also that would be self-explanatory as you looked at it—no mysteries, so that the techniques of how it was made would be part of the aesthetics. We felt very strongly about this, because at the time there were so many things made with the opposite idea in mind, that is, to disguise a thing as if it were made at the Gobelin factories in Paris, when in fact it had been manufactured by modern techniques.

So we had these things in mind. We had patents,

and at first the patents turned out to be valuable assets in terms of protection. But pretty soon we found that if we worked with a patent in mind—well, you know certain things are patentable and certain things not patentable. Now what divides the patentable from the nonpatentable is entirely different from what divides the good and appropriate from the bad and the inappropriate. If one has bitten the apple and been seduced into the idea of having a patentable item and royalties, there is always the temptation to make the design such as to be patentable rather than to be good.

There is a passage from the *Bhagavad Gita* that comes to mind: "Work done with anxiety about results is far inferior to work done in the calm of self-surrender." Anxiety about getting the approval of friends or the community, or about whether it will be patentable, always leads to inferior work.

OG *So you just stopped patenting chairs?*

CE It's unfair to the client if you say, "Don't patent them," so we arrived at the following principle: If the client wants to patent them, that's his problem. If it's to his interest, let him do it, but we will not put any of our effort into twisting the thing so that it's patentable. There are some surprising corollaries. When some of the blatant copies arrived, patent or not patent, there were refused by the government official at the pier just because they *were* detailed copies.

The original chair, the first called "the Eames chair," was molded plywood with very thin metal legs. If you look at any history of modern furniture, it is presented as a classic. It is probably the only chair we ever did that got the amount of attention from us that it deserved. The first imitations of the molded plastic shell that appeared in this country horrified the Herman Miller Furniture Company. They soon found it in their hearts not to be completely outraged, because each time a copy appeared, the sales of the original went up!

OG *Your most famous chair is very widely copied.*

CE The chair of which you speak, the black leather, down-stuffed lounge chair, I have never considered as good a solution as the other one, although it has apparently given a lot of pleasure to people. It has a sort of ugliness to it. I take a certain comfort in the fact that Picasso pointed out through Gertrude Stein (in the Alice B. Toklas book) that anything that is truly original must have a touch of ugliness because it has not had a chance to be honed to the elegance that comes with refinement. About ten years ago a German publication

published pictures of the original lounge chair and seventy-five different manufactured copies.

OG *But don't you have to worry about plagiarism?*

CE What you really worry about in the design of furniture or in architecture are the *bad* copies, when your idea is used in a kind of booby way. You don't mind if someone carries your idea further in a better way, although at first your nose may be a bit out of joint.

OG *I suppose that people whose opinions matter to you will recognize imitations for what they are. But how can you protect ideas that are still in an embryonic stage?*

CE There is a kind of moral patent that is taken out all over the world, within the circles of workers themselves. As you know, Eero Saarinen and I worked very closely together, especially when we were younger. (He died about ten years ago.) In 1939 we won the Organic Competition at the Museum of Modern Art by working on furniture together. As an architect he was known to be very competitive. He was a joy to compete along with, and a terror to compete against. Then Eero continued to design some furniture, and it was distributed by Hans Knoll, while our furniture was distributed by Herman Miller.

It was a healthy situation between us, but Eero would call me up in the middle of the night and would start telling me about a design for a chair he had in mind. He would be very explicit about the design, and then he would go down the list of all possible uses that this design could be put to, anything he could get in verbally to me—and I would be saying, "Don't tell me, I don't want to hear anything about it, I'm hanging up!"—and he would go on reciting this litany of uses, because if he told them to me, that was his moral patent. It's the kind of thing architects still practice. They throw an idea immediately to their friends, especially those who would be their greatest competitors.

OG *You were mentioning your earlier collaboration with Eero Saarinen . . .*

CE It used to be this way. In the middle of the night, at three o'clock in the morning—and this has something to do with what is known as the creative process—out of despair I would say something like, "If we can't do anything else, let's paint it brown." And then Eero would say, "What? Of course we'll make it round. It's obvious that's the solution. Why is it that I'm an idiot? I never thought of it. You take it and see it should be round."

And I say, "Wait a minute, you're mistaken. I just said a dumb thing about it being brown."

"You're always trying to make me feel good. I never have any ideas, you have all the ideas. Why didn't I think of it?"

"But I said 'brown.'"

"Don't give me that crap."

It reminds me of the fellow who reviews books so well that he pulls them up to another level. Then an author reads a review of his book and says, "Did I say that?"

OG *You said something earlier about the honesty of materials when you were discussing the molding of plywood for chairs. That is the same theme mentioned at the beginning of "Toccata for Toy Trains," your marvelous film that has many of your antique toys in it.*

CE The "Toy Trains" describes the unselfconscious use of materials in making an honest toy: "Tin is tin, what is wood is really wood, and what is cast is often beautifully cast." A toy tin train representing a complex locomotive does not try to make the tin look as though it were wrought iron or riveted plate or whatever. The material speaks for itself.

OG *From considering yourself an architect to being creative in designing toys—that's quite a wide step. Can you justify toys as miniature architecture?*

CE Rather than looking at toys as miniature architecture, I would look at them as miniature science. Much of hydraulics found its way into toys, displays, and tricks before it became a mechanical science. Static electricity went a long way in toys before being developed much as a science.

OG *Have you ever thought of an exhibit on toys as protoscience?*

CE Yes, especially of certain logical and mathematical games. We actually made an exhibit of that nature, although it was not seen by the public—we did it for an IBM training center. We have about thirty mathematical games here—many old, even ancient games.

An exhibit of toys and games can have important uses. Suppose, for example, we were to have an exhibition of sophisticated Japanese painting: the most sophisticated things are, in practice, removed from the primitive and are often exotic to our experience. At the beginning of such an exhibition, we have often thought of having a sort of decompression chamber that would show such toys as we've just described, or other games or ceremonies that are common to our experience. Our view is that if such things were seen before viewing the sophisticated art, and if indeed spectators did relate to them, that would be one very important step toward embracing the more sophisticated art.

[The conversation thus led to a discussion of the series of exhibitions that the Eames office has designed over the past twenty years, many on mathematical or scientific topics sponsored by IBM. The art and motivation for exhibit making are akin to multimedia productions, a concept invented and pioneered by the Eameses.]

OG *Multimedia seems to have mushroomed everywhere, like fast-food establishments. Do you sometimes think you have opened a Pandora's box?*

CE In a word, yes. It's something like the situation about twenty years ago when we thought of using wire technology to create a piece of furniture—wire technology had gone pretty far in terms of shopping center carts and that kind of thing—and so we did some wire furniture. It came back to haunt us, because afterward there was a rash of the kitschiest stuff, and we had to think, "Oh, my God, what have we done?" In some respects this is true of the multimedia.

OG *Isn't the term "multimedia" something of a misnomer?*

CE Yes. In most cases what they're talking about is the production of multiple images; by the same terms, any motion picture would be multimedia because it has both sound and images. The first thing that we did, which was entitled "A Rough Sketch for a Sample Lesson for a Hypothetical Course," was indeed multimedia. This was in 1950 or 1951. It had not only multiple images, including the relationship between still and motion pictures, but also sensory things—smell and music. We used a lot of sound, sometimes carried to a very high volume so you would actually feel the vibrations. So in the sense that we were introducing sounds, smells, and a different kind of imagery, we were introducing multimedia. We did it because we wanted to heighten awareness.

OG *Did you introduce the word at that time?*

CE No, we were anxious to treat multimedia as a tool and not as a show. The smells were quite effective. They did two things: they came on cue, and they heightened the illusion. It was quite interesting, because in some scenes that didn't have smell cues, but only smell suggestions in the script, a few people felt they had smelled things—for example, the oil in the machinery.

OG *What induced you to try such a show? Were your motivations any different from those of the multiplicity of multimedia we've got now?*

CE What has bothered us, if "bothered" is the word, is the frantic use of changing images and an abundance of images for psychedelic effect. The thing that separates our shows from some of the others is that we use multimedia for a very specific reason. In the case of the "Sample Lesson," we were trying to cram into a short time, a class hour, the most background material possible. George Nelson, Alexander Girard, Ray, and I had been asked by the University of Georgia to make a study of some of the problems of the schools where the students weren't getting a broad enough background for things having to do with a particular discipline. Instead of writing a report, we decided we would pool our fees and put together a show for a typical class. It would supply a very broad range of material upon which the teacher could then base his arguments; in other words, what happened in those fifty minutes would replace a certain amount of deficiency in background, but would leave the teacher free to make the connections.

OG *What subject did you pick?*

CE That's an interesting question. We made it clear that this was just the lesson for this particular day, and for this lesson we picked communications. Later we took out of it the "Communications Primer" for IBM, but that was just one little aspect.

For example, we asked ourselves whether indeed the Chartres Cathedral, as you see it now, a work of art from the past, is really communicating today the same kind of emotional reactions that it did in its time. We tried to evoke—with sound and smells and imagery—the interior of Chartres, what it might have been for an instant during the 1300s, but with the thought of letting the teacher develop the points. The Chartres thing was appropriate because we first presented this show down in Southern Baptist country where the people hadn't ever gotten close to what a fourteenth-century Catholic cathedral might have been.

OG *I remember very vividly your multi-screen show in the IBM pavilion at the 1964 New York World's Fair. That can't have been your first public multimedia show, because there were already quite a few other multiple-screen productions at the fair.*

CE The first large, broadly seen show was the one we did in Moscow in 1959, at the time of the Nixon kitchen debate. There our purpose for the multimedia was quite different. We had the very difficult problem of making the first statement from this country to the Soviet Union since the Russian Revolution. There had been no major statement from people to people until that time. We had to be very careful of what we did. We knew that words had their limitations; they could be used to the point of being almost without effect, certainly without the effect that we would intend to provide. We knew that some images were well known to the Russians. If, for example, we were to show a freeway interchange, somebody would look at it and say, "We have one at Smolensk and one at Minsk; we have two, they have one"—that kind of thing. So we conceived the idea of having the imagery come on in multiple forms, as in the "Rough Sketch for a Sample Lesson."

OG *But it wasn't so much for information as for credibility?*

CE We wanted to have a credible number of images, but not so many that they couldn't be scanned in the time allotted. At the same time, the number of images had to be large enough so that people wouldn't be exactly sure how many they had seen. We arrived at the number seven. With four images, you always knew there were four, but by the time you got up to eight images you weren't quite sure. They were very big images—the width across four of them was half the length of a football field.

OG *There is something so ephemeral about such a show. If someone had seven projectors and a wide wall, would it be possible to put it on again?*

CE We salvaged one set of prints, and we have a very crude composite. Elmer Bernstein wrote a marvelous musical score for it, and it was quite an emotional thing. Theoretically, it was a statement made by our State Department, and yet we did it entirely here and it was never seen by anyone from our government until they saw it in Moscow. It was a little touchy, but one of those things. If you ask for criticism, you get it. If you don't, there is a chance everyone will be too busy to worry about it.

OG *There is something intrinsically different about how your chairs are preserved compared to the multimedia shows. Someone can see your chairs in the Museum of Modern Art or the Stedelijk Museum in Amsterdam, for example, but the IBM show from the New York Fair can't be reexperienced with any ease.*

CE That's true. The fair itself falls into the category of the temporary triumphal arch, which is burned after it is used.

OG *Like Christo's art . . .*

CE The Christo experience, or a good birthday cake. There is a great value in how the thing disappears and can't be reproduced; it can't deteriorate and grow passé.

OG *Nowadays the multimedia techniques have been so widely copied and developed that it's impossible to think of a world without multiple projections in it.*

CE After you have made one multiple-image show, you're like a little boy who has been given a hammer—everything he encounters needs hammering! There is a tendency to apply your new system everywhere. But initially the multiple imagery had to perform very specific functions. In the IBM pavilion, for example, it was simultaneity. I think this is a very valuable device: to use multiple images to relate simultaneous happenings to the main theme. You get a feeling about relationships you didn't have previously. In thinking about decision making in the future—whether it be recombinant DNA or what have you—we believe some attention should be given to honing the techniques of showing critical things simultaneously. We had hoped that by now this might be a rather general procedure. I still think it's a good idea.

OG *I gather you feel that a lot of multimedia has lost sight of honest goals.*

CE In certain cases you don't mind that, if the thing has unity. Someone can switch goals and still do a good thing. But there are gray areas: shows may take on the trappings of information but not be really informative. These are the things that are disturbing. When information is not the goal, you often get an arbitrary cutting from image to image. In planning the Moscow show we tried our various tricks and rhythms in changing the images. We discovered that if you had seven images and changed one of them, this put an enormously wasteful, noninformative burden on the brain, because with every change the eye had to check every image to see which one had changed. When you're busy checking, you don't absorb information. Frantic-ness of cutting tends to degenerate the information quality. We have always been committed to information: it's not a psychedelic scene in any way.

[Like their multimedia shows, the Eameses' exhibitions have been committed to information. A series of exhibits made originally for the IBM display room on Madison Avenue has included the Computer Wall, Copernicus, On the Shoulders of Giants, and Newton. A much larger exhibition, made in connection with the American bicentennial, is The World of Franklin and Jefferson. Originally installed in Paris, it has subsequently been seen in Warsaw, London, New York, Chicago, Los Angeles, and Mexico City. It combines a certain number of original artifacts and art objects with an immense number of photographs and extensive captions.]

OG *Am I correct in thinking that much of the criticism of the Franklin and Jefferson show in the Metropolitan Museum arose from the fact that critics and some museum people are just unfamiliar with the idea of high information content in a museum setting?*

CE That may be true, but the reaction came as a surprise because the reception at the Louvre was so different—we opened at the Grand Palais, but it is under the same jurisdiction as the Louvre. There they recognized that they had both the material and the whole world of scholarship surrounding the material. Curators have access to complicated information about their objects, but often they have resisted including information with the material or showing any view of the setting from which the objects have been taken. I think it's still difficult for them to take that step, but at the Louvre they were terribly interested, and a whole group of curators was brought to the exhibition. I went back later and talked with them again because of their seeing this as a real problem: the commitment of the scholarly community to the visitors at large. In any event, they were not thrown by it; but, much to our surprise, in New York the art community as well as some of the curators were completely thrown.

OG *Do you feel that the intentions of the Franklin and Jefferson show were somehow misinterpreted?*

CE To avoid this very thing, we advertised the exhibition not as a show for historians (even though we owed very much to the historians) but as a citizens' exhibition. Actually it was not an art exhibition but more like a colored walk-through tabloid. We tried to make this purpose clear.

We used the captions to deal with problems and circumstances; that's why there were so many words. Had we been dealing with accomplishments, we could have done it in very few words. However, it is true that we set out originally to be quite critical and hard about the main characters, but as we went on, we were so impressed by how much someone like James Madison was able to pull off time and again that we came out pretty much all admiration.

We would, for example, have talked about Franklin's seemingly ribald verse or his essay on farting. In a sense, Franklin was doing the same thing as Jonathan Swift, except that Swift did it a hell of a lot better. Franklin was trying everything—it was part of his lifelong experimenting—but in these writings he tried something that wasn't very good. It seemed rather pointless to dwell on it when there was so much new we hadn't seen before, and so much we wanted to tell—for example, about Madison and Washington. Quite frankly, we swung over to what they managed to accomplish, not in an attempt to cover anything up but to show the importance of some of their ideas.

OG *Wasn't there criticism that the show was too "beautiful" to represent a wartime revolutionary movement?*

CE Yes, and we found this a little surprising, too, in light of the way the show was received in Paris. They saw it as a celebration, which was what we intended. We meant it to be colourful, but not garish. In Paris they perceived it as a celebration of that time when the eighteenth-century European Enlightenment was meeting up with American immediacy.

OG *They were prepared to think of the American Revolution in philosophical terms?*

CE Yes, absolutely. Then when the exhibit came back to the United States in 1976, we still thought of it as a celebration; but now what was uppermost as a quality that needed to be celebrated was the robust continuity in these people's lives—Franklin, Jefferson, and their whole circle. No discontinuity between their personal interests, their work, their public actions, their pleasures, and their passions.

OG *But what was the reaction of the American critics to all this?*

CE They didn't attack the content: that was almost disappointing to us, in a way. What was attacked—by the New York Times art critic, and then by a Chicago art critic quoting him—was the nature of the show itself, because it wasn't a real art exhibition. It was an architectural arrangement of words and photographs, with pockets of real things from the eighteenth century, chosen to reinforce the story. And apparently there's a fairly strong school of thought which says that only original, authentic art works have any business in the Met.

Then I believe also that it was seen as an intrusion on the museum by the sponsor—more than, say, a show of paintings sponsored by a big corpo-

ration would be. Maybe they felt that because there was a story, and IBM had paid for it, it must somehow be IBM talking—which was not at all the case, as you know.

I really don't know why a critic would be so defensive of the sacred enclosure around Art— I don't believe most good practicing artists would worry about this. We've always thought of the Met as a cultural history establishment, at least as much as an art museum. Think of all that great Egyptian stuff they have; it's not all fine art, or even applied art; some of it is just the equipment of everyday life. Also the Met, by its charter, has a commitment to offer information, not just to confront the visitor with objects. Certainly Charles Willson Peale in his museum didn't separate these two functions. He used his own paintings to give information: this is what Mr. So-and-so looked like; this is how the mastodon was dug up.

OG *Was there an objection to your using photographs rather than real objects?*

CE Naturally, there's never been any question for us of substituting photographs or words or films for the experience of real things. I don't think anybody who's visited the office could suspect us of that. In a ten-minute film we made for the Metropolitan we talked, among other things, about a small show of close-up photographs "that may help the eye to slow down when it comes to, say, a small sculpture at its real scale in the gallery." And we showed as an example the Rospigliosi cup, which at first glance is kind of uncongenial, I suppose, to many people's taste today. But if you're first exposed to enlarged details of that fine goldsmith's work and enameling, and the elegant profile of the statuette on top—her face is no bigger than my thumbnail—and if those images go by quite fast, then, when you come to the real thing, you're liable to think "now I can really see that." It's also true, though, that you can get satiated from too many juicy color pictures, especially if they just sit there.

I think it's easy to forget that art historians, in practice, are working with reproductions most of the time, in their research and in teaching. An art historian or a curator, comparing a drawing that's in the Louvre with another in New York, is not thinking all the time about the unique aesthetic impact of the original, he's counting dentils or something. If his photograph is sharp enough for that, he's content. But the layman, or the freshman, attending that scholar's lecture, hasn't seen

364

so many original drawings. He has to take a lot on trust, very often. Unless the teacher really tries to see that his slides are as good as possible, he's letting down his own discipline as well as his audience.

Maybe I'm jaundiced, but I find that many people whose subject has to do with visual aesthetics aren't visually literate when it comes to presentation. They don't extend their critical training to their own work as communicators. As long as audiences are looking at things through other means, what they get ought to be as informative as possible. And informative includes good-looking.

OG *I'm afraid we've grown accustomed to the idea that art museums are just repositories for aesthetic objects.*

CE I think that today our growing institutions have a growing commitment to give cogent information. I feel that anything that can be done to put art objects in their context without detracting from their rich qualities is helpful. Unlike Keats, who said that knowing about the rainbow shatters its beauty, I feel that knowledge about an object can only enrich your feeling for the object itself.

As far as I'm concerned, the ultimate use of any of these experiences is to plow them back into the business of life itself. What I find frustrating in some cases is that the presentation of exhibition material perpetuates and widens the gap between what is in the museum and what is the business of life for the viewer. To me this discontinuity is an outrageous thing: it is what we would like to dispel.

Source: Owen Gingerich, "A Conversation with Charles Eames," *American Scholar* 46, no. 3 (Summer 1977): 326–27.

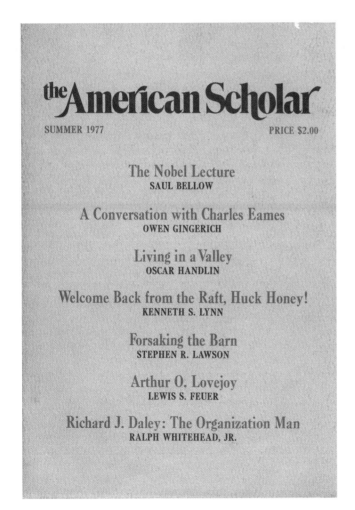

American Scholar cover.

St. Louis Oral History Project

INTERVIEW WITH CHARLES EAMES

October 13, 1977, Venice, California
Interviewer: Virginia Stith, St. Louis County
Parks and Recreation Department

VIRGINIA STITH *Let's start with talking about your earliest memories of when you lived in St. Louis.*

CHARLES EAMES My mother's family was a French family, and they had actually lived in Florissant and Cross Keys before the founding of St. Louis. This was the Aubuchon group and also the Chomeau group. The Aubuchons were sort of old ones, and as the tales would have it, one of the earliest of these guys was a guy named Kiercereau who built the original church and cathedral in St. Louis—that is, before the present Old Cathedral was built. You know, there's the Old Cathedral downtown. And our other friends and relatives would kid the family about being of those French pirates that came up the river.

That was my grandmother's side, which was the Aubuchons. My grandfather actually left Alsace at the time of the Franco-Prussian War, and he came to St. Louis because he had relatives, then met my grandmother in St. Louis.

Now, a lot of these families spoke French at that time. My mother didn't really learn to speak English until it came time to go to school. That was true, I think, of many of the families around what later became Cross Keys and Florissant.

VS *Were you brought up speaking French?*

CE No. I wasn't. My father was born near Lake Champlain in the East and grew up around New Haven. He came from a family of English descent, and he was a much older man than I was. Really—he was born in 1846, and *his* father was born in 1787. So, actually, my grandfather was born in the eighteenth century, my father in the nineteenth, and I was born in the twentieth; which made for a reasonably wide spread, and that's why my upbringing—in St. Louis, even—was largely nineteenth-century upbringing.

VS *Where did you attend elementary school?*

CE I was born about two blocks from Shaw's Garden, the Missouri Botanical Garden. By that time my father was reasonably well along, and he died when I was 11 or so. Prior to that time he had not been well, so the family fortune that kept us in reasonable state while we lived near Shaw's Garden all sort of disappeared. We were in the East for a little while and then moved to north St. Louis, so I attended the David Glasgow Farragut elementary school, which is just south of Fairgrounds Park.

But my very earliest memories—that is, when we still lived in south St. Louis—were of things like Halley's Comet. I'm speaking of myself as a child about three years old. Halley's Comet made a tremendous impression on me. I knew it was something very special, because my mother and father stopped in the middle of a piano-flute duet to go out and view it, so I knew it must have been something very awe-inspiring. Then when we went to the East, I watched the survivors of the ship come in, and so I became, then, a kind of *Titanic* buff. In St. Louis then I was doing some work with Frances Stadler, and she told me her father had been the guy who scooped the story of the sinking of the *Titanic*, and when she found out I was so interested in that she gave me one of the first editions of the *St. Louis Post-Dispatch* on the sinking of the *Titanic*. Carlos Hurd was her father's name—she was a Miss Hurd. So when she said her name was Hurd I said, "You're *not* related to Carlos Hurd, the great scoop man?"

VS *And then you went to high school in St. Louis, too?*

CE I lived in north St. Louis and went to what was then Yeatman High School near Fairgrounds Park. This was sort of a mixed bag. Fairgrounds had been literally a fairgrounds, there used to be an old bear pit there, I went skating on the ponds in Fairgrounds Park; there was sort of a mixture of good, housekeeping middle class, some quite good intelligent groups, and then there were also some pretty seamy elements. They weren't mixed along color lines, because in St. Louis the schools were segregated—completely segregated at that time. But in terms of the nature: there were a lot of Germans, of course, in north St. Louis, and the whole German community had pretty well expanded in that area. It was a good, healthy kind of neighborhood situation.

vs *Did you have any art training in high school?*

CE I didn't. We had the normal elementary school system. In the elementary school then, the kindergartens were conducted by the Froebel system. Are you familiar with Froebel? You should be. It's sort of the classic. Frank Lloyd Wright was raised on the Froebel system, and at that time it was very avant-garde. And it was a very good system. This had to do with elementary blocks of spheres and cones and pyramids and different kinds of exercises, and I was very grateful it came in. Oh, it was a classic St. Louis grammar school.

vs *What about the discipline in the schools?*

CE Oh, by today's standards, of course, it was highly disciplined. There were a lot of little affectionate attentions that were given by the schoolteachers. The art training consisted of that school of painting where once a week the class would paint flags, as we used to call it—these were the iris—with watercolors. I don't think I was ever particularly good at that, although I drew a lot: I used to draw cartoons and drew with the kids in school. My father *did* paint and draw, and he was an early photographer as well. He photographed during the nineteenth century; actually, when he died, this was one of the reasons that photography interested me. I was a great labels and instructions reader. You used to get patent medicine in fifteen languages, and I would try to figure out the languages: you'd have this ointment in Javanese or something, and I would try to compare the words. I was an instruction reader, and so when I came upon the cache of photographic equipment—

vs *Those were dry plates?*

CE They were actually glass plates which I would coat with emulsion and then take the photograph on the wet emulsion. This was a technique that had gone out of vogue for many years, but the chemicals were still good; and I was actually taking portraits and photographs on wet plates for a year before I found out that Mr. Eastman had invented film. Which was a very fine way to start out. . . .

vs *Your feeling about your early education was that it was a comfortable way for a boy to grow up and to learn?*

CE Oh, yes. I never had any negative feelings about my education, even in elementary school, even though people are very critical of that period. It is largely because there is always a teacher on the scene who takes the subject seriously and takes his pleasure seriously: I have never really analyzed it, but this is true of both high school and grade school. The children were not aware of a lot of things, but as far as I was concerned, I fared pretty well in the school system. I was not operating at the level that I was probably capable of, but that was because a lot was going on, and due to—I don't know what, the general circumstances—I guess I was 10 years old when I took my first after-school and summer regular job. At 10, I was working in a printing and envelope shop (Upton S. Cody) in downtown St. Louis.

vs *What did you do?*

CE I cleaned presses and I sorted type.

vs *Did you learn anything about the printing process in so doing?*

CE Not really, except that I printed some envelopes, and these were those presses where you had to damn well get your hands out of the way; there was nothing to really guard them. I succeeded in keeping all my fingers, which was learning something. In those days, my salary was $4.00 a week and the hours were something! Of course, that included Saturday. I'm not saying that I was in any way mistreated, because this was a going thing. But I remember, to save a nickel a day (with which I could then buy soda water instead of drinking that hot water that came up in the building), I used to ride downtown on a streetcar, but then I would ride what we used to call "bumpering a car" out. That meant that when the streetcar left downtown— this was the Cass Avenue Line—I had to fight the competition to climb on the bumper on the back of the streetcar, because usually there was so much business, the conductor was too busy. These were open cars, of course. I'd ride as far as I could on the bumper of the streetcar. One conductor got to me and by beating on my fingers with a punch. I fell off the streetcar on the cobblestones of the Cass Avenue Line and broke a rib which still sort of sticks out in a funny way. Everybody thought I was killed, and I thought they were going to put me in the penitentiary, so I managed to get the hell out of there.

vs *Were you aware, in those days, of going back and forth? Did you have any feeling, or develop any sense of respect, for the varied architecture in the street furniture with which that area of St. Louis is really exceptionally endowed?*

CE I suppose most of this was taken for granted. I was working in one of the old buildings, and I had tremendous affection for Eads Bridge. This is all within reason, because my grandfather was a French restaurateur, and I had seen—and

I've seen even recently—mention on the menus that they made in honor of Eads after completing the bridge.

VS *What was the name of the restaurant?*

CE Restaurant Porcher. It was the old Lucas mansion, which was on the southwest corner of Eighth and Olive where I think the Arcade building was built. My mother and my aunts all lived there.

VS *Let's go on to your decision to enter Washington University. Was that influenced by Adele Starbird, or was it the university at hand? What got you to Washington University?*

CE I'd been working during my high school years. I went from the print shop to working in a grocery shop [Hyke & Ebler], and then I worked in a drugstore [Ernst Niemoller] in north St. Louis. When I entered high school—I guess when I was 14—I started to work in a steel mill in Venice, Illinois.

VS *That was Laclede Steel?*

CE That was Laclede Steel, and it was a rail rerolling mill. I had gotten onto this by someone in the neighborhood who was an engineer. I got just a labouring job, and, as I say, I had just turned 14—although age didn't mean anything.

VS *There were no unions then?*

CE No.

VS *Were they paid decently? Was that better than the grocery store?*

CE Well, yes. I got 40 cents an hour.

VS *That was good for that time. That was really good.*

CE Yes, that was really good. It was hard work, but I got 40 cents an hour and that was much better. I worked from six in the morning to six at night.

VS *How did you go to school?*

CE Saturday and Sunday during the year, because they also worked on stuff Saturdays and Sundays and there was absolutely no union. I started out at a laboring job, which was to erect concrete forms of new construction, and one thing and another. And, then, I was still drawing. I'd draw things, and they found out I could draw, so the second or third year I would be put on patterns and some vague engineering work. So while I was still in high school I was making drawings at the steel mill and was no longer doing the same kind of laboring job—although it was surely fairly tough—and I would draw a lot. I had been introduced to the idea of architecture, and because of this combination of experience and things which

was a little in advance of what would normally be expected, I was given an architectural scholarship to the university.

VS *Had you shown a talent for mathematics, too?*

CE I had shown what was, I suppose, a talent for mathematics, but you have to remember that this was in a high school in north St. Louis. There is a mathematics teacher who is gratified that you have a certain understanding, but the general tendency was to not have it go a lot farther than that. However, that gratification is already something, and you get interested. I had a fairly good physics teacher; between the mathematics teacher, who was a woman, and the physics teacher, who was a man, you got a feeling that there was something there that had a certain basis of pleasure to it.

VS *To go on with enrolling in Washington University: you worked at Laclede Steel, and the idea had been introduced to you that maybe you should go on to school, and you were able to get a scholarship?*

CE Well, when I got out of high school, then that summer—instead of going to the steel mill, and knowing I was going into architecture—I got a job at the Edwin F. Guth Fixture Company. I think the Guth is still a good-size company. At the time old Guth himself was on deck, which I suppose is no longer the case, I don't know. I got a job designing lighting fixtures, which is kind of an interesting transition from steel mill to architecture.

VS *Was there any nepotism involved in the jobs you got? Were you recommended by somebody who knew somebody, or did you just go in on your own, cold, and tell them who you were and they hired you?*

CE Nobody knew who the hell I was, naturally. In the case of the steel mill, as I said, there was an engineer in the neighborhood, in north St. Louis, who got me the original job. The advances [I got] during that time [were] just because the job took. When it came to the Guth Company, I think that was absolutely cold. I just went in there cold, and I was whatever you are when you graduate from high school, and that worked very well. They were anxious to have me stay, and I was sort of committed. Also, the owners and the manager of the steel mill came in from the city someplace because the management on the level at the steel mill—this was bad . . . you can imagine the labor and racial conditions. They would be in Madison and Venice, Illinois; there would be blacks just murdered without any provocation. But the people in the mill responsible offered to get me an engineering fellowship or scholarship because, quite frankly, they had what was a very interesting idea: I had grown up with a lot of these people in the mill who were very reluctant to take advances in terms of conveyor systems and whatnot, and they thought that if I was educated as an engineer and came back, it would be a simpler matter to introduce refinements because I knew the mill and I knew the situation.

vs *Were the Aikens in the business at that point? They're still there.*

CE Yes. I didn't see much of the Aikens, but they were in the business, and they actually responded and were partially responsible, I suppose, for the offer I did get. But I was fascinated with the architectural idea, and while I was very grateful to the people in the steel mill, I then went into architecture and, as I said, used the Guth thing as a transition. When I started the university, . . . I already [had] a part-time job at Trueblood and Graf, the architects. So I was starting the university at the normal time, but I had already had four years in the steel mill and a summer working with this lighting fixture company, and I was already working in an office.

vs *Did you find the academic program somewhat stifling?*

CE Not really. You have to remember, I didn't have any preconceived ideas of either what an academic program was or wasn't, and I had been working. My mother was a Civil War widow. There weren't very many of those left; my father was in the Union Army. My mother received a thirty-dollar-a month pension as the widow of a Union soldier in the Civil War, and that's what the family lived on, except for what I brought in.

vs *It doesn't seem possible.*

CE And then, by the time she was in high school, my sister had a job in the city playgrounds, in Parks and Recreation. She had a knack for dealing with these kids, particularly tough kids. I don't know what the Soulard district is like now, but the Soulard district in St. Louis was pretty tough in those days. But she had these gangsters all working for her. . . . Well, even though Adele was living up in north St. Louis, she made a tremendous success down there as a young kid working in the playgrounds—and, as I say, these were very tough.

vs *That was a rather far-sighted parks department with playgrounds in that era.*

CE I have a feeling that it was. Because I remember going to some meetings and things with my sister, and I look back on it now as being pretty good.

vs *You were at Washington University along with Hari Van Hoefen and Roland Bockhorst, who is the building inspector for the City of Ladue now, I understand.*

CE Right, sure. I remember Roland. And there were other guys—I guess Gallion was just ahead of me, and there was a guy who was a real star, and there was a very large firm, Hellmuth . . .

vs *Obata, Kassabaum.*

CE And Kassabaum. Hellmuth . . . he's got a very successful firm, and Obata is quite a sensitive guy. Hellmuth, his uncle, and, I guess, his father were in the business. They used to go after all the big Catholic institutions, and they would grind those things out, and . . . at any rate, they're a very good sized firm. . . . I haven't seen George for many, many years, but I see Obata. In fact, Obata was just out here.

vs *They were the architects for the new library and herbarium at the Missouri Botanical Garden, and I believe they did the master plan. . . .*

CE There was also a guy, George Sansone, who was the son of a prominent St. Louis doctor. It was my first introduction to a part of St. Louis society where the mother had a certain social standing but was also a political activist; it was an introduction to a whole new kind of thing. I greatly admired her. The boy George had real talent, and he went up to Chicago and disappeared pretty much. But, yes, Bockhorst was there, and Hari, whom I've kept in touch with and seen for a long time. . . . Hari was interested and curious, and he was active from the very beginning.

vs *Who were the professors on the faculty at that point? I have a couple of names: Gabriel Ferrand and—*

CE Gabriel Ferrand. He was what you call the patron, because it was a French school; it was under the Beaux-Arts system. Then there was Lawrence Hill. He had an English background but he had certain exotic qualities in his makeup. He taught history and elements. I really consider Lawrence one of the greatest teachers I ever had, and probably he was very influential as far as I was concerned. And then there was a very small lively guy called Paul Valenti. He lived a mysterious domestic life in which the relationship was never clear. It was very mysterious, but very interesting and exotic. He could draw beautifully, and he really made—he was Italian, and he made the Italian Renaissance really come to life. He was the kind of professor who kind of enters into a plot with the students, and in that way gets them to work and do interesting things.

vs *Along this line, you obviously were either on your own or had read about the Bauhaus group, or had been influenced by Frank Lloyd Wright. In that Beaux-Arts atmosphere, where did you develop that interest? Who sparked that?*

CE Actually, I suppose the Bauhaus was not really that prominent. It just hadn't surfaced hardly at all in this country. Frank Lloyd Wright certainly had, and there had also been a competition for the Tribune Tower in 1925 in which Eliel Saarinen got the second prize and Gropius had a fairly undistinguished entry. It was quite interesting and sort of introduced us to the architects. But the Wright book came out, I guess, in '23 or '24, and it was a tremendous impression on me. Yet I didn't worry any about it as incompatible with the Beaux-Arts school because Wright knew architecture—I mean, he knew the history of architecture—and this seems still a perfectly good way of getting a background. I guess it was just a little bit more mysterious to me as to why, even though it was a Beaux-Arts school, they couldn't embrace people like Wright. Now I must say that Valenti did, but Ferrand was absolutely rabid on the subject. And actually Ferrand, in later years before he died, began to be taken by the modern school. The poetic justice came when, in one of the great architectural debates in St. Louis, Gabriel Ferrand took to defend the issue of the modern international style; and there was an architect, Louis La Beaume, in St. Louis, and he took up the defense of the classic architecture. The poetic justice came when Louis La Beaume, taking the classic side, actually cut Ferrand to ribbons because Ferrand demonstrated that, while he was a Beaux-Arts architect, he knew neither the modern nor the classic side of the argument. I think it just about killed Ferrand. It was, in a sense, a tragic thing, but as I say there were few architectural debates that take place in St. Louis.

vs *It might have been very good for the students at that particular time.*

CE Yes, it could have been. After leaving the school, I was invited back quite a few years later to give a lecture by the faculty, and Lawrence Hill was then the head of the school. And while I had tremendous admiration for Hill, why, whether he or Ferrand was the one who questioned my general tactics or direction most, I don't know. But I got a letter from Hill I don't know how many years later,

and he said, "My dear A: It has come to my attention that you have been the subject of some notoriety." He proceeded in this same manner to say that he didn't know why, but his faculty and students wanted me to come and lecture. So I wrote him a letter just as formal as his, acknowledging that what he said was probably true, but I would be interested in going back. When he made the introduction to my lecture, he pretty well spelled this whole thing out. He said that I had been asked to leave the school because I was prematurely interested and concerned with Frank Lloyd Wright, and he granted that it was valid but premature. And this time I visited him quite a bit, and we became quite good friends. In fact, there was a move to have him retire, and I remember going to Arthur Holly Crompton—at the time Compton was chancellor—and succeeded in part in having him held on to the faculty. I thought he was really great.

vs *Were you bitter at all when you left—when you were asked to leave?*

CE I think I only felt a little bitter about Ferrand. I think it's partially because I married Catherine Woermann, who was an architect, and she had already graduated—she got her bachelor's degree at Vassar—and then I was in the architectural school, and I think Ferrand had told her father that I could never be expected to amount to anything in the field. Naturally, this gives you a certain bias against a guy. Although he was one of the few people who—some of his acts I had resented, but when he died it was kind of with a sense of loss that I greeted it. I also felt a little badly about the tromping he had gotten from Louis La Beaume.

vs *Do you think the universities are learning at all to re-examine their judgments? They've been wrong so many times—as nearly as I can figure, there is no correlation between academic success and financial success, happiness, or any future measure.*

CE Well, I don't know, I think that the academic world's mistakes are reasonably predictable, or accountable, and I'm afraid if they would change their methods it might not be predictable and might be worse. I really don't know. The competition among faculty, or academic scholars even, as a scene—it's under the most unfortunate circumstance that you view them. They almost have no chance for being real human beings because they're sort of like competitive supplicants in an environment where the nature of the competition is embarrassing. It's not like competition in business, or out in work, or in the field outside. The individuals are much better than the institution and we use them; I work with individuals at the university a lot. I'd never work with the university, because everything breaks down like at the baby-sitter level. And the petty little competitions that grow—this gets to be part of the scene. Naturally, I'm interested in higher learning and scholarship and what happens in it, but in our own active work we're interested mainly in the kind of continuing found education that can be available not only to the people who are part of the academic world but to the people that aren't.

VS *You left university and immediately hung up your shingle as an architect. Did it work at all? What did you come out doing?*

CE Actually it's not quite that. I continued to work for Trueblood and Graf. They had a pretty good tradition. Trueblood had worked in T. C. Link's office, and Link had worked in one of the great offices and had built the St. Louis railroad station and also the Missouri capitol. One of my first jobs was sort of sorting the drawings of the St. Louis railroad station. Trueblood was very good; Graf was quite talented. I think Graf had married Melida Alice Gratiot, one of the Gratiot girls, and she's still on deck. Graf died, younger. Trueblood stayed on, and there is a third genera-tion of Trueblood practicing architecture, I think, in St. Louis. I'd like to see them sometime because Trueblood was a very strong and very good influ-ence on me. I had tremendous respect for him. People always assumed I was much closer to Graf because he had sort of a robust talent, and indeed, I was very close to him and enjoyed him. But I had tremendous respect for Trueblood.

VS *It was sort of an apprenticeship that you did.*

CE Yes. After the university I stayed on there for two years. In fact, I stayed on at Trueblood and Graf until 1930.

VS *Had Frank Lloyd Wright started his apprentice teaching by that time?*

CE Yes, he had Taliesin, and Taliesin was oper-ating, but that all seemed very removed from St. Louis. I would never think of going to—you know, right now kids feel they should call on the great so-and-so, and I never felt that. It always seemed— I always felt, before I knew Mies van der Rohe, I wouldn't want to go call on him until I had read everything he had written, which I couldn't do. You didn't feel that you wanted to take any of his energy, and why should you? And that was more or less a general feeling compared to now. People

think that they can go in, and I think it's a mistake.

VS *After you left Trueblood and Graf, was Robert Walsh your first associate?*

CE No, Robert Walsh and I had been together at Trueblood and Graf, and he was still there. I started in business with a guy by the name of Charles Gray who had also been in the Graf office. And then there was a little hiatus in which I went to Mexico for almost a year. I was in Monterrey, San Luis Potosi and around there. I arrived in Mexico with a total of 75 cents, and I lived there for about eight months and never got a cent from this coun-try. It was not easy. But then came back here in the spring, and when I came back I formed an office with Robert Walsh.

VS *Did that early experience in Mexico have any-thing to do with your humanistic philosophy?*

CE Oh, sure, there was a major difference. Before I went to Mexico I did all kinds of work and I worked on all kind of problems. I went to Mexico because, while we were struggling along, there was an awful lot of drinking. This was during the Depression—'32, '33—with John Meyer, who was later the president of a bank, in the South, and his wife, Alice Strauch. John was more secure, in a way, than the other brothers. And Bob Walsh— Bob Walsh's sister married one of the Meyers, Al Meyer, and there was a lot of drinking there. Then John's father committed suicide as a result of the Depression, and a younger brother tried to. And, as I say, although John and Alice led a pretty constrained life, there was an awful lot of drink-ing going on, and finally it got to be so much I thought, really, to hell with it, and I paid all the debts I could and had, took what was left, and took off for Mexico.

VS *What was left was 75 cents! Are there examples of the work before Mexico still standing? Had you built the house, for instance, for the Meyers?*

CE No. There was an engineering professor by the name of Ernest O. Sweetzer at Washington University, and I had built a little house for him out in that Wydown area.

VS *Is it still there?*

CE I suppose it is. It would be a fairly simple house with reasonably nice colonial—if you're going to say, "detailing." Otherwise it was fairly undistinguished, except for the way it was built— it was built very well. I did four or five things like that; I worked on a thing with Trueblood for a nutty guy in that area, and then the guy asked me to do some things there. It was after coming back that I did Alice's house, and also with Bob we did . . . some churches in the South—one in Paragould, Arkansas, and one in Helena, Arkansas.

vs *Are they still there?*

CE Yes, they're still in existence. That was a wild experience, doing these things. We would do the sculpture, the painting, the murals, and all the glass. We did all the vestments—we'd get fabrics up in St. Louis, take them down and make designs for the vestments. . . . I would supervise the women of the community, and they did marvelous things. I was a nut on the revival. While I had been never raised in the Catholic Church, my mother's family had been Catholic; and in the South there we did what later became very modern changes within the rubrics and ritual of the Church. Old Emil Frei was interested in that, and Emil got to be sort part of the scene.

vs *I looked at the house that you did for the Meyers, which now belongs to Bill Ford of Ford Hotel Supply. It's a beautiful house. It's one of the things you're still pleased with, I would think.*

CE I was pleased with it in many ways. Now, the house separated from the furnishings, this would be the only reason I wouldn't be too happy to go back. We designed a lot of the rugs and the furnishings particularly for the house. I designed the rugs and the tile, and that's really when I became closely acquainted with the Saarinens—I went up and had Loja Saarinen and her group weave the rugs I had designed. There was also a complete musical staff—about eight or ten bars of music—carved into the bricks of that house before they were baked. Josephine Johnson did some sculpture in the bricks, I did some sculpture; Carolyn Risque Janis, several people sculpted the bricks in the raw before they were baked, and they're spotted in an odd way throughout the whole building. We incised a whole section of a Beethoven symphony in the walls of that house. It was one of the first air-conditioned houses, and the first house using aluminum sash.

vs *That is one of the pieces of work in St. Louis, then, that is one of the most satisfactory?*

CE Oh, yes.

vs *You had other houses. Someone told me there was a house in Webster Groves, on Bristol—do you remember doing that?*

CE I don't. I vaguely remember the situation, and somebody was talking about it once and I was embarrassed not to remember it. Chip Reay has some stuff—he has some of the old files that he

had promised to send out. He also did a house that Bob did a lot of work on; the son-in-law—does the name Lippman?—and a guy whose name was Pinkus, and he was an entomologist or something. Lippman was a doctor, but a child educator. He belonged to the Viennese Freudian school. They were super-enthusiastic, fanatic almost. They all had an interesting force in the St. Louis cultural life. I had several Jewish friends in St. Louis, and it was a very positive introduction to a side of world culture which otherwise I would have completely missed.

vs *Where was the Lippmanns' house? Do you remember?*

CE No. It was close to an International style, because they were intellectually oriented. Then there was another doctor, Dr. Albert E. Auer. Dr. Auer had a great etching and lithograph collection; he was also a Jewish intellectual from that period, and these people were marvelously generous. His son was an architectural student, Jimmy Auer, who died fairly early in his career, and Dr. Auer did a lot for me in instruction in the whole world of prints and etchings and what not.

vs *St. Louis is surprisingly productive in many areas. That was at the beginning of the John Burroughs School, and the women's vote had a big group of—Edna Gellhorn, did you know her?*

CE Oh, yes.

vs *And Martha Gellhorn, who married Ernest Hemingway. Those women were an incredible group.*

CE Oh, yes. They were very, very important. And of course, I lived in a family where the women were very strong, as in many French families. I was raised essentially raised by my mother's sister and some French aunts, so that I'm used to having fairly strong women around.

vs *I think people in general would not see that as a byproduct of St. Louis, but it certainly is.*

CE Oh, yes. Also, for a family that was super middle-class respectable, they were not in any way puritanical from a standpoint of, oh, drinking and wine and even attitude toward sex. My mother was the motherly type of all time, and so were the French aunts, but there was a very healthy attitude towards sex so that it never became a problem. I would just encounter it from the differences between us and other kids in the neighborhood. My grandmother used to think that if a young boy didn't have a glass of claret with his soup, something was going to happen to his blood, and the neighbours would be horrified that their son had come to lunch and was given wine with his soup.

vs *Your first association with the Saarinens was, then, when you had the rugs woven for the Meyer house?*

CE Yes. I had gotten a note from Eliel because one of the churches had been published by the Architectural Forum.

vs *Do you remember which church it was?*

CE I think it was the one in Helena. There was some inquiry about the rugs for the house, and I just went up after the house had been built—and indeed they did make the rugs—I met Carl Milles, the sculptor. This was in about '35 or '36; Alice and John (Meyer) bought a silver and pewter casting of the head of the woman in the Orpheus fountain, and it was sort of a double thing—I had pulled off getting it through Milles, and Alice and John put up the funds to buy it. So with this background, Eliel asked me if I'd like a fellowship at Cranbrook. And now came the chance, because I had been going through a kind of turn of events with my own architectural practice; and I said that I'd like the fellowship if I could come and not really produce any work in the sense of work on a project but could go up and just plain read for a year. In a sense, it was a desire to make up what I had lost in the academic world. It was a question of just wishing I had the time to read. I actually stuck to this for about three months, and by that time there were interesting things to be done in Saarinen's own office, and by the end of the year he'd asked me to form what the school had not had—a design department. I put together a design department and headed that up for a year or two, and then I was working in his office and working with Eero and Eliel.

vs *By this time it was 1940. Was 1940 the Organic Furniture competition? There is a story that came from Girard regarding you someplace along the line: he was designing cabinets for radios, and you went in—apparently looking for a job—saw his designs, and left him a note that said "You don't need me here," and signed it "Charles Eames" before he even knew who you were. Do you remember at what point in time you did that?*

CE Yes, naturally. It was an entirely different point in time. This was not so far apart, but the nature of the time was considerably different because the 1930s and '39 was pre-war, and the Organic Furniture Competition was the last thing before the war. That was 1940—'39 and '40—and then in '41 Ray and I were both out here.

vs *Along that line there were the beginnings of some contemporary furniture in Europe, but here you came up with something that was radically new, and there had been virtually nothing new in furniture design since Duncan Phyfe—there had been a lot of reworking. What are the circumstances that bring forth the need to have a philosophy on furniture? The philosophy had to come before the design—or did it come the other way?*

CE The philosophy was an entirely different manifestation, as far as I was concerned. It was just like reading Frank Lloyd Wright's autobiography. He talked about building a windmill on a hill.

vs *We were talking about the Organic Furniture Competition, how you got started, and what prompted you to enter the competition. We didn't get that far, but that was my next question.*

CE You were talking about what had and hadn't been done, and I was about to point out that there were people like Alvar Aalto in Finland and a whole resurgence of furniture design in Sweden. In Alice and John Meyer's house we had designed quite a bit of furniture; it was along pretty classic lines, but in some way—

vs *Were you aware of the Swedish-Finnish movement? It seems to me that at that point we didn't exchange information as quickly as we do now.*

CE We didn't, but one of the buildings that had been quite an influence on people was the Stockholm City Hall. There were people in St. Louis who were aware of this whole thing in Sweden—Victor Proetz, and his brother's wife was Erma Proetz, who was an early strong career woman in the community, in the Gardner Advertising Company. He and Ralph Hall designed the Park Plaza Hotel, and the design of that coffee shop in the Park Plaza was absolutely great. Today it would be considered a real, historic—if it were in New York, the people would have kept it exactly the way it was. They painted a mural, and it was in a Wiener-Werkstatte Swedish mode. I was sort of influenced by that kind of style, and Emil Frei had also been exposed to it—the mosaic aspect of the Emil Frei company was responsible for the mosaics in the Gold Hall at Stockholm. So that there was this undercurrent, and some of the furniture for Alice Meyer had this influence. I ran into the furniture-maker who made that furniture back in the '30s—John Rausch in St. Louis. He was a German trained in veneers and furniture-making. He had a very small shop when I had him doing that, and, in fact, we were doing some great things.

There were so many people I didn't have that much of a chance to talk to him. I would have loved to have talked to him more. I'd like to know what his company is doing now. He was an absolute gem and did some marvelous inlays. So, then, that step from Sweden to Finland and the Alvar Aalto stuff is really quite a development. The Aalto, the Saarinens, and the Carl Milles form quite a bulk of influence. Much of that was showing in Alice Meyer's house.

vs *Still, it doesn't always happen. Someplace along the line the clue has to be in the temper of the times. Either an idea influences the people, or the people are ready to accept new ideas and it isn't always possible. Now, for instance, we're in the big nostalgia period.*

ce Well, the Organic Furniture Competition was quite something else. We were setting out to put the Frank Lloyd Wright theory, at least my own version of it, to work. It may have turned out looking more Miesian than Frank Lloyd Wright, but nevertheless it's one's own interpretation, and Ray and I had worked on that stuff pretty carefully. The stuff we did here was later. The Organic show that we did with Eero was more kind of a statement of principle. If it was built on anything, you could say it was built on the Aalto material, except that Aalto was all in one single plane, and ours had a lot of curvature built into it—and a shell principle, while Aalto's was a slab principle. We didn't expect it. From a merchandising standpoint, people had had a lot of criticism, and in New York the merchandising view was that the things we did would last about six months in the marketplace (now I'm speaking of the things we did later, not the Organic Design Competition). We were pretty much ready to come back and attack the whole problem again, but it didn't work that way; the fact is that the very first chairs we manufactured are still being manufactured, and those very same chairs are being produced in probably as great a volume as they ever were.

vs *This is an aside, but maybe it should go on the tape at the same time because I'd like to hear your reaction. We interviewed a man at Herman Miller named Stan Schrotenboer, and we asked him, "Well, when you think of Charles Eames, what do you think about?" He said in preparation to our coming, he had talked to a couple of other people who had been with the factory a long time, and one of them had answered, "Charles Eames is my job." Schrotenboer went on to say that what the man meant was that*

every other design comes and goes, but for our whole working career we've been manufacturing Charles Eames's things, and that's the bread and butter and that's our security. That's a very nice thing.

ce You don't often think of it that way, but it is true if you consider that when we first started doing these things Herman Miller had an annual gross of half a million dollars, and today they have an annual gross of sixty million.

vs *When you were struggling with the plywood-molding experiment, did you ever consider giving it up? Did you ever think, it won't work, I'll quit?*

ce Well, there were moments when there were some bombing scares out here—we thought that the Japanese were bombing the coast of California. In fact, about a hundred miles north, some U-boats did shell the coast. I remember some dreary nights I'd go home and I'd say, "God, dear God, I don't particularly want any bombs to drop on Los Angeles, or the United States, or any place. But if one must drop, wouldn't it be nice if it hit right in the middle of our plant." The problems at times had gotten to be fairly great.

vs *So that was working with the plywood, molding the plywood. You first had those chairs manufactured for you by Evans—is that correct?*

ce No, right in this building. We've been in this building for 35 years. We manufactured the first five thousand chairs right in this building. Evans Products, a company back in Detroit, had all that stuff we were doing in aircraft and whatnot; they had bought the company in that sense, but we maintained our own laboratory. After we built the first five thousand chairs to sort of prove the system—because we made all the tools and everything here ourselves—we shipped the tools back East and Evans Products started to manufacture in their plant in Grand Haven, Michigan. They weren't particularly interested in furniture like Herman Miller was, so Herman Miller sort of bought them out and we began doing it directly with Herman Miller. During the time that we had our laboratory, we were doing some work for Evans Products which included radio cabinets for Motorola. *That's* when I went back and saw the stuff that Sandro had done, and I said, "Look, you don't need me. I mean, you've got a great guy here, and this is marvelous stuff." This was before I had met him. Later I went out to dinner at their house, and then Ray came and visited them, and then Eero Saarinen. We became very close friends, all three of us.

vs *The little plywood elephant that you made—it*

was originally made for one of the Evans children, is that the story on that?

CE It wasn't made particularly for them, but one of the Evans children, Ed Evans, did get some. We were doing experiments in molding at that time, and we did some children's furniture. It was more or less a sculptural experiment in molding plywood.

VS *The folding screens came on about the same time? Were those manufactured, and for how long?*

CE In 1946 there was an exhibition at the Museum of Modern Art, and in that exhibition was all the material we had developed in the few years prior to that. It was at that exhibition that old D. J. De Pree saw it for the first time. He and his head of sales, Jim Eppinger, decided that they wanted to develop it, and that's when the first chairs were being manufactured. Jim Eppinger was from a Jewish family from Larchmont, New York, and a real salesman. He had sales in his blood, and he couldn't have been farther removed from this Dutch Reformed Michigan company, but he had respect for the material and did very well for them. Jim was enthusiastic about it.

VS *Then you actually started with Herman Miller in about 1946 and you were, in a sense, brought in by George Nelson?*

CE That's correct.

VS *What happened to George Nelson?*

CE I'd be interested in the story that you got, if anyone talked about George at Herman Miller. For a long time he was their chief design consultant, but he did a lot more than just furniture design. He really advised them as to how to expand, what property to buy, what things to do. Of course, we took part in this too, but George did an awful lot of general philosophical advice, but probably a lot of his advice on what they should do in advertising and promotion was a lot more valid than advice we would have given on that. D. J. De Pree had lost this designer that they had, Gilbert Rohde, who was very good and did very good for them. He went to New York trying to get advice, and George Nelson was then one of the editors of *Fortune* magazine. He later was also with *Architectural Forum*. And George spoke a language that architects speak, and D. J. asked him to criticize some of the pieces and he said, "O.K." He said, "These are good. I think they're good but I think you're probably not completely honest in the way you show the edge of a piece"—he used the terms of "honesty" and "material." This was kind of a new idea to D. J., and

it worried him to bring this moral content to the design. So he came back and George explained a little bit. He said, "I wasn't trying to criticize the morals of your plant, but there is a kind of way that you use material honestly." D. J. was completely impressed with this, and, as a result, it was through this moral issue that he brought George on board. Both our work and George's—the introduction of a kind of physical morality in handling material, this was the thing that really fascinated D. J. He'd never thought of it that way before. And there's a certain amount of larceny in the hearts of even the Dutch Reformed, and it looked like a way to bring morality to bear in a pretty good business proposition. That doesn't mean that he wasn't sincere about it—it was a genuine moral issue. It's just that people who look upon things that way would parlay the church or anything into a business thing.

VS *At the same time there were some other big-name designers doing sort of innovative things: Raymond Loewy, for one, Russell Wright, for another. Were they in the picture at all?*

CE No, I knew Russell Wright quite well. George had known Loewy, but Loewy was already a merchant at this point. He was in there good and contributing a lot of things to the issue. We had gotten to know Henry Dreyfuss fairly early in the game; Henry took the whole thing a little bit more seriously—he might even be said to have been a little pompous about it—but he was good, and he ran an awfully good shop. There was another character on the New York scene, Alfred Auerbach, who was the founding editor of *Women's Wear Daily* and a very, very alert and astute guy on the general art and design thing. Auerbach, along with a few others, had done an awful lot to help promote people like Dreyfuss and Dorothy Leibes, and Auerbach very early had a collection of paintings of Leger's and whatnot. I'd had some meetings with him and brought him on as a first kind of promotional and merchandising advisor for Herman Miller. He was on the scene with Herman Miller for several years while Eppinger was there.

VS *This was about the same time that the Niemeyer buildings were going up in South America. Had you seen the Niemeyer buildings or had a feeling about them?*

CE We had seen the same buildings that Niemeyer had seen, which were the Le Corbusier buildings. Niemeyer had worked with Le Corbusier . . . the Brasília buildings didn't—they actually weren't built for some time after that, but it was all going on about that same time. And as I say, our influence, if any, had been from Le Corbusier, which was the same influencing thing that had affected Niemeyer.

vs *According to Sandro Girard, you actually brought him into Herman Miller after you got there—George introduced D. J. to you, and you introduced D. J. to Sandro?*

ce I think that George was equally effective in getting Sandro. We certainly were enthusiastic about wanting him to come in, but George, too, wanted Sandro to come in.

vs *There must have been a certain amount of excitement in those days about working together on projects that were fresh and new and then seeing them all the way through to the end design concept. At what point did you diverge a little bit—or did you ever feel as if you diverged?*

ce Actually, George, Sandro, and I worked at the same time, but we have never worked together. We would use Sandro's fabrics, for instance, and he would use our chairs, but we have never worked together on any projects. We probably worked more closely with Sandro than we worked with George—George's offices were always fairly isolated. He was in New York, and Girard was at Grosse Pointe and then moved out to Santa Fe. I don't know where Sandro was when he started doing work for Herman Miller, but we worked in a reasonably isolated way. You know, work is affected by the pressures that are put on, and if other people or other interests start applying pressure of sorts, you respond to those. George was running an office, and he ran a much more sophisticated kind of office than we did.

For example, he would not only have Herman Miller for a client, but he would do something in furniture for another client. It was a perfectly good thing to do—he had these many clients which he was serving—and I think that in our own office we had arrived at a kind of a conclusion that we would never do anything for competing clients. As we got into work for ibm we would never do anything of a similar nature for Bell Labs; if we were going to be furniture for Herman Miller we wouldn't do anything remotely like furniture for anybody else.

vs *People at Herman Miller tell me that they never had a legal contract with you. As a matter of fact, both D. J. and Hugh were somewhat offended at the idea of a contract. They explained to me very carefully that there was a great deal of difference between a contract*

and a covenant, and that they thought that what they had with you was a covenant.

ce Well, of course, this can also be used to put a more exalted kind of screws on you if you want to. You put the screws in the covenant and you've really got something.

vs *But you're morally responsible for them.*

ce Yes. I think that—

vs *Still and all, it's an unusual company.*

ce It's an unusual company, but we have gone through over twenty years of service with ibm without any contract, either. It is an unusual company; so is ibm.

vs *Do you see changes happening in Herman Miller?*

ce Oh, I think so. It was a very strong family organization and it still is; there is a young management group in Herman Miller that has maintained a remarkable amount of genuine interest and concern, so you have people coming up who think very clearly. You know, if something goes right, it might change, but the general fundamental hasn't—the things that have made it good in the past, some of those are still there.

vs *When you're talking about those good things—human concern for each other, the quality of product—what else?*

ce Well, you see, you get a company that has for years thought and spoken of itself as a design-oriented company. And the fact is, the company has not been that design-oriented. They've done an awful lot to maintain good relations within the plant, and they've been concerned about quality in a kind of way by which they probably wished for it more than anything else. So you have people wishing for it and providing a background that would help induce it; and then you get a group of young management people who have been sort of schooled in that, and they, in much more precise ways, decide that they are going to try to put this into effect; and you see possibilities of real positive action. In a sense the early factory, like the primitive church, has something to offer, but very often this goes downhill. In the Herman Miller case, you see young people coming in with more precise ideas, and it could stand up very well.

vs *If I understand what I was told correctly, these young people tended to be people from Zeeland. Do you see Herman Miller hiring outside of Zeeland, or do you see them making a bid for young design people, as they did before? They have a designer now, the Action Office group—Propst, is that correct?*

CE Yes. Propst is a researcher. Actually, what would be nice is if they had a basic attitude towards furniture that would form a kind of anonymous good goods. I think that their weakest cases are where they attempt to go out and get designers. I think a much healthier thing for them would be to develop a habit of just making really good goods, not knocking themselves out to be innovative. I myself have always thought of innovation as a kind of a negative goal, and if we had a sign up over the door I would say, "Only Innovate As a Last Resort." Never set out to innovate, because more horror is done with that goal in mind than any other.

VS *There is an office building in St. Louis—the Laclede Building—which is stem-to-stern Herman Miller. That, I guess, is no longer possible. They're not doing that sort of thing anymore. They don't keep Girard fabrics; they're not doing the complete interior job that they used to do.*

CE You know, they have never really been a— they don't do a complete interior job. Correction: they did have a planning group that were doing it for a while. As a company, they have been doing well with the systems and they have gone a little bit overboard, but there's a lot of movement within the company now to get down back into residential pieces and bring more of a balance back into the line.

VS *Does this mean there will be more Charles Eames furniture? You haven't done anything since 1972, is that correct?*

CE That's largely our own fault. Whenever we have done anything, they have done it. We're working on some things now that the Vitra plant in Basel wants to do very much.

VS *Let's leave Herman Miller for a moment and go to IBM. You went to IBM at about the same time that you made that first trip to India; were those events interrelated, or were they two separate projects?*

CE Actually, I'd been working on some things with IBM for about two years before the India trip. In fact, we had finished that first film for the Brussels World's Fair before we left for India.

VS *What kind of an influence did that Indian trip have on you? You've done a lot of things that concerned India since then—you did a Nehru film, and then you went back, is that correct?*

CE I've probably made about five or six trips to India. We'd started by meeting people who would come from India, and then Sandro did that show in the Museum of Modern Art. Pupul Jayakar helped put that together—she was a close friend of Nehru's, and she was close to some of the philosophers and knew Gandhi fairly well. And she became a friend. Then we were brought to India in '56 or '57 to investigate the whole the problem of quality of design there.

VS *We were talking about India and your job.*

CE In India they felt that the general quality of things had been deteriorating in recent years, and they wanted some plan by which India itself could attack that problem through some kind of an institution, teaching or otherwise, that would raise the level of interest in quality and environment as such. Essentially, it's the same problem we have around us here. Ray and I spent five months in India, in which we worked from one end to the other and in the end wrote a position paper for a National Institute of Design. Probably the most characteristic thing about it was that it had to do with the attention given very small and simple problems in India, with the thought of building up an attitude towards design which was quite different from the traditional effect. In a country like India where it is highly tradition-oriented, there's no question of a problem of design—each particular situation in a person's life calls for a very special next situation to follow it. Everything is programmed, and as a result it's a beautiful and unified situation. Well, as this tends to go to pieces, they had to structure something there that would combat the degenerative influence of bringing in the effects of other cultures. Nehru was still alive when Ray and I were there, and we had many discussions with him and got to know Indira Gandhi. Later, when Nehru died, it was Indira Gandhi who got us to do the exhibition called Nehru: His Life and His India. That was in Washington and then New York, and then in London and several countries—it traveled. But the institute was a very interesting project. We did the basic design for it here—that is, the figuring out what the general motif would be—but then we constructed it in India, with Indian labor, and brought a group from the office here to India. It was a very interesting experience, and very good. The institute is now 10 years old, and we still keep in touch with it. It was initially funded by the Ford Foundation when they were in India.

VS *Was the exhibit preserved, or was it destroyed at the end of its show time?*

CE No, it was preserved in India. It's still in a building related to the Presidential Palace. . . .

vs *The political climate in India is precarious again. Do you think the institute will survive it?*

CE Oh, I believe it will. At this point, if they didn't have such an institute they would probably have to reinvent another one. The original document we wrote is little different in character than what they've carried out, although they bring out the old document regularly and publish it very often at the beginning of their annual reports. The goals are broad enough that I think it could last as kind of a guide for some time.

vs *We haven't talked very much about IBM, and that's a big portion of what you've done recently with the films. When did you start using films as a communication device in your work? I guess you've always been interested in photography since the dry plate experiments?*

CE We did an early film on the role of the computer called "A Communications Primer." This was before we'd done any work for IBM. We did that because we were interested in getting architects to use computer techniques in classifying and collecting data from which to attack a problem; we looked for a film we could use, couldn't find any and therefore made "Communications Primer." It became part of "A Rough Sketch for a Sample Lesson for a Hypothetical Course," the first multi-media show, which we did in '53 and '54. Architects in this country weren't too interested in the film, but it was a great success in London and Europe, and I think the Department of Agriculture bought 50 or 100 prints. From then on, we've been using film just as you would use architectural models. . . .

vs *How soon did IBM become a client and part of your life—which I think it really is, isn't it?*

CE It certainly has been for the last 20 years. We were called in by Eliot Noyes, who is a consultant to IBM, to look at and criticize a lot of design problems. We worked with Eliot as a consultant for some time, and then at the time of the Brussels World's Fair IBM had a pavilion but they didn't have a central statement to make in the pavilion. The time was short, and we wrote and produced a film called "The Information Machine." IBM used it at the fair and is still using it. From that time on, we've worked essentially in film and exhibition; we discuss all general problems of film and exhibition with IBM. And now it's been some time. It's been over twenty years.

vs *As busy as you are—and today I had a sample of that—when do you find time to do the research?*

CE Well, I don't do as much general reading as I'd like to. I can't do it because I get here usually about 8:30 in the morning and seldom ever leave before 10:00 o'clock at night, and we're usually on the projects. Years ago I used to sort of take the evening to read and mull over problems. Now, in a sense, I read only what is directly related to the work we're doing. But the work is usually general enough—at the moment we've just finished a film on Daumier in the nineteenth century, which involved an awful lot of photography in the Bibliothèque Nationale in Paris and all around, and for the Franklin-Jefferson thing, we were just steeped in the eighteenth century.

vs *You do use researchers, though, don't you?*

CE Not really. In the case of the Franklin-Jefferson exhibit we certainly did, but the people who really work on the problems are people that think about the central core. Like Jehane Burns, who is in London now; I wouldn't call her a researcher because she's sort of a lot more than that. We don't use researchers as they're sometimes used, where they're just sent out to gather material, because most of the people . . . like Alex Funke, working on "Powers of Ten." He had to produce a lot of the mechanics of the film, but he was also the one who would go and with him, why, I would go and we would talk to the biologists and the small particle physicists and the astronomers.

vs *That would stretch the average person's capability of understanding.*

CE Well, one thing builds on another; and, after all, if you're going to make a film or write a short story or an article, the trick is that as you reproduce or retell things, you have to actually limit yourself to those things that you do understand. Even though you may only understand just a fraction of what you get from the specialist, still—if you limit yourself to talking about those things that you do understand, it's a lot more effective than it would be if you tried to do a snow job.

vs *You have had innumerable honors and awards, but as I look at it one of the most exciting things was being the Norton Professor of Poetry at Harvard. How much time did you spend at Harvard, and could you describe that experience?*

CE Most awards, of course, tend to come along as compliments for having gotten other awards, so they tend to build up. Something like the Norton Professorship at Harvard is a little something else because Harvard is risking a lot when they do it. About once every four years they will go out of the field of poetry and into another field and pick someone to give the lectures, and it's a high risk if they get some maverick like myself to do it. Of course, it was a tremendous challenge for me.

vs *How many lectures?*

CE Six lectures, and they're spread throughout the entire year. At the time of each lecture I would spend two weeks on the campus; I gave a certain number of seminars and received and talked to a lot of students. I had quite an enthusiastic group at the lectures. The first two were given at the Loeb Theater, and then we ran out of room. We were also showing a lot of motion picture and visual material with the lectures, so the last four were given at the Harvard Square Motion Picture Theater. That was fun.

vs *I would think it would be exciting. Do you find the atmosphere on campus and the attitude of students greatly changed from when you were in school?*

CE Well, we gave the Harvard lectures at a time when student unrest was still fairly high. In fact, Dean Ford, who is dean of the College at Harvard, had his heart attack a week after he had made the appointment—the students had entered his office and sat in. I told him that I had a feeling that what he was doing this particular year was selecting a kind of human sacrifice to offer to the students. But the response was really marvelous. I've never felt closer to a group than I did at the end of this series of lectures, because the same students all came back.

vs *That would, I think, be an exciting period in your career.*

CE Well, a thing like this is very important because you work on it, then you do it, and then you feed off it for a long time—I mean, you feed off of it yourself. You do a concentrated amount of work, gather materials, develop some new ideas, then you use it. It was the same thing with the experimental course Ray and I gave at Berkeley quite a few years before—we did it, and in doing it we developed the whole concept of the use of multiple images, and then developed that more further on.

vs *You were at UCLA this last year or the year before last. Did you actually teach while you were there?*

CE No, I gave a series of seminars to graduate students. I had requested a group from multiple disciplines, so the group was made up of graduate students from many of the different colleges.

vs *In doing these interviews concerning your work, I've had an interesting point of view from almost everybody I've talked to so far, and one of the questions that keeps coming up is whether you've ever thought of yourself as a philosopher as opposed to an architect.*

CE Well, actually I use architect as a generic term, because for me it's come to mean just giving structure to anything. The fact of the matter is that we tend to think of ourselves as tradespeople, really. I mean we have a business; people come to us to get things, and what they usually come for are models of some sort or another. By models I mean ways of structuring certain problems. For instance, IBM will come. Right now we're working on the new building at 57th and Madison, and it calls for a kind of modeling of what the situation would be—what the young professional in midtown Manhattan could get from a museum at that kind of spot. It also calls for a certain amount of architecture and design, but that's really secondary to build a concept of what kind of service a corporation like that can be to the city.

vs *Isn't that in a sense a philosophy?*

CE Well, I would say that if you're going to attack a problem in teaching, you're part philosopher; if you're going to be a good physician, you're part philosopher; and certainly being a good parent in times like these calls for a bit of philosophy. So I wouldn't say that it didn't have some of that. But we wouldn't classify ourselves as trained philosophers.

vs *You have been described as a great teacher.*

CE That's probably because I haven't risked my record by attempting to teach too much. Ray and I did, actually, teach this experimental course in Berkeley that lasted for a year, and it was a rather grueling experience. We went up to Berkeley for five or six days each month and then we would come back and give criticisms and lectures. But after a day of teaching, why, I'd be more ready to go out and vomit . . . I'd come out of a day of teaching and not be able to eat dinner. Because it was just *so* debilitating. Just from the energy standpoint, I couldn't stand to really teach because I put so much into it.

vs *Do you think that's the general rule of people who hold those positions?*

CE Well, no. I think that the unfortunate part is that it's not the general rule of people that hold those positions. I was talking to a president of a university, a great, rascally president—I was asked to dinner after teaching a course, and I turned to him and said, "You'll have to excuse me, I can't eat, I've just had this day of teaching." And I said, "This is old stuff to you, you would have never . . ." He said, "Not at all," and explained what *he* went through. He was a pretty good teacher, so from then on I relaxed about it. It would still upset me to do a day of teaching, but I have seen . . . most mathematics teachers, particularly, in secondary school, must hate mathematics or they wouldn't teach it the way they do. And none of these people gets upset by an end of a day in teaching; I'd feel a little better if they did.

But nevertheless. In relation to teaching, myself—it's a terribly exhausting process. You end up going places and you give a lecture, and that's always disappointing, because you leave the place without ever seeing any students—like Washington University. I didn't say two words to a student there, and you don't get any feedback, you don't get any response. I'd like to go into a place where there is no lecture planned but where you get a general cross-questioning from students and faculty alike: it gives you an idea of the relationship between students and faculty in the place. That's the ideal situation, as far as I'm concerned. I don't mind how hard the grilling is—like if they set up a situation—but to have to go in and just give a spiel is absolutely pointless.

vs *I know that all of your exhibits are, in a sense, teaching exhibits, but the one that I thought particularly important and timed well—timed at a point where the country, and students particularly, had a pretty poor image of the American philosophy and the American contribution to the world—was the Franklin and Jefferson exhibit. Was the work on that exhausting or exhilarating? Or both?*

ce It was both exhausting and exhilarating for everybody that took part in it. It was certainly enriching. In the beginning, Ray and I were both Jeffersonian buffs and then were greatly rewarded by the work we did. We set out with the idea of being very critical—or, we didn't set out to be critical but we were not going to be uncritical—and gradually we got so impressed with the people themselves—for example, what Madison had done under great odds—that there was less and less room to be picky about the criticisms. Let's say, for example, you start out an exhibition on Franklin and decide that you're not going to just whitewash the dirty poetry he wrote; but then you get into it and you find a lot of people writing even much better stuff than Franklin of a highly shocking nature—Swift and people like that—and

it gets to be very unimportant relative to the other things because you're trying to sort of get in those important things. It wasn't always flattering, but it tended to reduce the amount of picky criticisms we expected to be doing. Everybody got into it, and the whole office was pretty well exhausted before we got through.

vs *Jefferson holds up, then, under that kind of scrutiny?*

ce Oh yes. And Franklin. Of course, I was interested in Jefferson in terms of architecture and other things, but there are a lot of surprises. In fact, somebody in Europe asked me the question: "After doing all this, if you were going to work with someone, who would it be? Would you rather work with Franklin or Jefferson?" Much to the questioner's surprise I said I'd rather work with Franklin. And I would.

vs *He had a more open mind?*

ce Well, I'd rather spend a weekend or a dinner party, maybe, with Jefferson, I don't know. But if I were going to work with somebody, I had a feeling that Franklin was a more open person in that sense. There were so many areas in which Jefferson was constantly questioning and whatnot, while Franklin, while questioning, was constantly probing in a very open way. I know enough about work to know that there are moments when you really want real action, you don't want somebody to have some great, broad, philosophical, beautiful, beautiful piece of prose.

vs *The other point on Jefferson is that he probably was so convinced that he was right about things that he was inflexible in many ways, and certainly many of the things that he said he believed in—and I'm convinced he believed in—he himself couldn't live up to. He simply had rules.*

ce I think that what you say is probably the key thing. With Franklin, it was a pretty open game. He was capable of great strategy, but even within the strategy it was quite an open game.

vs *There was an interesting climate in Virginia that produced so many people—Patrick Henry, James Madison, Thomas Jefferson, Washington, the whole Lee family.*

ce Yes. There was an awful lot of learning going on there which was certainly not predicated on teaching institutions. Teaching institutions were few and far between, but the intensity of the learning was great. You have a feeling that it was a combination of classic models that these families still went back to, and the immediacy of the problem.

They were not removed from the problem—they were, at the same time, not removed from the earth—and they took, essentially, the principles of the Enlightenment that were generated in Europe and, instead of taking them as armchair philosophers, nurtured and developed them under this situation. This was a point we tried to make in Paris. We tried to present the Revolution and the relationships of the people that formed it, and formed a government, as an aspect of eighteenth-century Enlightenment in Europe, nurtured and made immediate on a very rough and primitive soil.

vs *If you had to choose Jefferson's greatest achievement, what would you choose?*

CE What I would think of as his greatest piece of architecture . . . was the building of the Northwest Land Ordinance. That was the structure that divided the land into townships and sections and held certain parcels of land for the government and for education. It did several things. It put a kind of rationality to the division of land, which, in Europe was an absolute shambles, and it laid a groundwork that made a public educational system possible.

vs *What about Franklin?*

CE Well, Franklin, of course, is a slightly different case, because for many years people didn't take Franklin's science too seriously. It was viewed as . . . the kite experiment, and the foolish experiment. But he actually had a Newtonian view of science and did for electricity much what Newton did for the laws of motion. The thing that I still find most rewarding is his method of argument. I was in Sarge Shriver's outer office waiting for him to go to lunch in Paris, when he was ambassador to France, and I picked up a first edition of Franklin's letters. They were written at the time that he was trying to make peace with the British. You found that Franklin's method of relationship with an adversary was to work on the adversary's strength: he wouldn't try to find a weakness, he would try to pick out an argument that his adversary had made that had real logic, which, if pursued to its logical conclusion, would embrace *Franklin*'s point. This was at the time they were trying to solve the seating at the Vietnamese peace conference, and I handed this book to Sarge Shriver and said, "Look. Read this and do likewise."

Source: Charles Eames, Oral History, interview by Virginia Stith, St. Louis Department of Parks and Recreation, October 13, 1977, Eames Office LLC. Archives.

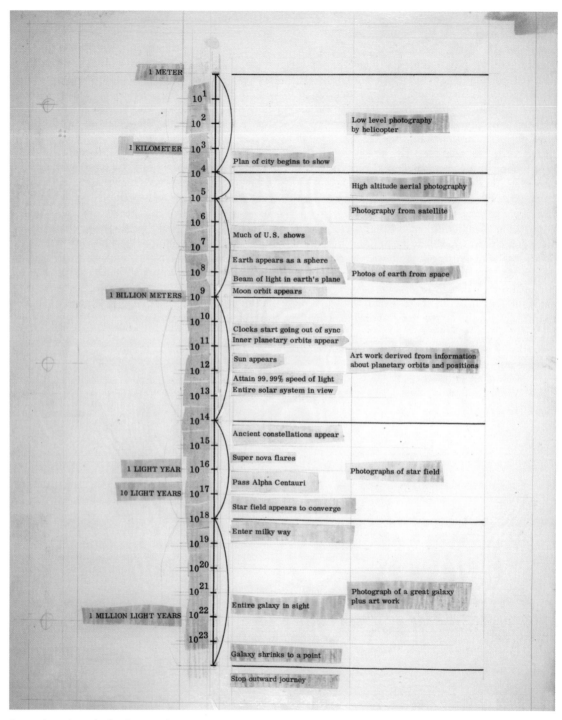

A page from the script for "Powers of Ten" by Charles and Ray Eames.

382

Notes on "Powers of Ten"

Particularly in the past fifty years the world has gradually been finding out something that architects have always known, that is—that *everything* is architecture.

The problems of environment have become more and more interrelated.

This is a sketch for a film that shows something of how large—and small—our environment is.

The largest and the smallest involve numbers too big and too little to conceive of.

But by using a logarithmic progression (the powers of ten) we can in a small and handleable number like 34 describe the whole universe.

It also shows the importance of the added *zero*.

It is interesting that most of the images in the last part of the film are of information that can be gathered by satellite.

It is also interesting that this information—which is absolutely necessary to guard the health of our earth—is the same information that nations keep as secrets.

What is *most* interesting is that the governments of the world will have to choose between their secrets and their planet earth.

Source: Charles Eames, handwritten notes, Container I: 217, Folder 11, Charles and Ray Eames Papers, Manuscript Division, Library of Congress, Washington, D.C., 1977.

Charles Eames on the crane, Ray
Eames to the left of the truck, during
production on "Powers of Ten."

RAY EAMES

U.S.-Japan Conference on Cultural and Educational Interchange

Editor's note: Draft of a speech to be delivered at U.S.-Japan Conference on Cultural and Educational Interchange, Tokyo, in July 1978.

One of the by-products of a new awareness of limits is that we begin to be more prudent about the nature of our inventions.

We begin to watch our new innovations for their possible irreversible side-effects.

The same sort of caution applies to what we're doing here.

We're talking about contributions to a culture that could tie a global unit together (which doesn't mean a unified global culture).

Common to all, like math, a common elegance.

An overall view of aesthetics.

We cannot take it for granted that such a culture would be based on anything like the fine arts as we or any other traditional society think of them now.

Steps toward an appropriate culture for spaceship earth are going to involve many TRANSFORMATIONS; and most of them look quite difficult from here.

One of the transformations is a transformation of the idea of craftsmanship.

A few years ago, at a meeting of a large crafts society, we heard members decrying the fact that there was not a sufficient demand for their work—that the need for craftsmen was disappearing.

On the contrary; this is a time when the need for a real, effective sense of craft in all our production has never been greater.

It requires a transformation of the idea of craftsmanship. A transformation which will embrace every manufactured object—every artifact on the landscape—every process and every system we devise.

This is a tragedy which we can't afford if people who have a grasp of tradition turn their backs on these new levels of responsibility.

There is a transformation in the idea of *hospitality*—so that the well-being of individuals is really anticipated in public structures—and above all to counteract the spirit of "don't look at me—I only work here"; so that more people would begin to act as *hosts*—act as if they really owned the place.

And there's also a transformation in the idea of *goods*: from an emphasis on things purchased with money to an emphasis on *skills and knowledge* bought with personal time and attention (which says Charles is the real coin of the realm).

In a situation of universal expectancy it helps to think of *Information* as a key resource, in relation to needs as well as pleasures.

• Because it makes low energy demands, and
• because once you have it, it works like the loaves and fishes: you can distribute it without diminishing it.

But [by the same token] you can't just order new information from a catalog. It isn't information unless it's *informative* to all the people concerned.

Right now, we have tremendous capacity for gathering and storing data; but our skills at *modeling data*—making it mean something—are way behind.

We need a whole new visual language using the existing communications hardware much more effectively.

In universities, the language of vision—even the art of diagrams and charts—is still neglected in favour of the written word.

But for any study of *process* one needs the resources of graphics, and color, and the *third dimension of time*, to convey a direct understanding, however abstract.

Source: Ray Eames, draft speech, July 1978, U.S.-Japan Conference on Cultural and Educational Interchange, Tokyo, Container I:218: Folder 13, Charles and Ray Eames Papers, Manuscript Division, Library of Congress, Washington, D.C.

Part Five

1980–1986

BILL N. LACY

"Warehouse Full of Ideas"

Editor's note: Architect Bill N. Lacy is a former president of three colleges: the American Academy in Rome, where he served from 1977–79; the Cooper Union, 1980–88; and the State University of New York College at Purchase, 1993–2001. From 1988 to 2005 he was the executive director of the Pritzker Architecture Prize.

I REMEMBER VIVIDLY my many visits to the Eames office, a warehouse-like arrangement located in the oceanside Los Angeles community called Venice. On the outside the office was a blank facade distinguished only by the bold, black-and-white, yard-high numerals "901." There was no other clue to the activity within the building, which was part museum, part funhouse, and part design and film studio. The Eameses' lives were everywhere on display in past projects frozen into exhibits and in work in process. There were toy trains, toy boats, wooden elephants, an aquarium. One room was a mock-up of a clown's dressing room; in others were seashells, wooden alphabet blocks, a sequined Indian doorway piece, and a model of the entrance of the new *Washington Post* building.

Charles Eames was a natural teacher, although not the kind who was comfortable in the classroom. Nevertheless, his Charles Eliot Norton lectures at Harvard University attracted such large numbers that they were moved to a local movie theater. Charles preferred small groups like those that visited his studio from UCLA and the University of Southern California. Students would sit in an informal circle around him and hear him tell how restraints in design were a welcome and necessary part of the process; that the terms good and bad should be replaced with scale, legibility, and workability; and that there was no such thing as an unimportant detail.

[Charles Eames] on education: "I don't believe in this 'gifted few' concept, just in people doing things they are really interested in doing. They have a way of getting good at whatever it is. The American educational system never tells a student that."

Source: Bill N. Lacy, "Warehouse Full of Ideas," *Horizon* 23, no. 9 (September 1980): 20–27.

RAY EAMES

Letter to Ronald Reagan

*Editor's note: A handwritten note on a copy of this letter
indicates that Ray Eames enclosed a Mathematica timeline
and a brochure for The World of Franklin and Jefferson
exhibition.*

**Ray Eames to President Ronald Reagan, The White House
September 24, 1981**

Dear Sir,

This is a plea—having heard your message on
the radio—returning from work this evening.

Your words seemed to come from conviction, so
I am giving you reasons you may not have thought
of because of concentrating on one idea—that of
budget-cutting where it is possible.

The need for a Department of Education is
not to take away initiative from states, but to
give a national standard for each state to strive
for. So that a child going to school in Mississippi
or Montana or Massachusetts or Michigan has
the same opportunity—and can move from New
Orleans to New York without missing a beat. And
that does not require a great amount of money.

Charles and I, while working on the U.S.
Bicentennial Exhibition—The World of Franklin and
Jefferson—became familiar with the group of extraordinary friends and cohorts who formed the government—and education was considered a necessity and
a responsibility. The E in HEW was taken out only to
make the H and W more handleable and let E do its
job with all eyes and hearts of the country watching.

All our wishes are with you in your enormous task.

Sincerely,

Ray Eames

Source: Ray Eames to Ronald Reagan, September 24, 1981,
Container I:116, Folder 11, Charles and Ray Eames Papers,
Manuscript Division, Library of Congress, Washington, D.C.

Note to Rolf Fehlbaum

Editor's note: Rolf Fehlbaum is chairman of Vitra, a family-owned furniture company with the exclusive license for Eames designs manufactured and distributed in Europe and the Middle East.

Ray Eames to Rolf Fehlbaum, Paris
January 7, 1986

It has been a great pleasure to be in Paris and to be a part of the announcement of Vitra taking over the task of producing our furniture for Europe.

I feel it could not be in better hands, for Rolf Fehlbaum has been an old and dear friend and was for many years and his sensitivity and concern is well understood.

We share a respect for quality and service to the consumer!

We look forward to a return visit.

Ray Eames

Source: Ray Eames, handwritten note to Rolf Fehlbaum, Paris, France, January 7, 1986, Vitra Archives, Basel, Switzerland.

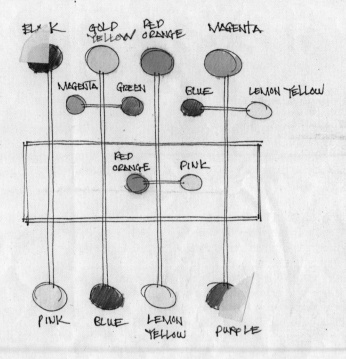

HUGH DE PREE

From *Business as Unusual*

Editor's note: Hugh De Pree, as President and Chief Executive Officer from 1962–80, led Herman Miller from a small, family-owned business to a large, publicly held corporation.

IN THE LAST SEVERAL years of our friendship, Charles and I seldom talked about design. He was obsessed with quality, with making every product better. He probed: Is the lounge chair being made as good as it can be? Who is deciding on changes in materials? Who at Herman Miller cares about quality? How do they show they care? What exactly are you doing, Hugh, about quality? Few answers would satisfy him. One time he was so persistent that I stood up and said I would leave if he did not ease off. He invited me to go. Only Ray Eames . . . doused the fire we had suddenly and uncharacteristically set. She persuaded us to resume the lunch. . . . We did but he still talked about quality. So my working with Charles Eames was a high for me and many others. One's level of understanding and care was raised beyond expectations. But it was not easy. It was difficult to deal with the contradictions of fun and intensity. But oh my, was it ever worth it.

Ralph Caplan once said, "Charles Eames was not always teaching, but when you were with him you were always learning."

At Charles's urging, we organized a technical center and staffed it with professional engineers. Charles gave them their objective: "Make our products unassailable in the marketplace."

When I think of Charles Eames today, I think of him as a teacher, more than as a designer.

Charles Eames believed we placed too much emphasis on innovation and argued that it was dangerous to try to be first or to be unique. He felt it required too much attention, leaving too little time to making things better. But he also gave us a valuable perspective of this aspiration when he said, "Hugh, the reason I am so frustrated with your drive for innovation is that true innovation is a function of a series of unexpected things coming together at a point in time." As an example, he used the French Revolution's seemingly unrelated but inexorable social and political causes. He was telling us that without these external dynamics, nothing will happen, and that you can't program major change. He added, "The only thing I can do is to try to help you recognize it when it happens, and then take advantage of it."

Ray pointed out that "Charles was drawn to [Herman Miller] because he thought they were very straightforward, honest business people, as opposed to the . . . idea of 'image' and 'international design.'"

She was putting into business terms an Eames concern that "what works good is better than what looks good, because what works good lasts." In other words, the people who had just designed the most revolutionary chair of the twentieth century felt that they were better off with a company that took that approach as a given and put it in the marketplace as simply a good chair. They felt uncomfortable asking people to buy the chair as a landmark of international design, or "design style"; they wanted them to buy it because it was comfortable and it worked.

Once, in discussing the design of Herman Miller's New York showroom, the words "good design" were used. Charles Eames said, "Don't give us that good design crap. You never hear us talk about that. The real questions are: Does it solve a problem? Is it serviceable? How is it going to look in ten years?"

Source: Hugh De Pree, *Business as Unusual* (Zeeland, Mich.: Herman Miller, 1986).

Index

Page numbers in italic type refer to photographs and illustrations. "CE" refers to Charles Eames. "RE" refers to Ray Eames. "C&RE" refers to Charles and Ray Eames. When these abbreviations begin a main entry, they are alphabetized as if they were full names, i.e., "CE" = "Eames, Charles," "C&RE" = "Eames, Charles and Ray," and "RE" = "Eames, Ray." Elsewhere in the index, these abbreviations are alphabetized as spelled.

Moses, Robert, 228
Motorola, 374
Muffat, Georg, 295
multimedia and multiple-image presentations, 193–94, 228, 241–43, *256,* 257–58, 282, 291, 313, 319, 330, 361–63
Murrow, Edward R., 170
Museum of Modern Art, XV, 38, 143, 316, 333, 339; design competitions sponsored by, XVI, 6, *7,* 29, 73, 130, 167, 344, 360, 373–74; Mies van der Rohe exhibition (1947), 26, *26;* New Furniture Designed by Charles Eames (exhibition, 1946), 333, 344, 375
Museum of Science and Industry, Los Angeles, 316
Museum of the City of New York, 151
music, 107, 121

National Aquarium, Washington, D.C., 270–71, 276, 280, *281,* 291–92, 315–16, 335
"National Aquarium Presentation" (C&RE), 280, 291–92, *293,* 297, 355
National Institute of Design, India, 176–87, 377–78
National Museum of Poland, XIII
natural environment, 276, 282, 286–87, 383
natural selection, 313
nature: architecture in relation to, 22–23, 31, 39, 60, 314; CE's commentary on, 79–80, 87–88; echoes of, in design, *320–21;* experience of, 20
Navajo, 246
Nazis, 33
Needham, Joseph, 323
needs: addressed by architecture, 22, 27, 29, 33; addressed by design, 5, 6, 32–33, 78–79, 115, 178
Nehru: His Life and His India (C&RE), 377
Nelson, George, 98, 112, 188, 192, 241, 288, 319, 332–36, *334, 337,* 344, 345, 362, 375–76
Neuhart, John and Marilyn, 192
Neutra, Richard, 29, 78, 89, 90, 244; Strathmore Apartments, 29, *36,* 37
Newby, Frank, 130
new covetables, 280, 307, 352
"A New Emergency Transport Splint of Plyformed Wood" (CE), 14–15
New Furniture Designed by Charles Eames (exhibition, 1946), 333, 344, 375
"A New Series of Storage Units Designed by Charles Eames" (CE), 75
Newton (C&RE), 363
New York Hall of Science, XIV
New York World's Fair (1964), 228, 248–58, 288, 291, 296. *See also* IBM World's Fair Pavilion (1964)

Niemeyer, Oscar, 375–76
Nixon, Richard, 198, 280, 362
noise (communication), 108
Northwest Land Ordinance, 340, 381
Norton Lectures, Harvard University, 313–14, 378–79, 388
Noyes, Eliot, 151, 316, 378

Obata (CE's college classmate), 369
oceanography, 105
O'Connell, James B., "A Visit with Charles Eames," 218–19
O'Hare International Airport, 232, 235–36, *236*
Oka, Hideyuki, 336
Omnibus (television show), 146–49
On the Shoulders of Giants (C&RE), 363
Oppenheimer, Frank, 342
Oppenheimer, J. Robert, 170, 352
"Organic Design" (CE), 6
Organic Furniture Competition (Museum of Modern Art, 1940), 6, *7,* 29, 167, 344, 360, 373–74
originality, 79, 98–99, 122, 158, 178, 206, 267, 313
Owens-Corning, 130

packaging, 106
Packard-Bell, 160
Paepcke, Walter, 94
painting, 13, 20, 106
Panel on Esthetic Qualities in Architecture (Ann Arbor, 1948), 27
"Parade" (C&RE), 121, 295, 316
Paragould, Arkansas, Eames-designed church in, 372
Paris Exposition (1925), 230
Passalaqua, Sam, *279*
pastries, 139
patents, 359–60
Payne Forced Air Heating System, 60
Peale, Charles Willson, 353
pedestal chair (Eero Saarinen), 188, 206, *207,* 346
peep shows, mathematical, 219, 243, 270, 294, 296
Penberthy Lumber Company, 60
Pencil Points (magazine), 335
Pepperidge Farm, 226
performance standards, 94–95, 97–98, 276
"The Perry Expedition" (C&RE), 297
Pett, Saul, 311
Pevsner, Nikolaus, 136
Phipps, William, 119
photography, 121, 282, 297, 367
"Photography and the City" (C&RE), 297, 355
Phyfe, Duncan, 373
physics, 106
physics experiments, 95–96
Picasso, Pablo, 106, 154, 230, 346, 360;

Guernica, 83, *83* (detail)
Pickens, Buford L., 129
Piel, Gerry, 328, 343
Piranesi, Giovanni Battista, 82
Pittsburgh Plate Glass Co., 130
plastics, 124, 244. *See also* molded plastic chairs
plastilene, 244
play and games, 106, 163, 219, 289, 323, 361
playgrounds, 163–64
pleasure, 226, 245–46, 314, 322, 328, 330
plyformed wood, 14
Plyon, 60
plywood: emergency transport splint, XVI, 14–15; laminating and molding of, 6, 8, 14, 24. *See also* molded plywood chairs
plywood dining chairs, *321*
plywood elephant, 374–75
Polaroid, XIII, 314
Ponti, Gio, 266
Portfolio (magazine), 76
"Powers of Ten" (C&RE), 291, 294, 297, 355, 378, *382, 383, 384*
preconceived ideas, dangers of, 6, 32–33, 35, 79, 89–90, 95, 99, 179, 229
"A Prediction: Less Self-Expression for the Designer" (CE), 206–7
Prestini, James, 157
probability, 136–37
"Problems of the Creative Artist" (panel, UCLA, 1963), XVI
problem solving: architecture as, 120–21, 127, 136; benefits of, 288; carried to conclusion, 39, 79, 89, 109; complexity involved in, 104–9; decision-making as aspect of, 288; design as, XIII, XIV, 5, 79, 89–90, 104, 115, 117, 179; disciplinary approaches to, 182; drawing as tool for, 122; game theory as tool for, 136–37; history as aid to, 125; "India Report" projects utilizing, 183–86; innovation as byproduct of, 291; in lota design, 179; role of restraints in, 244; Saarinen and, 309–10; statement of problem as initial step in, 176–77; theme and variations as tool for, 124; in UC Berkeley Architecture 1 and 2, *126,* 127, *128*
process man, 32
Proetz, Erma, 373
Proetz, Victor, 373
Progressive Architecture, 232–39
Propst, Robert, 376–77
Pruys, Simon M., 274–75
Ptolemy, 354
Public Broadcast Laboratory (television show), 269–71
public schools, art education in, 156
pueblos, *166,* 260
Puerto Rico, XIII